A Man that can Translate:
Joseph Smith and the Nephite Interpreters

Second Edition

Jonathan Neville, MS, JD

LDS Nonfiction by Jonathan Neville

The Lost City of Zarahemla
Moroni's America
Brought to Light
Letter VII: Joseph Smith and Oliver Cowdery Explain the Hill Cumorah
The Editors: Joseph, Don Carlos and William Smith
Whatever Happened to the Golden Plates?
Because of this Theory
Mesomania
Moroni's America (pocket edition)
The 2020 "seeing clearly" trilogy
- A Man that Can Translate: Joseph Smith and the Nephite Interpreters (2d edition)
- Infinite Goodness: Joseph Smith, Jonathan Edwards, and the Language of the Book of Mormon
- Between these Hills: A Case for the New York Cumorah

———

Novels by J.E. Neville (LDS)

The Joy Helpers
Moroni's Keys
Among All Nations
In Earthly Things

———

Novels by Jonathan Neville

The Mind Tamer
Caught Away
The Girl from Helper
The Perfect Mother
California Blues
The Mistake
The Clown House
The Rule of Equity

———

Nonfiction by Jonathan Neville

Legalines Series:
Constitutional Law
Contracts
Property Law
Torts
Criminal Law
Criminal Procedure
Civil Procedure

———

A Man that can Translate:

Joseph Smith and the Nephite Interpreters

Jonathan Neville, MS, JD

A Man that Can Translate: Joseph Smith and the Nephite Interpreters

Second Edition

This is a work of nonfiction. The author has made every effort to be accurate and complete and welcomes comments, suggestions, and corrections, which can be emailed to lostzarahemla@gmail.com.

All opinions expressed in this work are those of the author and do not necessarily reflect the opinions of any other individual or organization.

9-30-20

ISBN- 978-1-944200-79-4

Museum of the Book of Mormon Press
MOBOM.org Museum of the Book of Mormon

1-801-810-7718
www.digitalegend.com

To open-minded people everywhere.

Now Ammon said unto him: I can assuredly tell thee, O king, of **a man that can translate** the records; for he has wherewith that he can look, and translate all records that are of ancient date; and it is a gift from God. And **the things are called interpreters**, and no man can look in them except he be commanded, lest he should look for that he ought not and he should perish. And whosoever is commanded to look in them, the same is called seer.

(Mosiah 8:13)

The boldness of my plans and measures, can readily be tested by the touch-stone of all schemes, systems, projects, and adventures,— truth, for truth is a matter of fact— and **the fact is, that by the power of God I translated the book of Mormon from hieroglyphics**; the knowledge of which was lost to the world. In which wonderful event, I stood alone, an unlearned youth, to combat the worldly wisdom and multiplied ignorance of eighteen centuries

(Joseph Smith—Letter to James Arlington Bennet, 13 November 1843)

To the Reader:

The book covers four topics:
1. The controversy about the translation of the Book of Mormon.
2. The historical evidence about the translation.
3. The interpretation of that evidence.
4. The implications of the alternative interpretations.

In this book I briefly address the topic of the language of the text of the Book of Mormon. I discuss that topic in more depth in *Infinite Goodness: Joseph Smith, Jonathan Edwards and the Language of the Book of Mormon.*

———

I'm grateful to all the historians who have carefully preserved and compiled Church history resources, with special appreciation for the Joseph Smith Papers project. I look forward to even more discoveries. As always, any errors in this book are mine and I encourage you to call them to my attention.

I assume readers have some background in the history of the coming forth of the Book of Mormon. This book provides only brief overviews of relevant events before getting into details.

The notes and links in this book cite the best available sources for the referenced materials, regardless of the editorial stance of the creator(s) or publisher(s) of the sources.

To save space, I used numerous abbreviations and acronyms. See the list on pages ix and x.

Unless otherwise indicated, all **bold** lettering is my added emphasis.

I welcome your feedback and thoughts. You can email me at this address: lostzarahemla@gmail.com.

I've learned a lot from readers (and critics) and expect that we will all continue to "instruct and edify each other." (Doctrine and Covenants 43:8)

———

TABLE OF CONTENTS

TABLES and FIGURES

Preface

This book presents detailed evidence to corroborate what Joseph Smith wrote in the Wentworth letter about the translation of the Book of Mormon: "through the medium of the Urim and Thummim I translated the record by the gift and power of God."

Until recently, that proposition was a given for believers. Joseph, his principal scribe Oliver Cowdery, and their successors as leaders of the Church of Jesus Christ of Latter-day Saints, always taught what Joseph summarized in the Wentworth letter.

In recent years, the narrative has changed. Prominent LDS historians and scholars now teach that Joseph Smith did not actually translate the plates. Relying on historical accounts (but not the teachings of the prophets), they say Joseph did not even use the plates. Instead, he put a seer stone into his hat, covered his face with the hat, and read words that appeared either on the stone or in vision. Lately, both critics and many faithful LDS authors seem to have agreed to *reject* what Joseph and Oliver taught and *accept* what others said.

The result: many faithful members of the Church are confused. They don't know what to believe. They don't know what to tell their friends when they share the Restoration of the Gospel of Jesus Christ.

Some say it doesn't matter whether Joseph used the Urim and Thummim or the seer stone. Some say he used both to translate. Some say Joseph referred to the seer stone *as* the Urim and Thummim, which contradicts the plain language he and Oliver always employed.

I wrote this book because I (and many others) have been dissatisfied with these explanations. The translation is one of the merciful acts of God that Moroni exhorted us to ponder.

> Behold, I would exhort you that when ye shall read these things, if it be wisdom in God that ye should read them, that ye would remember how merciful the Lord hath been unto the children of men, from the creation of Adam **even down until the time that ye shall receive these things**, and ponder it in your hearts. (Moroni 10:3)

The translation of the Book of Mormon was a prerequisite for any of us to "receive these things."

———

President Russell M. Nelson has taught that "good inspiration is based upon good information."[1]

I start with the premise that what Joseph and Oliver wrote and taught was "good information." Ignoring what they taught, or re-defining terms to change the plain meaning of the words they used, does not seem likely to lead to "good inspiration" as we ponder the translation.

To the extent that their teachings contradict what others claimed, I asked myself, were these others lying? Confused? Mistaken? Or can the evidence be reconciled? If so, how?

Joseph Smith once explained, "I have a key by which I understand the Scriptures. I enquire what was the question which drew out the answer or caused Jesus to utter the parable."[2]

This book applies that approach to the available historical statements about the translation of the Book of Mormon. Throughout this book, we will assess dozens of statements by asking, what was the question, problem, issue, or context that "drew out" the statement?

When I practiced law, I observed that while it is usually easy to explain *some* of the facts, it is often difficult to explain *all* of the facts. In this book, we'll look at an explanation for all of the facts.

By applying Joseph's "key" I've concluded that Joseph and Oliver were correct and candid all along. Maybe more candid—and specific—than we realized.

See what you think after you consider the evidence.

———

[1]President Russell M. Nelson, "Revelation for the Church, Revelation for Our Lives" https://www.churchofjesuschrist.org/study/general-conference/2018/04/revelation-for-the-church-revelation-for-our-lives?lang=eng

[2] https://www.josephsmithpapers.org/paper-summary/history-1838-1856-volume-d-1-1-august-1842-1-july-1843/102

The stakes involved.

Long-time members of the Church of Jesus Christ of Latter-day Saints remember being taught that Joseph Smith translated the ancient plates by using the Nephite interpreters known as the Urim and Thummim. Artwork, lesson manuals, and teachings of Church leaders uniformly presented this narrative for many decades.

Younger members (and new converts) learn instead that Joseph used a seer stone that he placed into a hat. Joseph would dictate the words that appeared on the stone. The plates sat nearby, covered with a cloth the entire time. In the last decade, artwork, lesson manuals, videos, and even the *Ensign* magazine have depicted this scenario.

The dichotomy between old and new approaches leaves people with a sense of ambiguity and uncertainty.

For some faithful members, the question is unimportant. They believe the Book of Mormon is the word of God and it doesn't matter how it was produced. But other faithful members, plus those who have lost their faith and those outside the Church who investigate the truth claims, think the origin of the Book of Mormon is a core issue.

This is not merely a quibble about historical sources. The nature of the translation implicates theological and historical issues related to the historicity and divine authenticity of the Book of Mormon itself.

The controversy between the Urim and Thummim vs. the stone in the hat originated in the early days of the Church and has persisted for decades. Around 1880, William E. McLellin, one of the original Twelve Apostles who left the Church in 1838, wrote a document that listed 55 things he did not believe.[3] The first three involve the translation.

> 1. I do not believe that Joseph translated the book of Mormon. He only read the translation as it appeared before him. The Lord translated it for him, so says the book. "Wherefore, thou shalt read the words which I shall give unto thee" Page 111, of the Palmyra edition [2 Ne. 27:20]
> 2. I do not believe he ever possessed the Urim and Thummim during

---

[3]William E. McLellin "Some of the Reasons Why I Am Not a Mormon," ca. 1880. John L. Traughber, *Papers, 1854–1910*. Special Collections, J. Willard Marriott Library, University of Utah, Salt Lake City.

his whole life.
3. I do not believe he ever possessed the Interpreters after he lost the 116 pages first translated.

When we look at McLellin's list, we realize we've seen it recently. Numbers 1 and 3 are currently being widely taught. McLellin's reasons for not being a Mormon are being taught to new members and the youth of the Church today.

That should give everyone pause. We ought to be absolutely sure these things are correct if we're teaching them.

As an avid reader myself, I want to know authors' assumptions and biases. In a nutshell: I think Joseph Smith actually translated the Book of Mormon, but a lot of understandable misconceptions have arisen about the timing and methodology of the translation.

In this book we will consider interpretations that corroborate the teachings of the prophets, beginning with Joseph Smith and Oliver Cowdery. This includes a slightly different sequence of events for the translation than you are probably used to. See Chapter 1.

This is a hybrid book. The first section of each chapter offers an overview. You can read the eleven overviews now and get the gist of the book without getting into the details.

If you enjoy digging deeper, the balance of each chapter offers evidence and explanations, supported by extensive footnotes and Appendices.

Abbreviations and Acronyms Used

This book uses the following abbreviations and acronyms.

- References to scripture use customary abbreviations (Isa. means Isaiah).
- Citations in this book include Internet links when available.
- For further research, I recommend Wordcruncher, a BYU software tool with electronic texts, available at http://wordcruncher.com/.

———

CHL – Church History Library, Church of Jesus Christ of Latter-day Saints, Salt Lake City, Utah, USA.

CofC – Community of Christ. (See RLDS)

CR – Conference Reports (available on WordCruncher)

D&C – Doctrine and Covenants of the Church of Jesus Christ of Latter-day Saints (Salt Lake City, Utah: Intellectual Reserve, 1981)

EMD – *Early Mormon Documents*, ed. Dan Vogel, 5 vols. (Salt Lake City: Signature Books, 1996-2004)

EJ – *Elders' Journal of the Church of Latter Day Saints*, Kirtland, Ohio, October-November 1837, Far West, Missouri, July-August 1838.

EMS – *The Evening and the Morning Star*, Independence, Missouri, June 1832-July 1833; Kirtland, Ohio, December 1833-September 1834.

GR – *The Gospel Reflector*, Philadelphia, Pennyslvania, published by Benjamin Winchester

JoD – *Journal of Discourses*, an unofficial compilation of sermons by LDS leaders, England, 1845-1886. Accessible from several sources, including https://scriptures.byu.edu/#::j, http://wordcruncher.com/ http://www.josephsmithfoundation.org/journalofdiscourses/, and https://jod.mrm.org/1.

JSP – The Joseph Smith Papers (https://josephsmithpapers.org), a compilation of all known papers produced by or associated with Joseph Smith, Jr. *JSP* includes printed and digital records.

LDS – Acronym for "Latter-day Saints." Like the term *Mormon*, *LDS* refers members of the Church of Jesus Christ of Latter-day Saints and related beliefs and practices. Although currently disfavored by the Church, the terms are common in historical documents and commentaries.

M&A – *Latter Day Saints' Messenger and Advocate*, Kirtland, Oho, October 1834-September 1837.

MS – *Latter-day Saints' Millennial Star*, Manchester, England, May 1840-March 1842; Liverpool, England, April 1842-March 3, 1932; London, England, March 10, 1932-December 1970.

OM – Original Manuscript of the Book of Mormon (Harmony and Fayette).

OTH – *Opening the Heavens,* Second Edition, John W. Welch, Editor, (BYU Press and Deseret Book, 2017).

PM – Printer's Manuscript of the Book of Mormon

RLDS – Acronym for the Reorganized Church of Jesus Christ of Latter Day Saints from 1872 to 2001, when the organization changed its name to Community of Christ (CofC).

SITH – Acronym for the "stone-in-the-hat" theory of Book of Mormon translation.

T&S – *Times and Seasons,* Commerce/Nauvoo, Illinois, November 1839-February 1846.

U&T – Acronym for the Urim and Thummim.

Royal Skousen's *Critical Text of the Book of Mormon,* Volume 3, titled *The History of the Text of the Book of Mormon,* published by *BYU Studies*, is referenced by Part number.

Parts 1-2 - Grammatical Variation

Part 3-4 - The Nature of the Original Language

Part 5 - The King James Quotations in the Book of Mormon

Part 6 - Spelling in the Manuscripts and the Editions

1. A New Translation Timeline—1805-2020

Overview.

Traditionally, we've thought the translation of the current Book of Mormon took about 74 days over the three months of April, May and June 1829.

David Whitmer reportedly said the translation took eight months. Overlooked evidence supports that timeline. Joseph worked on the translation, with his wife Emma and others as scribes, from November 1828 to March 1829. In those five months, they translated much or all of the Book of Mosiah, but the work was slow.

Joseph needed a full-time scribe.

Oliver Cowdery, who arrived in Harmony, Pennsylvania, on April 5, 1829, was an answer to his prayers.

Detail.

The traditional timeline of the translation. The traditional understanding of the translation of the current text of the Book of Mormon starts on 7 April 1829 when Joseph Smith began dictating his translation of the abridged plates to Oliver Cowdery in Harmony, PA. They finished the abridged plates, including the Title Page on "the last leaf" of the plates, near the end of May.

In June, Oliver and Joseph relocated to the Whitmer farm in Fayette, NY. There, they translated the original plates of Nephi.

This scenario contemplates about 74 days of translation over three months:

- 53 days in Harmony for Mosiah through Moroni (8.2 pages/day using the 1830 edition pagination), and
- 21 days in Fayette for 1 Nephi through Words of Mormon (7.0 pages/day). That is the timeline most scholars accept.[4]

[4] E.g., "Almost all of the present Book of Mormon text was translated during a three-

The traditional timeline is serviceable as a simplified, easy-to-understand narrative. The problem: it ignores key historical evidence from Joseph Smith, Emma Smith, Lucy Mack Smith, and others.

The traditional timeline has also obscured an important aspect of the translation and its aftermath. In this chapter, I propose a new translation timeline that both (i) incorporates and (ii) harmonizes all of the historical accounts. The new timeline helps resolve the ongoing debate about whether Joseph Smith used the Urim and Thummim, the seer stone, or both, when he translated the Book of Mormon.

———

Toward a new timeline. We begin with David Whitmer, who reported a different time frame for the translation.

> The work of translating the tablets consumed **about eight months**, Smith acting as the seer and **Oliver Cowdery, Smith's wife, and Christian Whitmer,** brother of David, performing the duties of amanuenses [scribe], in whose handwriting the original manuscript now is.[5]

The "eight months" scenario significantly exceeds the traditional 74-day translation timeline. Although this is an isolated statement, Joseph, Oliver, and their contemporaries never said anything different. To the contrary: their statements support the eight-month timeline.

John H. Gilbert, the man who typeset the text of the Book of Mormon for Mr. E. B. Grandin, the printer, corroborated part of

---

month period between April and June 1829 with Oliver Cowdery as the scribe." https://www.churchofjesuschrist.org/study/history/topics/book-of-mormon-translation?lang=eng. See *OTH,* "Events Surrounding the Translation of the Book of Mormon" on p. 84 and "Estimated Day-by-Day Translation in 1829" on pp. 120-125. First edition online at BMC. https://bit.ly/2AKpiib. For a more detailed timeline that reaches a conclusion similar to the one I propose here, see Elden Watson's annotated timeline at https://www.eldenwatson.net/BoM.htm.

[5] Vol. XLV, *The Chicago Daily Tribune,* Thursday, December 17, 1885, discussed in Chapter 5. Oliver and Christian were scribes at the Whitmer home in Fayette. David could observe Emma's scribal work on the manuscript, even though she wrote in Harmony, not Fayette.

David's statement. Gilbert said of the manuscript from which he set the type, "I would know that manuscript today if I should see it. The most part of it was in Oliver Cowdery's handwriting. Some in Joseph's wife's; a small part, though."[6]

In 1877, Emma claimed she "frequently wrote day after day" and "hour after hour" as Joseph translated. The context of that statement indicates she referred to writing the Original Manuscript (OM) in Harmony. That's why the traditional timeline needs revision.

———

The sequence of translation. We first need to review the sequence of translation. As published, the Book of Mormon begins with the last part Joseph translated (1 Nephi). The first translation Joseph dictated—Mormon's abridgment of the Book of Lehi—was recorded on the 116 pages[7] that were lost by the scribe, Martin Harris, in June 1828.

Traditional Translation Sequence and Timeline (3 months for published Book of Mormon)		Location
Apr-Jun 1828	Abridged Book of Lehi (116 pages - lost)	Harmony
Apr-May 1829	Abridged plates (Mosiah-Moroni + Title Page)	Harmony
June 1829	Original plates of Nephi (1 Ne. – WofM)	Fayette

We know David's eight-month timeline did not refer to the first translation—the 116 pages—because those pages, having been lost, were not part of the Original Manuscript (OM) published as the Book of Mormon. When the 116 pages were lost, Joseph had to forfeit the Urim and Thummim (U&T). He could not translate until he received them back in September, 1828.

When he resumed translating in Harmony, Joseph continued where he left off, at Mormon's abridgment of the Book of Mosiah. He finished

[6] James T. Cobb interview with John H. Gilbert in "The Hill Cumorah," *The Saints' Herald* (Plano, ILL), Vol. 28, No. 11, June 1, 1881, p. 165. Online at http://www.sidneyrigdon.com/dbroadhu/IL/sain1872.htm#060181

[7] Some question the accuracy of the 116 page count, but that's not relevant to the question we're considering here.

translating the abridged plates (through Moroni and the Title Page, which was on the "last leaf" of the plates) in late May. Joseph then returned those plates to a divine messenger before leaving Harmony.

In June, Joseph and Oliver moved to the Whitmer farm in Fayette, NY. There, Joseph translated the original small plates of Nephi, known today as 1 Nephi through Words of Mormon.

Joseph's translation of both the abridged plates (in Harmony) and the original small plates of Nephi (in Fayette) was recorded by his scribes on sheets of paper that constitute the OM. Oliver Cowdery made a copy of the OM called the Printer's Manuscript (PM).

In 1841, the OM was placed in the cornerstone of the Nauvoo House in Nauvoo, Illinois. When it was recovered in 1882, most of it had been destroyed by mold and water. Parts of it were handed out as souvenirs to visitors to Nauvoo. Today, only about 28 percent of the OM is known to exist.[8] Table 1 below shows which parts of the OM still exist.

Oliver was the principal scribe on the OM, both in Harmony and in Fayette. David Whitmer's brothers John (JW) and Christian (CW) were probably the two additional scribes in Fayette on the existing part of the OM (mostly 1 Nephi). Emma was also a scribe in Fayette, as we'll see in Chapters 6 and 7. Of course, she was also one of the pre-Oliver scribes in Harmony.

Notice that Table 1 uses the current LDS chapters and verses. You are probably familiar with that organization of the text, and it works for both print and digital references, so we'll use it in this book. The original 1830 edition was divided only into books and chapters, not numbered verses. In 1879, Elder Orson Pratt (LDS) divided the text into smaller chapters and numbered verses. 1 Nephi had 7 chapters in the 1830 edition, but the current LDS edition has 22 chapters.[9]

---

[8] A sample page is available online at https://www.josephsmithpapers.org/paper-summary/book-of-mormon-manuscript-excerpt-circa-june-1829-1-nephi-22b-318a/1. Royal Skousen has published a "Typographical Facsimile of the Extant Text" in *The Original Manuscript of the Book of Mormon* (FARMS/BYU 2001). The JSP will publish a volume on the Original Manuscript around 2021-2.

[9] RLDS editions have retained the 1830 chapters but added numbered verses.

Table 1 - Scribes of the OM fragments in order of translation

Text (1981 edition)		Text (1981 edition)	
Harmony	**Scribe**	**Fayette**	**Scribe**
Mos.1-Alma 10:31	missing	1 Ne. 2:2-3:6	OC
Alma 10:31-13	OC	3:7-4:14	JW
Alma 14-21	missing	4:15-20	OC
Alma 22-60	OC	4:20-12:8	CW
[Alma 45:22]	JS	12:9-13:35a	JW
Alma 62-Hel. 3	OC	13:35b-14:11	Missing
Hel. 3-Hel. 13	missing	14:11b-16	JW
Hel. 13-3 Ne. 4	OC	14:15-20	OC
3 Ne. 5-Ether 2	Missing	14:20-23	Missing
Ether 3-Ether 15	OC	14:23-29	JW
Moroni	Missing	14:29-15:5	Missing
		15:5-16:1	JW
		16:1-2 Ne. 1:30	OC
		Fragments 2 Ne.-Enos	OC

The missing pages from Mosiah 1 through Alma 10:31 leave open many possibilities. The traditional timeline assumes Oliver Cowdery wrote all, or almost all, of the missing pages. This puts the commencement of the translation at April 7, 1829, two days after Oliver arrived in Harmony. For the rest of this chapter we'll discuss why I think that timeline is erroneous.

New (2020) Translation Sequence and Timeline (8 months for published Book of Mormon)		Location
Apr-Jun 1828	Abridged Book of Lehi (116 pages - lost)	Harmony
Nov 1828-May 1829	Abridged plates (Mosiah-Moroni + Title Page)	Harmony
June 1829	Original plates of Nephi (1 Ne. – WofM)	Fayette

Because the time frame for the translation in Fayette is well established, we will defer an analysis of those pages of the OM to Chapters 5-6.

The new (2020) timeline. When Joseph's parents visited Harmony in November 1828,[10] Joseph told them that the messenger had returned the plates with the U&T in September 1828 and that Emma was then writing for him.[11] Joseph separately reported that after he received the plates and U&T again, he "did not however go immediately to translating but went to laboring with my hands upon a small farm… to provide for my family."[12] Joseph likely worked on the farm during the last week of September and most or all of October during the harvest and preservation season.

If Emma had begun writing for Joseph by the time the Smith's visited in November, that leaves five months of possible translating before Oliver arrived in Harmony (Nov-Mar). When added to the traditional three months, we get David Whitmer's eight months.

Other scribes. Emma was apparently not the only scribe who wrote for Joseph during these five months. Emma later said her brother Reuben was a scribe, but she didn't specify whether this was for the 116 pages or the OM.

In his 1832 history, Joseph explained that before Oliver arrived in Harmony in April 1829, his brother Samuel scribed for him.

> my wife had written some for me to translate and also my Brothr Samuel H Smith but we had become reduced in poverty and my wives father was about to turn me out of doores & I had not where to go and I cried unto

---

10 Some historians think they visited in September, but Lucy quotes Joseph referring *back* to September.

11 Lucy Mack Smith, *History, 1845*, https://www.josephsmithpapers.org/paper-summary/lucy-mack-smith-history-1845/142

12 *History, circa June 1839-circa 1841*, https://www.josephsmithpapers.org/paper-summary/history-circa-june-1839-circa-1841-draft-2/13 , published in the *Times and Seasons*, 15 June 1842, p. 817, https://www.josephsmithpapers.org/paper-summary/times-and-seasons-15-june-1842/3

> the Lord that he would provide for me to accomplish the work whereunto he had commanded me[13]

Oliver Cowdery was an answer to this prayer.

Another pre-Oliver scribe might have been Martin Harris, who visited Harmony in March 1829 and requested a revelation. The revelation (D&C 5) includes this comment about the translation.

> 29 And if this be the case, I command you, my servant Joseph, that you shall say unto him [Martin Harris], that **he shall do no more**, nor trouble me any more concerning this matter.
> 30 And if this be the case, behold, I say unto thee Joseph, **when thou hast translated a few more pages thou shalt stop for a season, even until I command thee again; then thou mayest translate again.**

This raises the possibility that Martin resumed some scribal activity, leaving us with four potential pre-Oliver scribes for Joseph after he lost the 116 pages: Emma, her brother Reuben, Samuel Smith, and Martin Harris. Because the relevant pages of the OM are gone (Mosiah 1 through Alma 10:31), it is impossible to tell which of the pre-Oliver scribes may have written what portion of the OM. Both David Whitmer and John Gilbert mentioned only Emma's handwriting, so for purposes of the following analysis (and for simplicity), we consider all the pre-Oliver scribes as one unit, using Emma as the proxy.

The question is, what did Emma write?

Some may argue that whatever Emma wrote between November 1828 and March 1829, it was not the text of the published Book of Mormon. But that would contradict the statements from David and John that the OM included Emma's scribal work.[14]

The only thing we know for sure is that, however much Emma wrote, Oliver wrote from Alma 10:32 (page 251, line 22, in the 1830

---

[13] *History, circa Summer 1832*, https://www.josephsmithpapers.org/paper-summary/history-circa-summer-1832/6 .

[14] The "Events" table in *OTH* states that in March 1829 "A few pages may have been translated," such as "Mosiah chapter 1," but *OTH* does not identify a scribe. The *OTH* table apparently ignores what Joseph told his mother and what he wrote in his 1832 history about other scribes. As for Emma's work in Fayette, see Chapters 6-7.

edition) forward on the existing sheets of the OM that were translated from the abridged plates in Harmony. This means Emma wrote some or even all of the OM from Mosiah 1 through Alma 10:31. Using the 1830 edition pagination, this represents pages 153 through 251.

How much of the OM did Emma write? When he rejoined the Church in 1848, Oliver claimed he "wrote with my own pen the intire book of mormon (Save a few pages) as it fell from the Lips of the prophet."[15] Traditionally, "a few pages" has been understood to refer to the pages from the Fayette translation in the handwriting of two other scribes (presumably John and Christian Whitmer), plus Emma's writing in Fayette (missing). That corroborates Oliver's statement. But "a few pages" could *also* include a portion (or all) of Mosiah and Alma (up to Alma 10:31).

How many pages in the missing parts of the Original Manuscript are the "few pages" that Oliver Cowdery did not write?

Some authors recognize that "a few pages," such as Mosiah 1, may have been translated before Oliver arrived, but most stick with the three-month (74-day) timeline. In my view, that timeline *is certainly wrong.*

The question is, *how* wrong?

The traditional timeline assigns 53 days for dictating and writing Mosiah 1 (page 153 in the 1830 edition) through Moroni 10 (page 588).[16] This is 435 pages at an average of 8.2 pages/day.

When Oliver began writing on April 7, he would have picked up where Emma left off. If Emma wrote through Alma 10:31 (98 pages), Oliver's scribal work in Harmony could have covered as little as Alma 11 through Moroni 10. Instead of producing 8.2 pages/day, Joseph and

[15] Reuben Miller's account of Oliver Cowdery's speech. Online at https://catalog.churchofjesuschrist.org/assets/22222322-f4fe-41e3-aa86-bfc54b94df92/0/16. See Item #46 in Appendix 1.

[16] The Title Page was unnumbered and is only two paragraphs anyway.

Oliver might have produced as few as 6.3 pages/day.

If Emma wrote through the end of Mosiah (p. 221), she would have written 68 pages and Oliver would have written the balance (367 pages) in 53 days, and so forth.

Table 2 - Possible translation speeds – Oliver as scribe

Total Pages	Emma	Oliver	Days	Pages/day
435	0	435	53	8.2
435	35	400	53	7.5
435	68	367	53	6.9
435	98	337	53	6.3

The traditional timeline separately allocates 21 days in June 1829 for the 149 pages of the Fayette translation of the original small plates of Nephi (pages 5-153 in the 1830 edition.) This works out to 7 pages/day.

There are many variables in such averages, but depending on the extent of Emma's contribution, it appears the translation in Fayette was faster—perhaps significantly faster—than the translation in Harmony. In Chapter 7 we will discuss a likely reason for that.

Six or seven pages a day does not seem like much. It takes about 20-30 minutes to copy a page of text or write from dictation. (You should try it yourself.) That would amount to 3 to 4 hours per day.

Joseph Smith said of the work in Harmony, "During the month of April [1829] I continued to translate, and he [Oliver] to write, **with little cessation**, during which time we received several revelations."[17] David Whitmer told an interviewer that, in Fayette, "In regard to the translation, it was a **laborious work** for the weather was very warm, and the days were long and **they worked from morning till night**."[18]

If Joseph was actually translating the characters, and studying it out

---

17 "History of Joseph Smith," *Times and Seasons* (Nauvoo, IL) 15 July 1842, vol. 3, no. 18, pp. 847–862. https://www.josephsmithpapers.org/paper-summary/times-and-seasons-15-july-1842/7

18 James H. Hart, "About the Book of Mormon," *Deseret Evening News*, March 25, 1884. Appendix 1, #29

in his mind (D&C 9:8), and carefully putting it into his own words, and making corrections as he went or spelling proper nouns, we can see why the translation would take as long as he and David said it did.

In June in New York, the days are over 15 hours long. Working "from morning till night" to translate 7 pages a day gives around 2 hours/page, providing for an hour in break time. You can assume whatever work hours you want. If they worked 10.5 hours/day, they took 1.5 hours/page. That's still fast for a scholarly translation—the 47 King James translators took seven years.

But that pace is slow if all Joseph had to do was read the already-translated words off a stone. In that case what were he and his scribes doing the rest of the day?

Between November 1828 and March 1829, the most that Joseph could have translated with Emma was the 98 pages from Mosiah 1 to Alma 10:31. That is fewer than 20 pages/month. Understandable, given Emma's household duties, but at that rate it would have taken Joseph over two years to translate the entire Book of Mormon.

No wonder Joseph prayed for a scribe.

The beginning of the Book of Mosiah, which Joseph resumed editing after the 116 pages were lost, [19] is a bit of a mystery to historians.

When he copied the OM to create the PM, Oliver Cowdery did not number the chapter.[20] This makes sense because elsewhere on the OM, chapters were not originally numbered. Oliver copied the last line of the Words of Mormon, drew a long dash, wrote "Chapter," drew another long dash, and then began writing what is now Mosiah 1:1. He apparently went back later and inserted "the Book of Mosiah" above the long dash. An unidentified scribe wrote the Roman numerals for

[19] Joseph's sister Katherine said that when the angel returned the U&T, he told Joseph "to begin where he had left off." See Kyle R. Walker, "Katherine Smith Salisbury's Recollections of Joseph's Meetings with Moroni," *BYU Studies* 41, no. 3 (2002).

[20] See the facsimile of the PM: https://www.josephsmithpapers.org/paper-summary/printers-manuscript-of-the-book-of-mormon-circa-august-1829-circa-january-1830/121.

three "III" and then crossed off the last two digits to leave it as "Chapter I."

Figure 1 - Mosiah 1 in the OM

This sequence of events has led some to conclude that the current Chapter 1 of Mosiah was originally Chapter 3; i.e., Chapters 1-2 were part of the lost 116 pages. Maybe (as I think) verses 13-18 of Words of Mormon were originally part of Mosiah Chapter 2, with verse 12 being Joseph Smith's (i) summary of the pages lost with the 116 pages and (ii) his transition to the retained verses from the original Chapter 2.[21] It is also possible that the current Mosiah 1 was translated in 1828 with Martin Harris but *not* included in the 116 pages (that is, they were retained by Joseph Smith per D&C 10:41).

In this book, we assume Emma began writing at the current Mosiah 1:1, whether because she copied a previous translation (i.e., the "retained" material of D&C 10:41) or because Joseph resumed translating at that point after September 1828.

———

One indication that Emma wrote part of the OM comes from the errors Oliver made when he copied the OM to make the PM.

For example, when he copied Mosiah 18:14, Oliver mistakenly wrote *Helaman* instead of *Helam* three times in Mosiah 18:12-14. In Mosiah 23, he made the same mistake 11 more times. In each case he corrected the error by crossing out the *an*.

---

[21] I think of this as page 117. See Jonathan Neville, *Whatever Happened to the Golden Plates?*

His mistake suggests he had not previously seen the name *Helam* because it was Emma, not Oliver, who originally recorded the Book of Mosiah, at least through chapter 23. Had Oliver been the original scribe for Mosiah, the name *Helam* should not have been a surprise to him.

Some have speculated that when Oliver copied the Mosiah chapters into the PM (probably in December 1829), he remembered *Helaman* from having scribed Alma and Helaman the previous April or May. Those chapters use the name *Helaman* 86 times, so the theory is not implausible. But in that scenario, Oliver would also have written *Helam* a few weeks earlier in April when he recorded the Book of Mosiah the first time. Why would he forget he had written *Helam* if he was copying his own writing when he copied Mosiah into the PM?

Oliver's mistake makes more sense if he was copying from someone else's original scribal work. In that case, his frequent writing of *Helaman* from his original recording of Alma and Helaman may have led him to "see" *Helaman* when Emma had actually written *Helam*. It would have been the first time Oliver saw this name. Maybe he thought she had made a mistake and wrote *Helaman* as a correction, only to change it later after consulting with Joseph (or Emma).

Other spelling errors also suggest Oliver was copying from someone else's work when he copied Mosiah into the PM.

For example, in his Part Six, Royal Skousen discusses the word *angry*.[22] In the OM, Oliver spelled the word *angary* in Alma and Helaman, but then changed to *angery* in Ether and in 1 and 2 Nephi. When he copied the OM to create the PM, Oliver continued to spell it *angery* from 1 Nephi through 2 Nephi (15 instances). The next appearance of the term is in Mosiah 12:9, where he spelled it *angery*, but starting with Mosiah 13:4, he spelled it correctly as *angry*. He retained the correct spelling for the subsequent 48 times the word appears through the end of the PM (with one exception).

Skousen cites this as a case of Oliver learning correct spelling from proofing the typesetting of John Gilbert, and that's plausible. But it doesn't explain why he would misspell it until he got to Mosiah. More

[22] Skousen, *Part Six*, p. 506.

likely, he learned from Emma's spelling on the OM.

One more example. On page 560, Skousen writes "for most words that Oliver learned to spell correctly by omitting the silent *e*, [such as *comeing* corrected to *coming*] the point of transition usually occurred somewhere near the beginning of the book of Mosiah."

A more detailed analysis of spelling issues is beyond the scope of this book, but if you're interested, start with Skousen's *Part Six*.

Details in the PM, including the compositor's marks, indicate that although John Gilbert used the PM for most of the typesetting, he used the OM from Helaman 13 to the end of Mormon.[23] I propose that Gilbert also used the OM for part of Mosiah, which is why he remembered Emma Smith's handwriting on the manuscript. That is a detailed analysis you can read in Appendix 2.

———

The 116 pages. Apart from her work on the OM, Emma likely contributed to the lost 116 pages. She later talked about Joseph not knowing how to spell the name "Sar[i]ah" and him asking whether Jerusalem had walls, both elements of the Book of Lehi narrative later replaced by 1 Nephi on the original small plates.[24] She could have participated in these conversations when Joseph was dictating to Martin Harris—David Whitmer repeated the Jerusalem wall story, presumably from hearsay—but Emma told the accounts as if she was the scribe.

We have another hint in the letter Joseph wrote to Emma on June 4, 1834, in which he described "wandering over the plains of the Nephites, recounting occasionally the history of the Book of Mormon, roving over the mounds of that once beloved people of the Lord, picking up their skulls & their bones, as a proof of its divine authenticity."[25] Neither "plains of the Nephites" nor "mounds" occur

---

[23] Royal Skousen, https://journal.interpreterfoundation.org/why-was-one-sixth-of-the-1830-book-of-mormon-set-from-the-original-manuscript/

[24] Don Bradley explains this in his book *The Lost 116 Pages: Reconstructing the Book of Mormon's Missing Stories* (Greg Kofford Books, Salt Lake City, UT, 2019): 37-40.

[25] Joseph Smith, Jr., "Letter to Emma Smith," 4 June 1834, https://www.josephsmithpapers.org/paper-summary/letter-to-emma-smith-4-june-

in the text, yet Joseph wrote as if Emma was familiar with these terms.

The first reference to Nephite "plains" in the text is Alma 52:20, so if Joseph had been writing generically, Emma could be familiar with the term from the text Oliver originally scribed. But if Joseph used specific terms he knew Emma would recognize from her scribal work, they would have been in the 116 pages, which apparently referred to "mounds."[26] Of course, any scribal work on the 116 pages was separate from her writing on the OM after September 1828.

Conclusion: Emma said she "frequently" wrote "day after day" for Joseph. Oliver said he wrote all of the OM except "a few pages only."

These phrases reflect subjective memories. For Emma, acting as scribe even at a rate of 20 pages/month could have seemed like an eternity at the rate of two hours per page. Oliver, after writing most of the hundreds of pages of the OM, also copied most of those pages into the PM (over 384 pages in the PM alone). Emma's contributions could easily seem to Oliver, looking back from 1848, as "a few pages only."

Appendix 2 explains why I think Emma wrote most of the OM through Mosiah. The table on translation speeds indicates Emma (together with any other pre-Oliver scribes) wrote about 68 pages.

Pages in the 1830 edition average about 500 words. Emma could write such a page in 20-30 minutes. Producing 68 pages would take only 34 hours, less than two hours per week over five months. But if it took an hour or two per page, Emma's description suggests the translation required more effort than merely writing words Joseph read off a stone.[27]

We will use the following new (2020) translation timeline throughout the rest of this book.

1834/3.

[26] See the paper I presented at the June 2017 annual meeting of the Mormon History Association, online here: http://www.lettervii.com/2017/06/mormon-history-association-mounds-and.html.

[27] We will assess Emma's other statements about the translation in Chapter 9.

A New (2020) Translation Timeline

1805 – Joseph Smith, Jr. (JS) born 23 December in Sharon, Vermont.

1812 – JS has serious leg surgery, recuperates in Massachusetts, requires crutches until family moves to Palmyra.

1816 – Smith family moves to Palmyra, New York.

1820 – JS has First Vision.

1823 – JS visited by angel Moroni, views abridged plates with Urim and Thummim (U&T) and breastplate, 21-22 September.

1824-6 – JS visited by angel Moroni at the hill Cumorah each September.

1827 – JS marries Emma Hale in Jan., on Sept. 22 obtains abridged plates with U&T and breastplate, in Dec. moves to Harmony, Pennsylvania.

1828 – Using the U&T, JS begins copying and translating the characters from the engravings on the abridged plates.
– In Feb. Martin Harris (MH) takes transcript of characters to NYC.
– From Apr. 12-Jun. 14 JS translates plates with MH as scribe.
– In June MH loses the manuscript (the 116 pages). JS forfeits U&T.
– In July JS travels to the Palmyra area.
– On Sept. 22, JS receives back the U&T and the plates. He resumes translating with Emma and Samuel Smith as scribes.

1829 – In March, Martin Harris visits (D&C 5).
– On Apr. 5, Oliver Cowdery (OC) arrives in Harmony.
– On Apr. 7, JS translates the abridged plates into his own language (English) with OC as scribe.
– JS and OC receive Aaronic Priesthood from John the Baptist and baptize one another. Later, JS and OC receive Melchizedek Priesthood from Peter, James and John.
– Late May, JS commanded through U&T to contact David Whitmer (DW), requesting to move to the Whitmer home near Fayette, NY.
– Before leaving Harmony, JS translates the Title Page and has it printed (possibly in Binghamton, NY) for the copyright application.
– JS gives the abridged plates to a divine messenger.
– DW arrives. On the road to Fayette, JS, OC and DW encounter the divine messenger who has the abridged plates. The messenger says he is going to Cumorah. JS identifies him as one of the Nephites.

– The messenger brings the small plates of Nephi (original plates) to Fayette and shows them to Mary Whitmer, identifying himself as Brother Nephi. The messenger gives them to JS.
– JS and OC translate the small plates (1 Nephi through WoM).
– JS conducts demonstrations with a seer stone in a hat.
– The 3 witnesses view the abridged plates.
– The 8 witnesses view the plates of Nephi.
– OC copies the Original manuscript into the Printer's manuscript.

1830 – Book of Mormon published; Church organized; first missionaries sent to Lamanites (American Indians) in New York and Ohio.

1831 – LDS gather to Kirtland; New Jerusalem in Missouri revealed.

1832 – Grammar in the early revelations is changed (which to who, etc.).

1834 – In Painesville (near Kirtland) anti-Mormon book titled *Mormonism Unvailed* is published, establishing SITH as an alternative to U&T.
– Responding to *Mormonism Unvailed*, JS and OC publish the first formal history of the Church, affirming U&T.
– OC ordained Assistant President of the Church.

1837 – JS edits the Book of Mormon to correct grammar.

1840 – JS edits the Book of Mormon again.

1841 – The Cowdery letters are republished in the *GR*, *MS*, and *T&S*.

1842 – JS publishes "Church History" (the Wentworth letter), reiterating that he translated the plates with the U&T.

1844 – The Cowdery letters are republished in England and in *The Prophet.*
– Joseph and Hyrum Smith are martyred in Carthage, IL.

1848 – Oliver rejoins the Church, testifies of U&T.

1840s through 1890s – LDS leaders teach U&T while others teach SITH.

1877 – Emma Smith's "Last Testimony" (SITH); rebuttal of "Last Testimony" by Joseph F. Smith, Eliza R. Snow, etc.

1887 – David Whitmer's "An Address to All Believers in Christ" (SITH)

1900 through 2005 – LDS leaders teach U&T while others teach SITH.

2005 – *Rough Stone Rolling* rejects U&T in favor of SITH.

2007 – Final LDS General Conference address to teach that Joseph translated with U&T (Elder L. Tom Perry, April 2007).

2020 – SITH depicted in the *Ensign* and other Church media.

2. The translation problem

Overview.

A preliminary question about the translation of the Book of Mormon is whether Joseph Smith used the Urim and Thummim (U&T) or a seer stone in the hat (SITH). The two narratives were set out as alternatives in 1834 and have yet to be reconciled. We can analyze this question in the framework of thesis, antithesis, and synthesis.

The thesis: Joseph Smith and Oliver Cowdery claimed that Joseph Smith translated the ancient Nephite plates by the gift and power of God through the medium of the U&T that came with the plates.

The antithesis: Others, including David Whitmer and Emma Smith, claimed that Joseph produced the Book of Mormon by dictating words as he looked at a seer stone in a hat.

The synthesis: There are three alternatives:

(i) Redefine "Urim and Thummim" to mean both the interpreters that came with the plates *and* the seer stone Joseph found in a well.

(ii) Decide one explanation or the other was a lie.

(iii) Accept that Joseph translated with the U&T but he also used the seer stone to conduct a demonstration.

———

Detail.

The first (1830) edition of the Book of Mormon contains a Preface written by Joseph Smith, Jr., that is not included in modern editions.

> I would inform you that **I translated, by the gift and power of God**, and caused to be written, one hundred and sixteen pages, **the which I took from the Book of Lehi**, which was an account abridged from the plates of Lehi, by the hand of Mormon…

This plain declaration was one of several Joseph gave during his lifetime. Various scriptural passages corroborate his claims. The historical record includes roughly 200 statements about Joseph's translation of the Book of Mormon, and it is here that the narrative becomes murky because these statements offer an assortment of details, perspectives, assertions—and contradictions.

We all want to harmonize the historical evidence to derive an *objective* "truth" of what happened so everyone can agree, but historical evidence consists mostly of *subjective* personal accounts.[28] It is completely normal for different people to remember the same events differently. Individuals remember the same event differently at different times, emphasize one detail over another, etc.

Because the historical evidence supports multiple inferences, interpretations, and conclusions, we can organize them into a thesis, antithesis, and synthesis framework.

Framing the analysis

You have probably noticed a recent shift in the treatment of Joseph Smith's translation of the Book of Mormon. Traditionally, LDS Church leaders and historians taught the **thesis** set out below. Critics taught the **antithesis**. As early as 1834, the book *Mormonism Unvailed* presented both positions as alternative explanations for the Book of Mormon. Ever since, believers and critics have confirmed their respective biases by citing historical evidence that favors their respective interpretations.

In this book, we want to see whether and how the historical evidence supports what Joseph Smith claimed about the translation.

In doing this analysis, I recognize but do not address in any detail those who believe that Joseph composed or copied the Book of Mormon from another source. We'll discuss that issue in Chapter 10.

The thesis reflects my bias: I assume Joseph told the truth, so I begin by presenting supporting historical evidence.[29] Then I set out the antithesis with its supporting evidence. Finally, I consider three

---

[28] For an outstanding explanation of "Memory as History" see Ronald O. Barney, *Joseph Smith: History, Methods, & Memory* (University of Utah Press, Salt Lake City, Utah, 2020).

[29] Some academics claim they begin by analyzing all the evidence without a bias, but that is delusional thinking that fools no one. It is more transparent to acknowledge one's bias than to pretend one is unbiased.

categories of synthesis—three ways to reconcile the historical evidence.

Figure 1 - Thesis, Antithesis, Synthesis

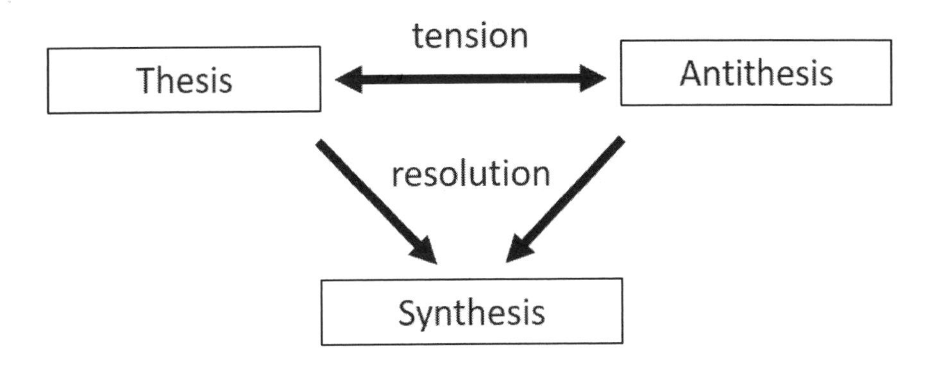

Thesis (U&T): By the gift and power of God, Joseph Smith translated an ancient text engraved on metal plates. Joseph and Oliver always claimed that Joseph used the Urim and Thummim (U&T) that Moroni deposited in the stone box with the original abridged plates. The U&T were also called the Nephite "interpreters" and the "spectacles." The Lord prepared the U&T specifically for the translation of the plates because "none other people knoweth our language" (Mormon 9:34) and the language was "confounded" and "no one can interpret them" (Ether 3:22, 24). Historical sources include Joseph Smith-History, Oliver Cowdery Letter I, the Wentworth letter, the *Elders Journal*, and Oliver Cowdery's last testimony.

Antithesis (SITH): Some contemporary observers claimed Joseph Smith dictated words that appeared on a seer stone (aka "peep stone") he placed in a hat (stone-in-the-hat or SITH). They say he did not use the plates (they sat nearby covered with a cloth) or the U&T (after the 116 pages were lost). This means Joseph did not *translate* the ancient plates in the normal sense of the term; instead, he *read English words*.[30]

[30] As used here, *read* expresses the idea that Joseph "read" words that appeared before him supernaturally, not in print or as ideas, but as visual words. Whether one believes the words appeared on the stone-in-the-hat or in vision, this concept of reading is

Some of the statements describing this scenario were compiled in the 1834 book *Mormonism Unvailed*, while others came around 50 years later in statements from Emma Smith, Martin Harris and David Whitmer.

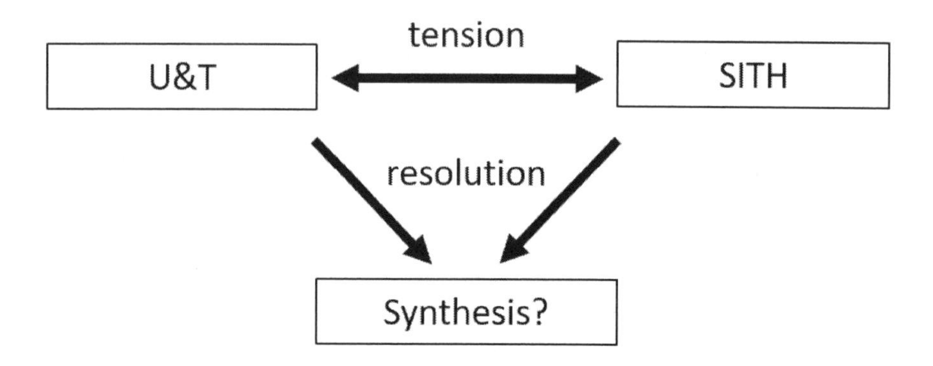

Discussion. The thesis/antithesis framing of the issue has caused confusion among Church members.

For older generations, learning about the SITH antithesis can be troubling and can disturb their faith because it contradicts the U&T thesis they had always been taught and always believed.

For younger generations who are being raised with the SITH scenario, it can be troubling when they learn that Joseph Smith and Oliver Cowdery always taught the U&T thesis.

In recent years, faithful Church members have sought to allay these concerns by reconciling the thesis and antithesis through synthesis. Here are three alternative possibilities for **synthesis**.

Synthesis #1: Both narratives are correct. A synthesis is possible by redefining terms; i.e., Joseph and Oliver used the term *Urim and Thummim* to refer to *both* the Nephite interpreters and the seer/peep stone in a hat. That is, Joseph used both instruments at various times.

Synthesis #2: Only one narrative can be correct. Those who believe Joseph and Oliver must reject the SITH narrative, while those who

---

neither *composing* nor *translating*.

believe the observers must reject the U&T narrative. Redefining terms is anachronistic because Joseph's contemporaries unambiguously distinguished between the two. One or the other side was lying.[31]

Synthesis #3: Both narratives are accurate observations, but some observers made incorrect inferences. Joseph Smith used the U&T that came with the plates to translate the engravings on the plates, but he also performed demonstrations with a stone in the hat to satisfy observers' curiosity about the process. That is, people who described the SITH proceedings *inferred* or *assumed* they watched the translation, but none of them recorded the words Joseph actually spoke or even asserted that Joseph *said* he was translating the plates on these occasions. (As we'll see later in the book, I propose that during the demonstrations, Joseph may have been reciting chapters of Isaiah from memory that are now contained in 2 Nephi.) Later, SITH evolved into a defense against the Solomon Spaulding theory.[32]

Most of us choose whichever synthesis confirms our beliefs, biases, and preferences, based on what we were taught when young or what we have heard from experts we trust (and agree with). Naturally, we defer to experts because we assume they have studied the issues and are unbiased (which usually means they share our biases).

Nevertheless, there remains a "tumult of opinions" about this topic because the conflicting evidence is difficult to reconcile—on its face. I hope the information in this book will enable you, the reader, to make an informed decision for yourself. If I've overlooked or ignored any facts you are aware of, let me know. We're all pursuing truth together.

---

[31] Those who reject any supernatural input suggest the peep stone was merely a prop Joseph used as he invented the text while he dictated, or recited the text from memory; i.e., they say he composed and dictated the text as a storyteller. E.g., William L. Davis, *Visions in a Seer Stone: Joseph Smith and the Making of the Book of Mormon* (University of North Carolina Press, Chapel Hill, NC, 2020).

[32] Early critics claimed Joseph Smith copied the Book of Mormon from a "lost manuscript" by Solomon Spaulding, provided by Sidney Rigdon. We'll discuss this more in Chapter 4.

Let's begin with my brief analysis of each proposed synthesis.

Analysis: Synthesis #1 is the approach taken by many LDS historians today and is set forth in recent LDS Church media and lesson manuals, including the Gospel Topics Essay on Book of Mormon Translation, *Saints* Volume 1, and the 2020 *Come Follow Me* manual. However, such a retroactive re-interpretation of the term *Urim and Thummim* contradicts the historical record.

In 1834 *Mormonism Unvailed* made a clear distinction between U&T and SITH, as we'll see in Chapter 4.

Joseph and Oliver responded promptly to *Mormonism Unvailed* by emphasizing that Joseph used *the* Urim and Thummim that *came with* the plates to *translate* the plates. They consistently claimed this throughout the rest of their lives.

Joseph and Oliver always claimed Joseph used *the* Urim and Thummim, not *a* Urim and Thummim, to translate the plates.

In connection with the translation of the Book of Mormon, they never referred to *a* Urim and Thummim as a generic term.[33] Neither of them claimed that Joseph read words that appeared on a seer/peep stone, that he didn't actually translate the plates, or that he had power to translate the plates with anything other than *the* Urim and Thummim.

Another problem with Synthesis #1 is it contradicts the scriptural narrative. If Joseph didn't need the U&T, there was no reason for Moroni to deposit the instrument. Instead of warning Joseph not to show the U&T to anyone, Moroni could have simply told Joseph to use the seer stone he already had and saved the trouble and risk.

For that matter, SITH maintains that Joseph didn't even use the plates, which puts in question all of the "plate" narratives.

Lately, SITH has combined with "linguistic evidence" to support

---

[33] D&C 130:9-10 refers to "a Urim and Thummim" in a different context. While there may be more than one Urim and Thummim, speaking generically, Joseph and Oliver never stated or implied that Joseph used more than one instrument for the translation of the Book of Mormon.

this proposition: "Based on the linguistic evidence, the translation must have involved serious intervention from the English-language translator, who was not Joseph Smith."[34]

Synthesis #1 means Joseph didn't use the Nephite interpreters, he didn't use the plates, and he didn't even translate anything.

Analysis: Synthesis #2 was implied in the original thesis; i.e., if Joseph used the U&T, he did not *also* use a seer stone. This means one version was true and the other was false, as set forth in *Mormonism Unvailed.*

Some people who accept Joseph Smith's account attribute statements about the seer stone to deliberate lies rooted in elements of the occult. However, there are numerous accounts by multiple observers, including David Whitmer, Martin Harris, and Emma Smith. Portraying all of these people—including two of the Three Witnesses—as liars influenced by the occult and/or their opposition to Joseph Smith is less historical analysis than mere mind-reading based on an ideological position.

This approach is the mirror-image of the argument by critics who claim Joseph and Oliver lied about the U&T; i.e., you decide in advance what you want to believe and reject all contrary evidence. This is the least persuasive type of analysis and cannot lead to agreement.

Analysis: Synthesis #3 accepts all the historical evidence for what it is, but distinguishes between statements of fact and statements of hearsay, opinion or belief. It considers bias, motives, and opportunity.

Joseph and Oliver always spoke of facts. Witness statements about SITH consist of both fact and opinion that can be separated for analysis; i.e., most people told the truth about what they observed (or heard others say), but they also made assumptions that led to the dual narratives set forth in *Mormonism Unvailed* and subsequent statements. From that point, SITH became a convenient way to refute the Spaulding theory.

---

[34] Royal Skousen, *Part Five*, p. 6.

I tested Synthesis #3 by examining the evidence and I think it is the best explanation. I wrote this book to explain why.

———

One important historical source is Zenas H. Gurley, who interviewed David Whitmer in January 1885 in Missouri and wrote an account of the testimonies of the witnesses of the Book of Mormon that was published as "The Book of Mormon" in *Autumn Leaves* 5 (1892): 451-55.

Gurley noted that Joseph could not allow anyone to see the plates or the Urim and Thummim except to certain individuals designated by God. "That Joseph had **another stone** called seers' stone, and 'peep stone,' is quite certain. **This stone was frequently exhibited to different ones and helped to assuage their awful curiosity; but the Urim and Thummim never, unless possibly to Oliver Cowdery**."

Gurley's observation makes sense. Joseph had been forbidden from the beginning from showing the plates or the U&T to anyone.

> Again, he told me, that when I got those plates of which he had spoken—for the time that they should be obtained was not yet fulfilled—I should not show them to any person; neither the breastplate with the Urim and Thummim; only to those to whom I should be commanded to show them; if I did I should be destroyed. (Joseph Smith-History 1:42)

And yet, Joseph's supporters were curious about the translation. How could he satisfy them and still comply with the commandment?

He could resolve the paradox by demonstrating with a seer stone.

> Joseph Smith could kill two birds with one seer stone.

One of those authorized to see the plates and the Urim and Thummim was Oliver Cowdery. The Lord said, "And, behold, I grant unto you a gift, if you desire of me, to translate, even as my servant Joseph." (D&C 6:25)

To translate, Oliver was surely authorized to see the plates and the

U&T. Oliver said as much in an 1848 interview with Samuel Whitney Richards.

Richards had returned from his first European mission in the fall of 1848. He joined his wife in Winter Quarters and spent the winter in Missouri. Oliver Cowdery and his wife stopped to visit during a snowstorm and stayed two weeks. They discussed the translation. Richards wrote his recollection in 1907.

> I was surprised to see the bright recollection he seemed to have of his early experiences with the Prophet Joseph, especially as relating to the translation of the Book of Mormon, some of which I will here relate.
>
> He represents Joseph as sitting by a table **with the plates before him, and he reading the record with the Urim & Thummim**. Oliver, his scribe, sits close beside to hear and write every word as translated. This is done by **holding the translators over the words of the written record, and the translation appears distinctly in the instrument**, which had been touched by the finger of God and dedicated and consecrated for the express purpose of translating languages. This instrument now used fully performed its mission. … To satisfy Oliver, Joseph with him went to the Lord in prayer until Oliver had the gift by which he could translate, and by so doing learned how it was that Joseph could correct him even in the spelling of words. [35]

Although Richards apparently wrote his account nearly sixty years later in 1907,[36] other evidence corroborates his account.

The heading to D&C 7 explains it was a "Revelation given to **Joseph Smith the Prophet and Oliver Cowdery**, at Harmony, Pennsylvania, April 1829, when **they** inquired through the Urim and Thummim."

They inquired.

---

[35] We can see from the Original Manuscript that spelling was erratic. Presumably Oliver meant the spelling of certain proper nouns in the text. The Richards statement is *Samuel W. Richards statement*, handwritten, May 21, 1907, available online at https://dcms.lds.org/delivery/DeliveryManagerServlet?dps_pid=IE4987076.

[36] The 1907 date does not preclude a prior written or oral statement. See an *Ensign* article here: https://www.churchofjesuschrist.org/study/ensign/1977/09/by-the-gift-and-power-of-god?lang=eng

From Harmony, Oliver wrote at least two letters to David Whitmer that suggest he, Oliver, progressed from being merely *convinced* Joseph had the records to *knowing of a certainty*—implying he had seen for himself. David related that shortly after Oliver arrived in Harmony,

> he wrote to me telling me that he was **convinced** that Smith had the records.... Joseph translated from the plates and he wrote it down. Shortly after this Cowdery wrote me another letter in which... he assured me that he **knew of a certainty that he had a record** of a people that inhabited this continent, and that the plates they were translating gave a complete history of these people.[37]

As Gurley explained, Joseph was not permitted to show the U&T to anyone else before the translation was completed in Fayette and the Three Witnesses had their experience.[38] Therefore, those who claimed to observe the translation process (aside from Oliver Cowdery) *could not have seen* the U&T.

On October 21, 1848 (shortly before stopping at the Richards home), Oliver rejoined the Church of Jesus Christ of Latter-day Saints. On that occasion, he reaffirmed his testimony about the translation and the U&T. At the time, he still possessed the brown seer stone Joseph had given him, the one Joseph used in the demonstrations. The stone was probably in his pocket.[39] Yet Oliver never mentioned it.

> I wrote with my own pen the entire Book of Mormon (save a few pages) as it fell from the lips of the Prophet as he translated it by the gift and power of God *by means of the Urim and Thummim, or as it is called*

---

[37] David Whitmer, *Kansas City Journal* (1881), #27 in Appendix 1.

[38] Mary Whitmer claimed an old man who called himself Brother Nephi—the same divine messenger who took the abridged plates from Harmony to Cumorah before bringing the plates of Nephi to Fayette—showed her the plates. The messenger could display the plates without violating the commandment given *to Joseph Smith*; presumably the messenger was not forbidden to show the plates to anyone.

[39] On March 3, 1850, Oliver died in Richmond, MO, at David Whitmer's home. Oliver's wife Elizabeth gave the seer stone to Oliver's brother-in-law, Phineas Young (brother of Brigham). https://www.josephsmithpapers.org/site/note-on-seer-stone-images and https://archive.org/details/historicalrecord79jens/page/622/mode/2up

> *by that book, holy interpreters.* I beheld with my eyes and *handled with my hands* the gold plates from which it was translated. I also beheld the Interpreters.[40] (emphasis added)

Had Joseph translated with the brown stone, Oliver could have declared as much and held it up for everyone to see. Instead, Oliver directly linked the U&T to the Nephite interpreters, using the same terminology as he did in the 1834 essay that is now canonized in the Pearl of Great Price as a note to Joseph Smith—History.

> Day after day I continued, uninterrupted, to write from his mouth, as he translated with the Urim and Thummim, or, as the Nephites would have said, 'Interpreters,' the history or record called 'The Book of Mormon.'

The 1834 essay was written partly to refute the claims in *Mormonism Unvailed*, which included SITH as an alternative to U&T. More than twenty years later, Oliver still deemed it important to reaffirm that the "Interpreters" Joseph used to translate the plates were the ones described in the Book of Mormon—the ones Moroni deposited with the abridged plates.

———

The term *interpreters* appears only four times in the 1830 Book of Mormon: three times in Mosiah and once in Ether.[41]

Mosiah 8:19 explains that "these interpreters were doubtless prepared for the purpose of unfolding all such mysteries to the children of men." Ether 4:5 relates the Lord's commandment to Moroni: "he also hath commanded that I should seal up the interpretation thereof; wherefore I have sealed up the interpreters, according to the commandment of the Lord."

Moroni explained that the record could be read only with the

---

[40] Reuben Miller's account of Oliver Cowdery's speech. Online at See Item #46 in Appendix 1.

[41] In modern LDS editions, the term "interpreters" also appears twice in Alma 37, but this was a change to the text beginning in 1921. Originally the term in Alma 37 was "directors."

interpreters, based on what the Lord said to the brother of Jared in Ether, Chapter 3.

> 22 And behold, when ye shall come unto me, ye shall write them and shall seal them up, that **no one can interpret them**; for ye shall write them in a language that they cannot be read.
> 23 And behold, these two stones will I give unto thee, and ye shall seal them up also with the things which ye shall write.
> 24 For behold, the language which ye shall write I have confounded; wherefore I will cause in my own due time that **these stones shall magnify to the eyes of men these things which ye shall write**.

We see that the Jaredite language could not be interpreted without "these stones." "Magnify" here presumably means more than merely enlarging the engravings like a magnifying glass. It connotes an expansion of understanding, conferring an ability to translate. That the stones would magnify to the "eyes of men" suggests multiple future translators—Mosiah, Moroni, and Joseph Smith.

Whether a stone found in a well could serve the same purpose as "these stones" that the Lord gave to the brother of Jared is a question we can each answer for ourselves.

Translation theories

The U&T vs. SITH debate is related to the theories of *how* Joseph produced the Book of Mormon.

1. Some think Joseph actually translated the characters on the plates; i.e., he studied the characters and learned the language well enough to convey the writings on the plates into his own words in English, guided by the Spirit to choose among alternative expressions.

2. Some think Joseph received spiritual impressions, thoughts, or pre-language concepts that he expressed in English, guided by the Spirit to choose among alternative expressions.

3. Some think Joseph "saw" actual words, whether appearing on the stone or in vision, and read the words out loud.

The debate is also framed in terms of "loose control, tight control, and iron-clad control," reflecting the varying degrees of freedom Joseph had to express what he understood, felt, or saw.[42]

All three options are consistent with U&T. SITH is consistent only with options 2 and 3. Therefore, acceptance of SITH means Joseph could not have translated in the ordinary sense of understanding the two languages.

Theological questions

Resolving the apparent contradictions raised by historical evidence is not merely a matter of curiosity. It implicates theological questions.

Synthesis #1 accepts *as fact* the proposition that Joseph read words that appeared on the seer/peep stone in a hat while the plates remained covered with a cloth nearby. As we discussed in the Preface, that proposition raises serious theological questions.

If Joseph didn't use the plates, why did they exist at all?

Why did Mormon and Moroni go to the trouble of abridging the Nephite records if the seer stone, functioning as a metaphysical teleprompter, provided Joseph all the words in the Book of Mormon?

And if Joseph didn't actually translate the plates, who did? If the plates were deposited in the hill Cumorah by Moroni and not removed until Joseph Smith found them, how could an intermediary translator translate the plates? Ether 3:22 says "no one can interpret them," without the interpreters. Did this person access the interpreters? Or was Moroni himself the translator, which might explain the inconsistent grammar in the text (because Moroni was not fluent in English).[43]

Such questions impact our interpretation of other historical evidence from the early days of the Restoration.

Evidentiary questions

---

[42] For a succinct overview with references, see Roger Terry, "Archaic Pronouns and Verbs in the Book of Mormon: What Inconsistent Usage Tells Us about Translation Theories," *Dialogue*, 47.3 (2014) https://www.dialoguejournal.com/wp-content/uploads/sbi/articles/Dialogue_V47N03_307.pdf

[43] Ibid.

To reconstruct historical events we must examine evidence, but evidence is inherently subjective and unreliable. Even first-person accounts are subject to bias, selective memory, ulterior motives, etc. Second-hand accounts, whether hearsay or interviews, are fraught with reliability problems.

In modern times, we have daily examples of reporters creating news instead of reporting facts. Whether driven by economic or personal considerations, reporters have strong incentives to create controversy and press a particular agenda. The same was true in the past.

In 1881, David Whitmer reluctantly consented to an interview with the *Kansas City Journal.* David started by telling the reporter, "I have been imposed upon and misrepresented so many times by persons claiming to be honorable newspapermen, that I feel a delicacy in allowing my name to come before the public in newspaper print again."

The reporter reassured him. "I am very sorry to hear that, but I **promise you** that we shall only give your statement as you make it and **will not misrepresent you** in any manner."

Nevertheless, the reporter promptly *misrepresented what David said*, even using quotation marks around David's alleged statements. David objected to the editor. Comparing the reporter's account with David's corrections side-by-side shows how easy it is for errors to creep in.[44]

Kansas City Journal	David Whitmer
David Whitmer, THE ONLY LIVING WITNESS, has resided since 1838 in Richmond, Ray county, Mo., and the JOURNAL dispatched a reporter to Richmond, to interview the "last of the eleven." The reporter called at the residence of Mr. Whitmer and found the patriarch resting in invalid's chair looking very pale and feeble, he having but just recovered from a long and very severe	To the Editor of the [Kansas City] Journal. RICHMOND, Mo., June 13 [1881].—**I notice several errors in the interview had with me** by one of your reporters as published in the Daily Journal of June 5th, '81, and wish to correct them.

[44] It is also possible the reporter accurately reported what David said but David changed his mind when he saw his words in print.

illness. In person, he is about medium height, of massive frame, though not at all corpulent, his shoulders slightly bent as with the weight of years. His manly, benevolent face was closely shaven, his hair snow-white, and his whole appearance denoted one of nature's noblemen. The education acquired during his boyhood days and his long life devoted to study and thought have stored his mind with a vast fund of information. After introducing himself, the reporter opened the conversation as follows: "Mr. Whitmer, knowing that you are the only living witness to the translation of the Book of Mormon and also that you were a resident of Jackson County during the Mormon troubles in 1833, I have been sent to you by the JOURNAL to get from your lips THE TRUE STATEMENT OF FACTS in regard to these matters. For nearly half a century the world has had but one side only, and it is now our desire to present to our readers for the first time the other side." "Young man, you are right. I am the only living witness to the Book of Mormon, but **I have been imposed upon and misrepresented so many times by persons claiming to be honorable newspapermen**, that I feel a delicacy in allowing my name to come before the public in newspaper print again." **"I am very sorry to hear that, but I promise you that we shall only give your statement as you make it and will not misrepresent you in any manner."**	
I went down to Harmony, and found everything just as they had written me. The next day after I got	. . . In regard to my going to Harmony, my statement was that "I found everything as Cowdery had written me,

there they packed up the plates and we proceeded on our journey to my father's house where we arrived in due time, and the day after we commenced upon the translation of the remainder of the plates.	and that they packed up next day and went to my father's, (**did not say 'packed up the plates'**) and that he, Smith, (not 'we') then commenced the translation of the remainder of the plates."
I, as well as all of my father's family, Smith's wife, Oliver Cowdery, and Martin Harris were present during the translation. The translation was by Smith and the manner as follows:	**I did not wish to be understood as saying that those referred to as being present were all of the time in the immediate presence of the translator,** but were at the place and saw how the translation was conducted.
"He had two small stones of a chocolate color, nearly egg shaped and perfectly smooth, but not transparent, called interpreters, which were given him with the plates.	I did not say that Smith used "two small stones," as stated nor did I call the stone "interpreters." I stated that "he used one stone (not two) and called it a sun stone." The "interpreters" were **as I understood**[46] taken from Smith and were not used by him after losing the first 116 pages as stated. **It is my understanding** that the stone referred to was furnished him when he commenced translating again after losing the 116 pages.
He did not use the plates in the translation, but would hold the interpreters to his eyes and cover his face with a hat, excluding all light, and before his eyes would appear what seemed to be parchment, on which would appear the characters of the plates in a line at the top, and immediately below would appear the translation in English, which Smith would read to his scribe, who wrote it down exactly as it fell from his lips. The scribe would then read the sentence written, and if any mistake had been made the characters would remain	My statement was and now is that in translating he put the stone in his hat and putting his face in his hat so as to exclude the light and that then the light and characters appeared in the hat together with the interpretation which he uttered and was written by the scribe and which was tested at the time as stated. Note.—It is but justice to the

[46] "I understood" constitutes hearsay, as does "it is my understanding."

visible to Smith until corrected, when they faded from sight to be replaced by another line. The translation at my father's occupied about one month, that is from June 1 to July 1, 1829."[45]	reporter who interviewed Mr. Whitmer to say that the errors above referred to were purely accidental and entirely unintentional, as it was his aim and desire as well as that of the *Journal* to publish Mr. Whitmer's statement just as he made it.—Ed[47]

This exchange demonstrates how communication errors can occur even when a professional reporter purportedly seeks accuracy.

We will see more examples of directly contradictory testimony regarding the translation of the Book of Mormon. For example, other witnesses report that David Whitmer explicitly testified that Joseph Smith translated the plates with the U&T and not with the seer stone. (See chapter 7.) Others spoke of the seer stone. I propose, as part of Synthesis #3, that many of the these sources told the truth about what they *observed* (even if they framed their inferences as observations), while others thought they had a noble reason to alter their stories.

Debates over the various accounts of the translation played out in the pages of the *Saints' Herald* (a publication of the Reorganized Church of Jesus Christ of Latter-day Saints) in the late 1800s. Those same debates persist to the present.

The consistency of what Joseph and Oliver said about the translation—that Joseph translated the plates with the U&T that came with the plates—contrasts with the confusing and contradictory evidence from other sources.

[45] "Mormonism," *Kansas City Daily Journal*, June 5, 1881; online at https://en.wikisource.org/wiki/Kansas_City_Journal,_June_5,_1881

[47] David Whitmer to the editor, *Kansas City Daily Journal*, June 13, 1881; at https://en.wikisource.org/wiki/Kansas_City_Journal,_June_5,_1881; cited in Cook, *David Whitmer Interviews*, 71–72.

3. Current Status

Overview.

Joseph Smith and Oliver Cowdery consistently taught that Joseph translated the plates with the Urim and Thummim that came with the plates.

After the deaths of Joseph 1844 and Oliver in 1850, LDS Church leaders frequently reiterated their claims in General Conference and other venues.

The last such testimony was in 2007.

Since then, the narrative has been changed to the idea that Joseph used both U&T and SITH. However, there are no historical accounts that support this narrative. Those who claim Joseph used the seer stone also say he did not use the U&T. Joseph and Oliver said Joseph used the U&T and never said he used a seer stone.

Detail.

For decades, leaders of the Church of Jesus Christ of Latter-day Saints taught that Joseph used the U&T. If you search the *Journal of Discourses* or LDS General Conference addresses, you get over 100 results of leaders testifying that Joseph translated the plates with the "Urim and Thummim" that he obtained from Moroni, which had been prepared for the purpose of translating the plates.[48]

On the other hand, the 1834 book *Mormonism Unvailed* described a different process.

> The translation finally commenced. They [the plates] were found to contain a language not now known upon the earth, which they termed "reformed Egyptian characters." The plates, therefore, which had been so much talked of, were found to be of no manner of use. After all, the Lord showed and communicated to him every word and letter of the Book.

[48] I recommend using WordCruncher to search LDS General Conference addresses. A good alternative is https://scriptures.byu.edu/ .

> Instead of looking at the characters inscribed upon the plates, the prophet was obliged to resort to the old "peep stone," which he formerly used in money - digging. This he placed in a hat, or box, into which he also thrust his face. Through the stone he could then discover a single word at a time, which he repeated aloud to his amanuensis, who committed it to paper, when another word would immediately appear, and thus the performance continued to the end of the book.[49]

This 1834 passage looks contemporary because it is the same narrative many modern historians have adopted.

The speakers in *Journal of Discourses* were familiar with *Mormonism Unvailed* and Oliver's eight essays that cited facts to rebut the claims of the critics (see Chapter 4). Many of them knew Oliver and Joseph personally and heard them testify that Joseph used the U&T to translate the plates.

In recent decades, however, faithful LDS scholars re-evaluated the historical evidence cited by critics regarding SITH. They decided the evidence was credible enough to warrant incorporation into standard Church history narratives, thereby implementing Synthesis #1.

Perhaps the most influential step in this process was the publication of *Rough Stone Rolling* in 2005. In January 2007, the author, Richard Bushman (RB)[50] was interviewed by John Dehlin (JD) of *Mormon Stories.* They discussed the thesis/antithesis dilemma and its impact.

> RB: **The stories of the stone in the hat were recorded very close to Joseph Smith's lifetime by the people who were there:** Oliver Cowdery, David Whitmer, and Emma Smith. So it's not like that we've sort of made up this new version. It's been there.
> **But I think what threw us off was our own embarrassment about Joseph Smith.**
> We so wanted him to be kind of a 19th century Protestant view of a prophet. A noble soul. Sort of partly ethereal, who speaks only spiritual wisdom, and not

---

[49] *Mormonism Unvailed,* p. 18, available online at. https://play.google.com/books/reader?id=KXJNAAAAYAAJ&printsec=frontcover&pg=GBS.PA18

[50] Professor Bushman is a member of the National Advisory Board for the Joseph Smith Papers and a general editor of the Papers from 2001 to 2013. He is the author of *Rough Stone Rolling* and other books and articles about Church history.

someone who's involved in magical practices, which is superstition, and which Protestants are dead set against in the 19th century.
That effort to kind of suppress anything that would scandalize Joseph Smith or turn him into a scandal I think motivated the desire to make it all sort of lovely and common sensical rather than anything that would be magical.

JD: So someone along the way maybe felt embarrassed, or said people aren't going to buy this, or people aren't going to believe it, or people are going to think we're goofy, and so let's re-write history and depict it in a way that is a little bit more palatable.

RB: I'm not sure it's quite that calculated, but it has that effect, that you kind of, just kind of bowdlerize the story, **you kind of whitewash it and it ends up this way.**

JD: I know that life is more complex than this, but I know a lot of people, it seems like a lot of the people who leave, they don't leave because they're weak or they're sinners or adulterers, they leave because they've got this view of what integrity and honesty is. They've always bought that integrity and honesty is absolute. There are blacks and whites, there is good and bad, and a lot of people say to me, John, Look, if the Church knows that they're depicting the translation process inaccurately, it is their duty and obligation to stand up, do it in General Conference, and tell everybody, all right, here's the deal, we were saying it wrong, here's how it is, and from now on, **whenever it is depicted in a motion picture or in the *Ensign*, we're going to stick his face in a hat with a stone in it.** I know you can't answer for them, but do you have any thoughts on that, or is that something you just have to leave to the way things are in life?

RB: I think your depiction of the disillusioned person is probably quite accurate. It's the absolutist, it's that personality that sees things as black and white that is going to be shocked and deeply offended by this whole thing. A personality that can't tolerate ambiguity and realize people get caught in situations and all sorts of strange things come out that is going to feel like you've got to lay down the law one way or another, and the Church has failed to do that, so while I was thoroughly devoted to it at one time in my absolutist way, I'm not thoroughly against it in my absolutist way.
I don't know what to do about that kind of personality because they're going to have troubles with the Church. That's quite true.[51]

[51] Transcript, 050: Richard Bushman—Experiences as a Mormon Historian, podcast, *Mormon Stories*, January 22, 2007, available online at https://www.mormonstories.org/podcast/richard-bushman-and-rough-stone-rolling-part-1-experiences-as-a-mormon-historian/

Is SITH a problem only for "absolutist personalities" or is it a problem in historical interpretation? I think the latter, obviously, and you'll see why by the time you finish this book.

Figure 2 - SITH in the *Ensign*, Jan. 2020

Thirteen years after this interview, in January 2020, the *Ensign* did publish an image of Joseph Smith translating with Oliver Cowdery, using the stone in a hat while the plates sat nearby on the table, covered with a cloth.

The article accompanying the illustration sets forth Synthesis #1. After quoting from Oliver Cowdery's Letter I (Joseph Smith—History 1:71, note), including Oliver's declaration that Joseph "translated with the Urim and Thummim, or, as the Nephites would have said, 'Interpreters,'" the article makes this claim:

> The "interpreters" used by Joseph during the translation process included the "two stones in silver bows" that were deposited by Moroni with the plates (see Joseph Smith—History 1:35.) In addition to these two seer stones, Joseph used at least one other seer stone that the Lord had provided.[52]

By expanding the definition of "interpreters" to include a seer stone *in addition to* the U&T, the article implements the Synthesis #1 technique of redefining terms. Notice, however, that the paragraph does not specifically state that Joseph used the "other seer stone" *for translation.* The vague wording accommodates the idea that Joseph used the "other

---

[52] LeGrand R. Curtis, Jr., "The Translation of the Book of Mormon: A Marvel and a Wonder, *Ensign*, January 2020, available online at https://www.churchofjesuschrist.org/study/ensign/2020/01/the-translation-of-the-book-of-mormon-a-marvel-and-a-wonder?lang=eng

seer stone" for other purposes (as I propose in this book).

But then the *Ensign* article actually paraphrases Joseph Smith to *change* what he said and replace the term "Urim and Thummim" with "interpreters."

***Ensign*, January 2020**	**Joseph Smith—History 1:35**
The "interpreters" used by Joseph during the translation process included the "two stones in silver bows" that were deposited by Moroni with the plates.	35 Also, that there were two stones in silver bows—and these stones, fastened to a breastplate, constituted what is called the Urim and Thummim—deposited with the plates; and the possession and use of these stones were what constituted "seers" in ancient or former times; and that God had prepared them for the purpose of translating the book.

To compound the problem, the next paragraph in the article is a direct quotation from David Whitmer's 1887 booklet titled *An Address to All Believers in Christ*. In that booklet, David specifically claims that Joseph used only the seer stone and never the U&T to translate the text published as the Book of Mormon. Whitmer's booklet also denounces Joseph and his successors for various reasons.

David's booklet (antithesis) directly contradicts Oliver's declaration (thesis). That's why the article resorts to Synthesis #1.

To assess the plausibility of Synthesis #1, we need to explore its development and implications. Then, in Chapter 4, we will review the historical background of the thesis and antithesis and how we arrived at the point where we are today.

> Synthesis #1 redefines the term "Urim and Thummim" to refer to *both* the Nephite "interpreters" and any other seer stone.

The recent acceptance of Synthesis #1 is puzzling to many long-time

Church members. Why has it become popular?

For many faithful members of the Church, Synthesis #1 is attractive as a relatively easy way to defuse the critics. By framing the translation as an unknowable mystery, believers can sort of accept all of the accounts, whether they relate SITH or U&T, and even when they conflict.

As shown by the *Ensign* article, members can avoid considering Joseph's specific claim that he used the U&T that came with the plates.

The accounts of the translation are so inconsistent and contradictory that we can say Joseph "used both instruments" because either way, the process had to be inspired and the details do not matter.

That is enough for many Church members.

But for other Church members (and for most people outside the Church) the idea that Joseph merely read words off a stone he put inside a hat not only contradicts what Joseph and Oliver said, but raises all the other historical and theological questions we've alluded to.

Synthesis #1 is unpalatable. Fortunately (from my perspective) no one is required to accept it. Especially because a better alternative exists.

One book that explains Synthesis #1 is *From Darkness unto Light: Joseph Smith's Translation and Publication of the Book of Mormon* by Michael Hubbard Mackay and Gerrit J. Dirkmaat. While I appreciate the detailed historical information and analysis in the book, in my view the authors' determination to establish Synthesis #1 led them to overlook the fact that in 1834, *Mormonism Unvailed* clearly distinguished between the two theories; i.e., that book presented the peep stone as an *alternative* to the U&T. There is no suggestion that the two instruments were the same, or that anyone used the terms interchangeably.

Against the backdrop of *Mormonism Unvailed*, the persistent and specific statements of Joseph and Oliver about *the* Urim and Thummim cannot plausibly be transformed into a SITH narrative by simply redefining the term as if Joseph and Oliver meant to testify (or should have testified) all along that Joseph used *a* Urim and Thummim.

Critics frame Synthesis #1 as a tacit admission that Joseph and

Oliver were less than candid when they claimed that Joseph translated with the Nephite interpreters that they called the Urim and Thummim. That is, if Joseph really produced the Book of Mormon by reading words that appeared on a seer stone he placed in a hat, then he did not use the Nephite interpreters after all. Nor did he use the plates they came with.

For critics, this narrative undermines the credibility of everything Joseph and Oliver claimed. The persuasiveness of the critical framing of Synthesis #1 has led some faithful Church members to adopt Synthesis #2 or Synthesis #3, both of which we'll discuss later in this chapter. First, though, let's look at how Synthesis #1 is currently being presented throughout the Church (in addition to the *Ensign*).

———

The first lesson in the 2020 *Come Follow Me* manual includes this section that sets out Synthesis #1:

> **How was the Book of Mormon translated?**
>
> The Book of Mormon was translated "by the gift and power of God." We don't know many details about the miraculous translation process, but we do know that Joseph Smith was a seer, **aided by instruments that God had prepared: two transparent stones called the Urim and Thummim and another stone called a seer stone.** Joseph saw in these stones the English interpretation of the characters on the plates, and he read the translation aloud while a scribe recorded it. Each of Joseph's scribes testified that God's power was manifest in the translation of this sacred work.
>
> See "Book of Mormon Translation," Gospel Topics, topics.ChurchofJesusChrist.org.

Naturally, Church members rely on Church curriculum material for reliable information. This passage from the *Come Follow Me* manual can be quickly passed over, but if we pause to read it carefully, we see some contradictions and confusion.

First, the passage distinguishes between the U&T and the seer stone, thereby preserving the distinction set forth in *Mormonism Unvailed* in 1834. By so doing, the manual seems to reject Synthesis #1. However, if the distinction is valid, and we accept what Joseph and Oliver taught, then Joseph *never* used a seer stone to translate the Book of Mormon. Yet the manual claims Joseph *did* use the seer stone to translate. The witnesses who said Joseph translated with the seer stone also said Joseph never used the U&T after the 116 pages were lost. That's why, without a synthesis, U&T is a direct conflict with SITH.

Second, the manual claims God prepared two separate instruments: the U&T (the Nephite "interpreters") and the seer stone. Moroni placed the U&T with the plates in the stone box on the hill Cumorah. That these interpreters were prepared by God for the translation is explained in the Book of Mormon, the Doctrine and Covenants, and the records of what Moroni told Joseph Smith. None of these references mention a seer stone, whether the one Joseph allegedly found while digging a well or another one. Consequently, the manual raises the question, in what way did God prepare the seer stone? Did God place it in the ground where Joseph would someday dig a well? And why did Joseph need the seer stone in addition to the U&T?

Third, the manual states as a fact that Joseph "saw in these stones the English interpretation of the characters on the plates." That is an inference based on hearsay because we have no direct statements by Joseph making such a claim.

The passage in the manual describes a supernatural teleprompter with words provided by an intermediary translator. But that claim introduces the theological questions we've already looked at, such as, if Joseph didn't actually translate the plates, who did?

The *Come Follow Me* manual tracks the language in *Saints*, Volume 1, which also frames the translation in terms of Synthesis #1. *Saints* closely follows David Whitmer's booklet, *An Address to All Believers in Christ*, although *Saints* does not cite this source.[53]

---

[53] Footnote 25 in *Saints* refers to the Gospel Topics Essay on Book of Mormon Translation and other sources, but not David Whitmer's account.

Saints, Volume 1	David Whitmer, *An Address to All Believers in Christ*
Sometimes Joseph translated by looking through the interpreters and reading in English the characters on the plates. Often he found a single seer stone to be more convenient. He **would put the seer stone in *his* hat, *place* his face into the hat** to ***block out*** **the light**, and peer at the stone. **Light** from the stone **would shine in the darkness**, revealing words that Joseph dictated as Oliver rapidly copied them down.[54]	Joseph Smith **would put the seer stone in*to a* hat, *and put* his face in the hat,** drawing it closely around his face ***to exclude*** **the light**; **and in the darkness** the spiritual **light would shine.**[55]

This account of Whitmer's is the only account of the translation that uses the phrase "in the darkness." The other similarities between the two versions are obvious. Notice how the authors of *Saints* switched the words *in* and *into* to create some difference: "stone in his hat" vs. "stone into a hat," then "face into the hat" vs. "face in the hat." Regardless, the key phrases are the same.

In his booklet, David wrote at length about why the "Latter Day Saints" in Utah were "in error" about various doctrines and practices. Denying that Joseph Smith used the U&T fit his objectives as we'll see in chapter 4.

Both *Come Follow Me* and *Saints* refer readers to the Gospel Topics Essay on "Book of Mormon Translation."[56] That essay makes a case for Synthesis #1 by quoting and citing historical statements from

[54] "The Gift and Power of God," Chapter 6 of *Saints*, Volume 1, page 61, online at https://www.churchofjesuschrist.org/bc/content/ldsorg/media-library/ebook-pdf/Saints-v1-English-PD60001624.pdf?lang=eng.

[55] David Whitmer, *An Address to All Believers in Christ*. See #33 in Appendix I.

[56] https://www.churchofjesuschrist.org/study/manual/gospel-topics-essays/book-of-mormon-translation?lang=eng

various observers, along with interpretations from modern scholars.

However, the essay never once quotes Joseph Smith or Oliver Cowdery when they explained that Joseph translated with the Urim and Thummim. Instead, it edits their teachings to avoid their references to the Urim and Thummim, just as the *Ensign* article did.

The Gospel Topics Essay is a useful resource, but it could be greatly improved by focusing on the teachings of Joseph Smith and Oliver Cowdery instead of the claims of others and the speculations of experts. To provide additional references and perspectives, I included an annotated version of the Gospel Topics Essay in Appendix 3 and my proposed revised essay in Appendix 4.

By now, you can understand why so many faithful members of the Church have difficulty with Synthesis #1.

Some prefer Synthesis #2.

One book that explains Synthesis #2 is *Seer Stone v. Urim & Thummim: Book of Mormon Translation on Trial* by Hannah L. Stoddard and James F. Stoddard. The authors have provided detailed historical research and analysis to support their theory that all of the observers who claimed Joseph translated by using SITH were involved with the occult and were lying.

I find their argument implausible and unpersuasive. Certainly, some of the observers were antagonistic to Joseph Smith, but Emma Smith, David Whitmer, and Martin Harris all sought to support the Book of Mormon. Each is a separate case, so I have separate chapters for each, but overall, I think they told the truth about what they observed, or at worst adopted others' statements for what they considered justifiable ends.

The other conceptual problem with Synthesis #2 is that it is the mirror image of the argument by critics that Joseph and Oliver lied. The critics claim they both knew Joseph merely dictated words (SITH), but they concocted the Urim and Thummim story because it sounded more plausible. This line of reasoning leads one to simply choose a side and stick with it, disregarding contrary evidence.

> Synthesis #2 rejects all the evidence that contradicts what Joseph and Oliver said about translating with the Urim and Thummim. It is the mirror image of the claim by critics that Joseph and Oliver were lying.

While I understand the desire among believers to disregard the statements about the seer stone in the hat, I don't think it is necessary to characterize all of these witnesses as liars with bad motives to reconcile the evidence and support what Joseph and Oliver said.

That's why I prefer Synthesis #3.

Synthesis #3 includes six points that we'll discuss in more detail in upcoming chapters.

1. Joseph Smith translated the engravings on the plates using the U&T that Moroni placed in the stone box with the plates. The Nephites referred to them as "interpreters." Joseph and others sometimes referred to them as "spectacles."

2. Joseph was under a strict command never to show the interpreters or the plates to anyone, except to certain people as designated by the Lord. One of these, presumably, was Oliver Cowdery, who was authorized to translate along with Joseph but was unsuccessful.

3. Many people were curious about the translation. Because he could not translate in the presence of others (because he used both the plates and the U&T), Joseph conducted demonstrations of the process to satisfy curiosity and explain the gift and power of God. He used a stone in a hat, a process with which his contemporaries were familiar, as a proxy to demonstrate how he could translate the engravings on the plates by means of the U&T and then dictate the English words to a scribe. This does not mean he literally "saw" words that he voiced.

4. Observers assumed they were watching the actual translation, but they did not record what words Joseph dictated, the duration or frequency of the demonstrations, or even a statement by Joseph that he was actually translating during these events. Joseph may have let them believe it was a translation without explicitly saying. More likely, he was

reciting Isaiah passages from memory (discussed in Chapter 5). Over time, statements from these observers coalesced into a consensus, and then ultimately into a defense against the Solomon Spaulding theory.

5. By 1834, the two different narratives (the thesis and antithesis) were explicitly identified in the anti-Mormon book *Mormonism Unvailed.* In response, Oliver and Joseph affirmed unequivocally that Joseph translated the plates by using the Nephite interpreters called the Urim and Thummim. They both reiterated that claim multiple times and never deviated from it.

6. After 1860, the U&T became an issue in the contest between the Church of Jesus Christ of Latter-day Saints (LDS) and the Reorganized Church of Jesus Christ of Latter Day Saints (RLDS). LDS authorities frequently testified that Joseph Smith translated the plates with the U&T. Heber C. Kimball declared in General Conference that Brigham Young possessed the U&T, indicating it enabled him to receive revelation. Partly to contest Brigham's claim of rightful successorship, RLDS authorities denied that Joseph used the U&T and assembled affidavits to support their position. These authorities also cited SITH as a defense against the Spaulding theory.

> Synthesis #3 accepts the evidence that Joseph translated the plates with the U&T. It also accepts evidence that he used SITH, but only for demonstrations, not for any actual translation of the plates.

By now, you may have already chosen which synthesis you prefer, but I encourage you to withhold judgment until you consider all the evidence in the next few chapters.

4. Historical Background - 1834

Overview.

The historical record includes numerous statements about both U&T and SITH, but in no case did any witness claim Joseph used both. The 1834 book *Mormonism Unvailed* presented U&T and SITH as explicitly alternative explanations.

Partly in response to *Mormonism Unvailed*, Oliver Cowdery wrote a series of eight essays about Church history, published serially in the *Messenger and Advocate* from 1834-5. In the first essay he specifically set forth the thesis: "Day after day I continued, uninterrupted, to write from his mouth, as he translated with the Urim and Thummim, or, as the Nephites would have said, 'Interpreters,' the history or record called 'The Book of Mormon.'" (Joseph Smith—History, Note, 1)

The antithesis is set forth in statements from several individuals, including David Whitmer, Emma Smith, and Martin Harris. Assessing the credibility and reliability of these statements involves questions of means, opportunity, and motive.

Detail.

The Translation Timeline at the beginning of this book provides an overview of key events. The Table of Translation Accounts in Appendix 1 includes relevant first- and second-hand accounts of the translation. This chapter frames the various accounts within the historical context.

One contemporary of Joseph Smith pointed out an inherent problem with these accounts. John A. Clark wrote a book titled *Gleanings by the Way* (1842) which includes a chapter titled "The Origin of the Mormon Delusion."[57] The chapter was adapted from an 1840 article, one of several articles Clark had written for the *Episcopal Recorder*,

[57] Online at https://archive.org/details/gleaningsbyway00clarrich/page/216.

a periodical for which he was one of the editors.

He prefaced his recitation of Martin Harris' narrative this way:

> **As far as I can now recollect**, the following was **an outline of the narrative** which he then communicated to me, and subsequently to scores of people in the village, from some of whom in my late visit to Palmyra, **I have been able to recall several particulars that had quite glided from my memory**.

Clark acknowledged he could remember only an "outline of the narrative" that Martin told him; the details had "quite glided" from his memory until he visited Palmyra and asked around. This is a good description of how a historical consensus develops. People "help" each other "remember" and thereby construct a collective narrative that they individually express as if based on their independent experiences.

Police, investigators and lawyers are all too familiar with such collective memories. While sometimes people deliberately collude to create a narrative—to get their stories "straight"—there are also innocent reasons why people help one another to remember. We all have gaps in our memories that we want to fill.

Psychologists have demonstrated that our memories are malleable because we reconstruct them each time we "remember" or relate a past experience. We don't record events like a video camera; there is no single location in the brain where complete memories are stored. Our memories can be distorted by social influences as well as our individual perceptions, to say nothing of bias, motive, capacity, etc.

Ronald O. Barney pointed out that

> Enthusiasts of history yearn for reliable, written-at-the-time records upon which to build their interpretations. But in the absence of primary documentation, memory is often called upon to fill the gaps left by those who, for a myriad of reasons, failed to create contemporaneous records.[58]

---

[58] Barney, *Joseph Smith: History, Methods & Memory*, pp 65-6.

Barney cites the example of George A. Smith, an Apostle and Church historian, who said, "I write from memory, most of the dates, names and distances being forgotten, but the principal facts are fresh in my mind."[59] It's natural for people to think their memories are accurate, but it's also unrealistic, except when there are specific details that make a particular memory memorable.

———

An article in the October 2015 *Ensign* titled "Joseph the Seer"[60] sets out the basic premise for Synthesis #1. The subheading reads "The historical record clarifies how Joseph Smith fulfilled his role as a seer and translated the Book of Mormon."

The article discusses the "stones" Joseph received along with the plates (which Joseph called the Urim and Thummim).

> The text of the Book of Mormon calls these stones "interpreters" and explains that they "were prepared from the beginning, and were handed down from generation to generation, for the purpose of interpreting languages," being "kept and preserved by the hand of the Lord" (Mosiah 28:14–15, 20).

But then the article cites Alma 37:21 ("Preserve these interpreters") without explaining that the term "interpreters" in Alma 37 was a change from the original edition, which used the term "directors" in chapter 37. The change was made in the 1920 LDS edition.

Next, the article introduces the seer stone.

> In fact, historical evidence shows[61] that in addition to the two seer stones known as "interpreters," Joseph Smith used at least one other

[59] George A. Smith, Memoir, draft 2 for June 5, 1835, 62, George A Smith Papers, ca. 1857, MS 1322, box 1, folder 2, CHL.

[60] Online at https://www.churchofjesuschrist.org/study/ensign/2015/10/joseph-the-seer?lang=eng

[61] The evidence "indicates" or "suggests" but does not "show" in the sense of proving this assertion because the "translation" element was an inference by the witnesses.

> seer stone in translating the Book of Mormon, often placing it into a hat in order to block out light. According to Joseph's contemporaries, he did this in order to better view the words on the stone.[62]
>
> By 1833, Joseph Smith and his associates began using the biblical term "Urim and Thummim" to refer to any stones used to receive divine revelations, including both the Nephite interpreters and the single seer stone.[63] This imprecise terminology[64] has complicated attempts to reconstruct the exact method by which Joseph Smith translated the Book of Mormon. In addition to using the interpreters, according to Martin Harris, Joseph also used one of his seer stones for convenience during the Book of Mormon translation. Other sources corroborate Joseph's changing translation instruments.[65]

The article's reference to 1833 ("by 1833") alludes to an article in the January 1833 Latter-day Saint newspaper *The Evening and the Morning Star*, edited by William W. Phelps, that equated "spectacles" and "interpreters" with the term "Urim and Thummim." Phelps explained that the Book of Mormon "was translated by the gift and power of God, by an unlearned man, through the aid of a pair of Interpreters, or spectacles— (known, perhaps, in ancient days as Teraphim, or Urim

[62] A footnote here refers to the Gospel Topics Essay on Book of Mormon Translation. The problem is that all the sources for SITH say Joseph did not use the Urim and Thummim after the 116 pages were lost; i.e., he did not use it (or the plates) to translate the Book of Mormon we have today. Yet Joseph and Oliver always said he used the Urim and Thummim and the plates.

[63] This claim is supported by a single example in a footnote in the article here, which reads: "Wilford Woodruff, for instance, called a seer stone he saw in Nauvoo a Urim and Thummim (Wilford Woodruff journal, Dec. 27, 1841, Church History Library). See also *Revelations and Translations, Volume 3: Printer's Manuscript of the Book of Mormon*, xix." The problem: Woodruff never said it was a seer stone. Modern scholars merely *assume* that's what he saw. See the discussion in Appendix 4.

[64] The terminology is not imprecise; Joseph and Oliver always said Joseph translated the plates with the Urim and Thummim that Moroni provided with the plates, which the Nephites called "Interpreters." Neither of them said Joseph used a seer stone; only others claimed that, and the distinction was crystal clear.

[65] Chapter 9 discusses Martin Harris.

and Thummim)."[66]

Some scholars have inferred that it was Phelps who coined the term *Urim and Thummim* for the interpreters that came with the plates. However, Phelps' article is also consistent with prior use of the term; i.e., instead of coining the term, he was explaining the term for readers who were familiar with the Bible.

Phelps may have thought up the term independently, but he was definitely not the first to use it. The first known use of the term *Urim and Thummim* to refer to the Nephite interpreters was reported on August 5, 1832, when Orson Hyde and Samuel Smith told an audience in Boston that the translation "was made known by the spirit of the Lord through the medium of the Urim and Thummim."[67] Orson and Samuel undoubtedly heard that from someone else—presumably Joseph or Oliver. Joseph wrote the identical clause in the 1842 Wentworth letter: "Through the medium of the Urim and Thummim I translated the record by the gift, and power of God."[68]

In my view, the writings of Joseph Smith and Oliver Cowdery establish that it was Moroni who first used the term. They related that Moroni told Joseph that it would be his "privilege, if obedient to the commandments of the Lord, to obtain and translate the same by the means of the Urim and Thummim, which were deposited for that purpose with the record."[69]

People can disagree about whether these words were Moroni's or a later interpretation and expansion of what Moroni said, but everyone should at least agree that this passage, like others from Joseph and Oliver, specifically ties the U&T to the Nephite interpreters.

---

[66] The Book of Mormon," *The Evening and the Morning Star*, January 1833, p. 2.

[67] "Questions Proposed to the Mormonite Preachers and Their Answers Obtained Before the Whole Assembly at Julian Hall, Sunday Evening, August 5, 1832," *Boston Investigator,* Vol. II, No. 20 (August 10, 1832). Online at http://www.sidneyrigdon.com/dbroadhu/NE/miscne01.htm

[68] https://www.josephsmithpapers.org/paper-summary/church-history-1-march-1842/2

[69] Letter IV, online at https://www.josephsmithpapers.org/paper-summary/history-1834-1836/68

———

There is an important reason why Joseph and Oliver always said Joseph translated the plates using the U&T. *They were refuting SITH.*

Although it is new to many Church members today, and although some modern scholars have revived SITH as if it was recently discovered, it is old news to anyone familiar with Church history. Contrary to modern notions of "imprecise terminology," early Church members and their critics alike have always recognized a clear distinction between the U&T (the Nephite interpreters) on one hand, and the seer or "peep" stones on the other hand.

As we've seen already, SITH originated in the early days of the Church. The 1834 book titled *Mormonism Unvailed*, published in Painesville, Ohio, just a few miles from Kirtland, sought every way possible to discredit Joseph Smith, his associates, and the Book of Mormon. It is difficult to overstate the significance of this book. Over 100 years later, on November 14, 1936, the Deseret Evening News in Salt Lake City published an editorial about *Mormonism Unvailed*, observing "For fifty years, this book was quoted by every anti-Mormon writer."[70]

The book made three basic claims against Joseph Smith that will be familiar to many modern readers.

1. It ridiculed the idea of the translation and identified SITH as an alternative to Joseph's account that he translated the plates with the U&T that Moroni put in the stone box with the plates.

2. It framed Joseph and his family as disreputable people.

3. It claimed the Book of Mormon was fiction based on a previous book by Solomon Spaulding.

---

[70] Dr. Francis W. Kirkham, "Two Significant Statements Attached to the Spaulding Manuscript," *Deseret Evening News*, November 14, 1936. http://www.sidneyrigdon.com/dbroadhu/LDS/ldsnews3.htm#111436

Joseph and Oliver promptly responded to these claims by publishing a series of eight essays about Church history in the *Messenger and Advocate*. (I call these the original Gospel Topics Essays)

The eight essays. These eight Church history essays were not ordinary, run-of-the-mill articles in a Church newspaper. They were written by Oliver Cowdery, with the explicit assistance of Joseph Smith. Two months later, in December 1834, Joseph ordained Oliver as Assistant President of the Church (senior in authority to the two counselors in the First Presidency). It was in that capacity that Oliver wrote and published the rest of the essays.

After the eight essays were published as letters in the *Messenger and Advocate* newspaper (as Letters I through VIII), Joseph had his scribes copy them into his journal as part of his life story. You can read them in the Joseph Smith Papers in *History 1834-1836*.[71]

To make sure all members of the Church were familiar with these essays, Joseph had them republished in every Church newspaper during his lifetime (except the short-lived *Elders' Journal*). The essays were republished in the *Millennial Star* (1840), the *Times and Seasons* (1841), the *Gospel Reflector* (1841), and the *Prophet* (1844). They were published as a separate booklet in England, and thousands of copies were sold. They were frequently quoted by Church leaders and authors.

In 1880, part of Letter I was canonized in the Pearl of Great Price as a note to JS-History 1:71. Later, President Joseph F. Smith republished all eight essays in the *Improvement Era* in Utah.

The essays are important because they address doctrinal and historical issues that are just as pressing today as they were when Joseph and Oliver wrote the essays in 1834-5.

Unfortunately, most Church members today are unfamiliar with these important essays, which have never been published in the *Ensign*

---

[71] https://www.josephsmithpapers.org/paper-summary/history-1834-1836/48

(so far). But they are easily available in the Joseph Smith Papers, both in print and online.

Oliver introduced the essays with this explanation:

> That our narrative may be correct, and particularly the introduction, it is proper to inform our patrons, that **our brother J. Smith Jr. has offered to assist us**. Indeed, there are many items connected with the fore part of this subject that render his labor indispensible. With his labor and with authentic documents now in our possession, we hope to render this a pleasing and agreeable narrative, well worth the examination and perusal of the Saints. —
>
> To do Justice to this subject will require time and space: we therefore ask the forbearance of our readers, **assuring them that it shall be founded upon facts**.

If you take the time to read these essays, be sure to compare and contrast the facts that Joseph and Oliver presented against what everyone else said.

Next, let's turn to the three criticisms from *Mormonism Unvailed* and see how Joseph and Oliver responded.

---

1. SITH. The first response to *Mormonism Unvailed* that Joseph and Oliver published addressed SITH. This was in Letter I, published in October 1834.

Setting aside the sarcasm of the following passage from *Mormonism Unvailed*, we can see that the first paragraph below from page 18 is essentially what some Church historians are teaching today.

> The translation finally commenced. They were found to contain a language not now known upon the earth, which they termed "reformed Egyptian characters." The plates, therefore, which had been so much talked of, were found to be of no manner of use. After all, the Lord showed and

> communicated to him [Joseph] every word and letter of the Book. **Instead of looking at the characters inscribed upon the plates, the prophet was obliged to resort to the old "peep stone," which he formerly used in money-digging.** This he placed in a hat, or box, into which he also thrust his face. Through the stone he could then discover a single word at a time, which he repeated aloud to his amanuensis, who committed it to paper, when another word would immediately appear, and thus the performance continued to the end of the book.[72]

This narrative, supplemented by later statements by David Whitmer and others, is the factual predicate for Synthesis #1. It represents what I referred to as the "antithesis" to the "thesis" that Joseph and Oliver taught, as we discussed in Chapter 1.

The second description of the translation found in *Mormonism Unvailed* is based on the explanation that Joseph and Oliver always gave. This is the "thesis," albeit embellished with the sarcasm typical of *Mormonism Unvailed.* This passage is also from page 18.

> **Another account they give of the transaction, is, that it was performed with the big spectacles before mentioned, and which were in fact, the identical Urim and Thumim** mentioned in Exodus 28 — 30, and were brought away from Jerusalem by the heroes of the book, handed down from one generation to another, and finally buried up in Ontario county, some fifteen centuries since, to enable Smith to translate the plates without looking at them![73]

Joseph's contemporaries who read this 1834 book understood these were two alternative, competing explanations of the translation of the Book of Mormon. Elsewhere in the book the authors distinguish between the "spectacles" (as a synonym for the U&T) and the "peep

---

[72] See https://archive.org/details/mormonismunvaile00howe/page/18

[73] Intentionally or not, the author missed the points that (i) the U&T that Joseph received was not brought from Jerusalem by Lehi but instead had been used by the Jaredites in America, and (ii) Joseph actually looked at the plates with the spectacles.

stone." There is no indication or implication that Joseph, Oliver, or anyone else referred to the "seer stone" or "peep stone" as *a* Urim and Thummim or vice versa. All contemporary accounts referred to the objects Moroni put in the stone box as *the* Urim and Thummim, the spectacles, or the Nephite interpreters.

Mormonism Unvailed pointed out some of the logical problems with SITH. This excerpt from pp. 77-8 of *Mormonism Unvailed* illustrates how the authors used the terms to attack the credibility of Joseph's account. Now that LDS historians have adopted SITH, critics today make the same arguments.

> Now, whether **the two methods for translating, one by a pair of stone spectacles "set in the rims of a bow," and the other by one stone,** were provided against accident, we cannot determine—perhaps they were limited in their appropriate uses—at all events the plan meets our approbation.
>
> We are informed that Smith used a stone in a hat, for the purpose of translating the plates. The **spectacles and plates were found together**, but were taken from him and hid up again before he had translated one word, and he has never seen them since — this is Smith's own story.[74] **Let us ask, what use have the plates been or the spectacles, so long as they have in no sense been used?** or what does the testimony of Martin Harris, Oliver Cowdery and David Whitmer amount to? They solemnly swear that they saw the plates, and that an angel showed them, and the engravings which were upon them.
>
> But if the plates were hid by the angel so that they have not been seen since, how do these witnesses know that **when Smith translated out of a hat, with a peep-stone,** that the contents of the plates were repeated and written down? Neither of the witnesses pretend that they could read the hieroglyphics with or without the stone; and, therefore, are not competent testimony….

---

[74] Joseph and Oliver responded to this claim by emphasizing that Joseph translated the entire Book of Mormon with the U&T. Separately, Joseph explained that the angel returned the U&T in September 1828 following the loss of the 116 pages.

Faced with *Mormonism Unvailed's* claim about SITH, Joseph and Oliver addressed the translation of the Book of Mormon with a simple statement of fact.

> These were days never to be forgotten—to sit under the sound of a voice dictated by the inspiration of heaven, awakened the utmost gratitude of this bosom! Day after day I continued, uninterrupted, to write from his mouth, as **he translated with the Urim and Thummim, or, as the Nephites should have said, "Interpreters,"** the history, or record, called "the book of Mormon."[75]

When considered in the context of *Mormonism Unvailed*, this statement is a powerful declaration of which narrative was correct. Oliver's rejection of SITH was obvious to his contemporary readers (unlike modern readers who are unaware of the context).

The response was so direct and clear they didn't need to elaborate.

2. Joseph's character. The second claim of *Mormonism Unvailed* focused on the character of Joseph Smith and his family, claiming they were not reputable people. The book supported this claim with a series of affidavits from former Smith neighbors in the Palmyra area, along with Emma's family and others in the vicinity of Harmony, Pennsylvania.

Oliver Cowdery's Letters II and VIII address some of the criticisms of Joseph Smith's character. The letters defused character criticisms by denying the worst of them, adding context, and pointing out that no one is perfect, not even the biblical prophets.

Oliver briefly discussed the opposition from Emma's father and relatives who provided statements published in *Mormonism Unvailed.*

> While employed here he became acquainted with the family of Isaac Hale, of whom you read in several of the productions of those who

---

[75] https://www.josephsmithpapers.org/paper-summary/history-1834-1836/49. Also found in JS-H, 1:71 footnote.

> have sought to destroy the validity of the book of Mormon. It may be necessary hereafter, to refer you more particularly to the conduct of this family, as their influence has been co[n]siderably exerted to destroy the reputation of our brother, probably because he married a daughter of the same, contrary to some of their wishes, and in connection with this, to certain statements of some others of the inhabitants of that section of count[r]y…

Addressing the attacks on the character of Joseph Smith and his family was an important part of the Church history that Oliver and Joseph wrote in these letters. Oliver emphasized that when not contradicted, slanderous reports may be believed by default.

> Though you may say, this is a digression from the subject proposed, I trust I shall be indulged, for the purpose of satisfying many, who have heard so many slanderous reports that they are <led to believe them true because they are> not contradicted; and besides, this generation are determined to oppose every item in the form or under the pretence of revelation, unless it comes throug[h] a man who has always been more pure than Michael the great prince; and as this is the fact, and my opposers have put me to the necessity, I shall be more prolix, and have no doubt, before I give up the point, shall prove to your satisfaction, and to that of every man, that **the translator of the book of Mormon is worthy the appelation of a seer and a prophet of the Lord.**
>
> In this I do not pretend that he is not a man subject to passions like other men, beset with infirmities and encompassed with weaknesses; but if he is, all men were so before him, and a pretence to the contrary would argue a more than mortal, which would at once destroy the whole system of the religion of the Lord Jesus; for he anciently chose the weak to overcome the strong, the foolish to confound the wise, (I mean considered so by this world,) and by the foolishness of preaching to save those who believe.[76]

Oliver's main point—that Joseph was an ordinary mortal who made

[76] https://www.josephsmithpapers.org/paper-summary/history-1834-1836/107

mistakes, but nevertheless a seer and prophet of God—should inform our own interpretations of the historical evidence.

You can read those letters in the Joseph Smith Papers and reach your own conclusions.[77] I think Oliver did a good job of refuting the claims in *Mormonism Unvailed* by putting Joseph's weaknesses and errors in proper context. Joseph added a personal letter, published in December 1834 in the *Messenger and Advocate*, to provide additional context.

3. Solomon Spalding theory. The last section of *Mormonism Unvailed* set out the theory that the Book of Mormon was copied, or at least derived, from a book written years earlier by Solomon Spalding (also spelled Spaulding). This theory immediately became a major issue for Joseph Smith and the Church and has persisted through the present.[78]

The Spalding theory dovetailed into the two previous claims. If Joseph had the bad character claimed, he could have dictated the Book of Mormon by reading the Rigdon manuscript from behind a curtain, pretending to use the U&T and the plates that no one was allowed to see.

SITH was a defense against the Spalding theory. If, as the SITH witnesses claimed, Joseph translated in full view of multiple witnesses, using a seer stone in a hat with no other manuscripts present, then he was not reading from a Spalding manuscript or any derivatives.

Because this theory plays such a significant role in the SITH saga, we will look at it in more detail in the next chapter.

Oliver Cowdery's essays did not satisfy the critics, of course. The

[77] Letter II: https://www.josephsmithpapers.org/paper-summary/history-1834-1836/52 Letter VIII: https://www.josephsmithpapers.org/paper-summary/history-1834-1836/93

[78] See Cowdery, Davis, and Vanick, *The Spalding Enigma: Investigating the Mysterious Origins of the Book of Mormon* (St. Polycarp Publishing House, 2018). With 597 pages of detailed references and explanation, this is the most comprehensive resource I know of. The authors conclude that the original *Manuscript Found* has never been found.

point/counterpoint between *Mormonism Unvailed* and the eight essays published between October 1834 and September 1835 came at a critical point in the course of the Restoration. The first Twelve Apostles were called and set apart in February through April 1835. In May they left on their first mission. In July, the Egyptian mummies were purchased. The Doctrine and Covenants was published in September.

Missionaries and members faced a constant barrage of negative publicity that would last throughout the 19th century (and persists today). The three criticisms and Oliver's responses were repeated over and over. Of the three, though, the Spalding theory endured the longest. I think it drove much of what people said when they discussed the translation.

Joseph and Oliver maintained that Joseph translated the plates with the U&T that came with the plates. Joseph's LDS successors consistently taught the same thing for decades, through 2007.

In my view, SITH originated from a demonstration Joseph Smith conducted in Fayette. While *Mormonism Unvailed* discussed both the U&T and SITH, SITH evolved into the dominant narrative.

Ironically, SITH offered the advantage that witnesses could testify they personally observed the translation and that, contrary to the Spalding theory, Joseph was not reading from any manuscript or notes. This became an important narrative for certain defenders of the Book of Mormon. I propose that, in the minds of several observers, that honorable end justified the means of altering their testimonies accordingly.

Appendix 1 in this book includes many of the accounts that specifically address the translation itself. You will see that these accounts contain contradictions and inconsistencies, which is perfectly normal with any collection of witness statements.

That's not the case with Joseph and Oliver, however. They consistently and persistently declared that Joseph translated the entire Book of Mormon by using the U&T Moroni provided with the plates.

In evaluating witness statements, components of credibility to consider for each witness include:

- **Context**: to whom were they speaking, under what circumstances.
- **Competency**: power to perceive, remember and communicate.
- **Opportunity**: a position to observe the events testified about.
- **Bias or partiality**: relationships, financial stakes, beliefs.
- **Motive**: an agenda to promote through testimony.
- **Prior inconsistent statements**: unreconcilable differences.
- **Contradictory facts**: demonstrable facts contrary to the testimony.

This book doesn't take the time to go through those considerations for each statement, but you can do that yourself now that you understand the historical context and prevailing motivations.

In subsequent chapters, we focus on David Whitmer, Emma Smith, and Martin Harris because these were three most influential observers and their statements have been quoted frequently in recent years.

To put their statements in context, we will first discuss the Spalding theory (chapter 5) and then, in chapter 6, we will examine the "demonstration" narrative that I call Synthesis #3.

"We are here, this lovely Easter morning, in the reconstructed farmhouse of Peter Whitmer, Sr....

"From the soil of Cumorah's Hill, a few miles to the west of here, Joseph obtained from the angel Moroni the records of a people who anciently inhabited this land; and, through the gift and power of God, he translated that record, now known as the Book of Mormon. A substantial part of that work of translation was accomplished in this Whitmer home."

President Spencer W. Kimball, General Conference, April 6, 1830

5. The Persistent Spalding Theory

Overview.

In the 1830s, opponents of the Book of Mormon developed a theory that the Book of Mormon was adapted from a manuscript written by Solomon Spalding (Spaulding), who died in 1816. According to this theory, Spalding wrote a novel that explained the Hebrew origins of the moundbuilders who left impressive earthworks in Ohio, where Spalding lived when he wrote the novel. Spalding read his manuscript to neighbors and left the manuscript at a printing company in Philadelphia, hoping they would publish it.

In 1832, Elder Orson Hyde was preaching in Ohio, quoting from and explaining the Book of Mormon. A man in the audience later claimed he remembered the names Lehi, Nephi, Lamanites and Nephites, as well as other elements of the Book of Mormon, from hearing Spalding read his book about 20 years previously.

Eventually a scenario was developed: Sidney Rigdon allegedly found the manuscript in Philadelphia, copied it, added Christian theology, and conspired with Joseph Smith to present it to the world as a long-lost record. A key claim was that Joseph read the manuscript to scribes from behind a curtain or sheet.

The 1834 book *Mormonism Unvailed* included affidavits to support the Spalding theory. Oliver's essays on Church history related facts to refute the theory, but opponents have persisted in advocating the Spalding theory through the present day.

Refuting the Spalding theory became an important priority. When he rejoined the Church in 1848, Oliver Cowdery again denounced the Spalding theory. More witnesses and new publicity arose in the late 1860s. Starting in 1870, David Whitmer, Emma Smith and others faithful to the Book of Mormon used SITH to prove Joseph could not have read from a manuscript.

Brigham Young and other LDS leaders continued to teach U&T. They denounced the Spalding theory without resorting to SITH.

———

Detail.

The Solomon Spalding (aka Spaulding) theory originated from an incident on February 13, 1832.[79] Orson Hyde preached that day in "Salem Village," which became Conneaut, Ohio, in 1833. The town is about 50 miles northeast of Kirtland, on the shore of Lake Erie.

Hyde preached from the Book of Mormon. A lawyer in the audience, Nehemiah King, left the meeting and allegedly told others that Hyde had been reading from the writings of Solomon Spaulding, a friend and neighbor of King's who had died in 1816.

An excommunicated Mormon, Doctor Philastus Hurlbut, learned about the allegation and collected affidavits from Spalding's family and neighbors to the effect that they recognized names such as Nephi, Lehi, Nephites and Lamanites from Spalding's book titled *Manuscript Found*, which they said explained how the first settlers of America came from Jerusalem and are the ancestors of the American Indians. The affidavits were published in October 1834 in *Mormonism Unvailed*, together with a purported link to the theory that Sidney Rigdon had obtained a copy of *Manuscript Found*, rewrote it to add "religious" content, met Joseph Smith's family, and set up the narrative about the plates and the translation. As early as 1831,[80] articles had been published claiming that Rigdon was the "true" author of the Book of Mormon, so the Spalding narrative blended in well.

The book and its claims did not catch Joseph and Oliver off guard.

In April, 1834, Oliver Cowdery published an editorial in *The Evening and the Morning Star* (then printed in Kirtland) alerting readers to the activities of Hurlbut.

---

[79] An overview from a faithful LDS source is Rex C. Reeve Jr., "What is 'Manuscript Found'? in *Manuscript Found: the Complete Original "Spaulding Manuscript,"* (BYU 1996), https://rsc.byu.edu/manuscript-found/what-manuscript-found

[80] "Rigdon was formerly a disciple of Campbell's ... but is probable he thought he should find it more advantageous to operate on his own capital, and therefore wrote, as it is believed the Book of Mormon." See "Mormonism," *Cleveland Advertiser*, Feb. 15, 1831, at http://www.sidneyrigdon.com/dbroadhu/OH/miscohio.htm

> We have not, till now, thought this man worthy a notice in our paper, neither would he at this time been noticed by us were it not to undeceive those at a distance who are unacquainted with him and may be deceived in consequence of the above mentioned title, of Doctor [Hurlbut's given name]. It is but just, that we should say, with regard to those individuals whose names are going the rounds in the public prints, as a committee, who have employed this Hurlbut **to expose, the "Origin of the book of mormon,"** that as citizens, and neighbors, they will be as forward to expose his character, and hold him up to the view of community, in the true light which his crimes merit, as they were first to employ him, and employ a more respectable agent, if they are calculating on success when they engage with the religion and characters of their neighbors. **We care not what he, or they preach or publish: we are in no fear that he will overturn the truth**: but let him conduct himself in a lawful manner, and hold in a proper estimation the lives, if not the characters of his fellowmen, and he is welcome to all the success which his ignorance or wisdom can gain.[81]

Because Spalding's *Manuscript Found* could not be located, the theory relied on the affidavits and circumstantial evidence about Rigdon's whereabouts, including his alleged access to the manuscript years in Philadelphia and his alleged meeting with Joseph Smith before Joseph translated the plates.

The absence of *Manuscript Found* left Joseph and Oliver with the dilemma of proving a negative; i.e., they could not prove Spalding's manuscript never existed, let alone that the missing manuscript had no relationship to the Book of Mormon. All they could do was testify about the translation of the plates with the U&T—and they did.

But truth is not always an effective defense.

In this case, the truth played into the hands of the critics. Unable to allow people to view the U&T and the plates, Joseph necessarily conducted the real translation in seclusion.

This led to somewhat of a stalemate. Joseph could not produce the original manuscript—the golden plates—but he could produce

---

[81] *Evening and Morning Star,* vol. II., no. 19 (April 1834):150 ¶3

witnesses who saw the plates and testified about them.

Hurlbut could not produce the original Spalding manuscript—*Manuscript Found*—but he could produce witnesses who read the manuscript and testified that it described Book of Mormon events and named specific people, including Lehi and Nephi, Lamanites and Nephites.

This equivalence left Moroni's promise (Moroni 10:3-5) as the deciding factor for those who read the Book of Mormon. Perhaps this is a reason why Joseph and Oliver never took stronger action to reject SITH. All they could do is relate the truth—that Joseph translated the plates with the U&T. Without endorsing SITH, they let it stand as a defense to the Spalding story.

Facts vs. theory. The essence of the Spalding theory is that the Book of Mormon is fiction, based on Spalding's novel.[82] To refute that claim, Oliver and Joseph cited facts. Oliver Cowdery introduced his eight essays on Church history by explaining that the narrative "shall be founded upon facts." He used the terms *fact* and *facts* 24 times in the eight letters.

> That our narrative may be correct, and particularly the introduction, it is proper to inform our patrons, that **our brother J. Smith Jr. has offered to assist us**. Indeed, there are many items connected with the fore part of this subject that render his labor indispensible. [sic] With his labor and with authentic documents now in our possession, we hope to render this a pleasing and agreeable narrative, well worth the examination and perusal of the Saints.—
>
> To do <justice to> this subject will require time and space: we therefore ask the forbearance of our readears, [sic] assuring them that **it shall be founded upon facts**.[83]

Spalding's book allegedly discussed the origins of the Indians who

[82] See an LDS view: https://www.churchofjesuschrist.org/study/manual/gospel-topics/spaulding-manuscript?lang=eng

[83] Joseph Smith, History, 1834-1836, https://www.josephsmithpapers.org/paper-summary/history-1834-1836/48

built the extensive earthworks in Ohio. One way to put space between the Book of Mormon and the Spalding theory would have been to distance the Book of Mormon from a North American setting, such as claiming the events took place in Central or South America. Instead, Oliver focused on the New York setting for the Hill Cumorah, a key landmark in the Book of Mormon because both major civilizations—the Nephites and the Jaredites—fought battles of extinction there.

In July 1835, Oliver published Letter VII, which (i) described the location of the hill Cumorah from which Joseph obtained the plates and (ii) directly linked that hill to the narrative in the Book of Mormon.

> You are acquainted with the mail road from Palmyra, Wayne Co. to Canandaigua, Ontario Co. N.Y. and also, as you pass from the former to the latter place, before arriving at the little village of Manchester, say from three to four, or **about four miles from Palmyra, you pass a large hill on the east side of the road**….
> At about one mile west rises another ridge of less height, running parallel with the former, leaving a beautiful vale between. The soil is of the first quality for the country, and under a state of cultivation, which gives a prospect at once imposing, when one reflects on **the fact, that here, between these hills, the entire power and national strength of both the Jaredites and Nephites were destroyed.**
> By turning to the 529th and 530th pages of the book of Mormon you will read Mormon's account of the last great struggle of his people, **as they were encamped round this hill Cumorah.** (it is printed Camorah, which is an error.) **In this valley fell the remaining strength and pride of a once powerful people, the Nephites…. This hill, by the Jaredites, was called Ramah: by it, or around it pitched the famous army of Coriantumr their tents.**[84]

Such statements of fact—declarations that the events in the Book of Mormon actually took place in a specific, recognizable location—directly refuted the Spalding theory and any other claim that the Book

[84] Oliver Cowdery, Letter VII, https://www.josephsmithpapers.org/paper-summary/history-1834-1836/90.

of Mormon was fiction.[85]

Spalding: 1835-1848. *Mormonism Unvailed* was published in October 1834 in Painesville, Ohio, ten miles northeast of Kirtland. Oliver's eight letters were published from October 1834 to October 1835 in Kirtland.

In December 1835, the *Latter Day Saints' Messenger and Advocate* published a letter from Joseph Smith "To the Elders of the Church of the Latter Day Saints." Joseph compared the Book of Mormon to

> an impenetrable, immovable rock in the midst of the mighty deep... braving the mountain waves of opposition... urged onward with redoubled fury by the enemy of righteousness, with his pitchfork of lies, as you will see fairly represented in a cut, contained in Mr. Howe's "Mormonism Unveiled?"...
>
> We might farther say that, we could introduce him to "Mormonism Unveiled." Also to the right honorable Doct. P. Hurlburt, who is the legitimate author of the same, who is not so much a doctor of physic, as of falsehood, or by name. We could also give him an introduction to the reverend Mr. Howe, the illegitimate author of "Mormonism Unveiled," in order to give currency to the publication, as Mr. Hurlburt, about this time, was bound over to court, for threatening life.
> (Messenger and Advocate II.3:228 ¶2)

In April 1836, Orson Hyde, whose sermon allegedly initiated the Spalding theory, dismissed the criticism in a letter to the editor.

> The cause of God will roll on in the face of an opposing world, and I cannot but make the expression of the Prophet, saying, "no weapon formed against thee shall prosper." The first weapon raised against the spread of truth, of any consideration in this country, was the wicked and scurrilous pamphlet published by A. Campbell. Next, perhaps, were the letters of E. Booth, and thirdly, Mormonism unveiled written by Mr. E.D. Howe, alias. Doct. P. Hulbert.
>
> These were designed severally in their turn for the exposure and overthrow

[85] Ironically, many LDS scholars today reject what Oliver wrote, claiming he was merely speculating. Obviously, such a position undermines Oliver's argument that the Book of Mormon is an actual history.

> of "Mormonism" as they termed it; but it appears that heaven has not blessed the means which they employed to effect their object, "No weapon raised against it shall prosper."
>
> The writings of the above named persons, I find have no influence in the world at all; for they are not even quoted by opposers, and I believe for no other reason than—that they are ashamed of them.[86]

Despite Hyde's dismissal, the Spalding theory found a receptive audience in the antagonistic media and among Christian ministers who felt obliged to defend their flocks against incursions by Mormon missionaries. In the ensuing years, Joseph Smith moved the Church to Missouri and then to Nauvoo, Illinois. Members of the Quorum of the Twelve went to England and found great success.

But the Spalding theory followed the Church everywhere.

In 1838, in New York City, Parley P. Pratt published *Mormonism Unveiled*, a partial response to *Mormonism Unvailed.* Pratt explained that he introduced Sidney Rigdon to the Book of Mormon in October 1830.

> The Spaulding story never was dreamed of until several years afterwards, when it appeared in Mormonism Unveiled -- a base forgery, by D. P. Hulburt, and others of similar character, who had long strove to account for the Book of Mormon, in some other way beside the truth. In the west, whole neighbourhoods embraced Mormonism, after this fable of the Spaulding story, had been circulated among them.[87]

That same year, the August 1838 *Elders' Journal*, published in Far West, Missouri, published a denunciation of Howe and Hurlburt [sic] without naming their book.

In 1840, Benjamin Winchester, an LDS leader in Philadelphia, wrote a booklet on the origin of the Spalding theory.[88] He knew Hurlbut personally and offered his own knowledge together with facts he had

---

[86] *Messenger and Advocate* II.7 (April 1836):296 ¶9–11

[87] Parley P. Pratt, *Mormonism Unveiled*, 2d Ed., (New York 1838), p. 42. http://www.solomonspalding.com/docs/prt1838b.htm#pg40b.

[88] Benjamin Winchester, *The Origin of the Spaulding Story*, (Philadelphia 1840), online at http://www.solomonspalding.com/docs/1840WinA.htm.

ascertained.

Winchester began the book with this observation.

> AS the public mind has been somewhat agitated, for the last nine or ten years, upon the subject of Mormonism, (so called,) and as there have been coined and put into circulation, innumerable statements respecting its origin, and all of them contrary the one to the other; I deem it an act of justice to a belied people, and a deceived public, knowing the facts of the case, **to present to them the truth of the matter**, and to show the contradictions and absurdities, which are swallowed greedily down, without question or examination, because men love darkness rather than light.
>
> **THE Spaulding tale of a 'manuscript found,' seems to be the basis, from which the vast multitude of ephemeral lies derive their very existence.** I shall therefore, address myself to the task of its entire demolition, so far as it has any thing to do with the book of Mormon; when the superstructure reared thereon, will fall to the ground of necessity.

Like Orson Hyde, Winchester claimed that *Mormonism Unvailed* had been a financial failure "in the west" [Ohio] but that new versions of the Spalding theory were published in New York and Massachusetts, along with newspaper articles. He set out the facts in some detail to support his claim that the "Spaulding Story" was "sheer fabrication."

The influence of the Spalding theory spread to England. An LDS missionary there, George J. Adams, republished Winchester's booklet in 1841 in Bedford, England, as *Plain Facts, shewing the origin of the Spaulding Story.*[89]

In 1843, Elder John E. Page published yet another rebuttal of the Spalding theory titled *The Spaulding Story, concerning the origin of the Book of Mormon.* Originally published in Pittsburgh, Page's book was republished by the RLDS in 1866 with some new material.

As we saw previously, Cowdery's response to Spalding (Letters I, IV, VII and VIII) were republished in England (*MS*, 1840), Philadelphia (Winchester's *GR*, 1841), Nauvoo (*T&S*, 1841) and New York (1844).

[89] http://www.solomonspalding.com/docs/1840WinA.htm#1841ed

Was all of this effort overkill?

Apparently not.

In 1842-3, six books were published that restated the Spalding theory to one degree or another. They are easily accessible online.

John C. Bennett, *Mormonism Exposed* (*History of the Saints*) (NY, 1842);
Henry Caswell, *The City of the Mormons* (London, 1843);
John A. Clark, *Gleanings By the Way* (Philadelphia, 1842);
Daniel P. Kidder, *Mormonism and the Mormons* (NY, 1842);
Jonathan B. Turner, *Mormonism in All Ages* (NY, 1842); and
Rev. Samuel Williams, *Mormonism Exposed.* (Philadelphia, 1842).

These books addressed several aspects of Mormonism in addition to the Spalding story. They briefly discuss the translation in the familiar terms of Joseph using spectacles or Urim and Thummim behind a curtain and/or using a stone in his hat.

The September 1, 1842, issue of the *Times and Seasons* replied to the Turner and Kidder books, lumping them with "the canine-like but powerless bite of Mormonism unveiled, by E.D. Howe."[90] On May 1, 1843, the *Times and Seasons* extracted "from Mr. Alexander Campbell's recommendation of 'Mormonism Unveiled'" and denounced it. The *Times and Seasons* listed Howe and the Spalding story as two of several failed efforts as "expositions of Mormonism."

Again, Oliver Cowdery's eight letters were called upon in rebuttal. In 1844, they were republished in England as a booklet, based on the version Benjamin Winchester published in his . That same year, another Mormon newspaper started in New York City named *The Prophet.* The paper serialized Oliver Cowdery's eight letters yet again. William Smith became the editor and published Letter VII in June, the same month Joseph and Hyrum were murdered in Carthage.

Oliver Cowdery's testimony. In 1846, when Oliver Cowdery rejoined the Church, the Spalding theory was still prominent.

---

[90] *Times and Seasons* III.21:906 ¶1

In chapter 2 we looked at Oliver's powerful and oft-quoted testimony, but only the first part. Look at what he said next.

> I wrote with my own pen the intire [sic] book of Mormon (save a few pages) as it fell from the lips of the prophet as he translated <it> by the gift and power of God. By means of the Urim and Thummim, or as it is called by that book, holy interpreters. I beheld with my eyes. And handled with my hands the gold plates from which it was translated. I also beheld the Interpreters. That book is true. **Sidney Rigdon did not write it. Mr. Spaulding did not write it.** I wrote it myself as it fell from the lips of the Prophet. It contains the everlasting gospel. And came in fulfilment of the revelations of John where he says he seen an angle [angel] come with the everlasting gospel to preach to every nation tongue and people. It contains principles of salvation.

Think about this a moment. When Oliver bore what turned out to be his final recorded testimony of the translation, he emphasized five key points. Two dealt with the Spalding theory.

- He wrote the translation as Joseph dictated it.
- Joseph used the U&T.
- He handled the gold plates and saw the interpreters.
- **Sidney Rigdon did not write it.**
- **Mr. Spalding did not write it.**

Because the Spalding theory was so significant to Oliver Cowdery on that momentous occasion, we should not be surprised that other witnesses, too, considered it an ongoing, serious problem.

Spalding: 1850s-1880s.

Oliver's testimony had no impact on the Spalding theory. Critics continued to write about it and solicit more information from witnesses (or their descendants), while LDS and RLDS leaders continued to denounce it.

In 1866, the RLDS republished an 1843 booklet written by John E.

Page when he was a member of the LDS Quorum of the Twelve.[91] The booklet refuted the Spalding theory on the typical grounds. The 1866 publication added some new material from 1857 and 1860.[92]

In 1869, newspapers in Pennsylvania published articles about the Spalding theory, including a new statement by Joseph Miller who claimed he had known Spalding, had read Spalding's "Manuscript Found," and recognized details from that manuscript when he read the Book of Mormon.

These articles may have prompted a new approach by believers in the Book of Mormon.

The next year, in February 1870, William E. McLellin visited David Whitmer in Richmond, Missouri. During that visit, McLellin met with Elizabeth Cowdery and copied part of an affidavit she had given that described SITH. (See Appendix 1.) Emma Smith wrote a letter on March 27, 1870, in which she claimed Joseph used a stone after the 116 pages were lost. (See Chapter 9.)

From 1870 forward, there are many accounts about SITH. In fact, there are no extant accounts about the seer stone from Emma or David prior to 1870. Most accounts from 1870 forward emphasized SITH and repudiated the Spalding account.

There is one notable exception. The only extant account by John Whitmer, one of the scribes for the Fayette Original Manuscript (OM), explained that Joseph used the Urim and Thummim. Zenas H. Gurley had interviewed John Whitmer and discussed John's testimony in a sermon that was reported in the *Saints' Herald* in 1879. Significantly, Gurley prefaced his discussion of John's testimony by saying, "The statement of the [three] witnesses is conclusive against the Spaulding Story. We have ceased to pay any regard to that."

With the Spalding theory dismissed, Gurley was free to relate what John Whitmer had told him.

> The speaker visited John Whitmer at Far West a few years ago. He is now dead;

[91] Hyde had been called as an Apostle in 1838 but was excommunicated in 1846.
[92] http://www.solomonspalding.com/docs/Page1843.htm#1866

> was then seventy years old. [John Whitmer died at Far West, Mo., on July 11, 1878.] He had seen the plates; and it was his especial pride and joy that he had written sixty [sixteen?] pages of the Book of Mormon. His neighbors all gave him a good character. He left the Church in 1837 or 1838, because of tendencies he could not approve; but had always remained true to the faith. **When the work of translation was going on he sat at one table with his writing material and Joseph at another with the breast-plate and Urim and Thummim. The latter were attached to the breast-plate and were two crystals or glasses, into which he looked and saw the words of the book.** The words remained in sight till correctly written, and mistakes of the scribe in spelling the names were corrected by the seer without diverting his gaze from the Urim and Thummim. Whitmer, at the time of the visit was receiving many letters from strangers, far and near. His characteristic answer to one of them was, "My testimony was true, is true, and will remain forever."[93]

Of course, this account from John Whitmer directly contradicts those who claimed Joseph did not use the U&T in Fayette. We will discuss the implications of that in Chapter 7.

What Gurley did not state is whether Joseph had a curtain or blanket between the two tables. We can assume that not mentioning a partition is equivalent to saying there was no partition, and that explains why John's description, as related by Gurley, appears to be the product of direct, personal observation, not of hearsay. And yet, only the three witnesses were supposed to see these objects—or was there an exception?

Recall Gurley's 1892 observations about the translation and Oliver Cowdery that we discussed in chapter 1. There, we discussed Gurley's point that Joseph could not allow anyone to see the plates or the U&T except certain individuals designated by God. "That Joseph had **another stone** called seers' stone, and 'peep stone,' is quite certain. **This stone was frequently exhibited to different ones and helped to assuage their awful curiosity; but the Urim and Thummim never, unless possibly to Oliver Cowdery**."

This was many years after his interview with John Whitmer. If John had seen the breastplate and U&T when he was serving as a scribe in

---

[93]https://archive.org/details/TheSaintsHerald_Volume_26_1879/page/n369/mode/2up

Fayette, Gurley surely would have remembered that.

Maybe Gurley considered the scribes, including John Whitmer, as people necessarily authorized to see the translation instruments, and that's what made him infer that Oliver, too, had seen them even though he was unaware of any statement to that effect from Oliver.

Of course, if there was a partition, John could have described the instruments based on how Joseph described them; i.e., his statement to Gurley was hearsay. Gurley could have avoided mentioning a partition to avoid giving ammunition to the Spalding advocates.

We can't make firm conclusions based on the evidence we have, but on balance, I think if there was a partition, Gurley would have mentioned it because he considered the Spalding theory to be dead.

Regardless, the Spalding theory marched on.

Spalding: 1880s-present.

In 1883, the RLDS leader, Joseph Smith III, wrote to a critic.

> You will pardon me when I state that no man living has a greater interest in the question whether the Book of Mormon is a fabrication from Rev. S. Spaulding's romance, or a discovery of deposited records of early inhabitants of this country as it purports to be, and came into being as my father, Sidney Rigdon, Martin Harris, Peter and David Whitmer, Oliver Cowdery and others, claim.... I have examined every work published against Joseph Smith, Mormonism, and the Mormons, that I could procure; from E. D. Howe's book to the last confession of John D. Lee, and Ann Eliza's exposure. I have given them all a close, and so far as I could, an analytical consideration... [There] is strong presumptive proof that the "Manuscript Found" would not bear out the claim that it was the origin of the Book of Mormon.[94]

Also in 1883, William Smith published a booklet titled *On Mormonism* in which he claimed that Joseph "translated them [the plates] by means of the Urim and Thummim, (which he obtained with the plates), and

[94] Letter to R. Patterson, *The Saints' Herald*, March 17, 1883, Vol. 30, No. 11. http://www.sidneyrigdon.com/dbroadhu/IA/sain1882.htm#031783

the power of God." Unless he was part of Joseph's family who was present for the demonstration in Fayette, William is not known to be a witness of the translation. Nevertheless, he described the translation.

> The manner in which this was done was by looking into the Urim and Thummim, which was placed in a hat to exclude the light, (the plates lying near by covered up), and reading off the translation, which appeared in the stone by the power of God. He was engaged in this business as he had opportunity for about two years and a half.... I was permitted to lift them [the plates] as they laid in a pillow-case... They weighed about sixty pounds according to the best of my judgment.[95]

Was William's account influenced by the Spalding theory? Spalding was definitely on his mind. On page 28, he wrote

> The story that Joseph Smith made up his revelation of the Book of Mormon out of a romance written by one Solomon Spaulding, like many other falsehoods told on the character of the Prophet, by the deceitful and lying stupidity of the people of the age in which we live must fall to the ground with the rest of their refuge of lies.[96]

The next year, in 1884, William was more emphatic about refuting the Spalding theory. He preached a sermon in Deloit, Iowa, on Jute 8, 1884, that was published in the *Saints' Herald* 31 (4 Oct 1884): 643-44. William said,

> Ministers take a great deal of pains to make it appear that this book was compiled from **a manuscript written by one Solomon Spaulding**. Many statements have been made and circulated far and wide, even printing some of them in books to be used in our schools. It has been printed and placed between the lids of the Bible, in order that in time it might become sanctified. They could not tell bigger lies. Ministers of old called Christ a winebibber. **I know that this Spaulding story is a falsehood.** I remember when Joseph called his father's family together, and told them that he had seen an angel, and what this angel had told him. When Joseph

[95] https://archive.org/details/williamsmithonmo00smit/page/10/mode/2up?

[96] https://archive.org/details/williamsmithonmo00smit/page/28/mode/2up?

> received the plates, he did not say they were the Spaulding manuscript.... Where is the Spaulding Story? I am a little too old a man to be telling stories. There is no money in telling this story. I expect to stand before angels and archangels and be judged for how I have told it. When Joseph received the plates he also received the Urim and Thummim, which he would place in a hat to exclude all light, and with the plates by his side he translated the characters, which were cut into the plates with some sharp instrument, into English. And thus, letter by letter, word by word, sentence by sentence, the whole book was translated.
>
> **It was not written from the Spaulding Romance. That story is false. Some say this romance was stolen by Sidney Rigdon while at Pittsburg. This is false. Sidney Rigdon knew· nothing about it.** He never saw or heard tell of the Book of Mormon until it was presented to him by P. P. Pratt and others. He was never at my father's house to see my brother until after the book was published. If he had wanted to see Joseph at that time and remained very long, be would have had to be in the field rolling logs or carrying brush.[97]

William said it was the U&T instead of a seer stone that Joseph put in the hat, but his purpose was the same: defeat the Spalding theory.

———

In August, 1884, a manuscript written by Solomon Spaulding was discovered in Hawaii by L.L. Rice, who had purchased the contents of Howe's printing shop in Ohio in 1839. The manuscript turned out to be the one that Hurlbut had obtained from the Spalding family, and it has nothing to with the Book of Mormon.[98]

For many LDS and RLDS, the Spalding theory was put to rest. Both churches published this Spalding manuscript to demonstrate that it could not have been the source for the Book of Mormon.[99]

---

[97] http://www.latterdaytruth.org/pdf/100198.pdf

[98] For a detailed account of the discovery and its aftermath, see http://solomonspalding.com/SRP/saga/saga11a.htm.

[99] An official entry on the LDS Church's web page presents this view. https://www.churchofjesuschrist.org/study/manual/gospel-topics/spaulding-manuscript?lang=eng

In 1887, David Whitmer addressed the Spalding theory in his final publication, *An Address to All Believers in Christ*, as he had in previous interviews. David's comment about SITH in that booklet is usually quoted out of context[100] by omitting the Spalding passage that precedes it and David's overall claims against Joseph Smith.

Critics were unpersuaded. An 1890 book, *The Mormon Delusion*, addressed the Spalding theory.[101] Another book published in 1890, *The Prophet of Palmyra* by Thomas Gregg,[102] opened with a reference to Solomon Spalding. Five chapters in the book explain the theory. On page 59, Gregg summarized a letter by Charles Anthon that showed how the translation with the U&T accommodated the Spalding theory.

> … the book of gold plates, held together with rings, had been dug up in Northern New York; that they were being translated by a young man behind a curtain, through the medium of the Urim and Thummim, which were generally talked of as spectacles…

Regarding the manuscript found in Hawaii, Gregg included statements from witnesses who claimed Spalding wrote multiple books and the manuscript found in Hawaii was not the one they had read, which they claim related Book of Mormon names and event. Those who accept the Spalding theory today rely on this "missing manuscript" version of the story.

The persistence of the Spalding theory may have led defenders of the Book of Mormon, including David Whitmer and Emma Smith, to conflate Joseph's SITH demonstration with the actual translation of the plates with the U&T. The totality of the evidence leads me to conclude that's exactly what did happen. We will consider specific examples in the next few chapters.

---

[100]E.g., see https://www.churchofjesuschrist.org/study/ensign/2020/01/the-translation-of-the-book-of-mormon-a-marvel-and-a-wonder?lang=eng

[101]https://archive.org/details/mormondelusionit00mont/page/24/mode/2up?q=blanket

[102] https://archive.org/details/GR_1666/page/n11/mode/2up

6. The Demonstration Narrative

Overview.

The idea that Joseph Smith used SITH as a demonstration of the translation process is new to many people, but it is consistent with the historical evidence.

The Whitmer household was disrupted when Joseph and Oliver arrived and began translating the small plates of Nephi. They worked upstairs, but their presence imposed extra burdens on Mother Whitmer and distractions from the day-to-day work on the farm. Two Whitmer sons, John and Christian, took turns as scribes, keeping them away from the farm work. A household servant threatened to leave unless someone explained what was going on.

Joseph was aware of the intense curiosity in what he was doing, but he was still under the strict command to not show the plates or the U&T to anyone.

People were familiar with the practice of using seer stones. Joseph realized he could demonstrate the process using SITH. Some in the audience inferred they were watching a translation, however.

Detail.

Synthesis #3 is my proposal that, for the benefit of some of his supporters, Joseph Smith conducted a demonstration of the translation process. Knowing he could not show them the actual plates or the U&T, Joseph used a stone—a seer stone—that he put into a hat.

I propose that for purposes of the demonstration, Joseph simply dictated—from memory—some of the chapters from Isaiah that are found in 2 Nephi today. (I think he recognized that Nephi was quoting from Isaiah and he saw this as an opportunity to conduct a demonstration.)

Synthesis #3 is supported not only by the statements of the observers, but also by evidence from the OM and the changes to Isaiah found in these chapters of 2 Nephi. We'll go through the evidence in the next chapter. Here, we need to frame the evidence.

Synthesis #3 reconciles the statements of Joseph and Oliver with those of other observers. Because Joseph dictated these Isaiah passages from memory, he did not *translate* them. This made it possible for Joseph and Oliver to truthfully say that Joseph translated the plates with the U&T, even though others observed him dictating Isaiah with SITH.

The most common objection I encounter to the "demonstration" narrative is that Joseph Smith would never mislead people like that.

I agree. But did he mislead them, or did they make an inference that gradually became a fact in their minds?

One way to interpret historical events is to make a hypothesis and then test it against the evidence—a version of the scientific method. That's what I've done here. For example, before conducting a demonstration proceeding, I don't think Joseph told people "I am now going to translate the plates as I place this stone in a hat and read the words that appear." No one quoted Joseph saying that. He certainly didn't write that, or anything like it. But I do think he (or someone else on his behalf) may have said something such as, "I will now show you how it is done." That would be easy for people to misinterpret.

Why would he conduct a demonstration?

As Zenas Gurley pointed out, Joseph was faced with a dilemma. On one hand, he was under a strict command to never show the plates or the U&T. Joseph had learned from his experience with the lost 116 pages that he could not jeopardize his standing with the Lord by ignoring or circumventing the commandments he was given.

On the other hand, his closest friends and family wanted to know how he was translating the plates, to the point of pestering and distracting him. Martin Harris was not the only one curious about how Joseph was translating. Joseph was imposing on the Whitmer family. They, along with his own family members, deserved an explanation.

According to contemporary sources, most people in western New York in the early 1800s were familiar with the concept of using a seer stone or "peep" stone in a hat. Joseph had participated in that activity enough to joke about it later.

The *Elders' Journal*, published in Far West, Missouri, in July 1838, listed Joseph Smith, Jr. as Editor. The issue published a series of questions and answers, including this one:

> Question 10. Was not Jo Smith a money digger.
> Answer. Yes, but it was never a very profitable job to him, as he only got fourteen dollars a month for it.[103]

Three years earlier, Oliver Cowdery, in Letter VIII, also made light of the accusations.

> Soon after this [Joseph's] visit to Cumorah, a gentleman from the south part of the State, employed our brother as a common laborer, and accordingly he visited that section of <the> country; and **had he not been accused of digging down all, or nearly so the mountains of Susquehannah [Susquehanna], or causing others to do it by some art of nicromancy, [sic]** I should leave this, for the present, unnoticed. You will remember, in the mean time, that those who seek to vilify his character, say that he has always been notorious for his idleness....

Joseph was known to joke around. Joseph Knight Sr. stayed at the Smith home overnight on the 22nd of September 1827 when Joseph took the plates and the artifacts from Moroni's stone box.

> After Brackfirst [breakfast] Joseph Cald me into the other Room and he set his foot on the Bed and leaned his head on his hand and says, "Well I am Dissopinted. "Well," says I, "I am sorrey." "Well," says he, I am greatly Dissopinted; it is ten times Better then I expected.[104]

Here are two examples from Joseph's life that reflect on the observer as much as on Joseph (similar to the way the accounts of the seer stone

---

[103] https://www.josephsmithpapers.org/paper-summary/elders-journal-july-1838/11. By comparison, Martin Harris paid Joseph Smith fifty cents a day to work on his farm, which is roughly equivalent to fourteen dollars a month.

[104] This is a first-person account by Joseph Knight, Sr., recorded around 1847. However, some of Knight's account is obviously hearsay, such as how Joseph translated and what he saw when he dictated. Joseph Knight, *Reminiscences*, online at https://dcms.lds.org/delivery/DeliveryManagerServlet?dps_pid=IE1276586, images 3-6.

in a hat reflect on the observers). These examples come from a sworn statement by Peter Ingersoll on pages 234-236 of *Mormonism Unvailed.*

The first one involves a journey to Pennsylvania.

> I then returned with Joseph and his wife to Manchester. One circumstance occurred on the road, worthy of notice, and I believe this is the only instance where Jo ever exhibited true yankee wit. On our journey to Pennsylvania, we could not make the exact change at the toll gate near Ithaca. Joseph told the gate tender, that he would "hand" him the toll on his return, as he was coming back in a few days. On our return, Joseph tendered to him 25 cents, the toll being 12½. He did not recognize Smith, so he accordingly gave him back the I2½ cents. After we had passed the gate, I asked him if he did not agree to pay double gatage on our return? No, said he, I agreed to "*hand*" it to him, and I did, but he handed it back again.[105]

Ingersoll's entire statement evinces deep contempt for the Smith family, so it's possible that he invented this story. One indicia of credibility, though, is Ingersoll's grudging admiration for Joseph's "true yankee wit" in this instance. The setting also fits Joseph's likely route between Palmyra and Harmony, Pennsylvania.

If true, as I assume it is, the story demonstrates Joseph's willingness to let others make inferences without correcting them.

In a similar vein, years later in a Nauvoo discourse on 26 May 1844, just a month before he was murdered, Joseph responded to polygamy-related charges by not directly answering the question and letting people infer from what he said that he had only one wife. "What a thing it is for a man to be accused of committing adultery and having seven wives, when I can only find one.[106]"

The second story from Ingersoll, if true, offers another example of Joseph Smith's "yankee wit," although not as Ingersoll intended.

> Joseph … seemed much perplexed as to the course he should pursue. In this dilemma, he made me his confident and told me what daily transpired in the family of Smiths. One day he came, and

---

[105] online at https://archive.org/details/mormonismunvaile00howe/page/234

[106] https://www.josephsmithpapers.org/paper-summary/discourse-26-may-1844-as-compiled-by-leo-hawkins/13

> greeted me with a joyful countenance. Upon asking the cause of his unusual happiness, he replied in the following language: "As I was passing, yesterday, across the woods, after a heavy shower of rain, I found, in a hollow, some beautiful white sand, that had been washed up by the water. I took off my frock, and tied up several quarts of it, and then went home. On my entering the house, I found the family at the table eating dinner; They were all anxious to know the contents of my frock. At that moment, I happened to think of what I had heard about a history found in Canada, called the golden Bible ; so I very gravely told them it was the golden Bible. To my surprise, they were credulous enough to believe what I said. Accordingly I told them that I had received a commandment to let no one see it, for, says I, no man can see it with the naked eye and live. However, I offered to take out the book and show it to them, but they refuse to see it, and left the room." Now, said Jo, "I have got the damned fools fixed, and will carry out the fun." Notwithstanding, he told me he had no such book, and believed there never was any such book, yet, he told me that he actually went to Willard Chase, to get him to make a chest, in which he might deposit his golden Bible. But, as Chase would not do it, he made a box himself, of clap-boards, and put it into a pillow case, and allowed people only to lift it, and feel of it through the case.[107]

When considered under the circumstances, this story includes elements that lead me to think it could be at least partly accurate. The joke was on Ingersoll, however.

Once Joseph brought the plates home, there were several attempts by third parties to find and steal them. It seems plausible that Joseph would seek to deter such efforts by spreading the word that he didn't really have plates. A confidant such as Ingersoll would be an effective method to spread such a rumor.

Of course, the sand in a sack story is patently ridiculous for obvious reasons; a bag of sand would hardly look like a book. The Smiths were a close family whose relationships were built on trust, not deception. By the time the Ingersoll account was published in 1834, members of Joseph's family had testified that they saw and handled the actual plates.

Assessing accounts such as Ingersoll's is within the realm of

---

[107] p. 235 at https://archive.org/details/mormonismunvaile00howe/page/234

subjective interpretation of historical evidence. Depending on your own bias, you may conclude Ingersoll was telling the literal truth or was a complete liar. Both alternatives are possible, but I think most people tend to tell a version of the truth, according to their subjective perception, as filtered through their memory, biases, agendas, etc.

In this case, a neighbor named Pomeroy Tucker remembered that at first, Ingersoll was "inclined to put faith" in Joseph's account of the gold plates.[108] If so, when Hurlbut came to town seeking affidavits critical of the Smiths, Ingersoll may have had an extra incentive to distance himself from Joseph Smith. He had apparently related a similar account in 1829 to support a lawsuit Lucy Harris filed against Joseph Smith that was heard in March 1829 at a court in Lyons, New York (about 15 miles east of Palmyra). Lucy Mack Smith's report states that

> The first [witness] arose and testified, that Joseph Smith told him that the box which he had, contained nothing but sand; and he, Joseph Smith, said it was gold, to deceive the people.
>
> Second witness swore, that Joseph Smith had told him it was nothing but a box of lead, and he was determined to use it as he saw fit.
>
> Third witness declared, that he once inquired of Joseph Smith what he had in that box, and Joseph Smith told him that there was nothing at all in the box, saying, that he had made fools of the whole of them, and all he wanted was, to get Martin Harris's money away from him, and that he (witness) was knowing to the fact that Joseph Smith had, by his persuasion, already got two or three hundred dollars.[109]

The magistrate told the court clerk to bring him "what had been written of the testimony already given. This he tore in pieces before their eyes, and told them to go home about their business, and trouble him no more with such ridiculous folly."

---

[108] Pomeroy Tucker, *The Origin, Rise and Progress of Mormonism* (New York: D. Appleton and Co., 1867):128. https://archive.org/details/originriseprogre00tuck/page/128

[109] Martin Harris testified he had given Joseph $50 voluntarily, and that Joseph had no disposition to take any man's money without giving him a reasonable compensation. https://www.josephsmithpapers.org/paper-summary/lucy-mack-smith-history-1845/154

We'll never know whether Ingersoll told the truth—but it doesn't matter. After referring to Ingersoll's account, Tucker wrote, "Testimony of the same tenor on this head might be multiplied, if it were not considered superfluous."

If we accept Joseph Smith's account of the plates, we don't have to also insist that Ingersoll and the others were liars. There is a plausible explanation that is consistent with seemingly contradictory accounts when considered in the historical context. These inconsistent statements could all be lies, but they could also be truthful accounts of the different ways Joseph deflected attention away from the plates. Using his associates to spread rumors that the plates did not exist, that he merely had collected sand, or lead, etc., would be a clever solution.

The existence of these stories illustrates the problem with accepting SITH for the proposition that Joseph *translated* with the seer stone. When we stick with the facts, the observers reported what they saw—Joseph putting a stone in a hat and dictating words—along with what they assumed or inferred—that Joseph was dictating a translation.

None of them read the stone themselves. None reported what words Joseph dictated. None even claimed Joseph said he was translating, although some reported what they thought Joseph "saw" in the stones.

The accumulation of accounts by witnesses that share an assumption does not constitute proof of the accuracy or veracity of that assumption.

———

There is another category of accounts that did arise from antagonism towards Joseph Smith and/or the Church of Jesus Christ of Latter-day Saints. These are accounts related by people who were not eyewitnesses to the translation. Nevertheless, they are presented as facts.

In 1841, Benjamin Winchester (author of the Spalding book we discussed in the last chapter) published a newspaper in Philadelphia. At the time, he was a zealous missionary, a close friend of Joseph and Hyrum Smith, etc. In the March 15 issue, he wrote:

> Moroni was then commanded to deposit this record in the earth, **together with the Urim and Thummim, or as the Nephites would have said, Interpreters**, which were instruments to assist in the work of the

translation.[110]

With Joseph Smith's express permission, Winchester republished Oliver Cowdery's eight essays on Church history. Part of Letter I, now found in the Pearl of Great Price, is on p. 138:

> Day after day I continued, uninterrupted, to write from his mouth, as he translated, with the Urim and Thummim, or, as the Nephites would have said, " Interpreters," the history, or record, called " The book of Mormon."

This important passage is from Letter IV (page 152):

> [Moroni] said this history was written and deposited not far from that place, and that it was our brother's privilege, if obedient to the commandments of the Lord, to obtain, and **translate the same by the means of the Urim and Thummim, which were deposited for that purpose with the record.**

Winchester was on solid ground. Not only did Joseph give him permission to republish Oliver's essays, but Joseph gave them to his brother Don Carlos to publish in the *Times and Seasons.* He had his scribes copy them into his own journal as part of his life history. His brother William republished them again in 1844 in New York City.

Winchester continued to publish books and articles defending the Church. He went on a mission to promote Joseph Smith's candidacy for U.S. President.

But then he became disgruntled, partly over polygamy and partly over disputes with his old friend William Smith (Joseph's brother). He was excommunicated.

Later in life, he changed his version of his experiences with Joseph Smith and Oliver Cowdery. Recall that Winchester was not a witness to any of the translation. He joined the Church years after the Book of Mormon was published. Nevertheless, he made statements as if he was

---

[110] Benjamin Winchester, "History of the Ancients of America, and Also of the Book of Mormon," *The Gospel Reflector*, (Philadelphia, March 15, 1841), v.1, no. 6: 138. https://archive.org/details/gospelreflectori00winc/page/126/mode/2up?q=Interpreters

a witness.

In 1900, Winchester dictated a final testimony.

> [Joseph] carried what he called a 'Peep stone' through which he claimed to see hidden treasure & etc. **This is what he afterwards called his 'Urim and Thummem.'** Finally he took the notion to get up a book. Then he claimed to have made the discovery of the plates. Then he got Cowdery, Harris and Whitmer into it."
>
> "Cowdery was his scribe, or the writer of the book, as Smith dictated it. It was done this way.... Smith was behind the blankets in the dark with this 'peep stone' in his hat and then his face in the hat. As he looked into the hat there would come sentence after sentence upon the stone, and he would dictate it to Cowdery, and Cowdery would write it down.

This account is a garbled version of the Spalding theory: Joseph writing a book, this time not with Rigdon but with "Cowdery, Harris and Whitmer," and dictated from behind blankets, but instead of reading a manuscript he used SITH. Winchester's claim—that Joseph called his "peep stone" his Urim and Thummim—contradicted what he had written when Joseph and Oliver were alive. Yet it is his *later* claim, not his *original* claim, that constitutes Synthesis #1, which some LDS scholars teach today.

———

Back in 1889, just two weeks after another of Winchester's articles came out in the *Salt Lake Tribune*, President Wilford Woodruff stood up in General Conference. He could have said, like some LDS historians today, "I now declare that Benjamin Winchester was correct. Joseph didn't really translate the Book of Mormon, and he didn't use the Urim and Thummim that came with the plates. He merely read words that appeared on a seer stone."

Instead, President Woodruff delivered this re-affirmation of what Joseph and Oliver always taught.

> And, as has been stated during this Conference, he brought forth the Book of Mormon-the stick of Joseph in the hands of Ephraim-in fulfillment of the testimony of Isaiah, **translating that record through the Urim and**

> **Thummim**, thereby revealing to us the history of the early inhabitants of this Continent.[111]

There is a long history of Church leaders defending and reiterating what Joseph and Oliver claimed. Here is one of over 100 examples from General Conference addresses.

> This book, that has been so despised by the world, was testified to by the Prophet Joseph when asked: "How and when did you obtain the Book of Mormon? Answer. Moroni, the person who deposited the plates, from which the Book of Mormon was translated, in a hill in Manchester, Ontario County, New York, being dead, and raised again therefrom, appeared unto me, and told me where they were; and gave me directions how to obtain them. **I obtained them, and the Urim and Thummim with them, by the means of which I translated the plates**, and thus came the Book of Mormon."
> It contains the simplest declaration and the best elucidation of the principles of the Gospel of the Lord Jesus Christ of any one book extant. And why should it not be? **translated word by word, sentence by sentence, line by line, page by page, through the Urim and Thummim?** We have no other book on earth that has such claims to our undivided confidence as the Book of Mormon.[112]

There are many sources in Church history that support what Joseph and Oliver said about the translation (the thesis). There are also sources, such as Benjamin Winchester's final testimonies, that contradict what Joseph and Oliver said (the antithesis).

So far in this book, we've reviewed enough information to allow you to make an informed decision about which synthesis you choose to accept. But there is much more information to consider.

In the next four chapters, we will look at three of the most significant people who discussed the translation: David Whitmer, Emma Smith, and Martin Harris.

---

[111] President Wilford Woodruff, Oct. 1889, 6th Session, CR.

[112] Elder Franklin D. Richards, Oct. 1896, 4th Session, CR.

7. David Whitmer, the Group Demonstration, and the Isaiah Chapters in 2 Nephi

Overview.

When Emma and some of Joseph's siblings arrived in Fayette, the Whitmers arranged for Joseph to show what he was doing. Everyone sat around the table in the living room downstairs. They stretched a curtain in front of the windows to block the view from outsiders. Joseph sat on one side of the table with his scribes on the opposite side. The scribes—Oliver Cowdery, Emma Smith, and Christian Whitmer—took turns writing because they tired quickly.

This demonstration raises the question, why would the scribes tire quickly, when each of them had previously written for days on end without relief?

An answer may be found in evidence from the Original Manuscript, which indicates that the demonstration probably involved the Isaiah chapters of 2 Nephi. When comparing these chapters to the KJV of Isaiah, there are inexplicable anomalies in chapters 13 to 21. Words and phrases are switched with no change in meaning and no support in the earliest Bible manuscripts. Words are omitted and added seemingly at random.

These anomalies are typical of memorization errors. It now appears that Joseph Smith recited these Isaiah chapters from memory to demonstrate the translation process. When Joseph and Oliver said Joseph translated with the Urim and Thummim, they told the literal truth because Joseph didn't translate these Isaiah chapters in 2 Nephi.

Detail.

There are multiple accounts of Joseph putting a stone in a hat, covering his face with the hat, and then reading out loud the words that appeared on the stone.

The accounts lack specifics about times and dates. None mention what words Joseph actually dictated during the observed performance, so it is impossible to determine what portion of the Book of Mormon was being dictated, if in fact it was Book of Mormon text.[113] None of the accounts even quote Joseph *saying* he was translating the Book of Mormon. We have a cascading series of inferences and assumptions.

All of these accounts describe activities at the Whitmer home near Fayette, New York (except accounts from Emma Smith and Martin Harris, discussed separately in chapters 8 and 9).

One Fayette account—a David Whitmer interview published in the *Chicago Tribune* in 1885—describes a group setting that may explain the observations that led to the various individual statements and rumors. The article contains only four brief quotations, interspersed among a narrative that contains numerous factual errors, probably attributable to the reporter's misunderstanding or assumptions (or agenda). These known factual errors cast doubt on the veracity of the balance of the article, but given the number of witnesses who made statements about the stone-in-the-hat procedure, we can assume some sort of public demonstration took place at Fayette.

Because the article is written in third person, it is impossible to determine whether David described the events first-hand or if he made hearsay declarations as if they were fact. A statement such as "Joseph did this or that" could be based on either personal observation or hearsay (i.e., what someone told him or what he inferred).

Notice how much emphasis is placed on making sure Joseph could not have been reading from another manuscript. That reflects the always-present Spalding theory.

I have inserted my comments on the article below in **bold**.

Vol. XLV, *The Chicago Daily Tribune*, Thursday, December 17, 1885, p. 3[114]

---

[113] There is no "chain of custody" of the documents to assure us that what scribes recorded during these demonstrations actually made it into the Original Manuscript.

[114] https://en.wikisource.org/wiki/Chicago_Daily_Tribune,_December_17,_1885

THE BOOK OF MORMON

David Whitmer, the Associate of Joseph Smith, Now on His Death-Bed. He Describes the Translation of the Golden Tablets at Which He Assisted. The Angel in the Pasture—His Hatred of Polygamy—His Services in the Church.

. . .

Mr. Whitmer then described Smith's story of the vision in which the location of the plates was revealed, with the history of the Nephites, Moroni's labor, and Smith's finding of the tablets, with which everyone is familiar.

TRANSLATING THE PLATES

Whitmer and Cowdery were greatly impressed by the recital of this strange story, and were conducted to the hill, where they personally viewed the receptacle in which Moroni, at the beginning of the fifth century, had concealed the history of his fathers.

[Oliver described the stone box in detail in Letter VIII.[115] He described his visit to the hill after the translation was completed, but he did not mention David accompanying him. This is an important event—one of many such events that people forgot to relate (or record), possibly because it was so widely known it was a "given" that "everyone knew."]

Smith also said that he had been commanded to at once begin the translation of the work in the presence of three witnesses.

[This is apparently a misunderstanding. Joseph waited four years after first discovering the plates before he was allowed to

---

115 Letter VIII is available online in the Joseph Smith Papers here: https://www.josephsmithpapers.org/paper-summary/history-1834-1836/93

translate them. There is no record that he was commanded to translate in the presence of three witnesses. Oliver, who was granted a gift to translate, presumably saw the plates during the translation; he said he saw them and the Urim and Thummim in Harmony. Beyond that, Joseph was explicitly commanded *not* to show the plates and other artifacts to anyone until after the translation was completed. Only then, in June 1829, did the three witnesses have the experience described in their testimony.]

In accordance with this command, Smith, Cowdery, and Whitmer proceeded to the latter's home, accompanied by Smith's wife, and bearing with them the precious plates and spectacles.

[This statement appears to refer to the time when David picked up Joseph and Oliver from Harmony, but on that occasion, they specifically did *not* have the plates with them because Joseph had given the plates to a divine messenger before leaving Harmony. By then, Joseph had translated the abridged plates all the way through the Title Page, which was on the last leaf of the plates he obtained from the stone box. Along the route, they encountered the messenger who said he was going to Cumorah, not directly to Fayette. Also, Emma apparently came to Fayette separately.]

The house of Senior Whitmer was a primitive and poorly designed structure, but it was deemed the most secure for the carrying out the sacred trust on account of the threats that had been made against Smith by his mercenary neighbors.

[This refers, possibly, to the "mercenary neighbors" in both Palmyra and Harmony. The description of the Whitmer house would apply to many farm homes of the period. Although it is not a large structure, the house does have a second story containing bedrooms. Recent excavations indicate it may have been a double cabin.]

In order to give privacy to the proceeding a blanket, which served as a portière, was stretched across the family living room to shelter the translators and the plates from the eyes of any who might call at the house while the work was in progress. This, Mr. Whitmer says, was the only use made of the blanket, and it was not for the purpose of concealing the plates or the translator from the eyes of the amanuensis.

[This account describes a "proceeding," singular. This suggests a one-time event. It refers to the family living room. If you've visited the restored Whitmer farm in Fayette, you've seen the large open room on the main floor. The upper floor is divided into smaller bedrooms. Other accounts have Joseph and Oliver working upstairs "all day," a more practical arrangement. They would come down with glowing countenances.[116]

In his 1881 correction of a published interview with the *Kansas City Journal* that we discussed in chapter 1, David wrote "I did not wish to be understood as saying that those referred to as being present were all of the time in the immediate presence of the translator, but were at the place and saw how the translation was conducted." This clarification corroborates the atypical nature of the proceeding described in this newspaper account.

Dictating and recording in an open, noisy and busy family living room for weeks on end would involve constant interruptions to both the Whitmer household and to Joseph and Oliver. A blanket would further impede family activities and would not block sound anyway.

The need to shelter the proceeding from the eyes of callers "while the work was in progress" is also consistent with a one-

---

[116] Sarah Conrad, a neighbor hired to help Mary Whitmer, "saw them [Joseph and Oliver] come down from the translating room several times when they looked so exceedingly white and strange." See Appendix 1 #78-9 and *OTH*, p. 185. The restored Whitmer home has recreated one of the upstairs rooms as a "translation setting." https://history.churchofjesuschrist.org/article/historic-sites/new-york/fayette/whitmer-farm?lang=eng..

time event; i.e., "while the demonstration was in progress." Using a blanket to conceal an activity from callers every day for weeks would arouse curiosity, not prevent it.

Notice the emphasis that the blanket was not used to hide the translator from the observers. David wanted to make sure readers would know Joseph could not have read another manuscript.

Another anomaly in this account is the presence of plates. If the plates were covered with a cloth the entire time (as some accounts claimed), a blanket would not be needed to shield them, but if they were uncovered, no one could have been present because Joseph was forbidden to show the plates to anyone until the translation was completed. David also said he never saw the plates before his experience as one of the Three Witnesses.

I infer from these incongruities that the reporter confused some of the details. Or else David was overzealous in refuting the Spalding theory.]

In fact, Smith was at no time hidden from his collaborators, and the translation was performed in the presence of not only the persons mentioned, but of the entire Whitmer household and several of Smith's relatives besides.

[More emphasis on how Joseph was never out of sight. This account is consistent with a demonstration because "the translation was performed" in the presence of a specific group of observers. For "the entire Whitmer household" to be present would require a temporary suspension of farm and other work. The presence of Smith's relatives also indicates it was a special event, likely prompted by a visit to the Whitmers. Because Joseph's parents did not come to Fayette until the translation was completed,[117] it is unclear who among his "relatives" participated,

[117] Lucy Mack Smith, *History*, 1844-5, https://www.josephsmithpapers.org/paper-summary/lucy-mack-smith-history-1844-1845/102; Lucy Mack Smith, *History*, 1845, https://www.josephsmithpapers.org/paper-summary/lucy-mack-smith-history-

but it could have been his siblings and Emma.

The term "translation" implies the audience was witnessing the actual translation, but this account does not quote Joseph Smith as *saying* it was a translation; the phrasing is consistent with an inference by David and/or the reporter.]

The work of translating the tablets consumed about eight months, Smith acting as the seer and Oliver Cowdery, Smith's wife, and Christian Whitmer, brother of David, performing the duties of amanuenses, in whose handwriting the original manuscript now is.

[In chapter 1, we reviewed the evidence and my conclusion that it did take eight months because Emma wrote at least some of the Harmony OM, starting with Mosiah 1. I concluded Emma (and the other pre-Oliver scribes) probably wrote all of Mosiah. This means that, on average, the Harmony translation proceeded more slowly than the translation in Fayette, although these averages are approximate.

This list of scribes helps us narrow down the possible material that Joseph dictated during the demonstration. On another occasion, David said "Martin Harris, Oliver Cowdery, Emma and my brother John each at different times wrote for Joseph as he translated."[118] The two lists can be reconciled if Christian, Oliver and Emma participated in the demonstration, but David also knew that John had served as scribe separately.]

Each time before resuming the work all present would kneel in prayer and invoke the Divine blessing on the proceeding.

["Each time" implies that demonstrations took place more than once, but how many times is not specified. It could have

---

1845/159

[118] P. Wilhelm Poulson, *Deseret Evening News*, August 15, 1878. https://whitmercollege.com/interviews/dr-p-wilhelm-poulson-1878/

been multiple sessions on a single day, or David could have said they kneeled in prayer and the reporter inferred they did so "each time." A prayer would naturally be part of a demonstration, just as we can assume Joseph and his scribes prayed before they began actual translation sessions.]

After prayer Smith would sit on one side of a table and the amanuenses, in turn as they became tired, on the other. Those present and not actively engaged in the work seated themselves around the room and then the work began.

[This account relates a demonstration, not a normal working procedure. The Whitmer family were busy farmers, especially in June. (David's father had been reluctant to have him take time off to fetch Joseph and Oliver from Harmony.) The messenger showed Mother Whitmer the plates precisely because she was so overworked. A busy farming family could not spend the month of June sitting around the table observing the translation.

Notice that the scribes took turns as they became tired. This also indicates it was a demonstration, probably of the Isaiah chapters in 2 Nephi.

This is a key point that requires a detailed explanation.

Here we will interrupt our analysis of the *Chicago Tribune* article to examine the evidence that Joseph dictated Isaiah chapters in 2 Nephi from memory.

We will return to the *Chicago Tribune* account on page 115. You can skip ahead if you don't want to read the details now.

What did Joseph "translate" with the stone in the hat?

The newspaper account of the demonstration could not be describing the translation of 1 Nephi for several reasons. The fragments of the OM we have for Jacob and Omni indicate Oliver wrote those books. That leaves primarily the middle of 2 Nephi (chapters 10-22) as the possible text Joseph dictated during the SITH demonstration.

Plates of Nephi. The Fayette translation involved only the unabridged small plates of Nephi (1 Nephi through Words of Mormon). We can tell this because (i) Joseph and Oliver completed the translation of the abridged plates in Harmony and (ii) John and Christian Whitmer served with Oliver Cowdery as scribes for parts of 1 Nephi.[119] These Whitmer brothers never went to Harmony.

We also know that the divine messenger who picked up the abridged plates from Joseph in Harmony took those plates back to the repository of Nephite records in the Hill Cumorah.[120] In my view, the messenger picked up the original plates of Nephi from that repository and brought them to Fayette so Joseph could translate them.[121] Even people who still think the unabridged plates were attached to the abridged plates agree that in Fayette, Joseph translated only the unabridged plates of Nephi.

Scribes present. The article says "the amanuenses, in turn as they became tired," sat across the table from Joseph. These scribes consisted of Oliver, Emma, and Christian Whitmer.

The article is corroborated by something David separately told James Hart. "Emma, Joseph's wife, came to my father's house a short time after Joseph and Oliver came, and she wrote a little of the translation, my brother Christian wrote some, but Oliver wrote the greater portion of it."

As we'll see below, we can tell from the OM that Emma was not a scribe for 1 Nephi. She couldn't have been; she didn't arrive in Fayette until "a short time after Joseph and Oliver came."

---

119 This is a tentative, but probably, identification made by Royal Skousen in his *Part Six*, p. 31.

120 For a list of references about the messenger, see http://www.lettervii.com/p/trip-to-fayette-references.html

121 A schematic of this scenario is online here: http://www.lettervii.com/p/the-two-sets-of-plates-schematic.html

The messenger gave Joseph the plates of Nephi shortly after he and Oliver arrived in Fayette. Presumably they began translating right away, before Emma came up from Harmony.

Family present. The *Chicago Tribune* article also said some of Joseph's family were present during the SITH event. This could not have happened within the first few days of Joseph's arrival. Joseph's brothers wouldn't have come to Fayette until they learned he was there. Like Emma, they likely came a short time later. Joseph's parents did not arrive at the Whitmer farm until near the end of the month when they learned the translation was complete, or nearly so.

Translation room. We previously saw that Sarah Conrad said she "saw them [Joseph and Oliver] come down from the translating room several times." She also told her granddaughter that "they would go up into the attic, and they would stay all day." David said, "In regard to the translation, it was a laborious work for the weather was very warm, and the days were long and they worked from morning till night."[122]

It wasn't until later, when Emma and Joseph's family members arrived, that Joseph conducted the demonstration in the Whitmer family room downstairs. The curiosity grew as the translation progressed. Sarah Conrad reached the point where she would not work in the house unless someone told her what was going on.

Evidence from John Whitmer. The handwriting of three people is found on the existing pages of the Fayette OM. Royal Skousen has updated the handwriting identification on these sheets of the OM.[123] He has identified John Whitmer as "very likely" and Christian Whitmer

---

[122] James H. Hart, "About the Book of Mormon," *Deseret Evening News*, March 25, 1884. Appendix 1, #29.

[123] For this breakdown, see Royal Skousen, "Oliver Cowdery as Book of Mormon Scribe," *Days Never to Be Forgotten: Oliver Cowdery*, online at https://rsc.byu.edu/days-never-be-forgotten-oliver-cowdery/oliver-cowdery-book-mormon-scribe. See also, Skousen, *The Original Manuscript of the Book of Mormon*, (FARMS, BYU, Provo, UT 2001), p. 14, and Skousen, *Part Six*, p. 31.

as "possibly." I agree with him, based partly on David Whitmer's recollections.

In chapter 5 we discussed the only extant record of John Whitmer's description of the translation: the report of a sermon by Zenas H. Gurley, published in 1879. According to Gurley, John described Joseph translating with the Urim and Thummim and the breast-plate, an indication that 1 Nephi, at least, was not translated during the demonstration David described.

The report claims John was proud to have written 60 pages of the Book of Mormon, but that looks like a reporting error. John's handwriting appears on only 14.3 pages, all in 1 Nephi. (See Table 1 below.) To have written 60 pages, John would have had to write about 45 of the 90 pages of 2 Nephi through Words of Mormon. While most of those pages are missing, the fragments that survived have Oliver's handwriting. That leaves little material available for the demonstration. I suggest the reporter heard *sixteen* but recorded *sixty*.

Evidence from the OM. The only part of the OM produced in Fayette that survives mostly complete is 1 Nephi 2 through 2 Nephi 1. Some fragments from 2 Nephi through Omni have been found. including 2 Nephi 7:1-9, all in Oliver's handwriting.[124] Oliver's is the only writing on the other fragments, but that does not preclude the participation of other scribes on the missing pages (such as Emma).

We are dealing with two pagination systems: the OM, and the 1830 edition. I used the 1830 edition to measure how much each scribe wrote because we can all access that edition, but we can't access the OM. However much of the commentary that follows refers to OM pages as well because the handwritten text provides important information.

Having written the translation of the Harmony plates (probably Alma through Moroni), Oliver was an experienced scribe so it is logical that he began writing Joseph's translation of the plates of Nephi in

124 An article about the challenge of recovering the Original Manuscript is here: https://www.churchofjesuschrist.org/church/news/church-acquires-more-fragments-of-original-book-of-mormon-manuscript?lang=eng

Fayette.[125] That's what I assume here.

Table 1 shows which Fayette scribe wrote which parts of the existing OM. Oliver wrote page 3 and the first 13 lines of page 4. Assuming he also wrote the first two pages of the OM, he wrote the first 5.9 pages of the 1830 edition, which I consider a day's work.

In the process, Oliver presumably trained John Whitmer, who began writing on Day 2 at 1 Nephi 3:7. He continued through 4:14, which is a few lines above the end of page 6 in the OM. Oliver finished off the page, ending at 4:20(a), which is a natural break, grammatically. I consider this a full day's work. Because John was new at this, I assume it would take a while for him to get comfortable taking Joseph's dictation.

Christian began on day 3 and wrote 1 Nephi 4:20 to 12:8. This is twelve pages of the OM, which works out to a little over 14 pages in the 1830 edition. I assume this took two days (days 3 and 4).

Next, on day 5, John wrote 12:9 through 16:1, a little over 11 pages in the 1830 edition. Oliver wrote the rest, through 2 Nephi 1:30, which I assume took 3 full days.

Obviously these are estimates that people can debate, but I rely in part on natural breaks, as I explain below.

---

[125] The first sheet (1 Ne. 1:1-2:1) is not extant. Dean C. Jessee itemized the scribes by sheet of manuscript in "The Original Book of Mormon Manuscript, *BYU Studies*, 10:3, https://byustudies.byu.edu/content/original-book-mormon-manuscript.

Table 3 - Fayette Scribes on the OM

Scribe	Verses	Page # 1830 ed.	Pages	Day
Oliver C.	1 Ne. 1:1-2:1 (1)	7.6	2.6	
Oliver C.	1 Ne. 2:2-3:6 (2)	9.9	2.3	1
John W.	1 Ne. 3:7-4:14 (3)	12.9	3	
Oliver C.	1 Ne. 4:15-4:20a (4)	13.2	.3	2
Christian W.	1 Ne. 4:20b-12:8 (5)	27.4	14.2	3-4
John W.	1 Ne. 12:9-16:1 (6) (7)	38.7	11.3	5-6
Oliver C.	1 Ne. 16:2-2 Ne. 1:30	62.8	24.1	7-9
Oliver C.	Fragments: 2 Nephi 4-9, 23-25, 33 Jacob 1-7 Enos 1			

1. Pages 1-2 of the OM are missing. I assume Oliver was the scribe for those pages. 1 Ne. 1:1 starts on p. 5 in the 1830 edition.
2. Transition on line 14/54 of p. 4 in the OM.
3. Transition on line 41/54 of p. 6 in the OM.
4. End of p. 6 in the OM.
5. End of p. 18 in the OM, but Christian wrote 3 words at the top of p. 19.
6. Transition on line 6/36, 1.5 lines after beginning of new chapter on p. 30 in the OM.
7. Because of missing and torn pages, these verses are lost: 1 Ne. 13:36-14:10, 14:19-14:22, and 14:30-15:4. Here I assume John wrote these lost verses.

According to the conventional understanding, the translation in Fayette started around June 5 and ended around June 28 (around 21 days, with Sundays off) to produce 149 pages in the 1830 edition.[126] This works out to about 7 pages a day on average, as we discussed in Chapter 1.

The table in *OTH* suggests Joseph translated only the first two chapters on the first day. [127] That is a reasonable assumption, considering Joseph and Oliver had to adjust to new surroundings, and close to what I estimate.

The first leaf of the Fayette OM is missing, but the second leaf has Oliver's handwriting through 1 Nephi 3:6. Table 2 shows the breakdown by scribe for the first 8 pages of the OM.

Table 4 - Fayette scribes on the OM, pages 3-8

Page of Fayette OM	Verses (current ed.)	Scribe
3 recto (front)	1 Ne. 2:2-23	Oliver Cowdery
4 verso (back)	1 Ne. 2:23-3:6	Oliver Cowdery
	1 Ne. 3:7-3:18	John Whitmer
5 recto	1 Nephi 3:18-4:3	John Whitmer
6 verso	1 Nephi 4:2-15	John Whitmer
	1 Nephi 4:15-20a	Oliver Cowdery
7 recto	1 Nephi 4:20b-37	Christian Whitmer
8 verso	1 Nephi 4:38-5:14	Christian Whitmer

To follow this discussion, I encourage you to look at the first existing leaf (pages 3-4) of the Fayette OM at this link:

https://www.josephsmithpapers.org/paper-summary/book-of-mormon-manuscript-excerpt-circa-june-1829-1-nephi-22b-318a/1

You can also go to JosephSmithPapers.org and search for "book of mormon manuscript."

On page 4, about one-third of the down (the 15th line) you can see the transition from Oliver Cowdery's handwriting to John Whitmer's.

[126] Mosiah starts on page 153, but 1 Nephi starts on page 5.
[127] See the table in *OTH*, p. 121-125.

Figure 3 - 1 Ne. 3:7 transition from OC to JW in the OM

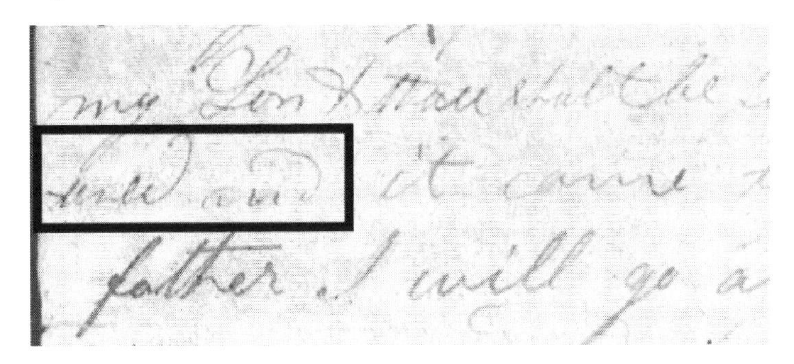

The transition is between the word Oliver finished writing, "mured" (the end of *murmured*), and the word "and" that John Whitmer wrote. You can see the difference in the way they wrote the letter *d*. Notice the lack of punctuation, spacing, etc. The scribes wrote in a continuous through most of the OM.

It is entirely possible that Joseph ended the day's work once Oliver wrote "mured" here.

Grammatically, this is a natural break in the text, but does that mean it is a natural stopping place for a day's work?

It could be. Although this break is in the middle of page 4 in the OM, it was typeset as a paragraph break in the 1830 edition near the bottom of page 9.

Figure 4 - 1 Ne. 3:7 1830 edition

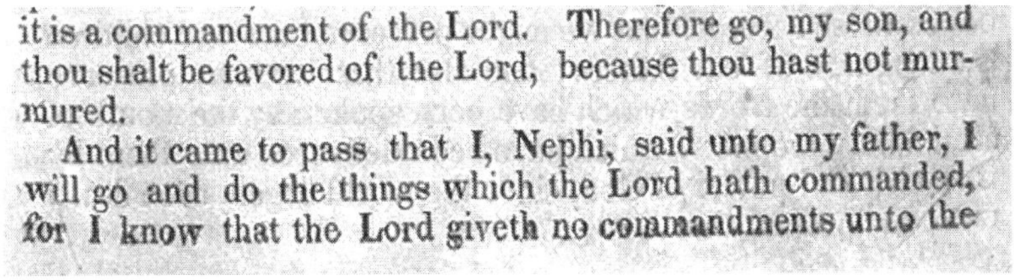

it is a commandment of the Lord. Therefore go, my son, and thou shalt be favored of the Lord, because thou hast not murmured.

And it came to pass that I, Nephi, said unto my father, I will go and do the things which the Lord hath commanded, for I know that the Lord giveth no commandments unto the

In the current LDS edition, it is a break between verses 6 and 7.

6 Therefore go, my son, and thou shalt be favored of the Lord, because thou hast not murmured.

> 7 And it came to pass that I, Nephi, said unto my father: I will go and do the things which the Lord hath commanded, for I know that the Lord giveth no commandments unto the children of men, save he shall prepare a way for them that they may accomplish the thing which he commandeth them.

If this transition from Oliver to John marked the end the first day, Oliver recorded 5 pages of text (about 2200 words). That's a little less than the 7 pages/day average, but reasonable.

The next day, day 2 of the translation, John Whitmer would have begun as scribe, picking up with verse 7 as Joseph dictated "and it came to pass…." John began writing just after Oliver's "mured" and continued writing from that point on.

Another possibility is visible at the end of page 4, verso, in the OM. Look at the bottom of the page. The last line ends with "behold he would also perish" (1 Ne. 3:18a) followed by an extended space, the only such space on the page.

Figure 5 - Space on page 4 of the OM

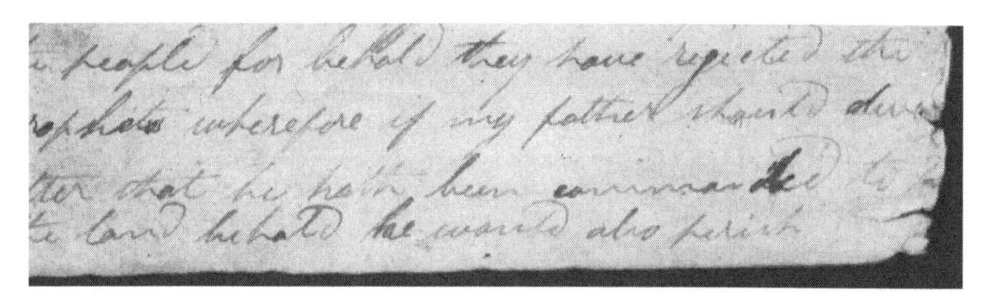
people for behold they have rejected the
phets wherefore if my father should dw
ter that he hath been commanded to
land behold he would also perish

This is also a good choice for a stopping place. John has reached the end of the page. He leaves a space because Joseph doesn't dictate the next word; they're finished for the day. Grammatically, this concludes the sentence (although it is not punctuated). This makes a little over 2600 words for the day, about six pages in the 1830 edition.

This example illustrates that we cannot tell for sure how much Joseph dictated on any given day, but it also shows a possible marker.

The handwritten text throughout the OM usually continues from one page to the next with no break in sentences, but in a few cases the writing concludes at the bottom of the page with a natural grammatical ending, sometimes even with a space. That's what happened with 1 Ne. 3:18a. Such a break could signify the conclusion of a day's work, or maybe the end of one of several sessions during a day.

A natural break might also explain why Oliver wrote the 5.5 verses from 1 Ne. 4:15-4:20a. 4:20a is a natural break at the end of page 6 in the OM. Perhaps John had written to verse 4:14 and stopped for any number of reasons. There was still some space at the end of the page. Oliver could have told Joseph, "Let's finish to the end of the page." Then Joseph dictated just enough to finish the page.

I counted 8 such natural breaks at the end of a page on the first 47 pages.

Table 5 - Natural grammatical breaks in the OM

Natural grammatical breaks at the end of a page in the OM				
Page (OM)	Page (1830)	Ending at Verse	Scribes	Day/ session
4	10 bottom	1 Ne. 3:18a	OC, JW	1
6	13 top	1 Ne. 4:20a	OC, JW	2
7	14 middle	1 Ne. 4:37	CW	
15	24 top	1 Ne. 11:1	CW	4-5
19	29 middle	1 Ne. 12:23	CW, JW	
21	30 middle	1 Ne. 13:29a	JW	6
35	46 middle	1 Ne. 17:48a	JW, OC	7-9
46	60 middle	2 Ne. 1:7	OC	

The last break is at the end of page 46 (2 Ne. 1:7). Page 47 ends with 2 Nephi 1:19 in mid-sentence, and the subsequent pages through Enos are too fragmentary to assess.

The natural breaks are not evenly spaced, but there's no reason to assume each day's translation covered exactly the same amount of material.

These breaks could be random, but that seems unlikely. Christian Whitmer began writing at the top of page 7 in the OM and finished at the end of page 18, except he wrote 3 words at the top of page 19 to finish the sentence.

There may be natural breaks within the pages as well. Further study may enable us to more closely estimate how long it took to translate these pages.

According to the OTH schedule, it took seven days to reach the end of 1 Nephi. I propose it took nine days instead. That is consistent with the slower pace of translation at Harmony, pursuant to the new 2020 translation timeline.

The point: if 1 Nephi was translated at the slower Harmony pace, the translation needed to speed up once Joseph reached 2 Nephi to finish according to the assumed overall timeline. Next we will discuss how and why that happened.

Scribes tiring. There is another reason why we can tell that the SITH demonstration did not take place in the first couple of days of the Fayette translation.

The *Chicago Tribune* article noted that the scribes traded off because they became tired. We can plainly see from the OM that, at least in 1 Nephi, the scribes did not write short passages and trade off during a single session of work because they "became tired." Instead, they wrote for entire days without alternating.

There is the one short transition from John to Oliver to Christian when Oliver wrote 1 Ne. 4:15-20b. That does not fit the demonstration narrative because Oliver would not have become "tired" after writing only five verses. Besides, David mentioned Emma, not John, as a scribe. Emma arrived after Joseph and Oliver, as we discussed above.

A better explanation for Oliver writing these verses is what we discussed above; i.e., he and Joseph just decided to fill in the rest of the page after John stopped writing verse 4:14.

———

Now that we can tell with a high degree of confidence that the events described in the *Chicago Tribune* did not involve Joseph dictating 1 Nephi, we need to look at the evidence for 2 Nephi.

We have only small fragments of the rest of the translation of the plates of Nephi, and only Oliver's handwriting appears on those fragments. However, 2 Nephi Chapters 10-22 are completely missing. Oliver, Emma, Christian and/or other scribes could have written some or all of those chapters.

The *Chicago Tribune* article noted that the scribes traded off because they became tired. Yet we can see from the OM in 1 Nephi that the scribes wrote continuous pages day after day. What would make scribes become tired during a single session of work?

The obvious answer is that, during the demonstration session, they had to write faster than normal.

As described in the *Chicago Tribune* article, the witnesses around the table were people normally busy with farm and house work. A sense of urgency would attend the proceeding. Time was of the essence. Scribes would be expected to write faster than usual and that would explain why they would tire out during a single session.

However, the scribes' capability was only one component of the timing of the dictation. Joseph also needed time to translate.

If, as some propose, Joseph merely read words that appeared on a stone, his role would require little time. He could read as fast as the scribes could write.

But if, as indicated by D&C 9, he had to "study it out in [his] mind" and ask if it was right, the deliberative part of the translation could have been time consuming. As we discussed above, it could have taken two hours per page.

We might think that, after two months of experience in Harmony, Joseph could translate faster. But in Fayette he was translating the plates of Nephi. Even if the language was the same as Mormon and Moroni wrote, the characters were undoubtedly different in the way handwriting varies from one person to the next.

Regardless of the reason, the schedule shows that the average pace of translating 1 Nephi was about 6.2 pages/day. This was roughly the same as it had been in Harmony (depending on how much Emma wrote).

1 Nephi 1:1 through 2 Nephi 1:7 takes up pages 5-60.5 in the 1830 edition of the Book of Mormon, which is 56 pages or about 38% of the plates of Nephi (Mosiah, translated in Harmony, begins on page 153). If it took 9 days to produce 38% of the text (6.2 pages/day), and they had only 12 days total to produce the other 62%, they would have had to translate around 7.7 pages/day to finish the plates of Nephi in 21 days.

This is consistent with the *Chicago Tribune* article, which said the scribes took turn because they got tired. For some reason, Joseph dictated fast enough during the demonstration to tire his scribes.

Let's not forget the translation problem we discussed in Chapter 2. Joseph and Oliver always claimed that Joseph translated the Book of Mormon with *the* Urim and Thummim that came with the plates. They never said he translated with *a* Urim and Thummim, let alone a seer stone he found in a well.

And yet, we have many eyewitness accounts of Joseph dictating words to a scribe as he looked at a stone in a hat.

Can we reconcile this?

I think we can.

We have identified four criteria to satisfy if the *Chicago Tribune* account correctly presented David Whitmer's testimony.

1. Joseph dictated in front of a group without consulting the Urim and Thummim or the plates.
2. Joseph dictated fast enough that his scribes tired and traded off.
3. Joseph dictated some part of the plates of Nephi after 1 Nephi.
4. Joseph translated the Book of Mormon with the Urim and Thummim.

How can all these criteria be met?

I propose that, for these demonstrations, Joseph dictated some of the Isaiah chapters in 2 Nephi from memory.

Furthermore, it is possible to determine, within a degree of probability, which chapters he dictated from memory.

1. If Joseph dictated from memory, he wouldn't have needed the Urim and Thummim or the plates.

2. Joseph could dictate from memory as fast as his scribes could write, which would tire them faster than the normal translation procedure.

3. There are sections of 2 Nephi that contain otherwise inexplicable omissions and word re-orderings that scholars can't make sense of, yet they are typical of an imperfect recitation from memory.

4. If Joseph recited this material from memory, he didn't translate it. Therefore, Joseph and Oliver told the truth when they said he *translated* the plates with the Urim and Thummim. Witnesses of the demonstration *also told the truth* about what they *saw*. But what they saw was not an actual translation. They merely *inferred* it was the actual translation.

In other words, the parts of the text that Joseph did not produce with the Urim and Thummim were not translations.

Point 3 requires more explanation.

When we examine the Isaiah material in the Book of Mormon, we notice that some passages have more numerous and more substantive changes, or variants, than others. For example, 1 Nephi 20-21 have significant variants, including new lines.

1 Ne. 20:14 adds this passage to Isaiah 48:14. "yea and he will fulfill his word which he hath declared by them and…."

1 Ne. 21:1 adds this to Isaiah 49:1. "and again hearken O ye house of Israel all ye that are broken off and are driven out because of the wickedness of the pastors of my people yea all ye that are broken off that are scattered abroad which are of my people O house of Israel."

That is the type of addition that a re-translation of an original text could produce. There are similar insertions in 2 Nephi 6, 7, and 12.

But from 2 Nephi 13 through 2 Nephi 23:21, the changes are minor. One author analyzed 2 Nephi 16-17 and wrote, "There are 29 differences, or variants, in these two Book of Mormon chapters relative to the KJV. None of these variants has any obvious purpose or value. Certainly, none clarifies Isaiah's message or substantially improves the grammar."[128]

Because the OM is missing for these chapters in 2 Nephi, we can only go by the PM. That means some of the variants may be attributable to copying errors or changes made by Oliver Cowdery.

In a rare example, Royal Skousen[129] points out that in the OM for 1 Ne. 20:11 (Isaiah 48:11) (1830 edition, 1 Nephi VI, page 53, line 26–28), Oliver originally wrote "for how should I suffer my name to be polluted" (OM1). Later, he crossed out "how should I" and wrote "I will not" above the crossout (OM2). Both are variants of the KJV. He copied the revised OM into the PM. The changes are in **bold** below.

KJV	OM1	OM2 & PM
For mine own sake *even* for mine own sake will I do *it*:	For mine own sake **yea** for mine own sake will I do **this**	For mine own sake yea for mine own sake will I do this
for how should *my name* be polluted?	for **how should I suffer** my name to be polluted	for **I will not suffer** my name to be polluted
and I will not give my glory unto another	and I will not give my glory unto another	and I will not give my glory unto another

For this analysis, I assume the PM for 2 Nephi 13 through 2 Nephi

[128] Stan Spencer, "Missing Words: King James Bible Italics, the Translation of the Book of Mormon, and Joseph Smith as an Unlearned Reader," *Interpreter:* 38 (2020): 45-106, https://journal.interpreterfoundation.org/missing-words-king-james-bible-italics-the-translation-of-the-book-of-mormon-and-joseph-smith-as-an-unlearned-reader/#sdfootnote15anc. Spencer proposed that these changes are attributable to the mysterious unknown supernatural translator (MUST) who provided the words that appeared on the seer stone.

[129] Royal Skousen, "Textual Variants in the Isaiah Quotations," *Isaiah in the Book of Mormon*, (FARMS: Provo, UT 1998): 383.

23:21 is an accurate copy of the OM, meaning that the variants between the PM and the KJV were dictated by Joseph Smith. If you're interested in doing a detailed comparison, I highly recommend Royal Skousen's Part 5, *The King James Quotations in the Book of Mormon*, which sets out all the differences in a side-by-side format.

In that book, Skousen makes five observations about the biblical quotations in the Book of Mormon.

1. He could not match the Book of Mormon text with any specific King James edition from the last part of the 1600s up to the 1820s.
2. He found 15 passages where the Book of Mormon quotation omits a significant phrase or clause from Isaiah. Although these omissions appear to be intentional rather than errors in transmission, there is no apparent reason for the omissions.
3. He found 29 passages containing a minor intentional difference between the biblical quotation and its KJV source, such as a single word, a minor change in the syntax, or a disagreement in number or tense.
4. He found differences that could have occurred during the dictation process.
5. He found examples of Book of Mormon quotations that were influenced by phrases elsewhere in the scriptures. (I discuss this more in Chapter 11).

Some of these observations make sense as the product of a new translation of an ancient text, but others make more sense as errors in reciting memorized material (or a scribe's error). Reciting from memory could also help explain why most of the italicized material in the KJV, which represents insertions by the translators, was retained in these chapters of 2 Nephi.

Here is an example from 2 Ne. 17 and Isaiah 7, of the type of errors one might make when reciting from memory, including repetition of expected words, omissions of words or phrases, and switching a word from one line to another. The differences are in bold.

Table 6 - 2 Nephi 17 vs Isaiah 7

2 Nephi	Isaiah
2 Nephi 17:1 Rezin king of Syria… went up **towards** Jerusalem	Isaiah 7:1 ***that*** Rezin the king of Syria went up **toward** Jerusalem
2 Nephi 17:6 **yea** the son of Tabeal	Isaiah 7:6 ***even*** the son of Tabeal
2 Nephi 17:11 ask either in the **depths** or in the **heights** above	Isaiah 7:11 ask **it** either in the depth or in the height above
2 Nephi 17:14 Behold a virgin shall conceive And **shall** bear a son	Isaiah 7:14 Behold a virgin shall conceive And bear a son
2 Nephi 17:15 That he may know to refuse the evil And **to** choose the good	Isaiah 7:15 That he may know to refuse the evil And choose the good
2 Nephi 17:18 that is in the uttermost part of Egypt	Isaiah 7:18 that *is* in the uttermost part **of the rivers** of Egypt
2 Nephi 17:20 that is hired	Isaiah 7:20 that is hired **namely**
2 Nephi 17:21 And it shall come to pass **That** in that day A man shall nourish A young cow and two sheep	Isaiah 7:21 And it shall come to pass in that day **That** a man shall nourish A young cow and two sheep
2 Nephi 17:22 And it shall come to pass for the abundance of milk they shall give he shall eat butter	Isaiah 7:22 And it shall come to pass for the abundance of milk **that** they shall give he shall eat butter
2 Nephi 17:23 And it shall come to pass in that day that every place shall be,	Isaiah 7:23 And it shall come to pass in that day that every place shall be,

where there were a thousand vines at a thousand silverlings, **which** shall be for briers and thorns	where there were a thousand vines at a thousand silverlings, **it** shall ***even*** be for briers and thorns.
2 Nephi 17:25 And all hills that shall be digged with the mattock there shall not come thither the fear of briers and thorns but it shall be for the sending forth of oxen, and for the treading of lesser cattle.	Isaiah 7:25 And **on** all hills that shall be digged with the mattock there shall not come thither the fear of briers and thorns but it shall be for the sending forth of oxen, and **for** the treading of lesser cattle.

Appendix 2 includes other chapters of 2 Nephi and Isaiah. Assuming these are not scribal errors (or pronunciation errors by Joseph), I think they show small lapses in an otherwise impressive memory.

Regarding Joseph's memory, historians estimate Joseph delivered more than 200 sermons without a written text. He quoted the Bible extensively. We've already seen how he recognized the scriptures Moroni quoted, chapter and verse, and well enough to recognize the changes. Memorizing these passages from Isaiah would not seem to be a significant challenge for Joseph.

An 1831 account in a Philadelphia newspaper, *The Sun*, discussed such a procedure. Despite the pejorative rhetoric typical of the day, the article describes an account by Martin Harris that is similar to other accounts Martin gave. In this account, Joseph puts the plates in a hat, applies "spectacles," and quotes the Bible from memory. The author frames this as deception by Joseph, but it looks to me instead like a demonstration of the process—exactly the type of demonstration Joseph conducted in Fayette.

> Finally, after frequent and fervent prayer, Jo's spectacles were restored to sight, and he again permitted to open the book. -- Jo had, during his spiritual blindness, by the assistance of some one, commited several chapters of the New Testament to memory; and, the better to carry on his deception with the deluded Harris, had inquired, and found out the words inserted by the translators; (which are distinguished by Italics, both in the New Testament and the Old.) So, in order to convince Harris that he could read from the plates, Jo deposits them in his hat, applies spectacles, and refers Harris to a chapter in the Bible which he had learned

> by rote; and which he read from the plates, with surprising accuracy; and what astonished Harris most, was, that Jo should omit all the words in the Bible that were printed in Italic. And, if Harris attempted to correct Jo, he persisted that the plates were right, and the Bible was wrong.
>
> Jo possessed a remarkably retentive memory; and having convinced Harris beyond the shadow of doubt, that he was commissioned by the Almighty, to reveal some hidden mysteries, he commenced translating, and Harris commenced transcribing, as Jo dictated; and; to avoid mistakes, Jo required his amanuensis to read what he had written; and nothing was allowed to pass, until Jo pronounced it correct. [130]

Reciting biblical passages from memory is not the same as translating the Book of Lehi (or the Book of Mosiah). There would be no "hidden mystery" in an ordinary Bible passage. But if Martin wanted to know how the translation worked, and Joseph could not show him the plates or the U&T, such a demonstration would be an effective solution—just as it was for the observers in Fayette.

Joseph also reportedly knew D&C 132 by heart.[131] That revelation consists of 66 verses and over 3200 words. This is about the same length as 2 Nephi 13-18 or 2 Nephi 16-20 (most of Chapter IX in the 1830 edition).

Speed of dictation. As we've seen, Joseph worked morning until night, a rate of 1.5 to 2 hours per page. Yet David Whitmer reported that the scribes tired and had to trade off during the demonstration. What explains why the scribes could write for days on end Harmony, and in early June in Fayette, but for only a short time in the presence of witnesses, as the article claims.

---

[130] "Mormonites," *The Sun* (Philadelphia), August 18, 1831, online at http://www.sidneyrigdon.com/dbroadhu/PA/Phil1830.htm#081831

[131] On July 12, 1843, Hyrum asked Joseph to write "the revelation on celestial marriage" so he could read it to Emma and convince her. "Hyrum very urgently requested Joseph to write the revelation by means of the Urim and Thummim, but Joseph, in reply, said he did not need to, for he knew the revelation perfectly from beginning to end. Joseph and Hyrum then sat down and Joseph commenced to dictate the revelation… I wrote it, sentence by sentence, as he dictated." William Clayton's Testimony, Feb. 16 1874, as reported in The Historical Record, 6 (May 1887): 225-26. https://archive.org/details/historicalrecord56jens_0/page/n469/mode/2up.

This detail corroborates the demonstration scenario. As we saw from the Harmony timeline, the translation process was slower than traditionally assumed. On average, Joseph translated faster in Fayette, but that's an average. If he translated 1 Nephi at the same rate as he translated in Harmony—and perhaps slower, given the new scribes—Joseph would have had to dictate the Isaiah chapters at a faster to reach an average rate faster than the Harmony rate. Presumably he could actually dictate from memory faster than he could when he was translating an original text. A faster pace would tire the scribes quicker, necessitating a hand-off sooner than normal, just as David described.

These are preliminary conclusions based on the evidence we have.

It is also possible that Joseph used the demonstration as an opportunity to exhort his listeners to faithfulness, as a preacher would, to prepare them to accept the actual text, or even to practice taking dictation. There are lots of possible explanations for the demonstration, but I think a memorized recitation of these chapters in 2 Nephi makes the most sense.

Now we return to the newspaper article.

———

Resuming with the *Chicago Tribune*:

After affixing the magical spectacles to his eyes, Smith would take the plates and translate the characters one at a time.

[This statement has David Whitmer describing Joseph's use of the Urim and Thummim and the plates. This contradicts the stone-in-the-hat (SITH) narrative.

But it also shows that the newspaper reporter was confused.

Joseph could not have used the plates or the Urim in Thummim in the presence of witnesses because he had been commanded not to show the plates or the interpreters to anyone. If all these people gathered around the table saw the plates and/or Urim and Thummim, the experiences of the Three

Witnesses and the Eight Witnesses would have been redundant and unnecessary.

Nevertheless, the article aligns with the description Joseph and Oliver consistently gave; i.e., that Joseph translated the plates with the U&T that Moroni put in the stone box for the purpose of translation. It also matches John Whitmer's account, as well as Lucy Mack Smith's account of how Joseph applied the U&T to his eyes and looked on the plates when he received the commandment to ask David Whitmer to come to Harmony and take Joseph and Oliver to Fayette.

We can only speculate about what David actually told the reporter. Perhaps David related what Joseph and Oliver told him about the actual translation as well as what happened during the demonstration and the reporter simply conflated the separate accounts. Alternatively, the reporter may have done his own research by reading *Mormonism Unvailed* or another report.]

The graven characters would appear in succession to the seer, and directly under the character, when viewed through the glasses, would be the translation in English. Sometimes the character would be a single word, and frequently an entire sentence.

[Because David never looked into the Urim and Thummim, this is either a hearsay account or pure speculation on David's part. The article does not say David claimed that Joseph told him this, although some accounts claim Joseph said things similar to this. There are no extant records from Joseph himself.]

In translating the characters, Smith, who was illiterate and but little versed in Biblical lore, was oft times compelled to spell the words out, not knowing the correct pronunciation, and Mr. Whitmer recalls the fact that at that time Smith did not even know that Jerusalem was a walled city. Cowdery, however, being a school teacher, rendered invaluable aid in pronouncing hard words and giving them their proper definition.

[The term "illiterate" in 1828 meant "ignorant of letters or books; untaught; unlearned." That could simply mean that Joseph did not attend much school. However, Joseph said he was "instructed in reading and writing" and his peers noted that he knew the scriptures well. He was familiar enough with the Bible that he recognized Moroni had quoted the prophets with distinct changes from the King James Version of those passages.

To support his point, David related the same Jerusalem wall anecdote that Emma did (discussed in Chapter 9). We can infer this incident took place when Joseph was translating the plates of Nephi, but it could also have been an anecdote carried over from the translation of the 116 pages.

The spelling detail raises the point that a person who reads a lot still may not know how to pronounce the words correctly. If accurate, the account indicates that Oliver would correct Joseph's pronunciation to make sure he had the exact word intended, including the definitions. Perhaps Joseph had a different accent than Oliver was used to. There are also homophones, meaning words that sound the same (or similar) but have different meanings, such as *straight* and *strait*.

"Giving them their proper definition" suggests an interactive process between Joseph and Oliver. Maybe Joseph was thinking out loud as he searched for the best English expression. The Book of the Mormon rarely defines terms, but thirteen times it uses the phrase "in other words" to explain a term or concept. (The D&C uses the phrase 23 times.) This could reflect *Mormon's* rethinking of a term or phrase. Writing on metal plates, he could not "erase" errors. That's plausible.

However, because the phrase is more common in the D&C, including a letter he wrote (D&C 128), it seem more likely that Joseph used when he thought the first expression did not capture the meaning he wanted to convey.]

MORE MIRACULOUS DEVELOPMENTS

A miracle is related by Mr. Whitmer as occurring while the translation was in progress. It seems that Smith, who was puffed up with his great importance as a confidential secretary to the Lord, displeased the Master by entering into some carnal confab in relation to the work.

[This apparently refers to the time in June 1828 when Joseph allowed Martin Harris to take the first 116 pages to show his wife and a few others. This was about a year before David ever met Joseph, so it's another hearsay account.]

For this offense he was punished by having the celestial visitant, who first commissioned him to inaugurate the work, suddenly appeared and carried off the plates and spectacles.

[Joseph explained that after the 116 pages were lost, the messenger did reclaim the plates. Joseph got them back with the U&T in September 1828.]

In this connection it might also be mentioned that Martin Harris, one of the witnesses to the translation, a farmer in the same county, and a man of simple mind and taste, was sent by Smith with a copy of the characters to Professor Anthon, a professor of languages in Columbia College, and author of several well known works, who pronounced the language inscribed on the plate Reformed Egyptian.

[This part of the article is fairly accurate, as far as it goes, except Joseph didn't send Martin to Professor Anthon. Martin was referred to Anthon. It is more likely that Joseph sent Martin to see Samuel Mitchill, who had provided an endorsement for *The Late War*. Martin first visited Luther Bradish, a state legislator in

Albany who had Palmyra connections. Bradish apparently gave Martin an introduction to the professors in New York City.]

About this time Harris, inspired by curiosity and elation, took sixteen of the golden tablets home to show his wife, who is alleged to have stolen them from a bureau drawer and peddled them among her friends. For this offense Harris was severely reprimanded by the Lord, through Smith, but the angel afterwards recovered the plates and restored them. Smith's offense of tattling the secrets of the works among his neighbors was less readily condoned, and for a long time the work was suspended, the angel being in possession of the plates and spectacles.

[This is a confused, erroneous version of the lost 116 pages. Harris did not take sixteen of the plates; he took the 116 manuscript pages. It seems unlikely that David would have related such an account, which is another indication that the reporter did separate research and conflated different accounts.]

Finally when Smith had fully repented of his rash conduct, he was forgiven. The plates, however, were not returned,

[This statement contradicts the first part of the article which claimed the plates were with the translator, shielded by the blanket. It also contradicts other narratives that have Joseph giving the Harmony plates to a divine messenger before leaving Harmony, the messenger taking those plates to Cumorah, and then the messenger bringing the plates of Nephi to Fayette for Joseph to translate. The messenger also showed the plates to David's mother, Mary Whitmer. However, it could be the reporter's misunderstanding of the two sets of plates.

It's possible that David told the reporter that the Harmony plates were not returned (because he saw the messenger who was taking them to Cumorah), and the reporter misunderstood, thinking that because the Harmony plates were not returned,

Joseph had no plates to translate from that point on. Separately, David said he knew the plates were in Fayette and explained that the messenger showed them to his mother.]

but instead Smith was given by the angel, a Urim and Thummim of another pattern, it being shaped in oval or kidney form.

[Other accounts have Joseph finding the seer stone in a well. Here, the angel gave Joseph "a Urim and Thummim of another pattern." It's possible that the messenger who brought the plates of Nephi from the hill Cumorah to Fayette also brought a different interpreter than the one Joseph used when translating the Harmony plates, but both Joseph and Oliver always said Joseph translated the plates with the Urim and Thummim that Moroni concealed with the original plates.

Either David or the reporter could have assumed this was the brown seer stone used in the demonstration.]

This seer's stone he was instructed to place in his hat, and on covering his face with the hat the character and translation would appear on the stone.

[Other accounts have Joseph using the "stone-in-the-hat" technique long before he obtained the plates, but here he learns the technique from an angel. The hearsay nature of this article prevents us from determining whether Joseph told people this provenance, or whether the observers assumed it, but the latter seems more probable because there are no records of Joseph claiming to have obtained a seer stone from an angel.

The technique described here is ideally suited for a public demonstration. Everyone can observe as Joseph shows the stone (perhaps passing it around), then places the stone in the hat, and then covers his face with the hat. They can hear Joseph dictate words that his scribe records. They likely would have recognized

the words of Isaiah, assuming Joseph was dictating 2 Nephi as we discussed above.]

This worked just as satisfactory as the old method, but at no time thereafter was the backsliding Joseph intrusted [sic] with the precious plates.

[This contradicts the first part of this very article. First, it was the plates and the spectacles; now it's the "seer's stone" and the hat.]

However, the entire portion of the golden volume, which the angel said might be translated, was reduced by the nimble amanuensis to readable manuscript. The other installment was withheld until the Lord could discover what the first had on the Gentiles. That He was not pleased with the result is manifested by the fact that the sealed portion has not yet been delivered to the world.

[Of course, if Joseph never used the plates to translate, there was no reason for any of them to be actually sealed. Joseph couldn't have known which portion of the plates were represented by the words that appeared on the stone in the hat.]

Assessment of David Whitmer as a witness:

Competency: As one of the Three Witnesses and a respectable citizen his entire life, we assume David Whitmer had the mental power to perceive, remember and communicate.

Opportunity: David was in a position to observe at least some of the events he testified about, but not others (such as what Joseph saw when he was translating). His testimony on those matters could be speculation, hearsay, or inference.

Bias or partiality: After he left the Church, David turned against Joseph and this may have affected his memory.

Motive: David sought to persuade people not to follow the LDS, but he also wanted people to accept the divine authenticity of the Book of Mormon. One of the most persistent threats to the Book of Mormon was the Spalding theory, and the best way to defeat the Spalding theory was to claim he actually watched the translation and there were no books or other manuscripts from which Joseph could read.

Prior inconsistent statements: David made several inconsistent statements over the years.

Contradictory facts: Inconsistencies don't necessarily amount to contradictory facts.

---

8. David Whitmer's Inconsistent Statements

Overview.

David Whitmer lived until 1888. Of all the witnesses to the Book of Mormon, he was interviewed by far the most often. David said he related his testimony hundreds of times, but the earliest known account from David Whitmer regarding the translation dates to 1872, over 40 years after the events.

With all that material, it's not surprising that there would be some discrepancies and inconsistencies. Some interviewers say David claimed Joseph translated with the U&T, or the spectacles, which he decribed in detail. Others say he claimed Joseph translated with SITH. Such differences may be attributed to his listeners' misunderstandings, but can they all be? Or did David change his accounts deliberately?

One thing David consistently related was his conviction of the divine authenticity of the Book of Mormon as one of the Three Witnesses. As I interpret the evidence, David's conviction (and sense of resposibility) led him to oppose the Spalding theory by expanding SITH from the demonstration he observed into a claim that this was the *only* method of translation Joseph used.

Detail.

David Whitmer said he related his testimony hundreds of times. Only a relatively few statements have survived, and they contain inconsistencies (even within some statements). A collection of these interviews, Lyndon Cook's *David Whitmer Interviews*, is 262 pages long. However, that book is out of print, difficult to find, and contains transcription errors. Appendix 1 has many of David's statements.[132]

[132] Two useful online compilations are found at: https://archive.bookofmormoncentral.org/content/miraculous-translation-book-mormon; https://josephsmithfoundation.org/papers/an-analysis-of-statements-by-david-whitmer-on-translation-of-the-book-of-mormon/

David always testified to the divine authenticity of the Book of Mormon as one of the Three Witnesses, but his explanations of the translation were inconsistent.

We expect any collection of witness statements to include some inconsistencies. Memory is not static; our brains reconstruct memory every time we try to remember something. We have all had the experience of remembering things differently from others who were present at the same event. Researchers have found that people even *misremember* information to match their own beliefs.[133]

Furthermore, 19th century accounts were rarely recorded verbatim. Many accounts are a reporter's version of what he/she heard from the witness, and reporters often have their own agenda to push. In Chapter 2, we considered an example where David specifically corrected a newspaper story that was incorrect in several details, but such corrections were not always forthcoming.

Things to look for include indicia of reliability, such as a specific detail that would make an event especially memorable. We can look for consistent elements across multiple accounts. We can consider means, motive and opportunity. We can also notice what is *not* said.

When evaluating David's statements, we assume he had the means, or ability, to observe and hear what was going on. He stated his motive directly: he was under an obligation as one of the Three Witnesses to testify to the divine authenticity of the Book of Mormon. We will discuss how that motive may have impacted his statements.

As for opportunity to observe and hear, we realize he was never a scribe. He did not see the plates or the U&T until after the translation was complete, when he was one of the Three Witnesses. David also admitted he wasn't present for much of the translation; he only saw what took place in the Whitmer living room, and Joseph and Oliver worked on the translation upstairs most of the time.

Therefore, much if not most of David's statements were probably hearsay, except for his description of the SITH demonstration in

---

133 E.g., a 2019 study from Dr. Jason C. Coronel at Ohio State University. https://phys.org/news/2019-12-facts-misremembered-personal-biases.html.

Fayette. As you read David's statements, think about the 1870 visit by William E. McLellin, when David's sister Elizabeth Cowdery was present. I'm not aware of specific evidence of an agreement among David, William and Elizabeth to promote SITH, but Elizabeth's affidavit and subsequent statements by David and William (as well as Emma) usually focus on SITH.

Most compilations of David's statements focus on his testimony as one of the Three Witnesses and his observations about the translation of the Book of Mormon. For reasons of space or perceived irrelevance, they usually omit David's discussions of the persistent Spalding theory, which David adamantly opposed. I suggest, however, that the need to refute the Spalding theory was *a*, if not *the*, reason why David usually emphasized SITH.

———

The best-known account from David Whitmer is probably the one he wrote in his booklet titled *An Address to All Believers in Christ*, published in 1887, some months before he died on January 28, 1888. This is the quotation found in the January 2020 *Ensign* and that was paraphrased in *Saints*, volume 1, etc., as we discussed in Chapter 3.

David wrote:

> I will now give you a description of the manner in which the Book of Mormon was translated. Joseph Smith would put the seer stone into a hat, and put his face in the hat, drawing it closely around his face to exclude the light; and in the darkness the spiritual light would shine. A piece of something resembling parchment would appear, and on that appeared the writing. One character at a time would appear, and under it was the interpretation in English. Brother Joseph would read off the English to Oliver Cowdery, who was his principal scribe, and when it was written down and repeated to Brother Joseph to see if it was correct, then it would disappear, and another character with the interpretation would appear. Thus the Book of Mormon was translated by the gift and power of God, and not by any power of man.[134]

---

[134] David Whitmer, *An Address to All Believers in Christ* (1887), p.12.

On its face, the account appears straightforward. But the quotation is usually taken out of context, at least in the *Ensign*, *Saints* book, and other recent materials.

The question readers should ask is, what immediately preceded this explanation? What led David to write, "I will now give you…" here?

The answer: David provided this description *specifically to refute the Spalding theory.*

If you read David's booklet, you will see that he started by discussing the three churches that believed in the Book of Mormon: his own Church of Christ, the RLDS, and the LDS. He pointed out that the LDS practice of polygamy was condemned in the Book of Mormon and said the practice was vileness.

He corrected a claim that he had repudiated his testimony of the Book of Mormon and strongly reaffirmed that testimony.

Then he turned to the Spaulding theory.

David discussed the translation only after explaining the Spalding theory in some detail. To understand David's motivation, we need to review his discussion of the Spalding theory. This is a long quotation so you can skip ahead if you want, but this context is critical for understanding David's description of the translation.

> p. 10. Besides other false statements that are in the two encyclopædias above mentioned is the old story of the Spaulding manuscript. That is, that one Solomon Spaulding, who died in Amity, Penn., in 1816, had written a romance, the scene of which was among the ancient Indians who lived in this country.
>
> That Spaulding died before he published his romance, and that Sydney Rigdon got hold of the manuscript in a printing office and copied it; that subsequently the manuscript was returned to Solomon Spaulding; that thirteen years after the death of Spaulding, in 1829, Rigdon became

---

https://archive.org/details/addresstoallbeli00whit

associated with Joseph Smith, who read the Spaulding manuscript from behind a blanket to Oliver Cowdery, his amanuensis, who wrote it down.

Hence the origin of the Book of Mormon.

This is what is claimed by the enemies of the book: Satan had to concoct some plan to account for the origin of that book.

I will say that all who desire to investigate the Spaulding manuscript story will not be obliged to go very far before they will see the entire [p. 11] falsity of that claim. **I testify to the world that I am an eye - witness to the translation of the greater part of the Book of Mormon.**[135] Part of it was translated in my father's house in Fayette, Seneca County, N. Y. **Farther on I give a description of the manner in which the book was translated.**

When the Spaulding story was made known to believers in the book, they called for the Spaulding manuscript, but it could not be found; but recently, thanks to the Lord, the original manuscript has been found and identified.[136] It has been placed in the library of Oberlin college, Oberlin, Ohio, for public inspection. All who have doubts about it being the original Spaulding manuscript, can satisfy themselves by visiting Oberlin and examining the proofs. The manuscript is in the hands of those who are not believers in the Book of Mormon. They have kindly allowed the believers in the book to publish a copy of the manuscript, with the proofs that it is the manuscript of Solomon Spaulding.[137] There is no similarity whatever between it and the Book of Mormon. Any one who investigates this question will see that the Spaulding manuscript story is a fabrication concocted by the enemies of the Book of Mormon, in order to account for the origin of that book.

Neither Joseph Smith, Oliver Cowdery, Martin Harris or myself ever met Sydney Rigdon until after the Book of Mormon was in print. I

---

[135] He exaggerated here. Most of the published Book of Mormon, and all of the 116 pages, were translated in Harmony. At most, David could have observed some of the translation in Fayette, but he also said he was not always present.

[136] There is ongoing debate whether this is the manuscript in question. Proponents of the Spalding theory claim Spalding wrote several manuscripts that remain lost.

[137] This manuscript is undoubtedly Spalding's, but witnesses claimed it was not the one they read or heard Spalding read publicly.

know this of my own personal knowledge, being with Joseph Smith, in Seneca County, N. Y., in the winter of 1830, when Sydney Rigdon and Edward Partridge came from Kirtland, Ohio, to see Joseph Smith, and where Rigdon and Partridge saw Joseph Smith for the first time in their lives.

The Spaulding manuscript story is a myth ; there being no direct testimony on record in regard to Rigdon's connection with the manuscript of Solomon Spaulding. I have in my possession the original manuscript of the Book of Mormon, in the handwriting of Oliver Cowdery and others,[138] also the original paper containing some of the characters transcribed from one of the golden plates, which paper Martin Harris took to Professor Anthon, of New York, for him to read " the words of a book that is sealed:" but the learned professor, although a great linguist could not read the language of the Nephites.

There is some evidence in the American Cyclopædia favorable to the Book of Mormon that I will speak of. It is as follows :

[David relates the Martin Harris visit to Prof. Anthon]

No man could read it, but God gave to an unlearned boy the gift to translate it.

I will now give you a description of the manner in which the Book of Mormon was translated.

David's understandable yet overzealous claim regarding how much of the translation he could have seen and his mistaken claim to possess the OM suggest his enthusiasm for testifying of the Book of Mormon overpowered adherence to strict veracity on some details.

The account has credibility problems for reasons in addition to David's agenda. Notice that nowhere in this account does David claim to write as a witness of the events.[139] He provides "a description" but does not say, "I observed." He describes what Joseph supposedly saw

[138] He actually had the Printer's Manuscript.

[139] Regarding another event, David wrote, "I was there also, and am an eye witness to these facts." *Address*, p. 31.

in the stone in the hat, something that David could not have seen, yet he does not explain the source of his knowledge. He does not write "Joseph told me he saw one character at a time." Consequently, it is impossible to determine which parts, if any, of this account are based on David's personal observations, what parts, if any, are second-hand accounts, and what parts, if any, are merely inferences or assumptions.

The reliability of this account is undermined by the discrepancies in David's prior statements, as we will see below. Furthermore, David could only have witnessed the translation of the plates of Nephi, which took place in Fayette. He was not present in Harmony where the abridged plates, Mosiah through the Title Page, were translated.

The quotation above is the only reference to a "seer stone" in *An Address to All Believers in Christ,* but David claimed some of the early revelations were "given through the stone." We infer he meant the "seer stone," but the wording is ambiguous because he also referred to the Urim and Thummim as a stone.

> Brother Joseph did not write a word of the Book of Mormon; it was already written by holy men of 'God who dwelt upon this land. God gave to Brother Joseph the gift to see the sentences in English, when he looked into the hat in which was placed the stone. Oliver Cowdery had the same gift at one time.[140]

> Now, brethren, I will ask you to read the early revelations that were given through the stone, up to June, 1829, and see if this matter is not just as I have told you;[141]

David once claimed to be present when Joseph received a revelation "through the stone," but he does not describe the method Joseph used.

> The next important change I will speak of, is made in a revelation which was given to Brothers Joseph Smith, Oliver Cowdery, and myself in Fayette, New York, June, 1829. I was present when Brother Joseph received it through the stone. It is Chapter 15 Book of Commandments, Sec. 16 Doctrine and Convenants.... I want

[140] *Address*, p. 37.
[141] *Address*, p. 55.

to repeat that I was present when Brother Joseph received this revelation through the stone: I am one of the persons to whom it was given, therefore I know of a surety that it was changed when printed in the Doctrine and Convenants in 1834. Likewise concerning all these changes of which I will speak, I know that these changes were made. I was present when nearly all the early revelations were received.[142]

David explained that Joseph gave the stone to Oliver.

After the translation of the Book of Mormon was finished, early in the spring of 1830, before April 6th, Joseph gave the stone to Oliver Cowdery and told me as well as the rest that he was through with it, and he did not use the stone any more. He said he was through the work that God had given him the gift to perform, except to preach the gospel.[143]

Although some authors have inferred that Joseph was "through with it" because he had translated the plates with the stone, it's equally consistent that he was "through with it" because he didn't need to do any more demonstrations.

David also mentioned the term "Urim and Thummim" once, implying the term described the stone Joseph used:

The people cannot understand why the Lord would bring forth his word from "a book (plates) that is sealed" and was buried in the ground by his ancient prophets on this land: and why He should have the words of the book delivered "to one that is learned," telling him to read it, etc. ; (see Isa. xxix) but the learned and wise men of the world could not read it; God gave to an unlearned boy, Joseph Smith, the gift to translate it by the means of a stone. See the following passages concerning the "Urim and Thummin," being' the same means and one by which the Ancients received the word of the Lord. (1 Sam. xxviii :6. Neh. vii : <i5. Ezra ii : 63. Num. xxvii : 21. Deut. xxxiii : 8. Exodus xxviii: 30. Lev. viii : 8 .).[144]

Elsewhere, David described the Urim and Thummim as the two stones set in "spectacles," the way others described them.

---

142 *Address*, p. 58.
143 *Address*, p. 32.
144 *Address*, p. 6.

> At times when Brother Joseph would attempt to translate, he would look into the hat in which the stone was placed, he found he was spiritually blind and could not translate. He told us that his mind dwelt too much on earthly things, and various causes would make him incapable of proceeding with the translation. When in this condition he would go out and pray, and when he became sufficiently humble before God, he could then proceed with the translation. Now we see how very strict the Lord is ; and how he requires the heart of man to be just right in His sight, before he can receive revelation from him.

In 1878, David was asked directly "Did Joseph use the Urim and Thummim when he translated?"

David answered by *describing* the U&T. This evasive answer suggests David didn't want to commit to yes or no.

> The Urim and Thummim were two white stones, each of them cased in as spectacles are, in a kind of silver casing, but the bow between the stones was more heavy, and longer apart between the stones, than we usually find it in spectacles. Martin Harris, Oliver Cowdery, Emma and my brother John each at different times wrote for Joseph as he translated.[145]

Many of David's statements are included in Appendix 1 to this book. Several are newspaper articles. As we saw in Chapter 1, newspaper accounts can contain errors, even when portraying statements as direct quotations.

In some cases what appear to be direct contradictions in David's statements may be nuance, word choice, or speculation. For example, according to a reporter's 1885 account of what David told him, after Martin Harris lost the 116 pages in the summer of 1828, Joseph gave the plates and "spectacles" to an angel. Once Joseph repented, he was forgiven.

> **The plates, however, were not returned**, but instead Smith was given by

---

145 P. Wilhelm Poulson, *Deseret Evening News*, August 15, 1878. https://whitmercollege.com/interviews/dr-p-wilhelm-poulson-1878/

> the angel a Urim and Thummim of another pattern, it being shaped in oval or kidney form. This seer's stone he was instructed to place in his hat, and on covering his face with the hat the character and translation would appear on the stone. This worked just as satisfactorily as the old method, but at no time thereafter was the backsliding Joseph intrusted with the precious plates.[146]

The article contradicts other statements by David. For example, David testified that in June 1829 he met the divine messenger—an old man—who was taking the plates from Harmony to Cumorah. David also said this messenger brought plates to Fayette and showed them to his mother. Perhaps David told the reporter that the *Harmony* plates were not returned when they arrived in Fayette and the reporter misunderstood that to mean no plates were returned after Joseph lost the 116 pages.

Regarding the return of the U&T, Joseph Smith's history, compiled by his scribes, says "Behold the former heavenly messenger appeared and handed to me the Urim and Thummin [sic] again."[147] The word "again" suggests Joseph received back the same Urim and Thummim he had given up; i.e., the one that accompanied the plates in Moroni's stone box, not "another pattern."

Joseph's parents visited Harmony after he left Palmyra (where Joseph had gone seeking Martin Harris). His mother, Lucy Mack Smith, related the events.

> when I entered his house the first thing that attracted my attention was a red morocco trunk, that set on Emma's bureau; which trunk Joseph shortly informed me, **contained the Urim and Thummim and the plates**. [Joseph explained that, after giving up the Urim and Thummim,] "I continued my supplications to God without cessation; and, on the 22d of September, I had the joy and satisfaction of **again receiving the Urim and Thummim**; and have commenced translating again, and Emma

---

146 1885 *Chicago Tribune* interview. Appendix 1, #30-31.

147 Joseph Smith History, circa June 1839-circa 1841 [Draft 2], available online at https://www.josephsmithpapers.org/paper-summary/history-circa-june-1839-circa-1841-draft-2/12

> writes for me; but the angel said that the Lord would send me a scribe, and <I> trust his promise will be verified. He also seemed pleased with me, when **he gave me back the Urim and Thummim**; and he told me that the Lord loved me, for my faithfulness and humility."[148]

The bolded passages affirm that Joseph had the plates and the Urim and Thummim. Lucy said nothing about "another pattern."

Such discrepancies are not uncommon in historical accounts. That's what makes them difficult to reconcile. Historians debate these things all the time. The best we can do is consider the accounts, assess credibility and reliability, and make up our own minds about what to believe.

The following excerpts show that David Whitmer gave a variety of descriptions of the translation.

Recall that in his 1878 interview with Poulson, David did not directly answer the question, but merely described the Urim and Thummim that came with the plates. In the newspaper account quoted above, David said Joseph received a Urim and Thummim of "another pattern." This description, however, matches that provided by other accounts of the Urim and Thummim that came with the plates.

In a sequence of articles published in the *Saints' Herald* in 1879-1880, two witnesses disagreed about whether David said Joseph translated with the Urim and Thummim. A third witness corroborated the claim that David once said Joseph used the Urim and Thummim.

Joseph used the U&T	Joseph did not use the U&T
Thomas Wood Smith (1879)	J. L. Traughber Jr. (1879)
I personally heard him [David] state, in Jan. 1876 in his own house in Richmond, Ray Co. Mo. . . . that **he saw Joseph translate, by the aid of the Urim and Thummim, time and again,** and he [David] then	I, too, have seen the "manuscripts" and examined them. I, too, have heard Father [David] Whitmer say that he was present many times while Joseph was translating; but **I never heard him say that the translation**

[148] Lucy Mack Smith, *History, 1845*, https://www.josephsmithpapers.org/paper-summary/lucy-mack-smith-history-1845/142

produced a large pile of foolscap paper closely written in a very fair hand, which he declared was the manuscript written mainly by Oliver Cowdery and Martin Harris, **as the translation was being read by the aid of the Urim and Thummim of the characters on the plates by Joseph Smith,** which work of translation and transcription he frequently saw.[149]

[Wood, 1880]
[U]nless my interview with David Whitmer in January, 1876, was only a dream, or that I failed to understand plain English, I believed then, and since, and now, that he said that Joseph possessed, and used the Urim and Thummim in the translation of the inscriptions referred to, and I remember of being much pleased with that statement, as I had heard of the "Seer stone" being used. And unless I dreamed the interview, or very soon after failed to recollect the occasion, he described the form and size of the said Urim and Thummim. The nearest approach to a retraction of my testimony as given in the Fall River Herald and that given publicly in many places from the stand from **was made by aid of Urim and Thummim;** but in every case, and his testimony is always the same, he declared that Joseph first offered prayer, then took a dark colored, opaque stone, called a "seer-stone," and placed it in the crown of his hat, then put his face into the hat, and read the translation as it appeared before him. **This was the daily method of procedure,** as I have often heard Father Whitmer declare; and, as it is generally agreed to by parties who know the facts, that a considerable portion of the work of translation was performed in a room of his father's house, where he then resided, there can be no doubt but what Father David Whitmer is a competent witness of the manner of translating. . . .
With the sanction of David Whitmer, and by his authority, **I now state that he does not say that Joseph Smith ever translated in his presence by aid of Urim and Thummim; but by means of one dark colored, opaque stone, called a "Seer Stone," which was placed in the crown of a hat, into which Joseph put his face, so as to exclude the external light.** Then, a spiritual light would shine forth, and parchment would appear before

[149] Thomas Wood Smith, "Origin of the Mormon Bible," *Fall River (MA) Herald*, 28 March 1879; reprinted in the *Saints' Herald* 26 (15 April 1879). https://archive.org/stream/TheSaintsHerald_Volume_26_1879/the%20saints%20herald%20volume%2026%201879#page/n125/mode/2up. This account is partly erroneous because while the manuscript David had was mostly written by Oliver and Martin, he actually had the Printers Manuscript, not the Original Manuscript.

January, 1876, till now, is, that unless I altogether misunderstood "Father Whitmer" on this point, **he said the translation was done by the aid of the Urim and Thummim.** If he says he did not intend to convey such an impression to my mind, then I say I regret that I misunderstood him, and unintentionally have misrepresented him. But that I understood him as represented by me frequently I still affirm. If Father Whitmer will say over his own signature, that he never said, or at least never intended to say, that Joseph possessed or used in translating the Book of Mormon, the Urim and Thummim, I will agree to not repeat my testimony as seen in the Fall River Herald on that point.[150]	Joseph, upon which was a line of characters from the plates, and under it, the translation in English; at least, so Joseph said.[151]
Eri B. Mullin (1880)	
Mr. D. Whitmer told me in the year 1874, that Joseph Smith used the Urim and Thummim when he was translating. . . . I for my part know he said that Joseph had the instrument Urim and Thummim. I asked him how they looked. He said they looked like spectacles, and he (Joseph) would put them on and look in a hat, or put his face in the hat and read. Says I, "Did he have the plates in there." "No, the words would appear, and if he failed to spell the word right, it	

[150] Thomas Wood Smith, Letter, *Saints' Herald* 27 (January 1, 1880): 13.

[151] 83. J. L. Traughber Jr., "Testimony of David Whitmer," *Saints' Herald* 26 (November 15, 1879): 341.

would stay till it was spelled right, then pass away; another come, and so on."[152]	

These conflicting accounts were published while David was alive. We think it should have been easy to reconcile them by simply asking David to explain the discrepancies, but apparently no one did.

It turns out that most of the Thomas Wood Smith article focuses on refuting the Spalding theory.

> The force of the opposition to our position and the point upon which the case of our opponents rests, is in the assertion, that Joseph Smith and Sydney Rigdon conjointly produced the Book of Mormon, from either a copy or the original manuscript of a certain retired clergyman, Rev. Solomon Spaulding.

I think Smith accurately reported what David said, perhaps when David was still working out the anti-Spalding narrative.

Notice that Traughber quoted David as saying "I now state that he does not say that Joseph Smith ever translated **in his presence** by aid of Urim and Thummim." That is consistent with David having observed a demonstration and with Joseph translating with the U&T both in the upstairs room in the Whitmer home and in Harmony.

Traughber and Smith could both have accurately reported what David said, but Traughber adamantly demanded a retraction. Why?

Traughber was a "devotee of William E. McLellin."[153] He received McLellin's papers from his widow and wrote of McLellin, "I valued him very much. He and I were true friends[;] yet for the last two years of his life we were as far apart in religion as the poles of the earth."[154]

McLellin's views of the translation changed over time. In March

[152] Eri B. Mullin, Letter to the editor, *Saints' Herald* 27 (March 1, 1880): 76.
[153] *The William E. McLellin Papers 1854-1880*, Larson and Passey, Editors (Signature Books: Salt Lake City, 2007): 34.
[154] The Journals of William E. McLellin, BYU Studies (1994): 257.

1847, McLellin published a newspaper titled the *Ensign of Liberty*. On page 2, he wrote "the record had been translated by Joseph Smith, jr., by the " inspiration of the Almighty," by the use of the means that the Lord had caused to be provided, viz. Interpreters, Directors, or more anciently called Urim and Thummim."[155]

The April 1837 edition of the same journal published this (p. 32):

> Who knows whether Joseph had the Interpreters, i. e. the Urim, and with that, by the inspiration of the Lord, translated the plates he had found? Answer—Oliver Cowdery, David Whitmer, and Martin Harris. How did these men know? The heavens were opened upon them, an holy Angel came down before them, in open day light, and laid before them the Plates, the Interpreters...

Twice more, the *Ensign of Liberty* reiterated the same message.

> When Joseph Smith found the plates of Mormon, he found with them in the same encasement the Interpreters, viz. the Urim and Thummim; and by the aid of that instrument he translated that sacred record called the book of Mormon. Hence holding these Interpreters, and having the gift from God to use them for sacred purposes he was called Seer. (p. 40)

> Joseph Smith, as we have shown, had been appointed, of God, a Seer, and had in his possession the Interpreters. He had translated the ancient record of the prophets of our American land, viz: the book of Mormon. (p. 42)

Later in life, however, as we saw in the Preface to this book, McLellin wrote "I do not believe he [Joseph] ever possessed the Urim and Thummim during his whole life." This was what Traughber supported.

McLellin was a complex man. "During a long life, he flitted from one Mormon faction to another, searching for what he perceived as the absolute truth of the gospel. His was a desperate and seemingly frustrating search for God."[156] Like David Whitmer, he retained a

---

[155] William E. McLellin, *The Ensign of Liberty of the Church of Christ*, March 1847, p. 2. https://archive.org/details/EnsignOfLiberty18471849/page/n1/mode/2up?

[156] Richard P. Howard, "Mormonism's 'Stormy Petrel,'" in *The William E. McLellin*

testimony of the truthfulness of the Book of Mormon, and it appears that this testimony may have led him to favor SITH over the U&T.

William E. McLellin attested to the veracity of David Whitmer's account in a letter he wrote to James T. Cobb dated 14 August 1880.[157]

> When I thoroughly examine a subject and settle my mind, then higher evidence must be produced before I change. I have set to my seal that the book of Mormon is a true, divine record and it will require more evidence than I have ever seen to ever shake me relative to its purity. I have read many "Exposes." I have seen all their arguments. But my evidences are above them all!... I have more confidence in the Book of Mormon than any book of this wide earth!...
> When I first joined the church in 1831, soon I became acquainted with all the Smith family and the Whitmer family, and I heard all their testimonies, which agreed in the main points; and I believed them then and I believe them yet...
> I saw him [David Whitmer] June 1879, and hear him bear his solemn testimony to the truth of the book—as sincerely and solemnly as when he bore it to me in Paris, Ill. In July 1831. I believed him then and still believe him....

McLellin had a close relationship with David Whitmer for many years. Both men were determined to refute the Spalding theory. In a postscript to this letter, McLellin responded once again to the Spalding theory, although he didn't mention Spalding by name.

> You seem to think S. Rigdon the bottom of all M.ism (Mormonism). Many people know better. He never heard of the work of Smith & Cowdery until C and P.P.Pratt brought the Book to him in Mentor, O. [Ohio]

———

The discrepancies in David's statements may also be attributed to his desire to corroborate Emma's testimony.

Papers, p. 3.

[157] Larry C. Porter, "William E. McLellan's Testimony of the Book of Mormon, *BYU Studies*, Volume 10, Issue 4, Article 15 (1970) at https://scholarsarchive.byu.edu/cgi/viewcontent.cgi?article=1426&context=byusq.

9. Emma Smith's "Last Testimony"

Overview.

There are no existing records that Emma Smith discussed the Book of Mormon translation during the lifetime of Joseph Smith or Oliver Cowdery (who died in 1850). Six such accounts from 1856-1879 do exist. The most detailed and lengthy is the "Last Testimony of Sister Emma."

In February 1879, Joseph Smith III, President of the RLDS church, interviewed his mother, Emma Smith. She died in April 1879 without independently authenticating the interview. On October 1, 1879, the RLDS published "Last Testimony of Sister Emma," purporting to be a transcript of the interview.

The interview addressed two main points: the Solomon Spalding theory and polygamy. Joseph Smith III had been heavily engaged in debating both topics. He used his mother's "Last Testimony" as proof to support his positions on both issues.

Shortly after the "Last Testimony" was published, LDS Church leaders in Salt Lake denounced it as a lie and questioned whether it was the authentic testimony of Emma Smith. They rebutted Emma's assertion that Joseph never practiced nor taught polygamy with contrary affidavits from women who claimed to be Joseph Smith's plural wives.

The Spalding elements of the "Last Testimony" received less attention in Salt Lake, possibly because the LDS leaders agreed with the efforts to debunk that theory. The "Last Testimony" claims Emma served as a scribe while Joseph dictated with his face buried in a hat (i.e., SITH), not using the plates at all. Emma also made a point of attesting to David Whitmer's veracity.

Both before and after the "Last Testimony" was published, LDS leaders in Salt Lake reaffirmed that Joseph "translated these records by the aid of the Urim and Thummim."

Whether it was Emma or her son who composed the "Last

Testimony," the article's objective of refuting the Spalding theory suggests the SITH narrative was driven by that objective, possibly in coordination with David Whitmer.

———

Detail.

As the wife of Joseph Smith, Jr., Emma accompanied him to the Hill Cumorah to get the plates in September, 1827. She served as a scribe for part of the 116 pages, as well as for the Harmony OM and the Fayette OM. She was directly involved with Joseph's activities through his murder in Carthage.

There are no known accounts of statements Emma made during the life of her husband, Joseph Smith, Jr. However, she gave three interviews between 1856 and 1879 and wrote one letter in 1870 that addressed the translation.

Emma's statements, which relate a version of SITH, have been widely accepted as authoritative by historians. A close examination of these statements led me first to question whether they should be accepted at face value, and then to conclude that they reflect a specific agenda of refuting the Spalding theory.

———

Here is a brief biography of Emma Smith.[158]

Emma Hale Smith Bidamon (July 10, 1804 – April 30, 1879) was the first wife of Joseph Smith. Upon Joseph's death, Emma was left a pregnant widow. Joseph had been trustee-in-trust for the church, so Emma had to untangle her personal finances from the church's. When Brigham Young, President of the Quorum of the Twelve, was chosen as Joseph's successor, Emma objected. She and Brigham had a rocky relationship. When Brigham led most of the Latter Day Saints from Nauvoo to Utah in early 1846, Emma and her children remained behind in the emptied town.

In 1847, Emma married the non-Mormon Major Lewis Crum

---

[158] The following bio is adapted from the Joseph Smith Papers and Wikipedia. https://www.josephsmithpapers.org/person/emma-hale-smith https://en.wikipedia.org/wiki/Emma_Smith.

Bidamon. The Bidamons struggled financially but remained in Nauvoo.
In 1860, Emma's 28-year-old son Joseph Smith III was sustained as president of the Church of Jesus Christ of Latter Day Saints, which added the word "Reorganized" to the name in 1872 (presently known as Community of Christ). Emma became a member of the RLDS Church. She remained in Nauvoo until she died on April 30, 1879.

In this chapter, we will consider six accounts attributed to Emma Smith. One is a handwritten letter; the other five are published accounts based on interviews.

As we've seen with David Whitmer's experiences, published accounts vary in accuracy and authenticity. On December 9, 1845, a year and a half after Joseph Smith died, a letter purportedly written by Emma was published in the *New York Sun*. Dated November 20, 1845, the letter included this paragraph:

> I must now say, that I have never for a moment believed in what my husband called his apparitions and revelations, as I thought him laboring under a diseased mind; yet they may all be true, as a Prophet is seldom without credence or honor, excepting in his own family or country, but as my conviction is to the contrary, I shall educate my children in a different faith, and teach them to obey and reverence the laws and institutions of their country.[159]

On January 15, 1846, the *Times and Seasons* in Nauvoo published a statement above the printed signature of Emma Smith:

> To the editor of the New York Sun; Sir: I wish to inform you, and the public through your paper, that the letter published Tuesday morning, December 9th, is a forgery, the whole of it, and I hope that

---

[159] The letter and commentary are available in Linda King Newell and Valeen Tippetts Avery, "New Light on the Sun: Emma Smith and the New York Sun Letter," *Journal of Mormon History* Vol. 6 (1979), pp. 23-35, online at JSTOR, www.jstor.org/stable/23286014.

this notice will put a stop to all such communications.

The *New York Sun* never published the disavowal. Historians have debated whether Emma wrote the original letter and whether the subsequent disavowal was published willingly. There is evidence to support multiple scenarios. This is another case of people believing whatever they want to believe by focusing on evidence that confirms their biases and ignoring evidence that does not.

This type of ambiguity and equivocation applies to the statements we will consider in this chapter.

The best-known statement about the translation attributed to Emma is titled "Last Testimony of Sister Emma." It was published on October 1, 1879, in the RLDS publication titled *Saints' Herald*[160] and in the *Saints' Advocate* in October 1879. The "Last Testimony" is quoted authoritatively in LDS Church materials including *Saints,* Volume 1, and the Gospel Topics Essay on Book of Mormon Translation, which frames it this way:

> Joseph's wife Emma explained that she "frequently wrote day after day" at a small table in their house in Harmony, Pennsylvania. She described Joseph "sitting with his face buried in his hat, with the stone in it, and dictating hour after hour with nothing between us."[161]

The Maxwell Institute rates Emma's "Last Testimony" so highly that its *Study Edition of the Book of Mormon* places her testimony right after the testimony of the Three and Eight Witnesses–and even before the Testimony of the Prophet Joseph Smith from JS-H.

Although many historians accept this testimony without

---

[160] The "Last Testimony of Sister Emma" is available online here: https://archive.org/stream/TheSaintsHerald_Volume_26_1879/the%20saints%20herald%20volume%2026%201879#page/n287/mode/2up

[161]https://www.churchofjesuschrist.org/manual/gospel-topics-essays/book-of-mormon-translation?lang=eng#note28. The entire interview is included in Appendix 5.

reservation, when considered in its historical context Emma's "Last Testimony" has significant problems that would ordinarily give historians pause.

Instead of accepting the "Last Testimony" on its face, we should apply Joseph Smith's "key" to "enquire what was the question which drew out the answer."

Circumstances. The interview with Emma was conducted in February 1879, shortly before she died on April 30.[162] She never signed it or publicly acknowledged it. It wasn't published until October 1879.

Why was publication delayed for eight months?

One factor may have been two sermons Orson Pratt delivered in September 1879 that reaffirmed Joseph's claim that he translated the plates with the U&T (see Appendix 5).

Joseph Smith III, Emma's son and the President of the RLDS Church, visited his mother for a week to conduct the interview. He took with him a list of questions prepared by H. A. Stebbins and other RLDS leaders.

The RLDS leaders were facing critics of the Book of Mormon, particularly those who promoted the Spalding theory.

They were also in an ongoing ecclesiastical battle with the LDS leadership in Utah over polygamy, right of succession, and other issues. Tensions were high. RLDS missionaries were proselyting in Utah. In General Conference, Brigham Young had warned the Saints against these missionaries, but they converted thousands of Utah Mormons.

This context helps explain the questions, the answers, and the response from the LDS community.

---

[162] The full interview is in Appendix 4.

Figure 6 - Questions for Emma, handwritten

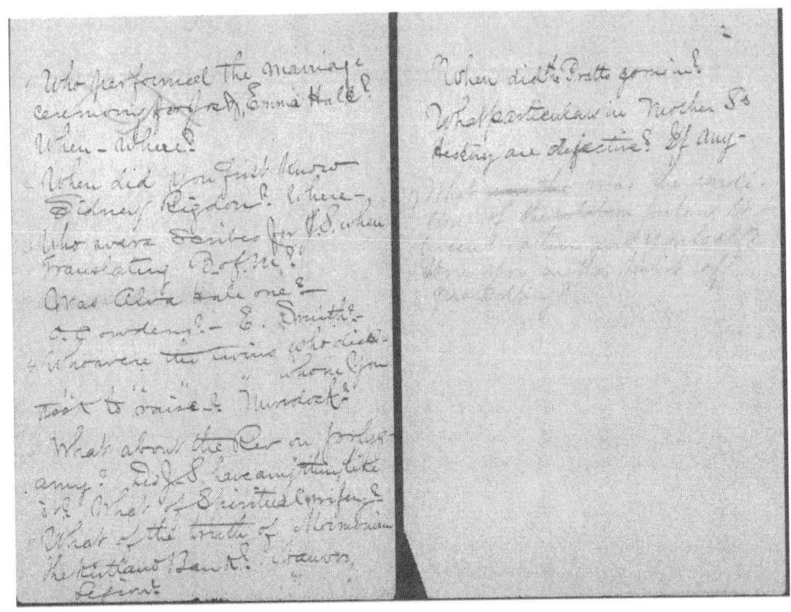

courtesy of the Community of Christ archives

1. Who performed the marriage ceremony for Jos & Emma Hale? When – Where?
2. When did you first know Sidney Rigdon? Where-
3. Who were scribes for J.S. when translating BofM? Was Alva Hale one? O. Cowdery? E. Smith?
4. Who were the twins who died?
   " " " " whom you took to raise? Murdock?
5. What about the Rev on polygamy? Did J.S. have anything like it? What of Spiritual wifery?
6. What of the truth of Mormonism? The Kirtland Bank? Nauvoo,

When did the Pratts come in?

What particulars in Mother S's History are defective? If any-

7. What was the condition of the feeling between father and yourself? Were you in the habit of quarrelling?

Objectives of the interview. Although the "Last Testimony" is often cited for the information about the translation, the original list of questions didn't ask how Joseph produced the Book of Mormon. Emma volunteered her comments about SITH after she answered the questions about Sidney Rigdon and the scribes. These questions were aimed at refuting the Spalding theory, which claimed Rigdon had copied the Spalding manuscript and colluded with Joseph to compose the Book of Mormon. Rumors that Rigdon married Joseph and Emma served to support the Spalding theory. Hence the questions about the marriage and when she first met Rigdon.

Two weeks after the interview, Joseph Smith III cited the interview to support his position in an exchange with a Spalding advocate.

We will return to this point after we consider the other major objective of the interview: debunking plural marriage.

Plural marriage. Plural marriage was a major difference between RLDS and LDS in the 19th century. Modern readers re usually unaware of the degree of animosity between the LDS and RLDS churches in the late 1800s.

In October, 1863, Brigham Young commented on Emma's son, Joseph Smith III.

> You have heard that Young Joseph Smith, the son of Joseph Smith the Prophet, has presented himself as the leader of the Latter-day Saints. I will take this for my text. In the first place I will say to the saints that I know more about Joseph Smith, the prophet of the last days, and his family, than all the apostates that ever did or ever will leave this church.... Joseph Smith that now is living in the state of Illinois, **the son of Joseph the Prophet, will never lead the Latter-day Saints: he may lead apostates, and will lead them to hell.**[163]

---

[163] Brigham Young October 7, 1863, address in the Salt Lake Bowery, at https://www.fairmormon.org/answers/Primary_sources/Brigham_Young/7

Regarding Emma, Brigham Young said this in the October 1866 General Conference.

> "To my certain knowledge, **Emma Smith is one of the damnedest liars** I know of on this earth; yet there is no good thing I would refuse to do for her, if she would only be a righteous woman; but she will continue in her wickedness."[164]

Another example of the ongoing dispute between the LDS and RLDS can be seen in an 1869 letter from George A. Smith to Joseph Smith III.[165]

In a section of the "Last Testimony" that the Maxwell Institute and the Gospel Topics Essay omit, Emma insisted that Joseph Smith never taught or practiced polygamy, never had another wife, and never received a revelation on polygamy. Those LDS historians who *accept* Emma's "Last Testimony" to support SITH also *reject* her testimony denying polygamy.

For Joseph Smith III, Emma's denial that Joseph ever practiced or taught polygamy was a major victory in his ongoing battle with Brigham Young and the Utah Mormons.

The publication of Emma's "Last Testimony" provoked an immediate response from Joseph F. Smith (JFS), Emma's nephew. JFS was the son of Hyrum and Mary Smith.[166] On October 17, 1879, just two weeks after the "Last Testimony" was published in the *Saints' Herald*, JFS wrote a letter to the editor of the *Deseret News*. The paper published his letter with this

October 1863

164 See http://www.eldenwatson.net/1860s.htm#14

165 https://archive.org/details/GeorgeASmithToJosephSmithIII9Oct1869/page/n7

166 In 1866 JFS had been sustained as a counselor to the LDS First Presidency and ordained an Apostle by Brigham Young, the President of the LDS Church.

introduction:

> THE following testimony in relation to the Prophet Joseph Smith's marital relations will be of great interest to the Latter-day Saints and should offer convincing proof to everyone who reads it that the martyred Seer not only taught but entered into the practice of plural marriage, and that he did so with the full knowledge, consent and assistance of his wife Emma whose **alleged** "last testimony" has been published, containing a denial of these facts. There is no need of these proofs to the saints who lived in Nauvoo, nor the great bulk of those who never resided there; but they are given for the benefit of all who may entertain any doubts whatsoever upon this important subject.[167] (emphasis added)

Like the editorial introduction to his letter, JFS suggested that Emma's "Last Testimony" may not have been hers. In his letter, he quoted from Emma's "Last Testimony" and then rebutted its claims about polygamy with sworn statements and affidavits. Among these were

> Two of the wives of the Prophet Joseph Smith, which I think, will assert quite as strong claims for belief and present a much better appearance of veracity than the published dialogue between Joseph Smith [III] and his mother, for this reason, if no other, these people, well known to this community, are mostly still living and can be cross-examined, **while "Sister Emma," whose lips are sealed in death, is represented as denying facts which it can be abundantly proven, were well known to her**, and to many now living in these mountains…

Although he focuses on the polygamy question, JFS's observations about the credibility of the "Last Testimony" and Emma's unavailability for questioning apply to the entire

---

[167] "Joseph the Seer's Plural Marriages," *Deseret News*, 22 October 1879, 604, online at https://newspapers.lib.utah.edu/details?id=2663429.

document.

On the same page of the *Deseret News* another letter to the editor questioned the authenticity of the "Last Testimony." This one was from Eliza R. Snow, who identified herself as "A wife of Joseph Smith the Prophet." Snow wrote:

> To my great astonishment, I read an article headed "Last Testimony of Sister Emma," published in the *Saints' Advocate*, a pamphlet issued in Plano, Ill.... I once dearly loved "Sister Emma," and now, for me to believe that she, a once highly honored woman, should have sunk so low, even in her own estimation, as to deny what she knew to be true, seems a palpable absurdity. **If what purports to be her "last testimony" was really her testimony, she died with a libel on her lips**—a libel against her husband—against his wives—against the truth, and a libel against God; and in publishing that libel, her son has fastened a stigma on the character of his mother that can never be erased.... So far as Sister Emma personally is concerned, I would gladly have been silent and let her memory rest in peace, **had not her misguided son, through a sinister policy, branded her name with gross wickedness**—charging her with the denial of a sacred principle which she had heretofore not only acknowledged but had acted upon....

At the end of Chapter Two I observed that LDS leaders throughout the 19th century repeatedly reaffirmed the teaching that Joseph used the U&T to translate the engravings on the plates. (Several examples are provided in Appendix 5.) Without understanding the historical context, we might wonder why they kept repeating something that Joseph and Oliver had made so plain.

The existence and usage of the U&T was a significant issue during that era. LDS Church leaders were all fully aware of SITH as it had been set out in *Mormonism Unvailed* and promoted by numerous other publications for decades. When they gave these sermons in General Conference and elsewhere, they were responding to critics (including Emma Smith) who denied that Joseph used the U&T to translate the plates.

They also denounced what they called "peep stones." For example, in a sermon on November 22, 1857, Heber C. Kimball mentioned that "When I came back from England there were but a few left in Kirtland. There was one little society of men that pretended to take the lead and oversight of the people, and they were **guided by a peep stone**."

OTH contains six entries under Emma Smith Bidamon (numbers 38-43, starting on page 129).[168] In this section we'll look at each of them, using the numbering system from *OTH,* with my notes set off in brackets.

There is one additional account from Emma, related by William E. McLellin. He spent 24 hours with Emma in Nauvoo in August, 1847. He asked her, "Have you any confidence in the book of Mormon, and the work of the last days?" He said her answer was prompt. "I have all confidence in that spirit of intelligence by which the book of Mormon was translated, and by which the revelations were given to the church in the beginning."[169]

38. Emma Smith Bidamon, as interviewed by Edmund C. Briggs (1856)

When my husband was translating the Book of Mormon, I wrote a part of it, as he dictated each sentence, word for word, and when he came to proper names he could not pronounce, or long words, he spelled them out, and while I was writing them, if I made any mistake in spelling, he would stop me and correct my spelling, although it was impossible for him to see how I was writing them down at the time. Even the word Sarah he could not pronounce at first, but had to spell it, and I would pronounce it for him.

---

168 https://archive.bookofmormoncentral.org/content/miraculous-translation-book-mormon

169 "Our Apology—and Our Tours," *Ensign of Liberty*, Dec. 1847: 34, online at https://archive.org/details/EnsignOfLiberty18471849/page/n33/mode/2up

When he stopped for any purpose at any time he would, when he commenced again, begin where he left off without any hesitation, and one time while he was translating he stopped suddenly, pale as a sheet, and said, "Emma, did Jerusalem have walls around it?" When I answered "Yes," he replied "Oh! I was afraid I had been deceived." He had such a limited knowledge of history at that time that he did not even know that Jerusalem was surrounded by walls.38

38. Edmund C. Briggs, "A Visit to Nauvoo in 1856," *Journal of History* 9 (October 1916): 454. Edmund C. Briggs and Samuel H. Gurley traveled to Nauvoo to visit Joseph Smith III and testify to him of the reorganization of the Church, which had recently occurred in Wisconsin. Briggs and Gurley arrived at the Mansion House in Nauvoo on December 5, 1856, and interviewed Emma Smith Bidamon three days later.

Comments. Although dated 1856, this account was first published 60 years after the interview in 1916. There is no record that Emma reviewed it or approved of it, and we have no original notes or other manuscript to compare to the published account.

The only example Emma gave of a proper noun Joseph could not pronounce is *Sarah*, but *Sarah* is mentioned only once in the 1830 edition of the Book of Mormon, in 2 Nephi 8:2 which was written in Fayette. The Fayette OM is missing this verse, but there is a fragment of 2 Nephi 8:6-17 in the handwriting of Oliver Cowdery, making it unlikely that Emma was a scribe for this passage. (Sarah is mentioned twice in D&C 132, a revelation that Emma denied Joseph ever received.)

Some scholars suggest that Emma probably said *Sariah* but the interviewers recorded it wrong. This is plausible because *Sarah* is a common biblical name but *Sariah* is not.

Sariah occurs 5 times in the Fayette OM in 1 Nephi. Each occurrence is in the handwriting of Oliver Cowdery or Christian Whitmer (except the introduction to 1 Nephi, which is missing but presumably in Oliver's handwriting). Emma was not in Fayette during the first part of the translation; she arrived after

Joseph and Oliver did.

Emma's reference to *Sarah* could have arisen from the translation of the 116 pages, which presumably mentioned *Sariah*.

Alternatively, this published account could be explained by Briggs incorporating accounts he heard from others, such as the Jerusalem wall question that David Whitmer also mentioned (discussed below).

Martin Harris also repeated the story, sort of. "He said it was impossible for the prophet Joseph to get up the 'Book of Mormon,' for he could not spell the word Sarah. He had him repeat the letters of the word. He was a very illiterate man." (see #54 in *OTH*.) Emma, of course, said he couldn't *pronounce* it; he spelled it out so she could pronounce it.

The *Sarah* story leaves us wondering whether Emma or Martin was the scribe involved. I lean toward Emma as scribe, with Martin repeating the story he heard from her.

The second element of this statement is the Jerusalem walls story, which David also related. This is an odd story. Presumably it refers to 1 Nephi 4:4, when Nephi and his brothers "came without the walls of Jerusalem."

Does the Bible say there were walls around Jerusalem when Lehi left Jerusalem? No. The Book of Mormon refers to the "first year of the reign of Zedekiah." This is in 2 Kings 24. There's nothing in the Bible about walls around Jerusalem in that year. Asking about walls around Jerusalem when Lehi left seems like a reasonable question to me.

2 Kings 25:1 skips to the ninth year of Zedekiah's reign, after Lehi had left. That chapter does discuss walls, but not when they were built. The 2 Chronicles 36:19 version of the history says the Chaldeans brake down the wall of Jerusalem, but again, that was several years after Lehi left. This detail is not a big deal, but I think it's a stretch to say Joseph didn't know the Bible because he didn't know if there were walls around Jerusalem when Lehi left the city.

Overall, this 1916 publication of an 1856 interview doesn't say much about the translation, but it does seem to incorporate some questionable statements.

39. Emma Smith Bidamon to Emma Pilgrim (1870)

Now, the first part my husband translated, was translated by the use of Urim and Thummim, and that was the part that Martin Harris lost. After that he used a small stone, not exactly black, but was rather a dark color.39

39. John T. Clark, "Translation of Nephite Records," *The Return* 4 (July 15, 1895): 2. Written from Nauvoo on March 27, 1870, the original letter is located in the Emma Smith Papers, Library-Archives, Community of Christ, Independence, Mo. (hereafter cited as Community of Christ Library-Archives).

Comments. The excerpt in *OTH* omits some important context. The Community of Christ Library-Archives sent me a photocopy of the original. (see a longer excerpt in Appendix 1). Emma wrote this letter as a response to an inquiry from Emma S. Pilgrim, who was the wife of the RLDS pastor in Independence, Missouri. The Pilgrim letter to which Emma responded is not extant so we can only infer that Emma Smith Bidamon was responding to a question about the translation.

Emma wrote the first page to explain why her response to Pilgrim was delayed. She had been attending sick family members in Plano. She assured Pilgrim that the delay "has not been willfull [sic] neglect or a wicked indifference to the subject of your inquiry as I always feel a peculiar satisfaction in giving all the information on that subject that I can."

Next she wrote the part that is often quoted.

> Now, the first part my husband translated, was translated by the use of Urim and Thummim, and that was the part that Martin Harris lost. After that he used a small stone, not exactly black, but was rather a dark color. I cannot tell whether that account in the Times and Seasons is correct or not because some one stole all my books and I have none to refer to at present, if I can find one that has that account I will tell you what is true and what is not.

Apparently Pilgrim's question arose from an unspecified account in the *Times and Seasons*, possibly Oliver Cowdery's Letter

I, the Wentworth letter, or Joseph Smith's History (now Joseph Smith—History in the Pearl of Great Price). Joseph's History was republished in the LDS Pearl of Great Price in 1851 (and canonized in 1881). Naturally, Emma did not refer to that source.

By 1870, when Emma wrote the letter, the divisions between RLDS and LDS were significant. Brigham Young and Orson Pratt had already reaffirmed in General Conference that Joseph used the U&T to translate the plates. Recall that it was in 1866 that Brigham said of Emma, "Emma Smith is one of the damnedest liars I know of on this earth."

In the letter, Emma does not claim she saw the U&T or the stone. She relates the account the same way anyone would who had heard someone else describe it. This passage can be read either as an eye-witness account by someone who forgot to mention she was an eye-witness, or as an explanation based on what she heard others say.

This seems strange because Emma was a scribe for both the 116 pages and part of both the Harmony OM and the Fayette OM. Lucy Mack Smith quotes Joseph saying Emma wrote for him after he recovered the U&T following the loss of the 116 pages. Lucy also explained that in May 1829, Joseph applied the U&T to his eyes to look on the plates but instead of the translation he received a commandment to write to David Whitmer. This was well after the 116 pages were lost.

Emma's reference to the *Times and Seasons* could mean either that she meant to say she could tell what was true or false about the account in the *Times and Seasons*, or that she needed that reference to refresh her recollection.

The *Times and Seasons* was published 10 years after the events of the translation. Emma wrote this letter nearly 30 years after the *Times and Seasons* was published, but she didn't know, or couldn't remember, what the newspaper's accounts said about the translation.

By 1870, numerous conflicting accounts of the translation had been published. The Spalding theory had been revitalized. Pilgrim's letter may have asked about Spalding. Emma's response—that Joseph used SITH for the Book of Mormon as published—was an effective refutation of the Spalding theory.

40. Emma Smith Bidamon, as interviewed by Nels Madsen and Parley P. Pratt Jr. (1877)

Q. Did he receive the plates from which he claimed to have translated the Book of Mormon?

A. Yes, they lay in a box under our bed for months but I never felt at liberty to look at them.

In regard to the Book of Mormon Mrs. Bidemon stated emphatically that he[r] husband, Joseph Smith could not have written such a book without inspiration. He had not read the Bible enough to know that there were walls around Jerusalem and he came and asked me if there were walls around the city of Jerusalem.40

40. Nels Madsen, "Visit to Mrs. Emma Smith Bidamon," 1931, Church Archives. Madsen and Parley Pratt Jr. visited Bidamon in Nauvoo while they were missionaries. Online at https://catalog.churchofjesuschrist.org/assets?id=0d0d3c56-50a1-4071-90f0-2bb08b753a7f&crate=0&index=0

Comment. The typewritten account of this interview is dated Nov. 27, 1931, 54 years after the interview took place. It is yet another version of the "walls around Jerusalem" story. In this version, Joseph "came and asked" about the walls, an indication that Emma was not the scribe when Joseph encountered this passage. Yet in the 1856 interview (reported in 1916), Emma claims Joseph turned white and asked her directly. The discrepancy suggests confusion on the part of Emma or her interviewers.

The Book of Mormon question came after Nels Madsen began this interview with questions about polygamy:

> Q. Did he have any more wives than you?
> A. Not to my knowledge.
> Q. Did he receive the revelation on plural marriage?
> A. Not to my knowledge.

We can assess Emma's credibility in light of the response to the next interview, which took place in 1879.

41. Emma Smith Bidamon, as interviewed by Joseph Smith III (1879)

Q. Who were scribes for father when translating the Book of Mormon?

A. Myself, Oliver Cowdery, Martin Harris, and my brother, Reuben Hale.

Q. Was Alva Hale one?

A. I think not. He may have written some; but if he did, I do not remember it. . . .

Q. What of the truth of Mormonism?

A. I know Mormonism to be the truth; and believe the Church to have been established by divine direction. I have complete faith in it. In writing for your father I frequently wrote day after day, often sitting at the table close by him, he sitting with his face buried in his hat, with the stone in it, and dictating hour after hour with nothing between us.

Q. Had he not a book or manuscript from which he read, or dictated to you?

A. He had neither manuscript nor book to read from.

Q. Could he not have had, and you not know it?

A. If he had had anything of the kind he could not have concealed it from me.

Q. Are you sure that he had the plates at the time you were writing for him?

A. The plates often lay on the table without any attempt at concealment, wrapped in a small linen table cloth, which I had given him to fold them in. I once felt of the plates, as they thus lay on the table, tracing their outline and shape. They seemed to be pliable like thick paper, and would rustle with a metalic sound when the edges were moved by the thumb, as one does sometimes thumb the edges of a book.

Q. Where did father and Oliver Cowdery write?

A. Oliver Cowdery and your father wrote in the room where I was at work.

Q. Could not father have dictated the Book of Mormon to you, Oliver Cowdery and the others who wrote for him, after having first written it, or having first read it out of some book?

A. Joseph Smith [and for the first time she used his name direct, having usually used the words, "your father," or "my husband"] could neither write nor dictate a coherent and well-worded letter; let alone dictating a book like the Book of Mormon. And, though I was an active participant in the scenes that transpired, and was present during the translation of the plates, and had cognizance of things as they transpired, it is marvelous to me, "a marvel and a wonder," as much so as to any one else.

Q. I should suppose that you would have uncovered the plates and examined them?

A. I did not attempt to handle the plates, other than I have told you, nor uncover them to look at them. I was satisfied that it was the work of God, and therefore did not feel it to be necessary to do so.

Major Bidamon here suggested: Did Mr. Smith forbid your examining the plates?

A. I do not think he did. I knew that he had them, and was not specially curious about them. I moved them from place to place on the table, as it was necessary in doing my work.

Q. Mother, what is your belief about the authenticity, or origin of the Book of Mormon?

A. My belief is that the Book of Mormon is of divine authenticity—I have not the slightest doubt of it. I am satisfied that no man could have dictated the writing of the manuscripts unless he was inspired; for, when acting as his scribe, your father would dictate to me hour after hour; and when returning after meals, or after interruptions, he would at once begin where he had left off, without either seeing the manuscript or having any portion of it read to him. This was a usual thing for him to do. It would have been improbable that a learned man could do this; and, for one so ignorant and unlearned as he was, it was simply impossible.41

41. Joseph Smith III, "Last Testimony of Sister Emma," *Saints' Herald* 26 (October 1, 1879): 289–90; and Joseph Smith III, "Last Testimony of Sister Emma," *Saints' Advocate* 2 (October 1879): 50–52. Joseph Smith III wrote that Emma reviewed the answers he had recorded for her. The answers "were affirmed by her" on the day before he left Nauvoo. Emma's husband Lewis C. Bidamon asserted that Emma's answers were "substantially what she had always stated" at times when they discussed the translation of the Book of Mormon.

Comment. The full interview is in Appendix 4. The ellipses in the excerpt above omit Emma's statement that

> there was no revelation on either polygamy, or spiritual wives.... No such thing as polygamy, or spiritual wifery, was taught, publicly or privately, before my husband's death, that I have now, or ever had any knowledge of.... [Joseph] assured me... that there was no such doctrine, and never should be with his knowledge, or consent. I know that he had no other wife or wives than myself, in any sense, either spiritual or otherwise.

We discussed the credibility of these statements at the beginning of this chapter.

In 1870, Emma claimed Joseph used the stone-in-the-hat after the 116 pages were lost. Here, she claims she wrote "hour after hour" and "day after day" as Joseph dictated from the stone-in-a-hat. If her 1870 statement was accurate, this means she had to have been recording Joseph's dictation beginning with Mosiah, which corroborates the conclusion that she wrote some or all of Mosiah.

We saw in Chapter 6 that Emma was one of the scribes during the SITH demonstration in Fayette. David Whitmer used that event to refute the Spalding theory. Emma endorsed David as a reliable witness. She believed in the divine authenticity of the Book of Mormon and had encouraged her son to assume the mantle from his father. Under the circumstances, it made perfect sense for Emma to embrace SITH.

Close observers would know that Emma's testimony contradicted that of her mother-in-law, Lucy Mack Smith, who died in 1856. Her memoir had been published in 1853 in England by Orson Pratt, but Brigham Young objected and many of the books were destroyed.

Recall that Lucy Mack Smith's *History, 1844-1845*, observes Emma wrote for Joseph *after* the 116 pages were lost.

> I ~~then~~ continued <said> Joseph my suplications to God without cessation that his mercy might again be exercised towards me and on the 22 of september **I had the Joy and satisfaction of again receiving the ~~record~~ <urim and Thummin> into my possession and I have commenced translating and Emma writes for me now** but the angel said that ~~if I got the plates again~~ that the Lord woul[d] send some one to write for me and I trust that ~~if~~ it will be so. he also said that ~~the~~ <he> ~~angel~~ ~~seemed~~ <was> rejoiced when he gave ~~him~~ <me> back the ~~plates~~ <urim and Thummim> and ~~said~~ that ~~he~~ <God> was pleased with ~~his~~ <my> faithfulness and humility ~~also that the Lord was pleased with him~~ and loved ~~him~~ <me> for ~~his~~ <my> penitence and dilligence in prayer in the which ~~he~~ <I> had performed his duty so well as to receive the ~~record~~ <urim and Thummin> and ~~be~~ <was> able to enter upon the work of translation again[170]

Lucy's *History 1845* revised the passage but kept the essence of her original history on this point.

> on the 22d of September, **I had the joy and satisfaction of again receiving the Urim and Thummim; and have commenced translating again, and Emma writes for me**; but the angel said that the Lord would send me a scribe, and < I> trust his promise will be verified. ~~The angel~~ He also seemed pleased with me, when he gave me back the Urim and

---

170 https://www.josephsmithpapers.org/paper-summary/lucy-mack-smith-history-1844-1845/91

> Thummim; and he told me that the Lord loved me, for my faithfulness and humility.[171]

Contrary to Lucy Mack Smith's account, William E. McLellin claimed that Joseph never got the U&T back after the 116 pages were lost. He wrote a letter[172] to Joseph Smith III in 1872 in which he claimed,

> When Joseph delivered the 116 pages of the translation to Martin Harris, his plates, his Interpreters, and his gift were taken from him for some two months. The Plates and gift of translation was restored to him, but not the Interpreters. He translated the entire book of Mormon by the use of a little stone he had in his possession before he obtained the plates.

His letter does not mention what Joseph and Oliver claimed. Instead, he refers to statements from John and David Whitmer, Emma Smith, Martin Harris, and Elizabeth Ann Whitmer Cowdery, the widow of Oliver (provided only by McLellin).

When we look at her "Last Testimony," Emma was not even sure who baptized her, a normally memorable event that took place after the translation of the plates. When asked whether Joseph forbade her from examining the plates, she replied "I do not think he did." She said she felt of the plates and thumbed them, but "was not specially curious about them." Although she moved them from place to place, she never uncovered them to look at them.

Of course, it is impossible to assess the credibility of a published statement made by a witness decades ago without cross examination. People remember some things and forget others. The best we can do is consider context, motives, bias, opportunity to observe, reliability, and other indicia of credibility.

---

[171] https://www.josephsmithpapers.org/paper-summary/lucy-mack-smith-history-1845/145

[172] William E. McLellin to Joseph Smith III, July 1872, *The William E. McLellin Papers 1854-1880* (Signature Books 2007), p. 484.

We cannot rule out the possibility that Emma was completely truthful in everything she said. But if so, her testimony directly opposes some of the core teachings of Brigham Young and his contemporaries, all of whom where frequently taught by Joseph Smith, as well as their successors as leaders of the Church—including their consistent affirmation of what Joseph and Oliver consistently taught about the U&T.]

42. Emma Smith Bidamon, as recorded by Joseph Smith III (1879)

She wrote for Joseph Smith during the work of translation, as did also Reuben Hale, her brother, and O[liver]. Cowdery; that the larger part of this labor was done in her presence, and where she could see and know what was being done; that during no part of it was did Joseph Smith have any Mss. [manuscripts] or Book of any kind from which to read, or dictate, except the metalic plates, which she knew he had.42

42. Joseph Smith III to James T. Cobb, February 14, 1879, Community of Christ Library-Archives; cited in Vogel, Early Mormon Documents, 1:544.

Comment. This letter to Cobb was written specifically to refute the Spalding theory, as we discussed above.

43. Emma Smith Bidamon, as recorded by Joseph Smith III (1900)

My mother [Emma Smith] told me that she saw the plates in the sack; for they lay on a small table in their living room in their cabin on her father's farm, and she would lift and move them when she swept and dusted the room and furniture. She even thumbed the leaves as one does the leaves of a book, and they rustled with a metalic sound. Yes, mother did some of the writing for father while he was translating[.] She testified that father found and had the plates, and translated them as the history states; that she had no doubt as to the truth of it.43

43. Joseph Smith III to Mrs. E. Horton, March 7, 1900, Community of Christ Library-Archives; cited in Vogel, Early Mormon Documents, 1:546–47.

Comment. This is another restatement of the Last Testimony that adds details omitted from the published interview.

In conclusion, we have only four statements from Emma, plus two statements from her son who elaborated on his interview with her. These are dated 1856 (published in 1916), 1870 (a brief letter answering an unknown question), 1877 (published in in 1931), and 1879 (published six months after her death).

All of these statements postdated Joseph's death and Emma's separation from the Church that accepted Brigham Young as leader. The statements support the RLDS position and contradict the LDS position regarding polygamy and the U&T.

The most significant statement, Emma's "Last Testimony," was published under circumstances relevant to the LDS/RLDS tensions. In September 1879, Orson Pratt delivered two sermons that specifically reaffirmed the testimony from Oliver Cowdery and Joseph Smith about the Urim and Thummim. The RLDS published Emma's interview in October 1879.

Joseph Smith III had strong reasons to elicit information from his mother that would support his theology and authority as President of the RLDS. Knowing that he later revealed additional information from that interview that he did not include in the published version suggests he could easily have modified or composed her answers. There is just no way to tell whether the Last Testimony is authentic.

In important details Emma's statements contradict those of her mother-in-law, Lucy Mack Smith, that were recorded in 1844-45. Of course, they also contradict the teachings of Oliver Cowdery and Joseph Smith about the Urim and Thummim.

Competency: Emma presumably had the mental capacity to perceive, remember and communicate, although the Last

Testimony was produced within a few months of her death.

Opportunity: Emma was certainly in a position to observe the events she testified about, at least the events in Harmony, although there is no record of her speaking or writing about them when Joseph was alive.

Bias or partiality: By the time she gave these statements, Emma was biased against Brigham Young and in favor of her son as President of the RLDS. Joseph Smith III conducted the interview, provided the only report of the interview, and published the interview after his mother's death.

Motive: Emma (or her son) had a strong motive to justify the RLDS positions and oppose the LDS positions. The prevailing concern about the Spalding theory gave Emma a motive to contradict accounts that Joseph dictated from behind a screen or blanket.

Prior inconsistent statements: Only one direct statement of Emma's exists—the letter she wrote. The reports of interviews with her may or may not be accurate, but they are not clearly inconsistent.

Contradictory facts: There are no objective facts that contradict or corroborate Emma's factual claims, apart from the existing statements of other witnesses.

In my view, concern about the Spalding theory drove this interview. Emma's statements about the translation seem designed to refute the Spalding theory. As such, they lack sufficient credibility to outweigh the relatively contemporaneous statements of Joseph and Oliver.

Emma's claims about polygamy were so credibly and adamantly contradicted by multiple affidavits and direct testimony that it is difficult to give credence to the "Last Testimony" on that issue. Whether or not Joseph Smith III influenced his mother (or edited her answers), the unreliability of the "Last Testimony" on that point casts doubt on its claims regarding the translation.

10. Martin Harris

Overview.

Martin Harris was the primary financial backer of Joseph Smith and the Book of Mormon. He took the characters to the scholars in New York City, served as scribe for the 116 pages, participated as one of the Three Witnesses, wrote some of the Printer's Manuscript, and helped oversee the publication of the Book of Mormon.

His affiliation with the Church was erratic, but toward the end of his life he moved to Utah and related his experiences with Joseph as they translated the plates.

Martin spoke of both the "spectacles" and the "seer stone." Over time, his SITH stories replaced his U&T accounts. In Utah, he famously claimed that he once swapped Joseph's seer stone for another stone he'd found, and that Joseph detected the false stone because it didn't work. That story was always problematic—it seems far more likely that Joseph was playing along to satisfy Martin's curiosity—and it fits within the framework of people who believed the Book of Mormon was true and sought ways to debunk the Spalding theory.

———

Detail.

In this chapter we'll look at translation-related statements made by, or attributed to, Martin Harris. Martin is a fascinating character who contributed much to the Restoration but also generated substantial confusion because of apparent contradictions in his statements. He left no known journal, personal remembrance, or even letter. The information we have is all filtered through the perceptions and perspectives of those who interviewed him or heard him speak.

John Gilbert, the compositor of the 1830 edition of the Book of Mormon, had an excellent memory of his interaction with Oliver

Cowdery, Hyrum Smith, and Martin Harris.[173] In 1892 Gilbert prepared a Memorandum for the upcoming World's Fair. He wrote,

> In the fall of I827. he [Martin] told us what wonderful discoveries Jo Smith had made, and of his finding plates in a hill in the town of Manchester, (three miles south of Palmyra,)—also found with the plates a large pair of "spectacles," by putting which on his nose and looking at the plates, the spectacles turned the hyroglyphics into good English. The question might be asked here whether Jo or the spectacles was the translator?[174]

Martin apparently related this account before becoming Joseph's scribe. He could only have heard it from Joseph himself, who in the fall of 1827 had just received the plates and "spectacles" and, as Joseph said, was copying and translating characters. Yet, as we'll see, Martin's account migrated toward SITH around 1870.

Martin's biographers, after comprehensive research, summarized their work: "Sifting through the new data and validating well-known information has helped us better understand Martin's bursts of religious zeal, unpredictable foibles, unchecked bitterness, and need for limelight."[175]

Martin's religious zeal becomes apparent from his participation in a variety of religious activities, as catalogued in the Joseph Smith Papers.[176]

> Born 18 May 1783 Easton, Albany Co., New York.
> Married first his first cousin Lucy Harris, 27 Mar. 1808, in Palmyra.
> Served in War of 1812 in New York militia.
> Became landowner of some 320 acres at Palmyra.

---

[173] Royal Skousen tested 13 of Gilbert's claims. "From these many examples, we can see that in every instance John Gilbert's recollections regarding the printing of the 1830 edition of the Book of Mormon are either precisely correct or, where wrong, the error is easily explained." Skousen, "Worthy of Another Look", p. 69.

[174] Ibid., p. 72.

[175] Susan Easton Black and Larry C. Porter, "Acknowledgements," *Martin Harris: Uncompromising Witness of the Book of Mormon*, (BYU Studies 2018), Kindle location 114.

[176] List adapted from https://www.josephsmithpapers.org/person/martin-harris.

Reportedly investigated Quakers, Universalists, Restorationists, Baptists, Methodists, and Presbyterians.
Took transcript of Book of Mormon characters to Luther Bradish, Samuel Latham Mitchill, and Charles Anthon, Feb. 1828.
Assisted JS as scribe during translation of first portion of Book of Mormon, ca. 12 Apr.–14 June 1828.
One of the Three Witnesses of the Book of Mormon, June 1829.
Baptized into Church of Jesus Christ of Latter-day Saints by Oliver Cowdery, 6 Apr. 1830.
Ordained a priest, by 9 June 1830.
Paid printing costs for publication of Book of Mormon through sale of 151 acres.
Led members of Manchester, Ontario Co., branch from Palmyra to Kirtland, Geauga Co., Ohio, May 1831.
Ordained a high priest by Lyman Wight, 4 June 1831, at Kirtland.
Appointed to serve mission to Missouri, 6 June 1831.
Participated in Camp of Israel expedition to Missouri, 1834.
Member of Kirtland high council, 1834.
Married Caroline Young, 22-year-old daughter of Brigham Young's brother John, Nov. 1, 1836. (They had seven children.)
Excommunicated, Dec. 1837.
Rebaptized into Church of Jesus Christ of Latter-day Saints, 1842, at Kirtland.
Joined the Shakers by Dec. 1844 (according to Phineas Young).
Member of high council of James J. Strang's Church of Jesus Christ of Latter Day Saints at Kirtland, 7 Aug. 1846.
Joined with William E. McLellin's religious movement, 1847.
Initiated a new movement with William Smith and Chilton Daniels at Kirtland, likely 1855.
Migrated to Salt Lake Valley, 1870, after Brigham Young asked Edward Stevenson to raise money for his transportation. Stevenson then accompanied Martin from Ohio to Utah.
Rebaptized into Church of Jesus Christ of Latter-day Saints, 1870.
Died at Clarkston, Cache Co., Utah Territory, 10 July 1875.

As noted in the summary, Martin joined the Shakers for a period. After the Shakers, Martin said he "tried Gladden Bishop, but no satisfaction."[177] He also joined with the Strangites in Kirtland, who sustained him to their Kirtland high council and sent him on a mission to England.

As a Strangite missionary, Martin planned to dissuade people from "Mormonism." In response, in November 1846 the Church newspaper in England, the *Millennial Star*, published a profile of Martin in an article titled "Sketches of Notorious Characters."

> MARTIN HARRIS
>
> One of the witnesses to the Book of Mormon, yielded to the spirit and temptation of the Devil a number of years ago—turned against Joseph Smith and became his bitter enemy. He was filled with the rage and madness of a demon. One day he would be one thing, and another day another thing. He soon became partially deranged or shattered, as many believed, flying from one thing to another, as if reason and common sense were thrown off their balance. In one of his fits of monomania, he went and joined the 'Shakers' or followers of Anne Lee. He tarried with them a year or two, or perhaps longer, having had some flare ups while among them; but since Strang has made his entry into the apostate ranks, and hoisted his standard for the rebellious to flock too [sic], Martin leaves the "Shakers," whom he knows to be right, and has known it for many years, as he said, and joins Strang in gathering out the tares of the field. We understand that he is appointed a mission to this country, but we do not feel to warn the Saints against him, for his own unbridled tongue will soon show out specimens of folly enough to give any person a true index to the character of the man; but if the Saints wish to know what the Lord hath said of him, they may turn to the 178th page of the Book of Doctrine and Covenants, and the person there called a "wicked man" is no other than Martin Harris, and he owned to it then, but probably might not now. It is not the first time the Lord chose a wicked man as a witness.[178]

---

[177] Thomas Colburn to Erastus Snow, letter, *St. Louis Luminary*, May 5, 1855, p. 2. Online at https://archive.org/details/StLouisLuminary18541855/page/n95

[178] "Sketches of Notorious Characters," *Millennial Star*, Vol. 8, No. 8 (Nov. 15, 1846): 124, online at https://contentdm.lib.byu.edu/digital/collection/MStar/id/938.

Martin left England after only a month. He returned to Kirtland and joined with William E. McLellin to form the Church of Christ. McLellin solicited David Whitmer to become President, but Whitmer declined. The Kirtland Church of Christ subsequently withdrew fellowship from McLellin, but Martin remained in the church.

In subsequent years, Martin occasionally met with Mormon missionaries who passed through Kirtland. He sometimes promised to go to Utah, but failed to do so. Apparently he accompanied his wife Caroline to Iowa in 1856, where she prepared to move to Utah, but Martin returned to Kirtland alone. Caroline proceeded to Utah in 1859.

Caroline's uncle, Brigham Young, knew Martin Harris well. In 1852, Brigham said,

> "Those who are acquainted with Martin Harris know his natural turn and disposition: he wanted to learn all things at once, was continually in pursuit of knowledge, and neglected to act upon that which he had already received. That is his true character, as far as I have known him. … [after quoting D&C 19:20]
>
> This language needs no particular explanation to those who ever knew Martin Harris.[179]

This background may help explain the inconsistencies among the statements attributed to Martin over his lifetime. In this book we focus mainly on statements about the translation itself.

At Harmony, Pennsylvania, Martin worked with Joseph in the winter/spring of 1828. Joseph Smith copied off some of the characters from the plates and translated them. Martin took the characters and translation to New York City, where he met with Professor Charles Anthon and Dr. Mitchill.

Martin claimed Anthon said the translation was correct. (Joseph

[179] Brigham Young, "Extensive Character of the Gospel," Discourse delivered in the Tabernacle, Great Salt Lake City, Aug. 15, 1852 (JD 6:283)

Smith—History 1:64-65) Anthon's version of the meeting was quite different; he told E.D. Howe, author of *Mormonism Unvailed*, that "upon examining the paper in question, I soon came to the conclusion that it was all a trick, perhaps a hoax."

This is the type of discrepancy that makes it difficult to sort out what really happened. Martin may have accurately reported the meeting. Or, his enthusiasm may have caused him to misunderstand Anthon's response. Or, he may have told Joseph what he thought Joseph wanted to hear. Regardless, Martin stuck to his story for the rest of his life.

Human nature being what it is, anything is possible. It seems unlikely that Anthon would say the translation is correct unless he knew the characters, but Moroni said "none other people knoweth our language," which was the reason why the Lord "prepared means for the interpretation thereof." (Mormon 9:34) Since we don't know for sure what characters Martin took, and we don't know what Joseph's translation was, we have no way to assess that part of the claim. But Martin's claim that Anthon objected only when Martin said the characters came from plates revealed by an angel is highly plausible.

Regardless of what actually happened, by 1834, Anthon could have changed his mind about the event; understandably, he didn't appreciate being cited as the expert who verified the authenticity of the Book of Mormon. Besides, if Anthon had agreed with what Martin said, Howe would not have put his account in *Mormonism Unvailed.*

Most likely, both Martin and Anthon related what they believed was the truth, from their own subjective points of view.

Upon his return to Harmony, Martin acted as scribe for some or all of the 116 pages. He famously asked Joseph Smith if he could take the pages to show his wife. Joseph later explained what happened.

> Some time after Mr Harris had began to write for me, he began to tease me to give him liberty to carry the writings home and shew them, and **desired of me that I would enquire of the Lord through the Urim and Thummin** if he might not do so. I did enquire, and the answer was that

> he must not. However he was not satisfied with this answer, and desired that I should enquire again. I did so, and the answer was as before. Still he could not be contented but insisted that I should enquire once more. After much solicitation I again enquired of the Lord, and permission was granted him to have the writings on certain conditions, which were, that he shew them only to his brother. Preserved Harris, his own wife [Lucy Harris], his father [Nathan Harris], and his mother [Rhoda Lapham Harris], and a Mrs [Mary (Polly) Harris] Cobb a sister to his wife.[180]

That Martin asked Joseph to inquire through the Urim and Thummim, and not through a seer stone, indicates that Martin was fully aware of the instrument Joseph used to translate and obtain revelation.

After the pages were stolen or lost, Martin may have acted as a scribe in Harmony in March, 1829, after Emma and before Oliver arrived.

David Whitmer said Martin was present at the Whitmer home in Fayette during the translation of the plates of Nephi, which led to speculation that Martin may have been one of the unknown scribes on the OM of part of 1 Nephi.[181] That speculation has been superseded by more recent study, as we discussed in Chapter 1. Besides, Martin never claimed that he wrote in Fayette; he only claimed first-hand knowledge of the translation of the characters[182] and the 116 pages that we no longer have. Plus, Lucy Mack Smith explained in her history that she and her husband took Martin with them when they visited Fayette after the translation was completed. They all read the manuscript together in the Whitmer home, which may explain David's recollection of who was

---

[180] Joseph Smith, *History, circa June 1839-circa 1841*, online at https://www.josephsmithpapers.org/paper-summary/history-circa-june-1839-circa-1841-draft-2/11.

[181] See the discussion in Black, Chapter Six, *Martin Harris: Uncompromising Witness of the Book of Mormon*, Kindle location 3210, especially note 41. This theory is based on comparing two unidentified handwriting samples that might have been Martin's work, but the theory contradicts Lucy Mack Smith's history. I consider the theory obsolete, superseded by Royal Skousen's identification of the Fayette OM scribes.

[182] The well-known "Caractors" document that still exists was apparently created in 1829, a year after Martin Harris took the copied characters and translation to New York. https://www.josephsmithpapers.org/paper-summary/appendix-2-document-1-characters-copied-by-john-whitmer-circa-1829-1831/1

present during the translation. Martin's handwriting is found on the PM, which fits this chronology (discussed in Chapter 1).

Whether or not Martin participated in the translation in Fayette, in all of his statements prior to 1870, the year when he emigrated to Utah, Martin claimed Joseph translated the writing on the plates with the U&T. This aligns with Emma's statement that Joseph used the U&T before the 116 pages were lost.

The earliest published statement from Martin Harris regarding the translation was his interview with John A. Clark, discussed in Chapter 3. According to Clark, [183]

> [Martin remarked] that there had been a revelation made to [Joseph Smith] by which he had discovered this sacred deposit, and **two transparent stones**, through which, as **a sort of spectacles**, he could read the Bible, although the box or ark that contained it, had not yet been opened; and that **by looking through those mysterious stones**, he had transcribed from one of the leaves of this book, the characters which Harris had so carefully wrapped in the package which he was drawing from his pocket. . . .
> . . . [Joseph] was already in possession of the **two transparent stones** laid up with the GOLDEN BIBLE, **by looking through which he was enabled to read the golden letters on the plates** in the box. How he obtained these **spectacles** without opening the chest, Harris could not tell. But still he had them; and by means of them he could read all the book contained....
> The way that Smith made his transcripts and transcriptions for Harris was the following. Although in the same room, a thick curtain or blanket was suspended between them, and Smith concealed behind the blanket, pretended to **look through his spectacles, or transparent stones**, and would then write down or repeat what he saw, which, when repeated aloud, was written down by Harris, who sat on the other side of the suspended blanket.[184]

---

[183] This statement is #49 in Appendix 1.

[184] Later, John H. Gilbert, Pomeroy Tucker, and Charles Anthon all said Joseph

Martin's use of the phrase "transparent stones" is significant because in 1831, Oliver Cowdery had reportedly referred to the Nephite interpreters as "two transparent stones."

> Oliver Cowdery, one of the three witnesses to the book, testified under oath, that said Smith found with the plates, from which he translated his book, **two transparent stones**, resembling glass, **set in silver bows**. That **by looking through these, he was able to read in English, the reformed Egyptian characters, which were engraved on the plates.**[185]

An 1841 report claimed that in October 1830, Oliver "stated that Smith looked into or through the **transparent stones** to translate what was on the plates."[186]

Joseph Smith also used that phrase to describe the U&T in the Wentworth Letter.

> With the records was found a curious instrument, which the ancients called "Urim and Thummim," which consisted of **two transparent stones** set in the rim of a **bow** fastened to a breastplate. Through the medium of the Urim and Thummim I translated the record by the gift and power of God.[187]

These three statements show that, at least as of 1840, Joseph, Oliver and Martin were aligned in their understanding that Joseph translated the plates with two transparent stones set in a bow to form spectacles.

---

translated from behind a curtain, an account they presumably heard from Martin Harris. The curtain accommodated the Spalding theory as well.

[185] From a letter published in *Evangelical Magazine and Gospel Advocate* (1831), cited in John Phillip Walker, ed., *Dale Morgan on Early Mormonism: Correspondence and a New History* (Salt Lake City: Signature Books, 1986), 338.

[186] Josiah Jones, "History of the Mormonites," *Evangelist* 9 (June 1, 1841), based on a history Jones wrote in 1831 when he lived in Kirtland.

[187] The Wentworth Letter is document #16 in Appendix 1.

After Joseph's death, Martin did not follow Brigham Young's group to Utah. Instead, he affiliated with James Strang, then William E. McLellin, and eventually William Smith prior to eventually joining the Saints in Utah in 1870.

During these years, he continued to repeat his testimony as one of the Three Witnesses. He gave several interviews, such as one to *Tiffany's Monthly* in January 1859. In this version, Martin changed his description from "transparent stones" to "white, like polished marble, with a few gray streaks," but he reaffirmed that Joseph translated with these two stones.

> [The plates] were placed in this way: four stones were set up and covered with a flat stone, oval on the upper side and flat on the bottom. Beneath this was a little platform upon which the plates were laid; and **the two stones set in a bow of silver by means of which the plates were translated**, were found underneath the plates….
> The **two stones set in a bow of silver** were about two inches in diameter, perfectly round, and about five-eighths of an inch thick at the centre; but not so thick at the edges where they came into the bow. They were joined by a round bar of silver, about three-eighths of an inch in diameter, and about four inches long, which, with the two stones, would make eight inches.
> "The stones were white, like polished marble, with a few gray streaks. I never dared to look into them by placing them in the hat…"

This statement, assuming it accurately reflects what Martin said, necessarily consists of hearsay, at least in part. Martin was not present when Joseph recovered the original plates. Martin could have read Oliver's description in Letter VIII, or he may have heard a description directly from Joseph, but he does not explain the source of his knowledge about how the plates were placed in the stone box. Nor does he explain how he could provide such a detailed description of the two stones set in a bow. He "never dared to look into them."

There is a serious disconnect in this statement. The description of two stones set in a bow necessarily refers to the Nephite interpreters; Martin says Joseph found them under the plates. However, the only time Martin could have seen the Nephite interpreters was when he was acting as one of the Three Witnesses; prior to that, Joseph was commanded not to show them to anyone. Martin claimed he saw the U&T as one of the Three Witnesses,[188] but by the time the Three Witnesses had their experience, the translation was completed. Martin would have had no occasion to "look into them by placing them in the hat."

If Martin had viewed the Nephite interpreters previously, such as when Joseph was transcribing the characters or translating the 116 pages, then Joseph had already violated the commandment not to show them to anyone and the promise of D&C 17:1 was a nullity, at least with respect to the U&T.

Martin never explained why he usually described the two stones as transparent, but here described them as like marble. Perhaps by "transparent" he meant "translucent." The detailed measurements in his description could have come from Joseph, or he could have handled and measured the U&T when the angel displayed them.

The next statements from Martin Harris were published after he had decided to join the Saints in Utah.

Edward Stevenson related how Martin returned to Utah.

> I was inspired to write to Martin Harris, and soon received a reply, that the Spirit of God, for the first time prompted him to go to Utah.

---

[188] David Whitmer claimed he saw the Urim and Thummim on this occasion, and he pointed out that Martin was not present for that viewing. Martin told William Pilkington that "I saw the gold plates, I saw him [the angel] turn the leaves over one by one, I saw the Urim and Thummim, the breast plate, the sword of Laban." William Pilkington, "A Dying Testimony Given by Martin Harris to William Pilkington, July 9, 1875," MS 8068, Church History Library.

> Several letters were afterward exchanged. President Brigham Young, having read the letter, through President G.A. Smith, requested me to get up a subscription and emigrate Martin to Utah, he subscribing twenty-five dollars for that purpose. Having raised the subscription to about $200, on the 19th of July, 1870, I took the railroad cars for Ohio, and on the 10th of August, filled my appointment, preaching twice in the Kirtland temple, finding Martin Harris elated with his prospective journey.
>
> A very singular incident occurred at this time. While Martin was visiting his friends, bidding them farewell, his pathway crossed a large pasture, in which he became bewildered, dizzy, faint and staggering through the blackberry vine that are so abundant in that vicinity, his clothes torn, bloody and faint, he lay down under a tree to die. After a time he revived, called on the Lord, and finally at 12 midnight, found his friend, and in his fearful condition was cared for and soon regained his strength. He related this incident as a snare of the adversary to hinder him from going to Salt Lake City. Although in his 88th year he possessed remarkable vigor and health, having recently worked in the garden, and dug potatoes by the day for some of his neighbors.

This "singular event" suggests a possibly serious health problem. Could it have affected Martin's memory? We'll never know, but it was after this that he claimed Joseph used a seer stone to translate the Book of Mormon.

Along the way to Utah, the travelers stopped in Des Moines, Iowa. The Iowa State Register published an interview that included this explanation:

> Mr. Harris describes the plates as being of thin leaves of gold, measuring seven by eight inches, and weighing altogether, from forty to sixty lbs. There was also found in the chest, **the Urim and Thummim, by means of which the writing upon the plates was translated… By means of the urim and thummim "a pair of large spectacles," as Mr. Harris termed them, the translation was made,** and Mr. Harris claims to have written, of the translations

as they were given by Smith, "116 solid pages of cap [foolscap]." The remainder was written by others.[189]

After he arrived in Salt Lake, Martin Harris addressed a congregation on September 5, 1870, together with Elder Edward Stevenson, President George A. Smith, and Elder John Taylor. The newspaper reported that "the house was crowded to overflowing."

The report includes three portions of Martin's address that I'll comment on separately.

> Martin Harris related an instance that occurred during the time that he wrote that portion of the translation of the Book of Mormon, which he was favored to write direct from the mouth of the Prophet Joseph Smith. He said that **the Prophet possessed a seer stone, by which he was enabled to translate as well as from the Urim and Thummim, and for convenience he then used the seer stone.**
>
> Martin explained the translating as follows: By aid of the seer stone, sentences would appear and were read by the Prophet and written by Martin, and when finished he would say, "Written," and if correctly written, that sentence would disappear and another appear in its place, but if not written correctly it remained until corrected, so that the translation was just as it was engraven on the plates, precisely in the language then used.

The second paragraph is necessarily hearsay; Martin said he never looked into the stone himself.

The first paragraph alludes to the two alternative explanations for the translation that had circulated for decades, as memorialized in 1834 in the book *Mormonism Unvailed.*

Some (notably, Joseph and Oliver, plus Martin before 1870) said

---

189 ("A Witness to the Book of Mormon," *Des Moines Iowa State Register*, August 28, 1870; cited in Vogel, *Early Mormon Documents*, 2:330. Available online at http://www.sidneyrigdon.com/dbroadhu/IA/misciow2.htm

Joseph translated the engravings on the plates by using the Urim and Thummim, meaning the Nephite interpreters, the spectacles, or the two stones set in a bow that Moroni had sealed up in the stone box on the hill Cumorah.

Others said Joseph merely read words that appeared on a stone in a hat (SITH).

By 1870, the competing interpretations were entrenched. On February 15, 1870, Elizabeth Whitmer Cowdery had given the alleged affidavit claiming that Joseph "would place the director in his hat, and then place his face in his hat, so as to exclude the light, and then [read the words?] as they appeared before him." William E. McLellin's copy of the affidavit is the only extant version.

McLellin, as we discussed previously, adamantly insisted that Joseph never had the U&T. It was one of his reasons for no longer being a Mormon.

Martin Harris had affiliated with McLellin for a period.

By the time Stevenson met Martin in Ohio in the summer of 1870, Martin could well have heard about Elizabeth's affidavit. By 1870, David Whitmer and Emma Smith were relating SITH as part of their effort to debunk the Spalding theory.

The historical record is scanty, especially with respect to the 1828 translation period, leaving room for several possibilities. Let's discuss three.

1. Maybe Martin sought reconciliation.

After joining the church, Martin spent most of his life in Kirtland, Ohio. Over the years he had affiliated with Strang, McLellin, and William Smith, and was now joining the Utah Mormons. Knowing the differences of opinion about the translation, he may have sought to unite the various camps in some way. Claiming that Joseph actually used both instruments would be a possible path toward reconciliation.

2. Maybe Martin told the truth, based on what he observed,

what he heard, or both. It was well known that Joseph possessed a seer stone. Recall what Zenas Gurley reported:

> That Joseph had **another stone** called seers' stone, and 'peep stone,' is quite certain. **This stone was frequently exhibited to different ones and helped to assuage their awful curiosity; but the Urim and Thummim never, unless possibly to Oliver Cowdery**.

This leads to two possibilities.

2a. Martin did observe Joseph use both the U&T and SITH. As we've discussed, Martin's personal knowledge was limited to Joseph's transcription and translation of the characters he took to New York and the 116 pages. The testimony of Joseph and Oliver that Joseph translated the plates with the U&T technically apply only to the Book of Mormon we have today. Oliver had no part of the characters document or the 116 pages. Although Joseph said he translated the characters and the Book of Mormon by means of the U&T, he could have left room for separately translating the characters or the 116 pages with a seer stone.

However, Joseph also said he lost the ability to translate when he forfeited the U&T after he lost the 116 pages, and regained the gift when the angel returned the instrument.

Presumably, Martin could not view the U&T; hence the curtain he described. Nevertheless, we cannot say it is impossible that Martin Harris observed Joseph using a seer stone and inferred that when Joseph was behind the curtain he used the interpreters.

2b. Martin did observe Joseph use a seer stone in a hat and dictate words, which Martin inferred was a translation of the plates. But in reality, Joseph was demonstrating the process to satisfy Martin's curiosity and conducted the actual translation behind the curtain, as Martin explained to others.

Martin's curiosity and desire for evidence is well documented. It's what led to the loss of the 116 pages.

The next part of Martin's sermon, in my view, corroborates the demonstration explanation.

> Martin said, after continued translation they would become weary and would go down to the river and exercise by throwing stones out on the river, etc. While so doing on one occasion, Martin found a stone very much resembling the one used for translating, and on resuming their labor of translation, Martin put in place the stone that he had found. He said that the Prophet remained silent unusually and intently gazing in darkness, no traces of the usual sentences appearing. Much surprised, Joseph exclaimed, "Martin! What is the matter! All is as dark as Egypt." Martin's countenance betrayed him, and the Prophet asked Martin why he had done so. Martin said, to stop the mouths of fools, who had told him that the Prophet had learned those sentences and was merely repeating them, etc.

Historians have long accepted this story on its face, but the story of the swapped stone is improbable at best—if used to support the claim that Joseph translated with a seer stone he found in a well. If Joseph was using a seer stone he'd had for years, a stone he stared at inches from his nose inside a hat many times, it is unimaginable that Martin could find a random stone identical enough that Joseph couldn't tell the difference. One wonders also why, if the seer stone was so valuable, Joseph would have left it out in such a manner that Martin could swap it without Joseph knowing.

The way Martin tells the story comes across as Joseph playing along with Martin's test. He sits, silently (as Martin infers he's unable to read anything on the stone). Then he looks up and asks Martin what the problem was.

Why would Joseph ask Martin what the problem was unless he knew what Martin had done?

Joseph surely was aware of Martin's urgent need for reassurance. Under a strict command to not show the plates or interpreters, conducting a demonstration with the seer stone would be a logical solution that, hopefully, would satisfy Martin. The stone swap was a fitting conclusion to the matter.

There is another reason to question Martin's account, however. The stone-swapping story was unknown before 1870—over 40 years after the fact. If Martin conducted the test to silence critics or satisfy his own curiosity, one would think he would have repeated the experience many times, from the outset. If he did, no one commented on it—including Joseph. Maybe Martin embellished an experience to entertain his audience, who packed the house to hear from one of the Three Witnesses. Maybe he saw this anecdote as a way to accomplish the noble objectives of refuting the Spalding theory and bringing together all believers in the Book of Mormon.

Or maybe he didn't relate the story all those decades because he realized Joseph was merely playing along with him.

We can't exclude the possibility that Martin misremembered the event, conflated separate incidents, or was merely confused, as he was when he fell in the field shortly before leaving for Utah.

———

There is one more factor to consider.

On September 17, 1870, shortly after he gave his sermon, Martin Harris was baptized in the Endowment House by Edward Stevenson. He was confirmed by Orson Pratt. Two months later, on November 27, 1870, Orson Pratt spoke in the Tabernacle. Without acknowledging Martin's seer stone account, Pratt reiterated Joseph's claim that he translated the plates with the U&T.

> Joseph Smith was not the only one, but there were three men besides him to whom the Lord sent his angel, clothed in glory, who exhibited the plates before their eyes after they had been translated, and commanded them to bear record of it to all people, nations and tongues. They have given their testimony in this book. These witnesses I am well acquainted with, as well as with Joseph Smith…
>
> And having revealed this book, and it having been translated by the gift and power of the Holy Ghost—the same gift and spirit which **enabled Joseph Smith to interpret the language of this record by the use of the Urim and Thummim**; I say, having done this, the

Lord commanded his servants to organize his Church.[190]

In subsequent years, Church leaders including Brigham Young, John Taylor, Wilford Woodruff, and Erastus Snow reaffirmed the testimony of Joseph Smith and Oliver Cowdery that Joseph translated the plates with the U&T that had been hidden up in the earth with the plates. Some of their teachings are included in Appendix 5.

Prior to—and after—his 1870 address, Martin always concurred with what Joseph and Oliver consistently taught; i.e., that Joseph translated the plates with the U&T. Even in the address, he made certain that there was no confusion about the existence of the two separate objects.

> Martin said further that **the seer stone differed in appearance entirely from the Urim and Thummim that was obtained with the plates, which were two clear stones set in two rims, very much resembled spectacles, only they were larger.** Martin said there were not many pages translated while he wrote; after which Oliver Cowdery and others did the writing.

This statement appears to refer not to the 116 pages, but to the few pages Martin wrote on the Harmony OM, presumably part of Mosiah, as we discussed in Chapter 1.

Martin's 1870 sermon was republished several times; the version I cited above appeared in the 1881 *Deseret Evening News*, six years after Martin died in 1875. Stevenson republished it in the *Millennial Star* in 1886. Andrew Jenson included it in the *Historical Record* in 1887.

It's easy to see why. The seer stone swap story is a fun anecdote, the kind of detail we all wish we had much more of. In Martin Harris' mind, the story validated his faith in the divinity of the translation he was writing as Joseph dictated it. That could be the very reason Joseph

---

[190] Journal of Discourses 14:299, online at https://jod.mrm.org/14/289.

played along with it.

In today's world, though, the story serves an entirely different purpose.

It is being used to *contradict* what Joseph and Oliver taught about the translation of the Book of Mormon. It is being used by critical and faithful scholars alike to support the idea that Joseph Smith didn't really translate the plates, didn't really use any Nephite interpreters, and didn't really even use the plates.

Instead, he merely read words that appeared on the seer stone.

That seems like a mistake to me.

Simon Smith visited Martin Harris shortly before Martin's death in July 1875. In his 1884 account of the interview, Smith quoted Martin as saying "I also wrote for him about one third of the first part of the translation of the plates as **he interpreted them by the Urim and Thummim.**"[191] Smith's account of Martin Harris' final statement about the translation said nothing about a seer stone.

———

[191] Simon Smith, #54 in Appendix 1.

11. The Language of the Translation

Composing, Translating, or Reading: new and overlooked evidence corroborates Joseph Smith's explanation

---

Overview.

If Joseph Smith translated the plates, the result would be largely indistinguishable from a composition—at least in terms of language. Translators work with the tools they have, consisting primarily of their personal mental language bank—the words in their minds. An English-speaker translating a foreign-language text into English can only draw upon his/her English vocabulary, grammar, etc. A translator might expand his/her mental language bank by consulting references, experts, etc., but ultimately whatever the translator expresses must come from the translator's mind.

Anecdotal accounts suggest that Joseph didn't know how to pronounce certain words, specified unusual spelling of other words, and may not have understood the meaning of yet other words. These accounts suggest—but don't require—that Joseph was seeing specific words, whether he consulted SITH or U&T. Misspellings in the text and frequent supplements (such as "in other words) suggest that Joseph was not "seeing" specific words.

The 700 non-biblical terms in the text can all be found in Joseph's local environment in Palmyra, circa 1817-1829. Hundreds of examples of "blending" of disparate biblical verses into passages in the Book of Mormon; many of these can be found in the works of Jonathan Edwards, whose 8-volume set was on sale in the Palmyra bookstore Joseph visited weekly to get the newspaper for his father.

In this chapter, I propose that the Lord prepared Joseph to act as translator by giving him the means, motives, and opportunity to read and listen to numerous Christian teachings. These terms, phrases, and arguments contributed to Joseph's mental language bank, upon which he drew to translate the plates after having studied the characters.

In other words, if Joseph translated the plates, we would expect the English text to reflect language common to western New York in the 1820s. To distinguish between a composition and a translation, we can assess the presence of antiquity in the text, such as indicia of Hebrew influence.

> *Anxiety and expectation regarding the need for divine direction was not uncommon among those religious reformers who set the stage for the Restoration of the gospel. One of the most famous of the New England preachers, Jonathan Edwards, said, "It seems to me a[n] ... unreasonable thing, to suppose that there should be a God ... that has so much concern [for us], ... and yet that he should never speak, ... that there should be no word [from him]."*
>
> (Jeffrey R. Holland, 'Prophets, Seers, and Revelators,' *Ensign*, November 2004)

———

Detail.

So far in this book we have considered historical accounts of the translation. In this chapter we briefly discuss the language of the text.

If, as he claimed, Joseph Smith translated the ancient records, we would expect the text to reflect Joseph's own language. To translate into English, he had to draw upon his own mental language bank; i.e., the words and phrases he had learned up to that point in his life. The gift of God could have included vocabulary and grammar unfamiliar to Joseph, but none of his scribes or contemporaries remarked that the text sounded unusual or unlike Joseph's ordinary speech. Joseph's brother William explained that Joseph translated "with an assistant to correct his English,"[192] suggesting that the scribes had input into the grammar and spelling. It's impossible to tell whether the text in the OM

[192] James Murdock, "The Mormons and Their Prophet," *Hartford and New Haven, Conn. Congregational Observer* 2 (July 3, 1841), online at http://contentdm.lib.byu.edu/cdm/ref/collection/BOMP/id/2555.

includes input from Joseph's scribes, but we can see that the spelling and grammar are inconsistent.

Joseph's uncle Jesse, who disapproved of Joseph's activities, wrote a letter to Hyrum, complaining that his brother (Joseph Smith Sr.) had not written to him. If he couldn't write, he could dictate, Jesse wrote, and "if more should be wanting he can employ the same scoundrel of a scribe, and then not only the matter but manner and style would be correct."[193]

Brigham Young explained that the scriptures reflect the language of the prophets through whom they are revealed.

> When God speaks to the people, he does it in a manner to suit their circumstances and capacities. He spoke to the children of Jacob through Moses, as a blind, stiffnecked people, and when Jesus and his Apostles came they talked with the Jews as a benighted, wicked, selfish people. They would not receive the Gospel, though presented to them by the Son of God in all its righteousness, beauty and glory. Should the Lord Almighty send an angel to rewrite the Bible, it would in many places be very different from what it now is. And I will even venture to say that **if the Book of Mormon were now to be rewritten, in many instances it would materially differ from the present translation.** According as people are willing to receive the things of God, so the heavens send forth their blessings. If the people are stiffnecked, the Lord can tell them but little. (emphasis added)[194]

"if the Book of Mormon were now to be rewritten, in many instances it would materially differ from the present translation." – Brigham Young

In this chapter, I propose that the language of the Book of Mormon is evidence that Joseph translated it because that language was part of Joseph Smith's mental language bank.

This involves three propositions based on the evidence:

---

[193] Jesse Smith to Hyrum Smith, June 17, 1829. http://www.josephsmithpapers.org/paper-summary/letterbook-2/65.

[194] Brigham Young, "The Kingdom of God," JD 9:311, July 13, 1862.

(i) Joseph Smith, Jr., was uniquely prepared by the Lord to translate the ancient Nephite record into English using his own vocabulary, including language and concepts acquired from specific sources;

(ii) Among the sources that Joseph was familiar with were his family, local newspapers, and the works of Jonathan Edwards and other Christian authors who set the stage for the Restoration of the gospel; and

(iii) evidence of both propositions is found throughout the text of the Book of Mormon, the Doctrine and Covenants, the Pearl of Great Price, and other writings of Joseph Smith, including his 1832 history.

Scholars and ordinary readers have long recognized the linguistic influence on the text of the Book of Mormon of the King James Version (KJV) of the Bible. With some modifications, complete chapters from Isaiah, Malachi and Matthew are duplicated from the KJV. Numerous biblical terms and phrases are present in the text of the Book of Mormon, often combined or woven into new expressions.

But the KJV is not the only influence we find.

The Book of Mormon text contains roughly 275,000 words,[195] consisting of around 5,600 individual terms of which about 1,700 appear only once. Excluding proper nouns, there are over 700 non-biblical terms in the Book of Mormon. There are over 58,000 verbatim biblical phrases (two to four words), many of which are blended to form unique passages in the Book of Mormon text. But there are also hundreds of non-biblical phrases common to the Book of Mormon and the works of Jonathan Edwards.

The text also includes specific variations of biblical passages—misquotations or paraphrases—that are identical to those in Edwards.

Book of Mormon language is similar to the language of other Christian books and sermons of the early 1800s. Authors and preachers learned from and responded to one another, exchanging ideas and terminology. Jonathan Edwards stood out as one of the most influential

[195] The specific number depends on the edition, the Preface (1830 only), the copyright notice, chapter headings, etc.

Christian authors in American religious history.

In my analysis, I focused on materials readily available to Joseph Smith during his early years. For example, the Palmyra printing shop that Joseph visited weekly to purchase a newspaper for his father from 1818-1821 offered a list of books for sale. Among these was an eight-volume set of Edwards' works, published in 1808, and the works of James Hervey. Most of the non-biblical terms and phrases in the Book of Mormon can be found in these two sources.

This evidence corroborates the consistent testimonies of Joseph Smith and Oliver Cowdery that Joseph Smith actually translated the ancient Nephite record into English.

Recognizing the influence of Jonathan Edwards also enhances the meaning of the Book of Mormon (and the Doctrine and Covenants), just as familiarity with the Bible does. To understand how, consider the law of Moses which is often referenced but never defined in the Book of Mormon. A reader must consult (or be familiar with) the Bible to know what the law of Moses is.

Several non-biblical Book of Mormon passages, such as Mosiah 3:19 ("the natural man is an enemy to God") acquire deeper meaning when their origins in Edwards' works are understood. The term "natural man" has been used in LDS General Conference over 300 times. The term is found once in the Bible ("But the natural man receiveth not the things of the Spirit of God" 1 Corinthians 2:14) but is not defined there. The term "enemy to God" occurs four times in the Book of Mormon but never in the Bible. ("Enemy of God" occurs once in the New Testament and once in the Bible.)

In this case, Edwards' sermon titled "Men Naturally God's Enemies," found in the 1808 collection, explains in detail how and why the natural man is an enemy to God. Mosiah 3:19 teaches how to overcome the natural man, but never explains what constitutes the natural man. Edwards supplies that information, the same way the Bible explains the law of Moses. I discuss this point in Appendix 8.

As we'll discuss, some critics may claim that these influences are evidence that Joseph Smith composed the text by copying or borrowing from these other sources. Despite these linguistic influences, however, the Book of Mormon does not adopt the theology of Jonathan Edwards or the other sources. This supports translation instead of composition.

———

Part 1: Origin theories.

Over the years, skeptics and believers have considered alternative explanations for the Book of Mormon. These alternatives boil down to composing, translating, or reading.[196]

Composing. Those who disbelieve Joseph's claims look for naturalistic explanations. They think Joseph and/or collaborators composed the Book of Mormon by borrowing from, or at least referring to, existing sources such as Spalding's *Lost Manuscript*, *The Late War* and/or *View of the Hebrews*. They argue that Joseph had access to hundreds[197] or thousands[198] of books in the vicinity of his home.

The composition theory includes such variations as plagiarism, collaboration, mental illness, genius, and "automatic writing."[199] One author suggested Joseph might have used a method "of oral composition that involved the use of private notes and the semi-extemporaneous amplification of skeletal narrative outlines."[200]

The skeptics recognize that the combination of a complex historical

---

196 For another perspective on the differing interpretations of the translation process, see Don Bradley, "Written by the Finger of God?" *Sunstone*, October 2011, online https://www.sunstonemagazine.com/written-by-the-finger-of-god-claims-and-controversies-of-book-of-mormon-translation/

197 Noel A. Carmack discusses floating bookstores on the Erie canal and the Palmyra bookstore and print shop. Noel A. Carmack "Joseph Smith, Captain Kidd Lore, and Treasure-Seeking," *Dialog: A Journal of Mormon Thought*, 46, no. 3 (Fall 2013): 108, https://www.dialoguejournal.com/wp-content/uploads/sbi/articles/Dialogue_V46N03_412b.pdf

198 D. Michael Quinn, *Early Mormonism and the Magic World View*, Signature Books (1998): 179.

199 Brian C. Hales, "Automatic Writing and the Book of Mormon: An Update," *Dialogue*, Vol. 52, No. 2, Summer 2019, https://www.dialoguejournal.com/wp-content/uploads/sbi/articles/Dialogue_V52N02_1.pdf.

200 *Visions in a Seer Stone*, p.184.

narrative with innovative theology sets the Book of Mormon apart from other 19th century works. But they note that lots of books are exceptional, and storytellers can relate long, complex narratives.

Believers reject composition because an entirely naturalistic explanation removes the basis for their belief. Instead, believers accept Joseph's explanation that, by the gift and power of God, he translated ancient metal records. However, they entertain different interpretations of the term *translation.*

Translating. Some believers think Joseph translated the engravings on the plates in the ordinary sense of the word; i.e., he studied and learned the characters and, with the assistance of the gift and power of God, translated them into English using his own vocabulary. The term *translation* was well understood in Joseph's day as a process of interpreting one language and rendering it in another. The first words on every King James Bible are "Translated out of the Original Tongues." Translation was a common experience, especially on the frontiers where local Indian tribes still spoke their native tongues.

Webster's 1828 *American Dictionary of the English Language*[201] defined *translation* this way:

> to render into another language; to express the sense of one language in the words of another. The Old Testament was translated into the Greek language more than two hundred years before Christ. The Scriptures are now translated into most of the languages of Europe and Asia.

Because the engravings were written in an unknown language, Joseph relied on the Nephite interpreters (which Joseph and Oliver Cowdery referred to as the Urim and Thummim) that Moroni provided with the plates. For months, Joseph studied the characters and translated them with the U&T. Later, he dictated his translation of the plates to his scribes. The translation was inspired both because of the aid of the interpreters and because, although Joseph had to study it out in his mind (D&C 9:8), the Spirit confirmed the translation he came up

---

[201] http://webstersdictionary1828.com/Dictionary/translate

with as he dictated it to his scribe.

Viewed this way, the idea that Joseph actually translated the Nephite records into English seems obvious. However, the issue is not so easily resolved because the similarities between the translated text and the 19th century sources are undeniable. As I'll show later in this chapter, they are even more extensive than previously reported.

These similarities support Joseph's claim that he translated the ancient records into English. And yet, faithful scholars have resisted this evidence, while skeptics have latched onto it.

What's going on?

Skeptics have been so intent on showing that Joseph (and/or others) composed the Book of Mormon that they didn't pause to realize that if Joseph actually translated the ancient record into English, we would find exactly the artifacts from other sources that are present in the text; i.e., as translator, Joseph could only draw from his own mental language bank. The language would be the same whether Joseph was composing the text or translating the plates.

Some faithful scholars have been so intent on showing that Joseph (and/or others) could not have composed the Book of Mormon that they quickly developed a bias against composition evidence. They reacted to the evidence of similarities by (i) denying their existence and (ii) claiming that Joseph was an unschooled farm boy who couldn't possibly have read all the source material cited by the skeptics.

In other words, the faithful scholars rejected the very evidence developed by the skeptics that supports Joseph's claim that he translated the plates. Instead, they have adopted a theory that Joseph was merely reading words that appeared on the U&T or seer stone.

Reading. In an effort to refute the evidence of composition, some believers interpret Joseph's use of the term *translate* to mean a supernatural phenomenon whereby Joseph read words that appeared on a seer stone he put in a hat (SITH).

These believers frame the debate this way: "To suggest that Joseph Smith, who lacked formal education and struggled to write a coherent letter in his early years, was the author of such unforgettable phrases at age twenty-three is simply untenable."[202] They tend to characterize Joseph as "poorly educated and unbookish."[203] They assert Joseph could not have known big words[204] or nuances of Early Modern English,[205] and that, at any rate, Harmony, Pennsylvania, Joseph's home when he dictated most of the text in 1828 and 1829, was a "resource vacuum."[206]

This line of reasoning has led to the currently popular faithful narrative that because Joseph Smith was unlearned, he could have produced the Book of Mormon *only* by reading English words that appeared on a seer stone he placed in a hat. The actual translation into English was performed supernaturally by unknown means—an intermediary translator—so that Joseph could simply read the words that appeared on the stone functioning as a metaphysical teleprompter.[207]

This narrative is supported by several eye-witness accounts who also reported that Joseph never consulted the plates during the process they observed, a point we've discussed in Chapter 6.

However, as Roger Terry[208] pointed out, none of the existing explanations for the translation account for all the evidence.

Why I reject the reading theory.

---

[202] Tad R. Callister, *A Case for the Book of Mormon*, Deseret Book (2019): 124.

[203] Richard L. Bushman, "The Mysteries of Mormonism," *Journal of the Early Republic* 15 (Autumn 1995): 506, quoted in Carmack (2013): 106.

[204] Terry, Roger (2014) "The Book of Mormon Translation Puzzle," *Journal of Book of Mormon Studies*: Vol. 23 : No. 1:182. https://scholarsarchive.byu.edu/jbms/vol23/iss1/10

[205] Royal Skousen, "The Language of the Original Text of the Book of Mormon," *BYU Studies* 57:3 (2018).

[206] John W. Welch, "Was There a Library in Harmony, Pennsylvania?" *Insights: An Ancient Window* (January 1994): 2, quoted in Carmack (2013): 106.

[207] This consensus has been described in Bushman (2005) *Rough Stone Rolling*, Skousen (2018), *The Nature of the Original Language*, and Mackay and Dirkmaat (2017) *From Darkness Unto Light*.

[208] Roger Terry, "The Book of Mormon Translation Puzzle," *Journal of Book of Mormon Studies*, Vol. 23, No. 1 (2014): 178. Available online at: https://scholarsarchive.byu.edu/jbms/vol23/iss1/10

The implications of composition evidence led faithful scholars to find alternative explanations. A sophisticated effort to deflect evidence of composition is the approach taken by Royal Skousen and Stanford Carmack. They claim that details in the grammar and syntax of the OM of the Book of Mormon (dictated by Joseph Smith) constitute indicia of Early Modern English that predated even the King James Bible, so they were obsolete by 1827. It would be impossible, they claim, for Joseph Smith or anyone else in his day to understand and properly implement these linguistic relics from Early Modern English.

Their research is impressively thorough. They used sophisticated statistical analysis of large databases.[209] They generated a two-volume, 1383-page work that documents, in detail, the basis for their theory.[210]

This chapter cannot discuss all the reasons why I disagree with their conclusions (although I accept all their data), but I can summarize my position with two points.

1. **Only verbatim record**. The only evidence we have of how Joseph Smith actually spoke is the (presumably) verbatim record of his actual speech; i.e., the text of the Book of Mormon and the early revelations that he dictated. No other verbatim transcripts of his speech patterns are extant; even the few records of his sermons from the 1840s are incomplete notes and summaries. When there are multiple accounts, such as the Zelph incident and the King Follet sermon, there are important variations that reflect the priorities and understanding of the individuals who recorded them.

Skousen and Carmack turn this evidence on its head by claiming the only verbatim record of what Joseph dictated is *not* evidence of how Joseph spoke. Instead, they cite Joseph's 1832 written history[211] and later written documents as evidence of how he spoke in 1829.

---

[209] For one critique of the statistical element, see https://www.timesandseasons.org/index.php/2019/04/of-early-modern-english-and-the-book-of-mormon/

[210] Royal Skousen, *The History of the Text of the Book of Mormon—Part Four—The Nature of the Original Language*, BYU Studies (2018).

[211] https://www.josephsmithpapers.org/paper-summary/history-circa-summer-1832/1

The problems are obvious. Speaking and writing are two different skills; people don't write the way they talk. Much of the 1832 history is in Joseph's own handwriting, suggesting it was not dictated. The extant document may have been copied from a prior draft (and was therefore likely edited). By 1832, Joseph was living in Kirtland among better educated people who taught him better grammar. The language of the revelations in the D&C shifted away from the "Early Modern English" elements around 1832, reflecting Joseph's improved understanding of English grammar. (Joseph's 1837 revisions to the Book of Mormon reflect the same type of changes that appear in the post-1832 revelations and also show he did not consider the original text unalterable.)

These realities leave little reason to assume that what Joseph *wrote* in 1832 is an accurate representation of how he *spoke* in 1829.

SITH maintains that Joseph "saw" the text, word-for-word, and merely read out loud the words he saw. The scriptural justification is 2 Nephi 27:20-24. "[T]hou shalt read the words which I shall give unto thee." But those verses also apply to Joseph reading the engravings on the plates that were given to him and then translating those words.

In the one brief extant example of Joseph writing what he saw (Alma 45:22), he misspelled *city* as *citty*. Oliver correctly wrote *city* 385 times between the OM and the PM.[212] Would the supernatural teleprompter misspell the word for Joseph but not for Oliver? If Joseph saw *citty*, why did he never correct Oliver's spelling to comport with what he saw in the stone?

Essentially, Skousen and Carmack claim that Joseph could not have normally spoken the way he dictated the Book of Mormon, but they offer no evidence of how he actually spoke. Instead, they expect us to take their word for it because of other publications.

2. **Publications vs. speech.** Recognizing the absence of verbatim evidence of how Joseph spoke (other than the recorded revelations and Book of Mormon text), Skousen and Carmack compared the text to

---

212 Royal Skousen, *Part Six, Spelling in the Manuscripts and Editions* (FARMS, BYU Studies, 2020): 136.

published materials. They concluded that the OM contains elements of Early Modern English that do not appear in published materials from the early 1800s. But this is merely an extension of the erroneous assumption that Joseph wrote the way he spoke. Consulting databases of published material to detect regional dialects and speech patterns would be difficult even in today's society, but there is no reason to assume that 19th century published material would capture everyday speech in rural New York.

John Gilbert recalled that

> On the second day—Harris and [Hyrum] Smith being in the office—I called their attention to a grammatical error, and asked whether I should correct it? Harris consulted with Smith a short time, and turned to me and said: "The Old Testament is ungrammatical, set it as it is written.[213]

Gilbert was a typesetter, not an editor, yet he instinctively sought to correct the grammar in the text. Every publisher would do the same. Comparing published text with a verbatim transcript is comparing apples with oranges.

The presence of elements of Early Modern English in the text does not logically require that Joseph would have had to intentionally replicate such elements. His speech patterns were the product of his environment. Colonial lag and other factors can account for elements of Early Modern English persisting among "common folk," even when these elements do not appear in published materials from 1827-1829. Daniel Webster observed that because of colonial lag, the American colonists could understand Shakespeare better than their British counterparts who stayed in England.

Like all people in every society, Joseph's normal speech patterns retained archaic elements he incorporated from his family and peers. (Today's baby boomers sometimes catch themselves saying "groovy," a term their children consider obsolete and embarrassing.)

In short, because the Early Modern English theory incorporates the

---

[213] Skousen, "Worthy of Another Look," p. 63.

"uneducated Joseph" and "stone-in-the-hat" theories, it cannot and does not answer the question of how and why the text of the Book of Mormon consists of vocabulary, phrases, concepts, and allusions from sources available in Joseph's environment.

Apart from linguistic problems, the reading theory conflicts with well-known historical sources.

First, the reading theory contradicts Joseph's direct claim that he translated the engravings on the plates with the Nephite interpreters (the U&T) that he obtained from Moroni when he obtained the plates. It contradicts Joseph's statement in the Preface to the 1830 edition that he "took" the translation "from the Book of Lehi." It also contradicts Joseph's statement that the Title Page is a "literal translation" of the last leaf of the plates because he couldn't have known that if he wasn't actually translating the plates.

Second, the reading theory requires the construction of a false historical narrative; i.e., Synthesis #1 that we discussed in Chapter 2. To reconcile the conflict between the Thesis and Antithesis, some historians have proposed that Joseph and Oliver used the term *Urim and Thummim* to apply to both the seer stone and the Nephite interpreters. But in 1834, there was already a clear distinction between the seer stone and the Urim and Thummim, as spelled out in *Mormonism Unvailed.* It was in response to the claims of that book that Joseph and Oliver specifically maintained Joseph used the U&T.

Oliver was responding to *Mormonism Unvailed* when he wrote Letter I – "Day after day I continued, uninterrupted, to write from his mouth, as he translated with the Urim and Thummim, or, as the Nephites would have said, 'Interpreters,' the history or record called 'The Book of Mormon.'"
(Joseph Smith—History, Note, 1)

Instead of creating a revisionist historical narrative to explain the conflict among the accounts, the conflict can be explained as the difference between a demonstration of the process (using SITH) and the actual process of translation (using the U&T). As we've seen in previous chapters, careful reading of the eye-witness accounts shows that they are all either (i) consistent with Joseph performing a demonstration to satisfy (or deflect) curiosity, leaving him and Oliver free to perform the actual translation with the U&T and the plates, or (ii) specifically designed to refute the Spaulding theory.

I don't expect this brief dismissal of the reading theory to satisfy its adherents, but I also don't expect the reading theory to survive the accumulating evidence of 19th century influences. Therefore, I proceed to consider the evidence of composing and translating.

Evidence of both Composing and Translating

Richard Bushman commented on the current framing of the issues regarding the production of the Book of Mormon.

> Modern Mormons read the Book of Mormon well aware of how critics think of the book… Perhaps the surest evidence of this condition is the frequently heard comment from educated Mormons that Joseph Smith could not have written the Book of Mormon. The affirmation implies that readers are constantly asking themselves: Did Joseph Smith write the book himself? The question is inescapable. Thus it is that modern readers go through the text thinking with two minds: the religious teachings of the prophets are processed with one mind, and the question about Joseph Smith's authorship is entertained in another…. Some [passages] may look very much like an insertion by the nineteenth-century Joseph.[214]

To date, studies of the text and Joseph's environment have detected a few possible influences (beyond the King James Bible). In addition to *The Late War* and the Spalding manuscript, some have suggested influences from *View of the Hebrews*, from history books, and from

[214] Richard Lyman Bushman, "Reading From the Gold Plates," *The Expanded Canon: Perspectives on Mormonism & Sacred Texts*, Greg Kofford Books (2018): 86.

religious authors.[215] Such evidence is consistent with both composing and translating.

This chapter expands on these sources and proposes that the language of the Book of Mormon—the English into which Joseph translated the plates—derives from specific sources contemporary with Joseph Smith, readily available to him in Vermont, Massachusetts, and New York. There are over 700 non-KJV words in the text of the Book of Mormon, and over 400 non-KJV phrases. All of these can be found in one or more of the five categories of sources readily available to Joseph Smith before he translated the plates: Palmyra newspapers, family traditions, the work of theologians from the First Great Awakening in the eighteenth century, history books written in the biblical style, and the King James Version of the Bible.

This chapter includes a few specific examples, but a detailed list is available in my book, *Infinite Goodness: Joseph Smith and Jonathan Edwards.*

Bushman's article referred to Blake Ostler's article that interprets the Book of Mormon as "a modern expansion of an ancient source."[216] This is the idea that the text Joseph dictated was a translation of an ancient document, yet, as Ostler explains,

> Joseph Smith gave us not merely the words of the Book of Mormon prophets, but also the true meaning of the text within a nineteenth-century thought-world. The translation was not merely from one language into another but was also a transformation from one thought-world to another that expands and explains the meaning of the original text in

---

[215] Thomas E. Donofrio itemized many of these in his article, "Early American Influences on the Book of Mormon," available at http://www.mormonthink.com/influences.htm#part2 (accessed June 3, 2019). A more comprehensive list is Rick Grunder, *Mormon Parallels* (2014) available at http://www.rickgrunder.com/parallels.htm.

[216] Blake T. Ostler, "The Book of Mormon as a Modern Expansion of an Ancient Source," *Dialogue: A Journal of Mormon Thought* 20, no. 1 (Spring 1987):66-123, https://www.dialoguejournal.com/wp-content/uploads/sbi/articles/Dialogue_V20N01_68.pdf, updated April 26, 2005, at https://www.timesandseasons.org/harchive/2005/04/updating-the-expansion-theory/

terms that Joseph Smith and his contemporaries would understand.[217]

Skeptics assert that 19th century language (including the King James Version excerpts) indicates a 19th century composition. Ostler claims the language and influences alone are not determinative.

> The conclusion that the Book of Mormon is pious fraud derived from nineteenth-century influences does not logically follow from the observation that it contains KJV quotations and is expressed in terms of a nineteenth-century world view.... All expressions of revelation must be communicated within their author's framework of thought, a framework limited by its assumptions. Nor does it follow that if the book derives from the revelation of an ancient source it must be explained exclusively in ancient terms.[218]

In my view, Ostler overstates his case because the "pious fraud" conclusion *does* logically follow from evidence of the 19th century influences; it just doesn't *necessarily* follow because other conclusions also logically follow from that evidence. Among these alternative conclusions is the one Joseph claimed; i.e., that he translated the ancient writings into English.

In other words, evidence of 19th century influences is consistent with *both* composing and translating.

This is a key point. Every time skeptics cite a source that predated the Book of Mormon as evidence of composition, *they are also citing evidence of translation.* This point seems self-evident, yet both skeptics and apologists have largely ignored or overlooked it because they have been talking past one another.

Skeptics think evidence of 19th-century influences contradicts Joseph's claim of divine participation in the translation, but what the evidence actually contradicts is the claim that Joseph did not translate the plates—did not even use the plates—but instead read words that appeared on the stone in the hat (SITH).

Apologists seek to refute evidence of 19th-century influence because

---

217 Ostler (1987): 107.

218 Ostler (1987): 115.

they buy into the skeptics' argument that such influence is evidence of composition, and that has led them to embrace SITH.

Neither skeptics nor apologists take Joseph's claim of actual translation seriously.

By contrast, consider the observations of a non-Mormon who wrote to the Editor of the *Millennial Star* in 1887.

> I know very well that whatever ideas an original writer or translator expressed, he could not go beyond his vocabulary. As Joseph Smith was confessedly a man of limited education, and the English Bible of 1611 was his one familiar book, of course he wrote or dictated to another to write in the very style and vocabulary which he possessed. An angel or spirit in using man's brain of course finds it a limited instrument, and can not make it act differently for him any more than an artist can sketch a fine cut line with a blunt pencil, or a course one with a fine point, or a musician draw from an instrument harmonies beyond its powers. Suffice it to say, thinking men should not rule a book out of a claim to genuineness on account of its style, when the style and stated facts of Joseph Smith's education are so consistent. [219]

The author here assumed that the King James Bible was the only book familiar to Joseph when he translated the plates, but as we'll see later in this chapter, the translated text can be linked directly to a handful of additional sources, all readily accessible to Joseph before he began translating.

To repeat: whether Joseph *composed* or *translated* the text, the evidence of outside 19th century influences would be the same.

To distinguish between composition and translation, we must consider factors other than outside influences on Joseph's language. Elements in the text that can help distinguish between composition and translation include instances of transliteration and Hebraic literary forms and allusions that are not found in the Bible or other outside influences.

---

[219] C (anonymous), "Are They of Israel," *Millennial Star*, No. 3, Vol. LXIX (49), Jan. 17, 1887: p. 37.

It has been suggested that the frequent use of the phrase "or rather" in the Book of Mormon indicates a translator's rephrasing immediately after expressing a particular rendition of the original text.[220] While that makes sense, Paul used the phrase when he composed one of his letters (Galatians 4:9). Jonathan Edwards used it over 200 times in his writing.[221] E.g., "For the saints in all their spiritual transactions with God act by the Spirit; *or rather*, it is the Spirit of God that acts in them." And: "none ever excited such images of terror in my mind, as the appearance of one who was a devout and zealous reformer, *or rather* restorer, of what he supposed was the ancient religion of the Indians."

Consequently, the phrase "or rather" is consistent with both composition and translation.

Presumably, the existence of this phrase would be another reason to reject SITH as implausible because a supernatural intermediary would have no reason to modify his/her thoughts mid-sentence.

Although this chapter focuses primarily on the language of the Book of Mormon to assess outside influences and to distinguish between composition and translation, substantive ideas in the text have invited comparisons of Joseph's theology with the theology of his contemporaries (the "Second Great Awakening"). Lynn Hilton Wilson suggests that Joseph's ideas were unique,[222] which can be considered evidence of translation as opposed to composition. Because Jonathan Edwards was involved with the First Great Awakening, comparisons to the Second Great Awakening may need to be reassessed.

Time frame.

---

[220] Samuel Brown, "Seeing the Voice of God," presentation to Faith Matter Foundation, published May 6, 2017, available online at https://www.youtube.com/watch?v=yWCz45qS-OU

[221] This chapter does not provide citations for the Edwards quotations because they can easily be found at the database accessible here: http://edwards.yale.edu/. Another source is the 1808 8-volume collection of Edwards' works that was on sale in Palmyra, NY, from 1818-1822, which has been digitized for Kindle, albeit with some errors.

[222] Lynne Hilton Wilson, "A New Pneumatology: Comparing Joseph Smith's Doctrine of the Spirit with His Contemporaries and the Bible," *BYU Studies Quarterly* 51, no. 1 (2012).

The back-and-forth between skeptics and believers, and different views among believers, involve speculation about how much time and ability Joseph would have had to read, incorporate, and reformulate the materials available to him, and then compose (or translate or read words on a stone) and dictate the text.[223]

For context, 47 scholars, divided into six committees, took four years to produce the KJV. They "translated out of the original tongues, and with the former translations diligently compared and revised."

Skeptics observe that Joseph had five and a half years between Moroni's first visit in September 1823 and the commencement of the translation in April 1829 to compose the narrative. Plus, he had practice in 1828 with the lost 116 pages. They claim this was enough time for Joseph to internalize the story so deeply he could recite it fluidly. Or, he could have simply dictated from a prepared manuscript (the Spalding theory). In their view, testimony from scribes that Joseph did not have a manuscript from which he read is simply an expected element of collaboration; i.e., either they lied, or Joseph somehow kept the manuscript hidden from sight.

Believers point to the traditional 90-day period (April 7 through June 1829), or the 8-month period (November 1828 through June 1829) in which Joseph dictated the entire text.[224] This is a rapid pace for both composing and translating, especially since the OM shows no signs of editing or revision. Hence the need for the "gift and power of God" to accomplish the task. And yet, believers also recognize that Joseph was instructed by Moroni about the content of the plates for years leading up to the actual translation. Joseph explained that on the night of Moroni's first visit,

> I was also informed concerning the aboriginal inhabitants of this country, and shown who they were, and from whence they came; a brief sketch of their origin, progress, civilization, laws, governments, of their

[223] In this chapter I set aside the question of collaboration on composition of the text because there is no evidence of such collaboration and because any such collaboration would still have collapsed into a single composition.
[224] See Chapter 1 and Appendix 1.

> righteousness and iniquity, and the blessings of God being finally withdrawn from them as a people was made known unto me.[225]

During the four years between Moroni's first visit and Joseph's acquisition of the plates, Joseph had further interactions with Moroni and, apparently, other Nephite individuals. The first published version of Joseph Smith—History named Nephi, not Moroni, as the divine messenger who appeared in September 1823. Brigham Young explained in an 1866 letter to his son that "There is really no discrepancy in the history about these names. It was Moroni who delivered the sacred records and Urim and Thummim to Joseph, but Nephi also visited him."[226]

Evidence from the text.

There is one fact everyone agrees with: Joseph claimed he translated the ancient plates.[227] Witnesses and circumstantial evidence both support and contradict Joseph's claim, leaving room for the composition and reading alternatives. Hence, everyone turns to the text itself.

People have analyzed the text of the Book of Mormon from a variety of perspectives. Some have conducted wordprint or stylometry studies. Some have compared the text to other books published before 1827. Some have carefully evaluated the grammar, syntax, and other features.

After reviewing many such studies, I decided to test the hypothesis

---

225 "Church History," (the Wentworth letter), *Times and Seasons*, 1 Mar. 1842, vol. 3, no. 9 (whole no. 45), pp. 706–710. https://www.josephsmithpapers.org/paper-summary/church-history-1-march-1842/2.

226 https://catalog.churchofjesuschrist.org/assets?id=b3c72fee-6f44-4ce6-8a9f-5cf38b6153d1&crate=0&index=387.

227 E.g., "Two days after the arrival of Mr. Cowdery (being the 7th of April) I commenced to translate the Book of Mormon, and he began to write for me." JS-H 1:67. "Day after day I continued, uninterrupted, to write from his mouth, as he translated with the Urim and Thummim, or, as the Nephites would have said, 'Interpreters,' the history or record called 'The Book of Mormon.'" (Note after JS-H 1:75, excepted from Letter I, *Messenger and Advocate*, vol. 1 (October 1834), pp. 14-16.

that, given the relatively limited vocabulary in the Book of Mormon (5,360 words, of which 2,219 are used only once or twice), it may be possible to ascertain sources for much, or all, of the vocabulary.

Biblical vocabulary has an obvious source: the King James Version. Significant portions of the Book of Mormon are direct copies from the KJV, with some minor alterations.

Much of the rest of the text consists of passages and phrases blended from disparate biblical verses. But there are about 750 non-biblical words in the text (depending on how one categorizes word forms) and hundreds of non-biblical phrases.

Chunking.

Experts on language acquisition use the term "chunking" to express the way people learn languages.[228] We don't learn to speak and write by memorizing lists of words; instead, we listen to or read words in combinations, or chunks. Then we reuse, reformulate, and rearrange these chunks to express our own ideas. To assess the origin of the language in the Book of Mormon, we should, therefore, look not only for specific words but for "chunks" of word groups and concepts. In the rest of this chapter, I use the term *vocabulary* to include both individual words and chunks.

The extent of biblical vocabulary in the text does not necessarily mean that Joseph copied directly from the Bible. Joseph could have learned the biblical vocabulary by reading sermons, books on theology, or Bible commentaries. Even direct biblical quotations in the text could, have come from Joseph's memory, whether he was acting as translator or composer. In his day, people memorized biblical passages.

The question is how to account for the 750 non-biblical words, plus several hundred non-biblical phrases.

If the non-biblical vocabulary in the Book of Mormon is present in Joseph's world in Palmyra circa 1817-1829 Palmyra, we can reasonably

---

[228] For an overview, see Richard Nordquist, "Chunk (Language Acquisition)," Glossary of Grammatical and Rhetorical Terms, Thought Co., online at https://www.thoughtco.com/chunk-language-acquisition-1689841.

infer that Joseph incorporated that vocabulary into the mental language bank he drew upon as either composer or translator.

Several researchers have pursued this line of inquiry. For example, Dale R. Broadhurst created a table of "Unique Textual Parallels" that consisted of 369 non-Biblical words (about half of the total) found in the 1830 Book of Mormon.[229] Broadhurst's table includes word lists from the 1737 *Works of Josephus*, the 1812 Solomon Spalding "Oberlin" manuscript, and the 1825 edition of Ethan Smith's *View of the Hebrews.* Of the 369 words, Broadhurst identified 37 that were found only in the Book of Mormon and the Spalding manuscript.[230] However, because most of these 37 words were commonly used elsewhere in pre-existing sources (such as Shakespeare), this study has little probative value.

Another study compared digital files of over 100,000 books that predated the 1830s.[231] The authors, Chris and Duane Johnson, conclude that, because of the number of similarities between the two books, "Joseph most likely grew up reading a school book called *The Late War* by Gilbert J. Hunt and it heavily influenced his writing of the Book of Mormon."

The Johnsons' conclusion about influence (setting aside the subjective term *heavily* and the ahistorical and rhetorical term *writing*) has provoked significant (and ongoing) reaction from believers and skeptics, but both sides have overreacted because they both misread the evidence.

The parallels in the Johnson study consist mostly of chunks of language sprinkled throughout the text of both books. The Johnsons extracted these chunks and combined them to create parallels that

---

229 Dale R. Broadhurst, Part 1, "Unique Textual Parallels," http://www.solomonspalding.com/bomstudies/part1.htm (accessed June 3, 2019).
230 Dale R. Broadhurst, Part 2, "Unique Textual Parallels," http://www.solomonspalding.com/bomstudies/part2.htm (accessed June 3, 2019)
231 Chris and Duane Johnson, "A Comparison of the Book of Mormon and The Late War Between the United States and Great Britain," Mar. 9, 2014, published at http://wordtree.org/thelatewar/. There is little explanation of methodology and no list of the 100,000 books studied or even the database used, and the link to the authors' notes is broken.

appear more striking than the chunks do in either text separately. Nevertheless, the parallels exist for everyone to see.

Such parallel chunks of language are exactly what we should expect if, as Joseph claimed, he translated the Book of Mormon into English.

We expect anyone's translation of any text into a target language to consist of vocabulary (terms and chunks of language and concepts) familiar to the translator. No one can write words that he or she has never seen before—except for transliterated words from the original that have no equivalent in the target language. (Transliteration is a clue we'll discuss below.)

A book copyrighted by the Corporation of the President of the Church of Jesus Christ of Latter-day Saints, made this point back in 1953.

> Joseph Smith in his translating under the inspiration of God obtained the meaning of the Book of Mormon text. [footnote omitted] Joseph Smith neither had a Ph.D. in English nor had he been trained as a linguist. He gave the ideas in the English language in such phraseology and diction as he could master, and not being learned in the knowledge of the English, his expressions were oftentimes ungrammatical and the local expressions of his community sometimes occurred.[232]

The totality of the evidence, including the linguistic parallels and the social context of *The Late War*, suggest that Joseph likely read *The Late War* and that the book formed part of Joseph's mental language bank.[233] Consequently, the Johnson study provides evidence that Joseph used his own English vocabulary to dictate the text of the Book of Mormon, whether as composer or translator.

The Johnson study received a strange reaction from LDS scholars. They raised two objections. First, they sought to distance Joseph Smith from *The Late War*, claiming there is no evidence he ever read the book.

---

[232] Franklin S. Harris, Jr., *The Book of Mormon: Messages and Evidences*, published by the Church of Jesus Christ of Latter-day Saints, Deseret News Press, Salt Lake City, Utah, 1953: 109.

[233] For more in-depth analysis, see *Infinite Goodness: Joseph Smith and Jonathan Edwards*.

Second, they claimed there were more differences than similarities.

For example, in his discussion of *The Late War*, Tad R. Callister, an emeritus LDS General Authority and former General Sunday School President, recently wrote, "I doubt that Joseph read any of the books alleged by the skeptics to be sources for the Book of Mormon before the translation process commenced. There is no historical evidence confirming that he did."[234]

When we consider the historical context, though, *The Late War* fits solidly into Joseph's environment in both Vermont and New York. The book covered the War of 1812, which lasted from 1812 to 1815. In August 1813, the British attempted an invasion of Burlington, Vermont, the site of a major U.S. military base, but were repelled. Burlington is about 95 miles north of Lebanon, Vermont, where the Smiths were living at the time. Vermont troops[235] served in both militia and U.S. Army regiments during the war.

Separately, the British invaded Pultneyville (located only 16 miles north of Palmyra) in 1814, killing two citizens, wounding three, and taking two prisoners. This was just two years before the Smiths arrived in Palmyra, where they lived among veterans of the war. Joseph's older brother Alvin, who died on November 19, 1823, was buried in the General John Swift Memorial Cemetery, named after a local hero of the War of 1812. Swift's tombstone explains that he was "killed by the Enemy of his Country [the British] July 12, 1814" in Canada.

The Late War was "Written in the Ancient Historical Style" (1816 and 1817 editions) or in the "Scriptural Style" (1819 edition), meaning it read like the King James Version (*It came to pass, the fourth day of the seventh month, the face of the whole earth*, etc.). The book contains an endorsement by Samuel L. Mitchill, the New York Professor whom Martin Harris visited to solicit a similar endorsement. Plus, the 1830 edition of the Book of Mormon resembles *The Late War* in design (Title

234 Callister (2019): 79.

235 These were the "Green Mountain Boys" that Joseph appealed to for assistance in 1843, claiming the rights of a "Green Mountain Boy." https://archive.org/stream/generaljosephsmi00smit#page/n1/mode/2up

page, full copyright notice, Preface).

Despite his belief that Joseph did not read the book, Callister recognized the possibility. "In the event that Joseph read any of these books, no doubt he learned some words or phrases that enhanced his vocabulary that would be available for future use in translation—that would seem natural to me."[236]

It does seem natural; in fact, this is evidence that Joseph *did* translate the text in his own language. One wonders, why did Callister first argue that Joseph didn't read the book?

Callister does not say, but we can infer that it could be because the current narrative accepted by many LDS scholars holds that Joseph *did not* translate the plates; instead, these scholars teach the reading theory (SITH).[237] Under SITH, Joseph wouldn't need an "enhanced vocabulary" from *The Late War* or any other source; he would merely read the words that appeared on the stone.

As explained previously in this chapter, in my view the evidence excludes reading (SITH) as a viable hypothesis, which leaves us with composing and translating.

The second argument by LDS scholars—that there are more differences than similarities between *The Late War* and the Book of Mormon—may be an argument against outright plagiarism, but it rings hollow because it does not refute the skeptics' point that *The Late War* influenced at least some of the vocabulary Joseph used in producing the Book of Mormon. Differences between the two books do not erase similarities, and the similarities are specific enough to raise a reasonable inference that there was at least some influence involved.

---

[236] Callister (2019): 79. Callister's equivocation may represent an unstated prudent approach based on multiple operating hypotheses.

[237] See the Gospel Topics Essay on Book of Mormon Translation, https://www.churchofjesuschrist.org/study/manual/gospel-topics-essays/book-of-mormon-translation?lang=eng&_r=1. The Church's web page teaches Primary children that "Joseph used a special rock called a seer stone to translate the plates" and that "Joseph didn't have much schooling, so he wasn't good at writing or spelling." https://www.churchofjesuschrist.org/study/friend/2017/02/golden-plates-to-book-of-mormon?lang=eng

If, as I propose, Joseph Smith actually translated the ancient plates into English, we should expect exactly the kind of evidence the Johnson study produced; i.e., chunks of language in the text of the Book of Mormon drawn from Joseph's mental language bank that he acquired by reading books such as (and probably including) *The Late War*.

Skeptics, of course, point to the same facts as evidence that Joseph composed the Book of Mormon. Composition is less persuasive than translation because of four factors.

First, the "influenced" vocabulary appears throughout both books in discrete chunks that are separated by intermittent text. They are not long passages or even complete sentences that could constitute plagiarism. The Johnson study merges the chunks together, but when put in context, the influence is less direct. This is classic chunking.

Here is an excerpt from the Johnson study that Callister evaluated.[238] The Johnson's used colors to show the corresponding vocabulary. Here I **bold** it.

The Late War	Book of Mormon
35:5-6	Alma 53:18-20
two thousand hardy **men**, who ... fought freely for **their country** ... Now the men **of war** ... were ... **men** of **dauntless courage**.	**two thousand** of those young **men** ... to defend **their country**. ... they took their weapons **of war**, ... were all young **men**, and they were exceeding **valiant for courage**, ...

Presented this way, the similarities appear significant. *Two thousand* is a specific number, *dauntless* is a rough synonym for *valiant*, etc.

Callister puts this example in context, which dilutes the similarities.[239]

The Late War	The Book of Mormon

238 Third entry at http://wordtree.org/thelatewar/

239 Callister (2019): 74.

The Late War 35:5–6	Alma 53:18-20
5 Immediately Jackson took **two thousand** hardy **men**, who were called volunteers, because they had, unsolicited, offered their services to **their country**, and led them against the savages. 6 Now the men **of war** that followed after him were mostly from the state of Tennessee, and **men of dauntless courage**.	18 Now behold, there were **two thousand** of those young **men**, who entered into this covenant and took their weapons of war to defend **their country**. 19 And now behold, as they never had hitherto been a disadvantage to the Nephites, they became now at this period of time also a great support; for they took their weapons **of war**, and they would that Helaman should be their leader. 20 And they were all young **men**, and they were exceedingly **valiant for courage**, and also for strength and activity; but behold, this was not all—they were men who were true at all times in whatsoever thing they were entrusted.

Other examples in the Johnson study may be more direct, but many of them are also common to the King James Bible. Consequently, this evidence does not support the Johnson's unquantified and subjective claim that *The Late War* "heavily influenced" the Book of Mormon, but instances of similarities are specific enough to suggest they came from Joseph's mental language bank.[240] A composition based on *The Late War* should have more similarities in theme and vocabulary than a translation of a foreign-language text in which the translator simply used his own vocabulary to convert the source material into English.

[240] I've included some of these instances in my upcoming book, *Infinite Goodness: Joseph Smith and Jonathan Edwards.* I used BYU's Wordcruncher program, which includes *The Late War* in the database so anyone can compare words and phrases. https://www.wordcruncher.com/

The second factor that favors translation over composition is the absence of evidence that Joseph (or anyone close to him) had all of these sources available during the dictation process in Harmony (1828 and 1829) or in Fayette (1829). To compose the text by copying from multiple sources as the skeptics argue, Joseph would have needed the sources available during the dictation. Yet no one, not even the skeptics, can cite evidence that Joseph brought books to Harmony or Fayette or that such sources were available to him there.

This means that Joseph would have had to compose the text from memory; i.e., that he drew upon his own mental language bank. But once skeptics concede that point, distinguishing between composition and translation becomes easier. All the evidence points to a continuous dictation of a coherent document. That is exactly what we would expect if Joseph translated an original, edited text from the plates as he claimed. Translators use the organization, structure, concepts, and narrative from the original text. They just convert one language to another. By contrast, dictating such a complex document from one's imagination without making changes or edits is, well, unimaginable—and unprecedented.[241]

The third factor that favors translation is the presence of transliteration in the text. "Transliteration is the process of transferring a word from the alphabet of one language to another."[242] Translators use transliteration when there is no known equivalent in the target language. By one count, there are 188 unique proper names in the text,[243] including kinds of animals that appear as transliterations such as *curelom* and *cumom*. These are non-English words. While it's possible to create non-English words when composing a manuscript in English, Joseph's scribes reported that he spelled out some of these names, exactly as one would do if transliterating the original language.

---

241 *Visions in a Seer Stone* proposes that Joseph used mnemonic clues to keep track of an extended oral performance, but the Book of Mormon is far more extensive and complex than the sermons cited in that book as examples.

242 "transliteration", https://www.vocabulary.com/dictionary/transliteration (2019)

243 Paul Y. Hoskisson, "Book of Mormon Names," *Encyclopedia of Mormonism* (1992) https://eom.byu.edu/index.php/Book_of_Mormon_Names

The fourth factor is the presence of subtle Hebrew linguistic patterns, structures and themes, as outlined by Ostler, Welch, and others, which would be unexpected in a 19th century composition. That topic has been thoroughly examined in many books and papers and is beyond the scope of this chapter (although I mention it in the Conclusion).

Part 2: Preparation of a Prophet.

As previously noted, there is a long tradition of characterizing Joseph Smith as an unlearned farm boy who was a blank slate upon which the Lord could write.

The historical evidence supports an alternative framing. I propose that Joseph Smith was well prepared for his calling as translator of the Nephite plates, that this preparation began at a young age, and that by the time he began the translation, he was "intimately familiar" with Christian theology, vocabulary and rhetoric. This influence was additional to the influence of the Bible.

In his 1832 history, Joseph wrote that his "goodly Parents… spared no pains to instructing me in the Christian religion."[244] We lack details to know what this instruction consisted of, but apparently it began at an early age because Joseph once declared "It is a love of libe[r]ty which inspires my soul. civil and religious liberty— were diffused into my soul by my grandfathers. while they dandld me on their knees."[245]

Joseph's leg surgery in 1813 may have played a key role in his preparation to become a prophet. Due to complications from the surgery, Joseph went with his uncle Jesse Smith to Salem, Massachusetts, for convalescence.[246] Although only seven years old at

---

[244] Joseph Smith, History, circa Summer 1832, https://www.josephsmithpapers.org/paper-summary/history-circa-summer-1832/1

[245] https://www.josephsmithpapers.org/paper-summary/journal-december-1842-june-1844-book-2-10-march-1843-14-july-1843/309

[246] Lucy Mack Smith, History, 1844-1845, p. 2, book 3, online at https://www.josephsmithpapers.org/paper-summary/lucy-mack-smith-history-1844-1845/32

the time, Joseph was old enough to read and he was laid up with nothing else to do.

By comparison, Parley P. Pratt wrote that as a child, he always had a book. "At the age of seven years my mother gave me lessons to read in the scriptures; I read of Joseph in Egypt,--his dreams, his servitude, his temptation and exaltation… All this inspired me with love, and with the noblest sentiments ever planted in the bosom of man."[247]

Joseph's journal relates an event from November 14, 1835, that includes an interesting detail about his young life.

> A Gentleman called this after noon by the name of Erastus Holmes of Newbury Clemon [Clermont] Co. Ohio, he called to make enquiry about the establishment of the Church of the latter-day Saints and to be instructed more perfectly in our doctrine &c I commenced and gave him a brief relation of my experience while in my juvenile years, say from 6, years old up to the time I received the first visitation of Angels which was when I was about 14, years old and also the the [sic] visitations that I received afterward, concerning the book of Mormon, and a short account of the rise and progress of the church, up to this, date.[248]

Holmes inquired about the "establishment of the Church," so it is curious that Joseph began with his juvenile years, "say from 6." That time frame corresponds with his leg surgery, but what did that surgery have to do with the establishment of the Church?

There is circumstantial evidence that Joseph read Christian materials while staying in Salem. Samuel Deane delivered a series of four sermons for young men that were collected and published as a booklet in Salem, Massachusetts, in 1774.[249] Joseph's uncle Jesse was known for his strong religious beliefs.[250] Would he not give such

---

247 Autobiography of Parley P. Pratt, 1888 edition, page 19, online at https://archive.org/details/autobiographyofp00prat/page/18.

248 Joseph Smith, Journa, 1835-1836, p. 36-7. Online at https://www.josephsmithpapers.org/paper-summary/journal-1835-1836/37

249 *Four Sermons to Young Men, from Titus II.6. preached at Falmouth*, by Samuel Deane. Salem (Samuel and Ebenezer Hall) 1774.

250 John W. Welch, "Jesse Smith's 1814 Protest," *BYU Studies* Vol. 33, 1 (1993): 131, https://scholarsarchive.byu.edu/cgi/viewcontent.cgi?article=2892&context=byusq

reading material to his recuperating nephew? The booklet contains non-biblical language that appears in the Book of Mormon, including *design, anxious, tendency, rising generation, opposite, in other words, on the other hand, garb, regulation, faculties, lay before, state of probation, everlasting damnation, soften, reluctance, look forward, ignominious, thoughtless,* and more. As suggested by this terminology, the sermons focus on Book of Mormon themes.

Joseph's convalescence didn't conclude in Massachusetts. He wrote that after the doctors removed "a large portion of the bone from my left leg… fourteen additional pieces of bone afterwards worked out before my leg healed, during which time I was reduced so very low that my mother could carry me with ease. & after I began to get about I went on crutches till I started for the State of New York."[251]

These years of disability compromised Joseph's usefulness for farm work, leaving him more time to read and engage in what his mother Lucy Mack Smith later called "meditation and deep study."

Writing about events after Moroni's first visit, she observed that

> From this time forth, Joseph continued to receive instructions from the Lord; and we, to get the children together every evening for the purpose of listening while he imparted the same to the family. I presume we presented an aspect as singular, as any family that ever lived upon the face of the Earth: all seated in a circle, father, mother, sons, and daughters, and giving the most profound attention to a boy, eighteen years of age, who had never read the Bible through in his life; for he was much less inclined to the perusals of books then any of the rest of our children, but far more given to meditation and deep study. [252]

Note that books were not unavailable to the Smith family; all the kids had books. Lucy commented on Joseph's different approach.

Scholars usually interpret this passage to mean that Joseph was

---

[251] Joseph Smith, *History, 1838-1856*, volume A-1, Addenda, Note A (handwriting of Willard Richards) https://www.josephsmithpapers.org/paper-summary/history-1838-1856-volume-a-1-23-december-1805-30-august-1834/137

[252] Lucy Mack Smith, *History*, 1845, p. 86, online at https://www.josephsmithpapers.org/paper-summary/lucy-mack-smith-history-1845/93

"unbookish" as we saw at the beginning of this chapter, in contrast to his siblings who "perused" books. However, I propose an alternative reading, starting with the term *perusal.*

Webster's 1828 dictionary defines *perusal* as "the act of reading."[253] That appears to be the connotation of the term as used in documents collected in the Joseph Smith Papers, including letters and newspaper articles.

However, *peruse* is a contronym, meaning "a word that has two meanings which seem to contradict each other." It can mean "to look at or read (something) in an informal or relaxed way" or "to examine or read (something) in a very careful way."[254]

To clarify which meaning they intend, writers use adjectives such as "attentively" or "negligently." In a letter dated April 13, 1833, Joseph Smith wrote "Dear Broth Carter your letter to Broth Jared is just put into my hand and I have **carefully purrused** [sic] its contents, and imbrace [sic] this oppertunity [sic] to answer it."[255] [emphasis added]. The adverb *carefully* would be redundant if the term had the meaning commonly ascribed to Lucy's statement.

Lucy contrasted "the perusals of books" with "meditation and deep study." This suggests she meant that the other children's perusals were more relaxed and informal than Joseph's "deep study." This connotation is consistent with her observation that Joseph hadn't "read the Bible through," because "meditation and deep study" requires more detailed examination of cross-references and commentaries than merely reading it through.

Furthermore, Joseph explained, in his own handwriting, that

> At about the age of twelve years my mind become [sic] seriously imprest with

---

[253] "Perusal," *Webster's Dictionary 1828*, Online Edition, online at: http://webstersdictionary1828.com/Dictionary/meditation

[254] "Peruse," Merriam-Webster.com, accessed April 27, 2019, https://www.merriam-webster.com/words-at-play/peruse-usage

[255] Letter to John S. Carter, 13 April 1833, Joseph Smith Papers, Letterbook 1, p. 29. https://www.josephsmithpapers.org/paper-summary/letter-to-john-s-carter-13-april-1833/1

> regard to the all importent concerns of for the wellfare of my immortal Soul which led me to searching the scriptures believeing as I was taught, that they contained the word of God thus applying myself to them and my **intimate acquaintance with those of differant denominations** led me to marvel exceedingly…[256]

Even if he didn't "read the Bible through," Joseph was "searching the scriptures" between the ages of 12 and 15. Later in the same history, he writes, "by searching the scriptures I found that mankind did not come unto the Lord but that they had apostatized from the true and living faith"[257] and "I learned in the scriptures that God was the same yesterday to day and forever."

Joseph's familiarity with the scriptures enabled him to detect that Moroni quoted Malachi "with a little variation from the way it reads in our Bibles."[258] In his 1838 history, Joseph quoted Moroni's version of the passages exactly. This doesn't necessarily mean he had a photographic memory because he could have referred to notes he had made, such as the "authentic documents now in our possession" that Oliver Cowdery used to write his eight essays on the Priesthood and early Church history.[259] But the larger point, that Joseph knew the Bible well, is established by these comments.

When Joseph referred to "my intimate acquaintance with those of different denominations," he could have meant (i) members or ministers of different denominations he personally knew in Palmyra, and/or (ii) the writings of Christian ministers and theologians he had read. I think he meant both because his *History, circa Summer 1832*, like the Book of Mormon and the revelations in the D&C, is replete with the vocabulary of Christian theologians such as Jonathan Edwards and

---

[256] Smith, *History*, circa Summer 1832, https://www.josephsmithpapers.org/paper-summary/history-circa-summer-1832/2.

[257] "True and living" is a non-biblical Book of Mormon phrase. "True and living faith" is a nonscriptural phrase that appears in the work of Jonathan Edwards, a theologian whose work is second only to the KJV in terms of its influence on the text of the Book of Mormon.

[258] Joseph Smith – History 1:36.

[259] Oliver Cowdery, Letter I, History, 1834-1836, https://www.josephsmithpapers.org/paper-summary/history-1834-1836/48.

James Hervey.[260]

Joseph's early preparation armed him with a mental language bank that enabled him to deliver an English translation of the ancient Nephite text that fits squarely within the Christian tradition. As we should expect, nearly every verse in the Book of Mormon contains language and concepts found in five discrete categories of sources, all available to Joseph before he translated the plates.

1. The King James Version of the Bible.

2. Books and other publications sold in Palmyra between 1818 and 1823, such as the works of Jonathan Edwards and James Hervey,[261] and publications available in Vermont and Massachusetts before the Smiths moved to Palmyra, such as the Deane sermons discussed above and the works of Ethan Smith, including *View of the Hebrews.*

3. Newspapers published in the Palmyra area between 1818 and 1828.

4. So-called "pseudo-Biblical" books including *The Late War*, *The American Revolution*, *The First Book of Napoleon*, and *The First Book of the American Chronicles of the Times.*

5. Family speech as documented in their writings, primarily Lucy Mack Smith's history.

---

[260] An annotated version of Joseph's 1832 History is in an appendix in *Infinite Goodness: Joseph Smith and Jonathan Edwards.* I started with the annotated version in the JSP and added over 100 footnotes showing connections between the 1832 History and terms and phrases from the Bible, the modern scriptures, and Jonathan Edwards. Much of the vocabulary is found only in Jonathan Edwards, such as the phrase "true and living faith" noted above.

[261] James Hervey is the only author common to both the list of books on sale in Palmyra in 1818-1823 and the list of books Joseph Smith donated to the Nauvoo library in 1844.

Most of these sources have attracted some attention from skeptics and apologists. For my book *Infinite Goodness*, I've prepared extensive annotations to illustrate how these sources contributed to Joseph's mental language bank. In this chapter, we have looked at the example of the Deane sermons from Salem. We will look at more examples below, but before discussing the examples, let's consider how my proposal creates a new paradigm.

This new evidence supports the following propositions:

> Joseph Smith, by the gift and power of God, using the interpreters that had been prepared anciently and placed by Moroni in the stone box along with the plates, translated ancient engravings on metal plates and dictated his own English version of the text.

> Joseph was prepared from a young age to accomplish the translation by reading, studying, and meditating upon the works of well-known theologians, including Jonathan Edwards and James Hervey.

At first glance, this proposition may appear apologetic in nature because as we've seen, evidence of translation is also evidence of composition. I maintain that evidence extrinsic to the language itself tips the scale toward translation, but I also recognize there is an element of faith involved with my preference for translation.

The new evidence changes both current understanding (the reading theory) and traditional views (such as Joseph's supposed ignorance). I don't see this as mere deconstruction in the mode of New Mormon History. Patrick Q. Mason has observed how the New Mormon History served as a "historiographical bridge between an older style of apologetics and Mormon studies."[262] Applying these new facts involves

[262] Patrick Q. Mason, "Mormon Studies: The Emergence and State of the Field,"

a multidisciplinary approach that is squarely within the modern concept of Mormon studies.

I propose instead that the historical evidence and the language of the text support Joseph's persistent claim that he translated the ancient Nephite plates into English.

Part 3: Examples of influences

Blending is a technique of incorporating phrases from unrelated passages in source material.

Royal Skousen has identified connections between the Book of Mormon and the KJV through "blending" of biblical phrases, which we'll examine below.

In my analysis, the entire Book of Mormon consists of blending of identifiable sources.

1. The King James Bible.

Soon after the Book of Mormon was published in 1830, skeptics noticed it had many similarities to the Bible, including entire passages copied nearly verbatim from Isaiah and Matthew, as well as phrases from the Old and New Testament sprinkled throughout the text.

We would expect any book of scripture that originated with ancient Hebrews to share attributes with the Old Testament. Because Lehi left Jerusalem before the Babylonian exile, and because he took the "brass plates" containing the books of Moses and the pre-exhilic law and prophets, we would expect Book of Mormon passages to include material from the Old Testament.

However, much of the Book of Mormon includes terms and phrases from the New Testament (as well as the mostly verbatim Sermon on the Mount material from Matthew). Skeptics claim this is

---

in *Directions for Mormon Studies in the Twenty-First Century*, University of Utah Press, Salt Lake City, 2016: 3.

evidence that the Book of Mormon is not the translation of an ancient source, but instead a modern composition. "The fact that so great a proportion of the whole book being made from quotations from the Bible, a part of which was not written until six hundred years after the pretended period of our author, places the matter beyond controversy, and is conclusive testimony that the author was an infidel."[263]

Believers argue there is no reason why the Lord could not have delivered the same Sermon on the Mount to the Nephites that he gave to his followers in Jerusalem.

Another possibility is that the Nephite text contained teachings similar enough to Matthew that Joseph drew on his mental language bank to render it the way he had memorized it. This could account for the variations from KJV in the Book of Mormon. Similar variations from the KJV are found in the works of Jonathan Edwards and other theologians who misquoted or paraphrased the Bible and whose work Joseph likely read.

Beyond that, though, other passages in the text include bits of New and Old Testament phrases joined together to compose a single verse in the Book of Mormon. Royal Skousen describes this as "blending."

> [Blending] is quite different from a paraphrastic quoting of a single King James passage (or a midrash-like commentary on it). It is as if the translator knows the King James Bible so well that hardly anything can be translated without using biblical phrases and expressions. Thus the Book of Mormon translation is much more than a literal rendition of what was originally on the plates. It is a highly creative translation affected by a thoroughly absorbed knowledge of the King James Bible.[264]

The concept of *blending* is comparable to the concept of *chunking*. In both cases, the author or speaker rearranges terms, phrases and concepts drawn from his/her mental language bank to express his/her thoughts that often have little or nothing to do with the original source.

The blending in the Book of Mormon is fluid. The manuscripts

---

263 https://archive.org/details/mormonismunvaile00howe/page/64.
264 Skousen, *Part 4* (2018): 1031.

show no evidence of trial-and-error dictation or collaboration. And this is exactly how language works in our minds. We formulate thoughts by arranging and rearranging chunks of language we have heard or read elsewhere, converting those chunks into our own unique expressions.

The first example of blending Skousen offers is from Mosiah 18:21, "having their hearts knit together in unity and in love one towards another."

This passage contains the only usage of the term *knit* in the Book of Mormon. The term appears seven times in the KJV. Three of these involve the term *heart(s)*.

Epistle Dedicatory. "is that which hath so bound and firmly *knit* the *hearts* of all Your Majesty's loyal and religious people unto You..."

1 Chronicles 12:17. "If ye become peaceably unto me to help me, mine *heart* shall be *knit* unto you..."

Colossians 2:2. "That *their hearts* might be comforted, being *knit together* in love..."

Skousen demonstrates the blending this way:[265]

Mosiah 18:21	having *their hearts*	*knit together* in unity and	*in love* one towards another
Colossians 2:2	... *their hearts*...	being *knit together*	*in love*

Skousen points out that other writers used similar phrases.

1652, John Clarke, "and had their *hearts knit together* in a more than ordinary bond of love."

1656, Alexander Grosse, "and to have our *hearts knit together* in love."

Of course, both of these authors postdated the 1611 King James Version and the Epistle Dedicatory, so they represent blending of biblical passages themselves.

There is another element of Mosiah 18:21 that has a relationship to a Biblical passage. The phrase "in unity" appears only once in the Book of Mormon and once in the Bible. Psalm 133:1 reads, "Behold, how

265 Skousen, *Part 4* (2018): 1032.

good and how pleasant it is for brethren to dwell together in unity!"

Adding this passage to the blending gives us a more complete accounting for the passage:

Mosiah 18:21	having *their hearts*		*knit together in unity* and	*in love* one towards another
Colossians 2:2	… *their hearts…*	being	*knit together*	*in love*
Psalm 133:1		…dwell	*together in unity*	

Whether he composed the text or translated it, Joseph could have blended Colossians and Psalms subconsciously, by randomly choosing passages from different parts of the Bible, or by coincidence. The combination of Old and New Testament verses is problematic for a literal translation because the Book of Mormon authors presumably had no access to New Testament texts. That's why this is good evidence of both composition and translation. Note, however, that we still must omit much of Colossians and Psalms to make the blending work.

Skousen treats KJV blending as evidence that Joseph did not translate the text.

> It is as if the translator knows the King James Bible so well that hardly anything can be translated without using biblical phrases and expressions… Each example provides an extraordinary demonstration of linguistic gymnastics. Of course, all of this is quite amazing, perhaps even miraculous, if one assumes that Joseph Smith must have been the one responsible for all of this textual manipulation.[266]

Without discounting the spiritual element involved with the translation ("the gift and power of God"), there is a source of blending in the Book of Mormon that Skousen did not consider. That is, the text of the Book of Mormon could blend not only the KJV, but also the writings of prominent Christian theologians such as Jonathan Edwards and James Hervey.

---

266 Skousen, *Part 4* (2018): 1031.

2. 18th century theologians.

As a rule, preachers and theologians quote, paraphrase, and rearrange passages from the Bible. The blending in the Book of Mormon is different, though, in the sense that passages (chunks) of biblical and theological language are used not to borrow authority from the original, but instead to repurpose the chunks for an entirely different document. That distinction is key to understanding how Joseph translated the text.

Let's start with Jonathan Edwards, the "father of American theology."[267] He introduced Colossians 2:2 with his own preface and paraphrased the rest.[268] Separately, he spoke of counsel to live in unity and love one another. His work offers a simpler and cleaner blending than one derived solely from the KJV.

Jonathan Edwards: "and seemed, by their discourse and behavior after public worship, to have their *'hearts knit together in love'* Colossians 2:2." Also: "giving of them counsel, to live *in unity and love one another*, as one that was going from them…"

Combining these quotations, we see a closer fit than the KJV verses, and without the omissions those verses require. Plus, the Edwards phrase starts with a form of the verb *have.*

Mosiah 18:21	having *their hearts*		*knit together* in unity and	*in love*
Colossians 2:2	… *their hearts…*	being	*knit together*	*in love*
Psalm 133:1		… dwell	*together in unity*	
		———		
Mosiah 18:21	having *their hearts*		*knit together* in unity and	*in love*
Edwards	*have their hearts*		*knit together*	*in love*
Edwards			*in unity and*	*love*

To be sure, Edwards used the Bible here, but he did so in chunks,

[267] Wilson (2012): 132.

[268] For the original source, enter search terms at http://edwards.yale.edu/.

putting biblical passages in his own construction to paraphrase rather than directly quote the Bible, much the same way that the Book of Mormon does. Because the original chunks are so diverse, I suggest this blending in the Book of Mormon is not evidence of *copying* from the Bible (or from Edwards) but instead is evidence of *composition* or *translation* from Joseph's mental language bank.

Earlier in this chapter we noted Lucy Mack Smith's observation that Joseph "had never read the Bible through in his life." The evidence in the text suggests that, instead of blending passages directly from the KJV, Joseph may have blended passages from the theologians whose work he read.

Mosiah 18:21 offers a clue. The conclusion of Mosiah 18:21 reads *having their hearts knit together in unity and in love one towards another.* This is close, but not identical to, the conclusion of the Edwards passage—to *live in unity and love one another.*

Mosiah 18:21 is one of three instances in the Book of Mormon of the phrase *one towards another.* The phrase *one towards another* does not appear in the KJV. It is a non-biblical phrase.

But Edwards uses the phrase often. Here are some examples.

"When religion therefore prevails among a people, there will be seen much of a spirit of love *one towards another* amongst them…"

"The love of men *one towards another* oftentimes grows up suddenly…"

"all living in love, studying to promote one another's good, abounding in deeds of righteousness and mercy, apt to forbear with one another, apt to forgive one another, ready to deny themselves one for another, living together like a society of brethren in all Christian and holy behavior *one towards another.*"

While Joseph could have added this phrase to his mental language bank from a variety of sources, Jonathan Edwards is a likely candidate. If we search for similar phrases instead of the exact phrase, we find that the phrase *one toward another* (without the s) appears in the Bible five times, but never in the Book of Mormon. The non-biblical phrase *one towards another* appears in Edwards 76 times.

	KJV Bible	Book of Mormon	Edwards
One **towards** another	0	3	76
One **toward** another	5	0	3

Statistically, we see that Edwards is far more likely to use *towards* than *toward*, but he still uses both. A qualitative analysis suggests a more specific reason for the difference between the Bible and the Book of Mormon, however.

Edwards misquoted the Bible the same way the Book of Mormon does.

One of the biblical passages is 1 Thessalonians 3:12. "And the Lord make you to increase and abound in love *one toward another*, and toward all men, even as we do toward you:"

Jonathan Edwards misquoted the passage this way:

"The Lord make you to increase and abound in love *one towards another*, and towards all men, even as we do toward you."

Another biblical passage is Romans 12:16. "Be of the same mind *one toward another.* Mind not high things, but condescend to men of low estate."

Edwards never quoted this passage from Romans accurately, but twice, he misquoted it in a paraphrase:

(i) "with Brotherly Love be of the same mind *one towards another* in Love serving one another."

(ii) "Here we are exhorted to unanimity, and to be of the same mind *one towards another*, not to mind high things, but to condescend to men of low degree."

In fact, two of the three times Edwards wrote "one toward another" he was misquoting (or paraphrasing) John 13:35.

John 13:35. "By this shall all men know that ye are my disciples, if ye have love one to another."

Edwards. "that particular token of their being the disciples of Christ, viz., of their 'having love one toward another' John 13:35"

Edwards. "Their hearts were full of 'love one toward another' John

13:35."

This example of blending shows both that Mosiah 18:21 is closer to Edwards than to the KJV, and that the last phrase of verse 21 does not appear in the KJV but does appear in Edwards many times—including in his misquotes of Romans 12:16.

This evidence leads me to conclude that Jonathan Edwards is a more likely source for the blending in Mosiah 18:21 than the KJV.

Straight and narrow.

Another example of blending or paraphrasing not only shows the influence of Edwards, but also helps resolve an ongoing debate among believers about how to revise the text.

The non-biblical phrase "straight and narrow" appears four times in the 1830 Book of Mormon. In the 1981 LDS edition, these passages are spelled "strait and narrow," which is also non-biblical, but which reflects the Printer's Manuscript.

Strait (straight) and narrow				
	OM	PM	1830	1981
1 Ne. 8:20	Strait	strait	straight	strait
2 Ne. 31:18	-	strait	straight	strait
2 Ne. 31:19	-	strait	straight	strait
Hel. 3:29	-	strait	straight	strait

Royal Skousen identified "27 instances of the words *strait* and *straight* in the text of the Book of Mormon… we have two different words here, strait 'narrow' and straight 'not crooked'.[269]

Because "strait" and "straight" are homophones, Joseph could have intended either word when he dictated the text. The extant OM and the PM spell it *strait* everywhere except in Alma 50:8, where the OM spells it *straight* but the PM spells it *strait.* Yet in every case, the 1830 edition spells it *straight*, presumably because Gilbert, the typesetter, chose that

[269] Skousen, *Part 6*, p. 543.

spelling.

Most scholars assume these Book of Mormon passages are a blending or paraphrase of Matthew 7:13-14.

> *Enter* ye *in at the strait* gate: for wide is the gate, and broad is the way, that leadeth to destruction and many there be which go in thereat: Because *strait* is the gate, and *narrow* is the way, *which leadeth unto life*, and few there be that find it.

3 Nephi 14:14 and 27:33 are word-for-word replications of Matt. 7:14 (except 27:33 uses *that leads to life*).

Although Book of Mormon passages share specific elements with Matthew 7:14, Matthew 7 lacks the references to *eternal life* and the repeated phrase *straight and narrow.*

Consider 2 Nephi 31:18 (1830 ed.): "And then are ye in this *straight* and *narrow* path *which leads to eternal life,*" and Jacob 6:11 "*enter in at the straight gate*, and continue in the *way* which is *narrow*, until ye shall obtain *eternal life.*"

This blending or paraphrasing could be attributed to Joseph Smith's creativity with the KJV, but there is another possibility. In the early 1700s,[270] Jonathan Edwards paraphrased Matt. 7:14 this way: "Matthew 7:14(a). 'The entrance *into eternal life* is *a strait and narrow passage.*'"

Here we have two key Book of Mormon elements not found in Matt. 7:14: *eternal life* and *strait and narrow.*

In another publication, Edwards wrote: "it would above all things tend to the conviction of deluded hypocrites, and to prevent the delusion of those whose hearts were never brought to a thorough compliance with *the strait and narrow way which leads to life*; it would tend to deliver us from innumerable perplexities."

Another: "There are but two that are competitors for the possession of us, either Christ or the devil. There are but two paths, one of which you are to travel in, either *the strait and narrow way* that *leads*

[270] Based on a database search, Edwards appears to have been the first to use the phrase *strait and narrow* in a religious sense.

to life, or the broad way to destruction."

Another: "The cross is the way to the crown. A way of having the cross is *the strait and narrow way* that *leads to life*."

These examples from Edwards are closer to the Book of Mormon than is Matthew 7:14. They suggest that Joseph Smith, when translating the Nephite plates, relied upon his familiarity with Edwards' work, drawn from Joseph's own mental language bank.

The OM and PM used *strait*, the way Edwards spelled it. However, Edwards did spell the phrase "straight and narrow way" one time:

> Some men spend their whole lives, from their infancy to their dying day, in going down the broad way to destruction. They don't only draw nearer to hell, but they every day grow more and more ripe for destruction; they are more assimilated to the inhabitants of the infernal world. While others press forward in the *straight and narrow way* to life, towards Zion, and laboriously travel up the hill against the inclination and tendency of the flesh, these run with a swift career down towards the valley of eternal death, towards the lake of fire, towards the bottomless pit.

Because Edwards spelled the phrase both ways, maybe he considered the alternate spellings to be synonyms. Webster's 1828 dictionary equates the two words, although it also notes some different connotations.

LDS scholars have debated which of these two terms is correct.[271] Paul Y. Hoskisson cited ancient Hebrew as determinative.

> In the ten verses in the Book of Mormon where the words *strai(gh)t* and *narrow* occur in the same verse, there are compelling reasons in nine of them to read *strait*, while the tenth verse could take either reading. Reading *strait* in the expressions *strait gate and narrow way* and *strait and narrow way* preserves the poetic parallelism, accords with a biblical Hebrew analog, and

---

[271] A summary of the debate is in "Is the Path to Eternal Life 'Strait' or "Straight'?", Book of Mormon Central KnoWhy #456, online at https://knowhy.bookofmormoncentral.org/knowhy/is-the-path-to-eternal-life-strait-or-straight.

is consistent within the Book of Mormon.[272]

Hoskisson's observation about Hebrew parallelism also supports Edwards as the source of this phrase, although not as he intended. Wilson H. Kimnach wrote of Edwards that he

> seems always to have liked juxtaposition of opposites and other varieties of parallelism, and was inclined to render the pattern of juxtaposition in such an outline form... Most obvious and simple, yet frequently most important and effective, are the rhythmic devices of repetition and parallelism. Indeed, it has been remarked that "repetition of words and constructions is the essence of his style." Faust and Johnson, Selections, p. cxii.[273]

Careful readers of the last Edwards quotation above may have noticed two non-biblical Book of Mormon phrases: *ripe for destruction* (used two times by Edwards) and *press forward* (used four times by Edwards). These are among hundreds of examples of non-biblical Book of Mormon phrases that appear in Edwards' works.

Let's examine *press forward* and *pressing forward.* The term *pressing* does not appear in the KJV. *Press* as a verb appears in the New Testament twice. We'll consider these verses after looking at the Book of Mormon verses.

> "And I saw numberless concourses of people, many of whom were *pressing forward*, that they might obtain the path which led unto the tree by which I stood." (1 Nephi 8:21)
> "And it came to pass that I beheld others *pressing forward*, and they came forth and caught hold of the end of the rod of iron; and they did *press forward* through the mist of darkness, clinging to the rod of iron, even until

---

[272] Paul Y. Hoskisson, "Straightening Things Out: The Use of *Strait* and *Straight* in the Book of Mormon," *Journal of Book of Mormon Studies* 12, no. 2 (2003): 66.

[273] Wilson H. Kimnach, General Introduction to the Sermons: Jonathan Edwards' Art of Prophesying, *Sermons and Discourses 1720-1723* (WJE Online Vol. 10), online at https://bit.ly/2RwFrf3.

they did come forth and partake of the fruit of the tree." (1 Nephi 8:24)
"But, to be short in writing, behold, he saw other multitudes *pressing forward*; and they came and caught hold of the end of the rod of iron; and they did *press* their way *forward*, continually holding fast to the rod of iron, until they came forth and fell down and partook of the fruit of the tree." (1 Nephi 8:30)
"Wherefore, ye must *press forward* with a steadfastness in Christ, having a perfect brightness of hope, and a love of God and of all men. Wherefore, if ye shall *press forward*, feasting upon the word of Christ, and endure to the end, behold, thus saith the Father: Ye shall have eternal life." (2 Nephi 31:20)
"And it came to pass that he fought with Lib, in which Lib did smite upon his arm that he was wounded; nevertheless, the army of Coriantumr did *press forward* upon Lib, that he fled to the borders upon the seashore." (Ether 14:12)

As mentioned above, the verb *press* does appear twice in the New Testament. In Luke 8:45 Peter said, "Master, the multitude throng thee and *press* thee." This has little if any relevance to the Book of Mormon passages.

Paul writes in Philippians 3:14, "I *press toward* the mark for the prize of the high calling of God in Christ Jesus." This verse may be a candidate for a blending or paraphrase in the Book of Mormon verses. *Toward* sounds and looks similar to *forward* and suggests movement ahead. It doesn't work as a synonym in the Book of Mormon passages, however.

Paul's "I press toward" requires a direct object; i.e., the mark. Nephi's "ye must press forward" has no direct object.

Once again, we find a likely answer in a paraphrase from Jonathan Edwards. He used the phrase *press forward* over 50 times, but once in particular, he used it specifically in connection with Philippians 3:14, replacing Paul's "I press toward" with "You must *press forward* towards."

> The work of a Christian is compared to running, and wrestling, and fighting, and those exercises which require the greatest labor. *You must press forward* "towards the mark for the prize of the high calling" (Philippians 3:14). And in all, you must go forth in God's strength.

It's an easy step to go from Edwards' "*you must press forward* towards the mark" to Nephi's "*you must press forward* with a steadfastness in Christ."

Other examples from Edwards' work evoke images and concepts that appear in the Book of Mormon passages above.

> "'Tis the cold, carnal, and lifeless that are most likely to be blind and walk in *darkness*. Let us *press forward* and not stay and hinder the good work."
> "*hold on* till we are arrived to the place we seek. We ought not to be discouraged with the length and difficulties of the way, as the children of Israel were, and be for turning back again. All our thought and design should be to get along; we should be engaged and resolved to *press forward* till we arrive."
>
> "The consideration of it should stir you up effectually to *press forward* , and still to *press forward*, and to resolve to *press forward* forever, let what will be in [the] way; and hearken to no temptation; and never look back, or in any wise slacken or abate your endeavors, as long as you live, but if possible increase more and more."

One additional side note. 2 Nephi 31:20 contains the non-biblical phrase "endure to the end." That phrase appears in eight Book of Mormon passages (and two sections of the D&C).

The KJV has one passage in Matthew 24:13, repeated in Mark 13:13, that uses a similar phrase. "But he that shall *endure unto the end*, the same shall be saved."[274]

What accounts for the difference between "endure *to* the end" and "endure *unto* the end?" (Note: there is one Book of Mormon instance of "endure unto the end" in 1 Nephi 13:37.)

Once again, we can look at a misquote from Jonathan Edwards as a possible answer.

"They have a spirit to suffer the ill will and hatred of men. Matthew

---

[274] Joseph Smith—Matthew changes the original Matthew 24:13 to read 24:11 "But he that remaineth steadfast and is not overcome, the same shall be saved."

10:22, 'Ye shall be hated of all men for my name's sake: but he that shall *endure to the end*, shall be saved.'"

"how few are saved out of the mass of mankind, and particularly how few are sincere, of professing Christians, that never wither away but *endure to the end*, and how, of the many that are called, few are chosen."

Readers may notice "*many are called but few are chosen*" which is common to both Matthew 22:14 and D&C 121:34, 40.

The Edwards phrase *wither away* in the quotation above is another non-biblical Book of Mormon term in Jacob 5:7.

We could continue with many more examples, but the purpose of this chapter is to introduce the proposition that Edwards and other similar sources played a major role in preparing Joseph Smith to translate the text the way he did.

I mentioned above that Roger Terry identified a list of non-biblical terms that he thinks Joseph could not have known. This was one of his four objections to the idea that Joseph translated the Nephite records into his own language.

> Joseph's ability to craft (or dictate) an extensive and intricate English document was rather limited. According to [Brant] Gardner's theory, Joseph was receiving ideas that he had to formulate in coherent English sentences. But Joseph's formal language abilities at this point in his life were limited. According to his wife, Emma, he could not even pronounce names like Sarah and had to spell them out. According to Gardner's theory, "As the generation of language moved from Joseph's subconscious to his conscious awareness, it accessed Joseph's available vocabulary and grammar" (p. 308). I would argue, however, that the vocabulary of the Book of Mormon was far beyond Joseph's "available vocabulary" in 1829. Consider the following list of words that appear in the Book of Mormon, most of which do not appear in the Bible: *abhorrence, abridgment, affrighted, anxiety, arraigned, breastwork, cimeters, commencement, condescension, consignation, delightsome, depravity, derangement, discernible, disposition, distinguished, embassy, encompassed, enumerated, frenzied, hinderment, ignominious, impenetrable, iniquitous, insensibility, interposition, loftiness, management, nothingness, overbearance, petition,*

> *priestcraft, probationary, proclamation, provocation, regulation, relinquished, repugnant, scantiness, serviceable, stratagem, typifying, unquenchable,* and *unwearyingness.* I find it unlikely that Joseph would be able to conjure up this level of vocabulary and use these words correctly in context as he dictated the Book of Mormon.

With five exceptions, all of these words appear in the writings of Jonathan Edwards and/or the local Palmyra newspapers. They are a subgroup of the 750 non-biblical Book of Mormon words that were used by Edwards and the other sources I've described in this chapter. The exceptions are *cimeters, consignation* (a legal term in continual use since the 1600s), *hinderment* (although *hinder* is common in Edwards), *overbearance* (Edwards uses *overbear*), and *unwearyingness* (although Edwards uses *weary* hundreds of times). Apart from *cimeters*, these words can be explained as derivatives of words readers of Edwards would be familiar with.

There are several other examples of the influence of Jonathan Edwards. For example, the Book of Mormon frequently refers to "types," a non-biblical phrase meaning "the characteristics of … people, things, or groups that share particular characteristics."[275]

Alma 25:15. "Yea, and they did keep the law of Moses; for it was expedient that they should keep the law of Moses as yet, for it was not all fulfilled. But notwithstanding the law of Moses, they did look forward to the coming of Christ, considering that the law of Moses was a **type** of his coming, and believing that they must keep those outward performances until the time that he should be revealed unto them."

Jonathan Edwards wrote extensively about such types from the Old Testament. For example, he explained that

> [t]here are a multitude of things in the Old Testament which the church then did not understand, but were reserved to be unfolded to the Christian church, such as the most of their **types and shadows** and prophecies, which make up the greatest part of the Old Testament; so I believe there are many now thus veiled, that remain to [be] discovered by the church in

---

[275] https://dictionary.cambridge.org/us/dictionary/english/type

the coming glorious times."

Absent direct evidence that Joseph read Edwards' writings, we can only make inferences from the written record.

We should note that, at least by 1838, Joseph Smith had a substantial personal library. In November 1838, William E. McLellin ransacked Joseph's home. Joseph sued to recover five hundred dollars. A Declaration related to the suit includes this description:

> Joseph Smith jr. complains of William E McCleland [McLellin] being in the custody of &c of a plea of trespass on the case.2 For that whereas the said plaintiff heretofore to wit: on the first day of September in the year of our Lord eighteen hundred and thirty eight at the county of Clay aforesaid was lawfully possessed as of his own property of certain goods and chattles to wit of **a Library of books part of which were in the Hebrew and Syriac languages the balance in the English language treating of history, divinty and general Literature**...[276] (emphasis added)

Because there is no known itemized list of these books, we'll never know whether they included books that were on sale in Palmyra before Joseph moved to Kirtland, but the possibility exists.

---

3. Local Newspapers.

In his 1832 history, Joseph wrote that "At about the age of twelve years my mind become seriously impressed with regard to the all-important concerns for the welfare of my immortal Soul."

Joseph turned twelve in December 1817, right about the time when the family moved to Palmyra. Perhaps the move prompted his concerns for the welfare of his "immortal Soul."

A newspaper titled the *Palmyra Register* began publication in Palmyra on November 26, 1817. A worker there, Orsamus Turner, reported that

---

[276] Declaration, circa 6 March 1839 [JS v. McLellin], https://www.josephsmithpapers.org/paper-summary/declaration-circa-6-march-1839-js-v-mclellin/1

Joseph Smith, Jr., came into the printing shop every week to get the newspaper for his father.[277] The newspaper featured articles on local, national and international news, but also contained sermons and morality lessons with themes common to the Book of Mormon. Articles in the newspaper include numerous non-biblical terms and phrases found in the Book of Mormon. My book *Infinite Goodness* has a lengthy list. Here are two examples.

Alma 30:16 "Ye look forward and say, that ye see a remission of your sins. But behold, it is the effects of a phrensied mind; and this *derangement* of your minds comes because of the traditions of your fathers, which lead you away into a belief of things which are not so."

The *Palmyra Register*, Sep 29, 1818, included an article with this passage:

..."some symptoms of *mental derangement*, and has not since been heard of..."

The *Palmyra Register*, Mar 17, 1819

"The prisoner it is said has been *deranged in his mind* for almost eighteen months past."

Moroni 9:18 "O the *depravity* of my people! They are without order and without mercy."

The *Palmyra Register*, April 7, 1818

"Yes--all the sickness & waste & poverty and war, that ardent spirits produce, may be traced to one general cause; viz. the deep & desperate *depravity* of the heart. If the heart was right, everything else would be right."

---

4. Pseudo-biblical books.

Previously in this chapter we looked at *The Late War* as an example of a pseudo-biblical book—a book written in the "biblical," "scriptural," or "ancient historical style"—which some skeptics

[277] Orsamus Turner, *History of the Pioneer Settlement* (Rochester, NY 1851): 214. Available online at https://archive.org/details/historyofpioneer00turn/page/214

propose as a source of the Book of Mormon. As we observed there, any such evidence of composition is also evidence of translation. *The Late War* stands out among the pseudo-biblical books because of the timely subject matter (the War of 1812), the design similarities to the Book of Mormon, and the endorsement of Samuel Mitchill, but other pseudo-biblical books also include non-biblical material that appears in the Book of Mormon.

These books describe history (mostly wars) using language designed to emulate the KJV:

The First Book of Napoleon—the story of Napoleon

The American Revolution – the Revolutionary War

The First Book of the American Chronicles of the Times—the Revolutionary War

The Late War – War of 1812

The non-biblical Book of Mormon terms found in these books involve primarily military affairs. Such terms are rarely used in the works of Jonathan Edwards and other theologians, except in a metaphorical sense. These pseudo-biblical books use the terms to describe actual military adventures, just as the terms are used in the Book of Mormon.

For example, the non-biblical term *stratagem* appears 7 times in the 1830 Book of Mormon. (It also appears in Joseph Smith-History 1:60.) The term does not appear in *The Late War*, but it does appear in *The American Revolution*: "The Indians retreat with precipitation (occasioned by a Stratagem of Arnold) and the British follow their example."

Other non-biblical military terms found in these books and the Book of Mormon include *surrounded, encompassed, rehearsed* (as in relating an account), *strong and mighty* (referring to men instead of God), *send a proclamation* (KJV only makes a proclamation), *interposition, distinguished, sally, provisions, commencement, weighed down, countenance, and encircle.*

---

5. Family sources.

Probably the best-known example of family influences are the dreams of Joseph Smith Sr., related by Lucy Mack Smith in her *History*, that parallel Lehi's dream in the Book of Mormon. Lucy's history also includes a poem written by her sister Lovisa in 1794 that includes the term *adieu*,[278] a term that skeptics have focused on as an anachronism in the text.

In her *History*, Lucy included extracts of her father's brief autobiography.[279] However, Solomon Mack's full history[280] includes references to *redeeming love*, a non-biblical Book of Mormon term.

Alma 5:9 says, "they did sing redeeming love." Alma 26:13 recounts how "they are brought to sing redeeming love."

Solomon Mack included a series of hymns, two of which contain the lines "where we shall sing redeeming love"[281] and "there we'll sing redeeming love."[282]

Summary of the language of the translation

I propose that Joseph Smith was prepared from a young age for his role as prophet and translator of the ancient Nephite plates. The documentary evidence shows a close connection between the vocabulary in the text and the vocabulary of Joseph's specific environment, which I infer became part of his mental language bank from which he drew when he translated the plates.

I've identified five categories of sources that can account for most of the vocabulary, including terms and phrases, that appear in the Book of Mormon. The primary influences are the KJV and the works of Jonathan Edwards, but the writings of other theologians, Palmyra

---

278 See Lucy Mack Smith, *History*, 1845, p. 19, online at https://www.josephsmithpapers.org/paper-summary/lucy-mack-smith-history-1845/26

279 Lucy Mack Smith, History, 1845, p. 2, online at https://www.josephsmithpapers.org/paper-summary/lucy-mack-smith-history-1845/8

280 Solomon Mack, *A Narraitve [sic] of the Life of Solomon Mack* (Windsor, VT, 1811), available online at https://archive.org/details/narraitvesicofli00mack/page/n1

281 Solomon Mack, p. 40.

282 Solomon Mack, p. 42.

newspapers, books written in the "biblical style" such as *The Late War*, and the influence of Joseph's family are evident in the text.

This evidence supports both the composition and translation origins of the Book of Mormon. By themselves, composition and translation would generate similar if not identical evidence; i.e., the outcome of Joseph's work-product would reflect his own mental language bank whether he composed or translated the text.

Choosing between composition and translation involves assessing several factors. A detailed analysis is beyond the scope of this chapter, but here are three elements to consider.

Joseph's opportunity to compose vs translate. Given the three months in which Joseph dictated the manuscript (not including the Book of Mosiah), composition would be virtually impossible. Some suggest Joseph worked out the story long in advance.[283] Evidence along those lines is also consistent with his having been tutored by Moroni and Nephi for years before he got the plates. But knowing a story in advance and dictating it coherently in a short time are two different things. By comparison, translating an existing text would presumably proceed relatively quickly once Joseph understood the Nephite characters and learned how to rely on the Spirit to guide his word choice and placement. Translation also explains how Joseph could begin each session where he left off, especially if he ended previous sessions at the bottom of a particular plate.

Transliteration. As discussed above, instances of transliteration indicate translation instead of composition.

Artifacts of ancient writing. Some scholars have identified poetic word forms such as chiasmus in the text. While some Christian authors, including Jonathan Edwards, discussed Hebrew patterns and parallelisms, and even employed them in their own writings, the examples in the Book of Mormon are more complex and intricate. The Book of Mormon text also includes references to formal legal and religious practices known in ancient times but not in the early 1800s.

283 E.g., William L. Davis, *Visions in a Seer Stone: Joseph Smith and the Making of the Book of Mormon* (University of North Carolina Press, Chapel Hill, NC, 2020).

Some of these are so subtle they are unlikely to have been intentional.[284]

Unique doctrines. Although the text contains nonbiblical language common to Jonathan Edwards and the other sources, the Book of Mormon does not adopt their theology. This is important evidence of translation because the theological implications of the Book of Mormon are so profound. It is implausible that young Joseph Smith, in his first production, could so effectively engage theologically with Jonathan Edwards. By comparison, Mormon's abridgment of a thousand years of Jewish/Christian history could plausibly provide such answers and insights.

Identification of two separate civilizations. The societies described in the Book of Mormon differ significantly from the Moundbuilder legends that were contemporary with Joseph Smith, but the Book of Mormon account fits the archaeological record developed after 1830. The chronology of the Jaredites and the Nephites corresponds to the chronology of the ancient Adena and Hopewell civilizations in North America. These separate civilizations were not identified until after the Book of Mormon was published. The Adena culture is "named after the estate in Ohio where its remnants were first discovered in 1901."[285] The name Hopewell was coined in 1891 because certain earthworks in Ohio were owned by a family named Hopewell.

———

The evidence cited by skeptics to justify their claims that Joseph composed the Book of Mormon is equally compatible with Joseph's own claim that he translated ancient plates. Ultimately, one's acceptance or rejection of the divine authenticity of the Book of Mormon is a matter of faith.

---

[284] Several examples are in Don Bradley's *The Lost 116 Pages: Reconstructing the Book of Mormon's Missing Stories* (Greg Kofford Books, Salt Lake City, UT, 2019).

[285] https://www.encyclopedia.com/humanities/encyclopedias-almanacs-transcripts-and-maps/mound-builders-poverty-point-adena-hopewell-and-mississippian-cultures

12. Conclusion

The historical record regarding the translation of the Book of Mormon includes around 200 statements from a wide variety of participants, observers, and people who heard one thing or another. The record contains apparent contradictions that can be reconciled as the product of a demonstration and defense against the Spalding theory.

In this book I've explained why I have settled on Synthesis #3 as the most plausible explanation for the evidence, based on my assessment of credibility, reliability, opportunity, bias, motive—all the normal factors that bear on the believability of someone's testimony.

You will reach your own conclusions.

Another approach is the hierarchy of reliability, based on theological considerations. The following table categorizes the major witnesses/observers in descending order of reliability.

	Translation of:			
Evidence ranked by reliability	116 pages		BofM	
	SITH	UT	SITH	UT
Moroni (Ether, JS-H, Letter IV, etc.)				
D&C (Sections 3, 6, 7, 10, 11, 14, 17)				
Joseph Smith, Jr.				
Oliver Cowdery				
Lucy Mack Smith				
Martin Harris				
David Whitmer				
Emma Smith				
Mormonism Unvailed statements				
Elizabeth Cowdery				
William E. McLellin				

Those who accept the scriptures as divine would by definition consider them reliable. Next would be Joseph Smith and Oliver Cowdery, the principle participants in the translation.

The table shows that the most reliable evidence concurred that the U&T—the Nephite interpreters—were provided by the Lord specifically for the purpose of translating the plates. They also concur that Joseph used the U&T to translate the plates.

Lucy may have been an observer of some events, but her primary role was as Joseph's confidant. In her account she quotes his statements about the U&T.

The 1834 book *Mormonism Unvailed* described two alternative methods of translation: SITH and U&T. David Whitmer, Martin Harris, and Emma Smith also distinguished SITH from U&T.

Mormonism Unvailed also described the Spalding theory. Those who sought to bolster faith in the divine authenticity of the Book of Mormon were cognizant of the claims of the Spalding theory. Their efforts to refute the Spalding theory apparently led them to emphasize SITH, based on the demonstration Joseph conducted.

———

All of this leaves you, the reader, with lots of options.

Choose wisely.

———

Appendix 1: Table of translation accounts

The following overview of the accounts of the translation process is reprinted here with permission of its author, Scott Woodward.

Accounts of the Translation Process

It is difficult to assess with certainty the exact process, or processes, by which Joseph Smith translated the Book of Mormon. The few extant first-hand accounts from those who participated directly in the translation process provide little insight into the granular details of the process. Those accounts which provide the greatest amount of detail are typically 2nd hand accounts obtained from interviews or other interactions with eyewitnesses. The 2nd-hand nature of these accounts introduces the question of reporter accuracy when reporting the details of the account. Did the interviewer/note-taker record the details correctly? There is a desire to trust those accounts which were written by non-participants, such as Joseph Knight and David Whitmer, who were close to, but not directly involved in, the translation process. In several such accounts, however, the details contradict one another. For instance, were the plates present while Joseph translated, or were they not? Did he ever look at the plates, or did he always look into his hat? Did Joseph put the Nephite interpreters (the spectacles) into his hat, or did he only place his seer stone into the hat? Perhaps Joseph did some of all of these things at different times in the process, thus accounting for the contradictions. It's hard to assess with certainty. Then there are also many accounts from antagonistic sources which provide additional details. But should we trust those who are reporting the translation process with the intent to ridicule it? All of these hazards notwithstanding, several accounts are provided below for the reader to consider for themselves and to draw their own conclusions about the translation process.

https://scottwoodward.org/bookofmormon_translationprocess_accounts.html

The table is adapted from scottwoodward.org, with added scriptural material, edited content and links.

There are similarities in wording among these accounts that suggest some are derivative of others. For example, in 1834 Oliver Cowdery wrote "**Day after day** I continued, uninterrupted, to write from his mouth, as he translated." This account was republished in the 1840 *Millennial Star*, the 1841 *Gospel Reflector*, the 1841 *Times and Seasons*, and the 1844 *The Prophet*, so it was widely known.

The 1879 "Last Testimony of Sister Emma" says she, too, wrote while Joseph dictated "**day after day**."

Accounts by three individuals—Elizabeth Cowdery (Oliver's wife), David Whitmer, and William Smith—use the identical phrase "exclude the light." Each account mentions the "manner" of the translation and says Joseph "placed" or "put" the translation instrument into a hat.

The only extant version of Elizabeth's account is a copy made by William E. McLellin, who was visiting Elizabeth and her brother David Whitmer when he made the copy.

1870 Elizabeth Ann Whitmer Cowdery, as reported by William E. McLellin.	1883 William Smith	1887 David Whitmer.
I cheerfully certify that I was familiar with the **manner** of Joseph Smith's **translating the book of Mormon**…	The **manner in which** this was done was by	I will now give you a description of the **manner in which** the **Book of Mormon was translated**.
He **would place the director in his hat**, and then **place his face in his hat**, so as **to exclude the light,** and then [read?] to his scribe the words (he said) as they **appeared** before him."	looking into the Urim and Thummim, which was **placed in a hat to exclude the light**, (the plates lying near by covered up), and reading off the translation, which **appeared** in the stone by the power of God.	Joseph Smith **would put the seer stone into a hat,** and **put his face in the hat,** drawing it closely around his face **to exclude the light;** and in the darkness the spiritual light would shine.

Elizabeth was fourteen years old in 1829 when Joseph and Oliver translated the plates of Nephi at her father's home in Fayette. She married Oliver three years later, in December 1832.

Forty-one years later, in 1870, William E. McLellin was visiting Elizabeth's brother David Whitmer in Richmond, Missouri. Elizabeth was also there and she purportedly showed McLellin an affidavit she had made regarding her statement about the translation. McLellin's copy is the only extant version of her affidavit, and there are no other known statements from her. Elizabeth died in January 1892.

McLellin insisted that Joseph never used the U&T to translate the Book of Mormon. His opinion could have been based partly on Elizabeth's account and conversations with David, but he may also have influenced their statements. He quoted the affidavit in a letter he wrote claiming that "it never was Urim nor Thummim."

One wonders what the original purpose of the affidavit was. McLellin's excerpt lacks context, but the part of the affidavit omitted in the table above suggests Elizabeth was trying to refute the Spalding theory.

> He translated the most of it at my Father's house. I often sat by and saw and heard them translate and write for hours together. Joseph never had a curtain drawn between him and his scribe while he was translating.

Without the Spalding context, Elizabeth's emphasis that there was no "curtain drawn between them" is superfluous.

David's account specifically responded to the Spalding theory, as we discussed in Chapter 8. William Smith, as we discussed in Chapter 5, also had the Spalding theory in mind.

None of these statements indicate what words Joseph dictated. Elizabeth's affidavit referred only to "his scribe" instead of Oliver by name, which leaves open the possibility that she observed the demonstration David described.

An anomaly in Elizabeth's account is her claim that Joseph translated *most* of the Book of Mormon at her father's house in Fayette. However, the translation of the plates of Nephi in Fayette consisted of only 153 pages out of 588 pages of the entire book.

One significant difference among these accounts is the nomenclature for the translation instrument. Elizabeth's affidavit referred to "the director," an apparent allusion to Alma 37:21, 24, which originally mentioned *directors* (before the 1920 edition changed the wording to *interpreters).* Her future husband, Oliver Cowdery, always said Joseph used the Nephite *interpreters* (the Urim and Thummim), as described in Mosiah and Ether.

William said Joseph "translated them [the golden plates] by means of the Urim and Thummim, (which he obtained with the plates), and the power of God." This tracks with Joseph's own terminology. William was not present for any of the translation, unless he was among the family members who observed the demonstration at the Whitmer home.

David referred to the "seer stone," as he usually did after 1870.

The similarities between Elizabeth's account and those of William and David could be coincidences. All three could have a common earlier source. They could be the natural consequence of these individuals reminiscing together at some point.

For David and William, the Spalding theory was an important issue to address. That suggests that Elizabeth, too, may have been motivated to refute the Spalding theory. David and Elizabeth were together when Elizabeth showed McLellin her affidavit in 1870. Emma Smith's letter in which she claimed Joseph used a stone after the 116 pages were lost was dated March 27, 1870. There are no extant accounts about the seer stone from Emma or David prior to 1870.

As I read the various accounts, it is apparent to me that Joseph, Oliver and Lucy Mack Smith related consistent accounts that were closer in time to the translation. Others related inconsistent accounts much later in time. When considered in light of the desire to refute the Spalding theory, these later accounts make sense to me.

See what you think.

Table of Accounts of the Translation

1st Hand Accounts	
Source	***Method***
1. Lucy Mack Smith *(mother of Joseph Smith, Jr.)* **1827 [recorded in 1844-5]** Mother said he do not be uneasy all is right see here Said he I have got the key I knew not what he meant but took the article in my hands and upon after examing it <*> <(*with no covering but a silk handkerchief)> <found> that it consisted of 2 smooth < 3 cornered diamonds set in glass and the glass was set in silver bows> con[n]ected with each other in the same way that old fashioned spectacles are made… https://www.josephsmithpapers.org/paper-summary/lucy-mack-smith-history-1844-1845/61 The thing which spoke of it had that Joseph termed a Key was indeed nothing more nor less than **a urim and Thummim** by which the angel manifested those things to <him> that were shown him in vision by the which also he could at any time ascertain the approach of danger Either to himself or the record and for this cause he kept these things constantly about his person. https://www.josephsmithpapers.org/paper-summary/lucy-mack-smith-history-1844-1845/69	Description of Urim and Thummim ——— could ascertain danger
2. Joseph Smith (*Translator*) **1828.** Martin Harris returned again to my house about the twelfth of April, eighteen hundred and twenty eight, and commenced writing for me, while **I translated from the plates**, which we continued until the fourteenth of June following, by which time he had written one hundred and sixteen pages of manuscript on foolscap paper. Some time after Mr. Harris had begun to write for me he began to teaze me to give him liberty to carry the writings home and shew them, and desired of me that **I would enquire of the Lord through the Urim and Thummim if he might not do so. I did enquire,** and the answer was that he must not… in the mean time while Martin Harris was	***Method*** By means of the Urim and Thummim ——— Sight and power to translate

gone with the writings, I went to visit my father's family at Manchester. I continued there for a short season and then returned to my place in Pennsylvania. Immediately after my return home I was walking out a little distance when behold the former heavenly messenger appeared and **handed to me the Urim and Thummim again, (for it had been taken from me** in consequence of my having wearied the Lord in asking for the privilege of letting Martin Harris take the writings which he lost by transgression,) and **I enquired of the Lord through them** and obtained the following revelation:

[D&C 3] Revelation to Joseph Smith, Jr. given July, 1828, concerning certain manuscripts on the first part of the book of Mormon, which had been taken from the possession of Martin Harris.

3 [current verse 8]. **Behold, you have been intrusted with these things,** but how strict were your commandments; and remember, also, the promises which were made to you…

5 [current verse 12]. And when thou deliveredst up **that which God had given thee sight and power to translate,** thou deliveredst up that which was sacred, into the hands of a wicked man… and this is the reason that **thou hast lost thy privileges for a season**, for thou hast suffered the counsel of thy director to be trampled upon from the beginning.

6 [current verse 16]. Nevertheless my work shall go forth, for, inasmuch as the knowledge of a Saviour has come unto the world, through the testimony of the Jews, even so shall the knowledge of a Saviour come unto my people… **and for this very purpose are these plates preserved which contain these records,** that the promises of the Lord might be fulfilled, which he made to his people;

Also published in the *Times and Seasons*:
https://www.josephsmithpapers.org/paper-summary/times-and-seasons-16-may-1842/4

3. Joseph Smith (*Translator*) **March 1829 [D&C 5].** … as my servant Martin Harris has desired a witness at my hand, that you, my servant Joseph Smith, jr. **have got the plates of which you have testified and borne record that you have received of me…** I the Lord am God, and **have given these things unto you**, my servant Joseph Smith, jr. and have commanded you that **you shall stand as a witness of these things**, and I have caused you that you should enter into a covenant with me that **you should not show them except to those persons to whom I command you**; and you have no power over them except I grant it unto you. And **you have a gift to translate the plates**; and this is the first gift that I bestowed upon you… Verily I say unto you, that wo shall come unto the inhabitants of the earth if they will not hearken unto my words: for hereafter you shall be ordained and go forth and **deliver my words** unto the children of men. Behold if they will not believe my words, they would not believe you, my servant Joseph, if it were possible that you could **show them all these things** which I have committed unto you…. 3 Behold verily, I say unto you, **I have reserved those things which I have entrusted unto you**, my servant Joseph, for a wise purpose in me, and it shall be made known unto future generations; but **this generation shall have my word through you**; in addition to your testimony the testimony of three of my servants, whom I shall call and ordain, **unto whom I will show these things**: and they shall go forth with **my words that are given through you**, yea, they shall know of a surety that these things are true: for from heaven will I declare it unto them: I will give them power that **they may behold and view these things as they are; and to none else will I grant this power, to receive this same testimony**, among this generation, in this, the beginning of the rising up, and the coming forth of my church out of the wilderness—clear as the moon and fair as the sun, and terrible as an army with banners. And the testimony of three witnesses will I send forth of my word;	***Method*** Gift to translate the plates

4 And now I command you, my servant Joseph, to repent and walk more uprightly before me, and yield to the persuasions of men no more… 5 …if he [Harris] will bow down before me, and humble himself in mighty prayer and faith, in the sincerity of his heart, then will **I grant unto him a view of the things which he desires to see.** And then he shall say unto the people of this generation, behold **I have seen the things which the Lord has shown unto Joseph Smith, jr.** and I know of a surety that they are true, for **I have seen them: for they have been shown unto me by the power of God and not of man.** And I the Lord command him, my servant Martin Harris, that he shall say no more unto them concerning these things, except he shall **say I have seen them, and they have been shown unto me by the power of God:** and these are the words which he shall say. But if he deny this he will break the covenant which he has before covenanted with me, and behold he is condemned. And now except he humble himself and acknowledge unto me the things that he has done which are wrong, and covenant with me that he will keep my commandments, and exercise faith in me, behold, I say unto him, he shall have no such views; for I will grant unto him no views of the things which I have spoken. And if this be the case I command you, my servant Joseph, that you shall say unto him, that he shall do no more, nor trouble me any more concerning this matter. 6 And if this be the case, behold I say unto thee Joseph, **when thou hast translated a few more pages thou shalt stop for a season, even until I command thee again: then thou mayest translate again.** And except thou do this, behold thou shalt have no more gift, and I will take away the things which I have intrusted with thee. https://www.josephsmithpapers.org/paper-summary/doctrine-and-covenants-1835/166	

4. Joseph Smith (*Translator*) **April 1829. [D&C 6]** Introduction: Revelation given to Joseph Smith the Prophet and Oliver Cowdery, at Harmony, Pennsylvania, April 1829. Oliver Cowdery began his labors as scribe in the translation of the Book of Mormon, April 7, 1829. He had already received a divine manifestation of the truth of the Prophet's testimony respecting the plates on which was engraved the Book of Mormon record. **The Prophet inquired of the Lord through the Urim and Thummim and received this response.** … 10 Behold thou hast a gift, and blessed art thou because of thy gift. Remember it is sacred and cometh from above— 11 And **if thou wilt inquire, thou shalt know mysteries** which are great and marvelous; therefore thou shalt **exercise thy gift, that thou mayest find out mysteries**, that thou mayest bring many to the knowledge of the truth, yea, convince them of the error of their ways. 12 **Make not thy gift known** unto any save it be those who are of thy faith. Trifle not with sacred things. 15 Behold, thou knowest that **thou hast inquired of me and I did enlighten thy mind**; and now I tell thee these things that thou mayest know that **thou hast been enlightened by the Spirit of truth**; 16 Yea, I tell thee, that thou mayest know that there is none else save God that knowest thy thoughts and the intents of thy heart. 17 I tell thee these things as a witness unto thee—that **the words or the work which thou hast been writing are true**. 25 And, behold, **I grant unto you a gift, if you desire of me, to translate, even as my servant Joseph**. 26 Verily, verily, I say unto you, that there are records which contain much of my gospel, which have been kept back because of the wickedness of the people; 27 And now I command you, that if you have good desires—a desire to lay up treasures for yourself in heaven—then **shall you assist in bringing to light, with your gift, those parts of my scriptures which have**	***Method*** Through the Urim and Thummim ——— Gift to translate

been hidden because of iniquity. 28 And now, behold, I give unto you, and also unto my servant Joseph, **the keys of this gift, which shall bring to light this ministry**; and in the mouth of two or three witnesses shall every word be established. https://www.lds.org/scriptures/dc-testament/dc/6?lang=eng	
5. Joseph Smith (*Translator*) **April 1829. [D&C 7]** Introduction: Revelation given to Joseph Smith the Prophet and Oliver Cowdery, at Harmony, Pennsylvania, April 1829, **when they inquired through the Urim and Thummim** as to whether John, the beloved disciple, tarried in the flesh or had died. The revelation is a translated version of the record made on parchment by John and hidden up by himself. https://www.lds.org/scriptures/dc-testament/dc/7?lang=eng	***Method*** Through the Urim and Thummim
6. Joseph Smith (*Translator*) **April 1829. [D&C 8]** A Revelation to Oliver [Cowdery] he being desirous to know whether the Lord would grant him **the gift of Translation** given in Harmony Susquehannah Pennsylvania. Oliver Verily Verily I say unto you that as Shuredly as the Lord liveth which is your God & your Redeemer even so shure shall ye receive a knowledge of whatsoever things ye shall ask with an honest heart believeing that ye Shall receive, a knowledge concerning **the engraveings of old Records which are ancient** which contain those parts of my Scriptures **of which hath been spoken by the manifestation of my Spirit** yea Behold **I will tell you in your mind & in your heart by the Holy Ghost** which Shall come upon you & which shall dwell in your heart now Behold **this is the spirit of Revelation** Behold this is the spirit by which Moses brought the children of Israel through the red Sea on dry ground therefore **this is thy gift** apply unto it & blessed art thou for [it] shall deliver you out of the hands of your	***Method*** in your mind and in your heart ——— Spirit of revelation ——— Through the sprout, rod, gift of Aaron

enemies when if it were not so they would sley thee & bring thy soul to distruction

O remember these words & keep my commandments remember **this is thy gift**

———

A. [Revelation Book 1] now this is not all for **thou hast another gift which is the gift of working with the sprout**

Behold it hath told you things

Behold t**here is no other power save God that can cause this thing of Nature to work in your hands for it is the work of God** & therefore **whatsoever ye shall ask to tell you by that means that will he grant unto you that ye shall know**

B. [Book of Commandments 1835] Now this is not all, **for you have another gift, which is the gift of working with the rod:**

behold it has told you things:

behold **there is no other power save God, that can cause this rod of nature, to work in your hands, for it is the work of God;** and therefore **whatsoever you shall ask me to tell you by that means, that will I grant unto you, that you shall know.**

C. [Doctrine and Covenants, current] 6 Now this is not all thy gift; **for you have another gift, which is the gift of Aaron;**

behold, it has told you many things;

7 Behold, there is no other power, save the power of God, that can cause this gift of Aaron to be with you.

8 Therefore, doubt not, for it is the gift of God; and you shall hold it in your hands, and do marvelous works; and no power shall be able to take it away out of your hands, for it is the work of God.

9 And, therefore, **whatsoever you shall ask me to tell you by that means, that will I grant unto you, and you shall have knowledge concerning it.**

———

remember that without faith ye can do nothing trifle not with these things do not ask for that which ye had not ought ask that ye may know the mysteries of God & that **ye may Translate [and receive knowledge from] all those ancient Records which have been hid up which are Sacred** & according to your faith shall it be done unto you Behold it is I that have spoken it & I am the same which spake unto you from the begining amen Revelation Book 1 https://www.josephsmithpapers.org/paper-summary/revelation-book-1/6 Book of Commandments https://www.josephsmithpapers.org/paper-summary/book-of-commandments-1833/23 Doctrine and Covenants https://www.lds.org/scriptures/dc-testament/dc/8?lang=eng	
7. Joseph Smith (*Translator*) **April 1829. [D&C 9]** A Revelation to Oliver [Cowdery] he was disrous [desirous] to know the reason **why he could not Translate** <&> thus said the Lord unto him Recd. in harmony Susquehannah County Pennsylvania Behol[d] I say unto you my Son that **because ye did not Translate** according to that which ye desired of me & did commence again to write for my servent Joseph even so I would that ye Should **continue until ye have finished this Record which I have entrusted unto you** & then Behold **other Records have I that I will give unto you power that ye may assist to Translate** be patient my Son for it is wisdom in me & **it is not expedient that ye should translate** at this time Behold this is the work which ye are called to do is to write for my Servent & Behold it is **because that ye did not continue as**	***Method*** study it out in your mind and ask Bosom shall burn within you ——— Given from God

ye commenced when ye commenced to Translate that I have taken away this privilege from you do not murmer my Son for it is wisdom in me that I have dealt with you after this manner Behold ye have not understood **ye have Supposed that I would give it unto you when ye took no thought save it was to ask me** **but Behold I say unto you that ye must study it out in your mind then ye must ask me if it be right & if it is right I will cause that your bosom shall burn within you therefore ye shall feel that it is right** but if it be not right ye shall have no such feelings but ye shall have stupor of thought that shall cause you to forget the thing which is wrong there **ye cannot wriete that which is sacred save it be given unto you** [end of page, continuing with D&C] **from me**. 10 Now, **if you had known this you could have translated**; nevertheless, it is not expedient that you should translate now. 11 Behold, it was expedient when you commenced; **but you feared**, and the time is past, and it is not expedient now; 12 For, do you not behold that **I have given unto my servant Joseph sufficient strength**, whereby it is made up? And neither of you have I condemned. 13 Do this thing which I have commanded you, and you shall prosper. Be faithful, and yield to no temptation. 14 Stand fast in the work wherewith I have called you, and a hair of your head shall not be lost, and you shall be lifted up at the last day. Amen. Revelation Book 1 https://www.josephsmithpapers.org/paper-summary/revelation-book-1/8 D&C https://www.lds.org/scriptures/dc-testament/dc/9?lang=eng	

8. Joseph Smith (*Translator*) **Summer 1828-May 1829 [D&C 10].** 1 Now, behold, I say unto you, that because you delivered up those writings which you had **power given unto you to translate by the means of the Urim and Thummim**, into the hands of a wicked man, you have lost them. 2 And you also **lost your gift at the same time, and your mind became darkened**. 3 Nevertheless, **it is now restored unto you again**; therefore see that you are faithful and **continue on unto the finishing of the remainder of the work of translation as you have begun**. 4 Do not run faster or labor more than you **have strength and means provided to enable you to translate**; but be diligent unto the end… 7 And for this cause I said that he is a wicked man, for he has sought to take away **the things wherewith you have been entrusted**; and he has also sought to destroy **your gift**…. 15 For behold, he has put it into their hearts to get thee to **tempt the Lord thy God, in asking to translate it over again**. 16 And then, behold, they say and think in their hearts—We will see if God has **given him power to translate; if so, he will also give him power again**; 17 And if God giveth him power again, or **if he translates again, or, in other words, if he bringeth forth the same words**, behold, we have the same with us, and we have altered them; 18 Therefore they will not agree, and we will say that he has lied in his words, and that he has no gift, and that he has no power… 29 Now, behold, they have altered these words, because Satan saith unto them: He hath deceived you—and thus he flattereth them away to do iniquity, to get thee to tempt the Lord thy God. 30 Behold, I say unto you, that **you shall not translate again those words which have gone forth out of your hands**;	***Method*** translate by means of the Urim and Thummim ——— Translate the engravings on the plates of Nephi

31 For, behold, they shall not accomplish their evil designs in lying against those words. For, behold, **if you should bring forth the same words they will say that you have lied and that you have pretended to translate**, but that you have contradicted yourself.

32 And, behold, they will publish this, and Satan will harden the hearts of the people to stir them up to anger against you, that they will not believe my words…

38 And now, verily I say unto you, that **an account of those things that you have written**, which have gone out of your hands, **is engraven upon the plates of Nephi**;

39 Yea, and you remember it was said in those writings that a more particular account was given of these things **upon the plates of Nephi**.

40 And now, because **the account which is engraven upon the plates of Nephi** is more particular concerning the things which, in my wisdom, I would bring to the knowledge of the people in this account—

41 Therefore, **you shall translate the engravings which are on the plates of Nephi, down even till you come to the reign of king Benjamin, or until you come to that which you have translated, which you have retained**;

42 And behold, **you shall publish it as the record of Nephi**; and thus I will confound those who have altered my words….

44 Behold, they have only got a part, or **an abridgment of the account of Nephi**.

45 Behold, **there are many things engraven upon the plates of Nephi** which do throw greater views upon my gospel; therefore, it is wisdom in me that **you should translate this first part of the engravings of Nephi, and send forth in this work**.

46 And, behold, **all the remainder of this work** does contain all those parts of my gospel which my holy prophets, yea, and also my disciples, desired in their prayers should come forth unto this people.

47 And I said unto them, that it should be granted unto them according to their faith in their prayers;

48 Yea, and this was their faith—that my gospel, which

I gave unto them that they might preach in their days, might come unto their brethren the Lamanites, and also all that had become Lamanites because of their dissensions. 49 Now, this is not all—their faith in their prayers was that **this gospel should be made known also, if it were possible that other nations should possess this land**; 50 And thus they did leave a blessing upon this land in their prayers, that whosoever should believe in this gospel in this land might have eternal life; 51 Yea, that it might be free unto all of whatsoever nation, kindred, tongue, or people they may be. 52 And now, behold, according to their faith in their prayers **will I bring this part of my gospel to the knowledge of my people. Behold, I do not bring it to destroy that which they have received, but to build it up**.... 62 Yea, and I will also bring to light my gospel which was ministered unto them, and, behold, **they shall not deny that which you have received, but they shall build it up, and shall bring to light the true points of my doctrine**, yea, and the only doctrine which is in me. 63 And this I do that I may establish my gospel, that there may not be so much contention; yea, Satan doth stir up the hearts of the people to contention concerning the points of my doctrine; and **in these things they do err, for they do wrest the scriptures and do not understand them**. https://www.lds.org/scriptures/dc-testament/dc/10?lang=eng	
9. Joseph Smith (*Prophet*) **1829-June.** **[D&C 14-16]** Introduction. [D&C 14] and the two following (sections 15 and 16) were given in answer to an inquiry through the Urim and Thummim. **[D&C 17]** Introduction. Revelation given through Joseph Smith the Prophet to Oliver Cowdery, David Whitmer, and Martin Harris, at Fayette, New York, June 1829, prior to their viewing the engraved plates that contained the Book of Mormon record. Joseph and his	***Method*** answer through the Urim and Thummim

scribe, Oliver Cowdery, had learned from the translation of the Book of Mormon plates that three special witnesses would be designated (see Ether 5:2–4; 2 Nephi 11:3; 27:12). Oliver Cowdery, David Whitmer, and Martin Harris were moved upon by an inspired desire to be the three special witnesses. The Prophet inquired of the Lord, and this revelation was given in answer **through the Urim and Thummim**. 1 Behold, I say unto you, that you must rely upon my word, which if you do with full purpose of heart, you shall have **a view of the plates**, and also of the breastplate, the sword of Laban, the **Urim and Thummim, which were given to the brother of Jared upon the mount**, when he talked with the Lord face to face, and the miraculous directors which were given to Lehi while in the wilderness, on the borders of the Red Sea. 2 And it is by your faith that you shall obtain a view of them, even by that faith which was had by the prophets of old... 5 And ye shall testify that you have seen them, even as my servant Joseph Smith, Jun., has seen them; for it is by my power that he has seen them, and it is because he had faith. 6 And **he has translated the book**, even that part which I have commanded him, and as your Lord and your God liveth it is true. https://www.lds.org/scriptures/dc-testament/dc/17.1?lang=eng&clang=eng#p1	
10. Joseph Smith (*Translator*) **1829.** I would inform you that **I translated, by the gift and power of God**, and caused to be written, one hundred and sixteen pages, the which I took from the Book of Lehi, which was an account abridged from the plates of Lehi, by the hand of Mormon; (Preface to the Book of Mormon, circa August 1829) https://www.josephsmithpapers.org/paper-summary/preface-to-book-of-mormon-circa-august-1829/1)	***Method*** Gift and power of God.
11. Joseph Smith (*Prophet*)	***Method***

1830-April **[D&C 20]** 8 And gave him **power from on high, by the means which were before prepared, to translate the Book of Mormon**; 9 Which contains a record of a fallen people, and the fulness of the gospel of Jesus Christ to the Gentiles and to the Jews also; 10 Which was given by inspiration, and is confirmed to others by the ministering of angels, and is declared unto the world by them—11 Proving to the world that the holy scriptures are true, and that God does inspire men and call them to his holy work in this age and generation, as well as in generations of old;.	Power from on high, by means which were before prepared.
12. Joseph Smith (*Translator*) **1832**. [Martin Harris] returned to me [from New York] and gave them to <me to> translate and I said [I] cannot for I am not learned but **the Lord had prepared spectacles for to read the Book therefore I commenced translating the characters** and thus the Prop[h]icy of Isaiah was fulfilled. (History, circa Summer 1832) https://www.josephsmithpapers.org/paper-summary/history-circa-summer-1832/5	***Method*** Used spectacles which the Lord had prepared.
13. Joseph Smith (*Translator*) **1833**. The Book of Mormon is a record of the forefathers of our western tribes of Indians; having been found through the ministration of an holy angel, and **translated into our own language by the gift and power of God**. (Letter to Noah C. Saxton, 4 January 1833) https://www.josephsmithpapers.org/paper-summary/letter-to-noah-c-saxton-4-january-1833/4	***Method*** Gift and power of God.
14. Joseph Smith (*Translator*) **1835**. [The Angel told me] that **the Urim and Thumim, was hid up with the record, and that God would give me power to translate it, with the assistance of this instrument**.... The Angel told me, that the reason why I could not obtain the plates at this time [1823], was because I was under transgression, but to come again in one year from that time. I did so but did not obtain them, also the third and	***Method*** With the assistance of the Urim and Thummim by the gift and power of God.

the fourth year the last of which time **I obtained them, and translated them into <the> english language by the gift and power of God** and have been preaching it ever since. (Interview, 9 November 1835) https://www.josephsmithpapers.org/paper-summary/conversations-with-robert-matthews-9-11-november-1835/4	
15. Joseph Smith (*Translator*) **1838**. How, and where did you obtain the book of Mormon? Moroni, the person who deposited the plates, from whence the book of Mormon was translated, in a hill in Manchester, Ontario County, New York, being dead; and raised again therefrom, appeared unto me, and told me where they were, and gave me directions how to obtain them. I obtained them, and **the Urim and Thummim with them, by the means of which, I translated the plates**; and thus came the Book of Mormon. (*Elders' Journal*, July 1838) https://www.josephsmithpapers.org/paper-summary/elders-journal-july-1838/10	***Method*** Translated plates by the means of the Urim and Thummim.
16. Joseph Smith (*Translator*) **1842**. These records were engraven on plates which had the appearance of gold, each plate was six inches wide and eight inches long, and not quite so thick as common tin. They were filled with engravings, in Egyptian characters and bound together in a volume as the leaves of a book, with three rings running through the whole. The volume was something near six inches in thickness, a part of which was sealed. The characters on the unsealed part were small, and beautifully engraved. The whole book exhibited many marks of antiquity in its construction, and much skill in the art of engraving. **With the records** was found **a curious instrument, which the ancients called "Urim and Thummim,"** which consisted of **two transparent stones** set in the rim of a bow fastened to a breast plate. **Through the medium of the Urim and Thummim I translated the record by the gift and power of God**. ("Church History," [aka the Wentworth Letter], *Times and Seasons*,	***Method*** Through the medium of the Urim and Thummim.

March 1, 1842) https://www.josephsmithpapers.org/paper-summary/church-history-1-march-1842/2	
17. Joseph Smith (*Translator*) **1842**. **JS-H 1:35**. He [Moroni] said there were two stones in silver bows—and these stones, fastened to a breastplate, constituted what is called **the Urim and Thummim**—deposited with the plates; and the possession and use of these stones were what constituted "seers" in ancient or former times; and that **God had prepared them for the purpose of translating the book**. **42** Again, he told me, that when I got those plates of which he had spoken—for the time that they should be obtained was not yet fulfilled—I should not show them to any person; neither the breastplate **with the Urim and Thummim**; only to those to whom I should be commanded to show them; if I did I should be destroyed…. **62** By this timely aid was I enabled to reach the place of my destination in Pennsylvania; and immediately after my arrival there I commenced copying the characters off the plates. I copied a considerable number of them, and **by means of the Urim and Thummim I translated some of them**, which I did between the time I arrived at the house of my wife's father, in the month of December, and the February following. https://www.lds.org/scriptures/pgp/js-h/1?lang=eng	***Method*** By means of the Urim and Thummim
18. Joseph Smith (*Translator*) **1843**. SIR:—Through the medium of your paper, I wish to correct an error.... The error I speak of, is the definition of the word "MORMON." It has been stated that this word was derived from the Greek word mormo. This is not the case. There was no Greek or Latin upon the plates from which **I, through the grace of God, translated the Book of Mormon**.... Here then the subject is put to silence, for "none other people knoweth our language," [Morm. 9:34] therefore **the Lord, and not man, had to interpret**, after the people were all dead. https://www.josephsmithpapers.org/paper-	***Method*** By the grace of God; the Lord interpreted it.

summary/letter-to-editor-circa-15-may-1843/1	
19. Joseph Smith (*Translator*) **1843, Nov. 13**. [T]he fact is, that **by the power of God I translated the Book of Mormon from hieroglyphics**, the knowledge of which was lost to the world, in which wonderful event I stood alone, an unlearned youth, to combat the worldly wisdom and multiplied ignorance of eighteen centuries, with a new revelation, which (if they would receive the everlasting Gospel,) would open the eyes of more than eight hundred millions of people, and make "plain the old paths," wherein if a man walk in all the ordinances of God blameless, he shall inherit eternal life. (letter, Nov. 13, 1843, in *History, 1838-1856,* Vol. E-1) https://www.josephsmithpapers.org/paper-summary/history-1838-1856-volume-e-1-1-july-1843-30-april-1844/147	***Method*** Translated hieroglyphics by the power of God.
20. Oliver Cowdery (*Scribe*) **1829, Nov. 9**. Now Joseph Smith Jr., certainly was the writer of the work, called the book of Mormon, which was written in ancient Egyptian characters,--which was a dead record to us until translated. **And he, by a gift from God, has translated it into our language**.... This record which gives an account of the first inhabitants of this continent, is engraved on plates, which have the appearance of gold; and they are of very curious workmanship.... And after that which was not sealed, was translated, the book should again be hid-up, unto the Lord, that it might not be destroyed; and come forth again, in the own due time of him, who knows all things unto the children of men. (Letter Oliver H.P. Cowdery to Cornelius, C. Blatchly, Nov. 9, 1829, Gospel Luminary 2, no. 49 (Dec. 10, 1829): 194, in the Juvenile Instructor (blog), August 21, 2012, **https://juvenileinstructor.org/1829-mormon-discovery-brought-to-you-by-guest-erin-jennings/**)	***Method*** Translated ancient Egyptian characters by a gift from God.
21. Oliver Cowdery (*Scribe*) **1834**. On Tuesday the 7th [I] commenced to write the Book of Mormon. These were days never to be forgotten to sit under the sound of a voice dictated by the	***Method*** With the Urim and Thummim, or Interpreters

inspiration of heaven, awakened the utmost gratitude of this bosom! Day after day I continued, uninterrupted, to write from his mouth, as **he translated, with the Urim and Thummim, or, as the Nephites would have said, "Interpreters,"** the history or record called "The book of Mormon." (*Messenger and Advocate*, 1:14) https://www.josephsmithpapers.org/paper-summary/history-1834-1836/49 also in the Pearl of Great Price, Joseph Smith – History, footnote. https://www.lds.org/scriptures/pgp/js-h/1?lang=eng	
22. The Three Witnesses (*Oliver Cowdery, Martin Harris, & David Whitmer*) **1829**. [We], through the grace of God the Father, and our Lord Jesus Christ, have seen the plates which contain this record, which is a record of the people of Nephi, and also of the Lamanites, their brethren, and also of the people of Jared, who came from the tower of which hath been spoken. And we also know that they have **been translated by the gift and power of God**, for his voice hath declared it unto us; wherefore we know of a surety that the work is true. ("Testimony of the Three Witnesses") https://www.lds.org/scriptures/bofm/three?lang=eng	***Method*** By the gift and power of God.
23. Oliver Cowdery (newspaper report) **1831 April 9.** "During the trial it was shown that the Book of Mormon was brought to light by the same magic power by which he pretended to tell fortunes, discover hidden treasures, &c. Oliver Cowdery, one of the three witnesses to the book, testified under oath, that said Smith found with the plates, from which he translated his book, two transparent stones, resembling glass, set in silver bows. **That by looking through these, he was able to read in English, the reformed Egyptian characters, which were engraved on the plates.** So much for the gift and power of God, by which Smith says he translated his book. **Two transparent stones**, undoubtedly of the same properties, and the gift of the same spirit as the one in which he looked to find his neighbor's goods.	***Method*** By looking through the stones he read in English the characters engraved on the plates

("Mormonites," *Evangelical Magazine and Gospel Advocate*, Utica, NY, April 9, 1831.) http://www.sidneyrigdon.com/dbroadhu/NY/miscNYSe.htm#040931	
1870s and later	
24. David Whitmer. After 1870, David Whitmer made many statements about the translation that have been compiled and summarized by L. H. Pearson, Ph.D.. His work is available here: David Whitmer: Man of Contradictions – An Analysis of Statements by David Whitmer on Translation of the Book of Mormon. https://josephsmithfoundation.org/papers/an-analysis-of-statements-by-david-whitmer-on-translation-of-the-book-of-mormon/	
Note: Statements made around 1870 and later appear to have been influenced by William E. McLellin, a harsh opponent of Joseph Smith but a firm believer in the divine authenticity of the Book of Mormon. **25. William E. McLellin.** In 1872, McLellin wrote a letter to Joseph Smith III, President of the RLDS. He challenged Joseph Smith Jr.'s role as prophet. Years earlier, McLellin had affirmed that Joseph used the Urim and Thummim, but he wrote this: **Now all L.D.Sism claims that Joseph Smith translated the Book with Urim and Thummim, when he did not even have or retain the Nephite or Jaredite Interpreters, but translated the entire Book of M. by means of a small stone.** I have certificates to that effect from E. A. Cowdery (Oliver's widow,) Martin Harris, and Emma Bidamon. And I have the testimony of John and David Whitmer. The Urim was never on this Continent. Its use was to inquire and receive the word of the Lord direct. Num 27:21. I Sam 28:6. 30:7. 8. But was never used to translate languages. The Directors or Interpreters seem to have been prepared for the special purpose of interpreting or translating languages, but not to inquire and get revelations from God….	***Method*** by means of a small stone

The Urim was used alone for the purpose of inquiring of God. The Interpreters were used alone for the purpose of interpreting languages. They were not used interchangeably. Now by this we see how all L.D. Saints have been deceived, and believed erroneously in this item. (Larson and Passey, Editors, *The William E. McLellin Papers 1854-1880* (Signature Books (2007), p. 492-3.)	
26. Emma Smith (*in a letter to Emma Pilgrim*) **1870**. …I always feel a peculiar satisfaction in giving all the information on that subject that I can. Now the first that my <husband> translated, was **translated by the use of Urim, and Thummim**, and that was the part that Martin Harris lost, after that **he used a small stone, not exactly, black, but was rather a dark color**, I can not tell whether that account in the Times and Seasons is correct or not because some one stole <all> my books and I have none to refer to at present, if I can find one that has that account I will tell you what is true and what is not. (Emma Smith Bidamon, Nauvoo, IL, to Emma Pilgrim, 27 Mar. 1870, in Vogel, *Early Mormon Documents*, 1:532)	***Method*** 116 pages by Urim and Thummim. The remainder by using a small dark colored stone.
27. David Whitmer (*an observer of the process (?) in his home in Fayette, New York; 1st hand account*) **1881**. My statement was and now is that in translating **he put the stone in his hat** and putting his face in his hat so as to exclude the light and that then the light and **characters appeared in the hat together with the interpretation** which he uttered and was written by the scribe and which was tested at the time as stated. (David Whitmer to the editor, *Kansas City Daily Journal*, June 19, 1881; cited in Cook, *David Whitmer Interviews*, 71-72) https://whitmercollege.com/published/interviews/kansas-city-journal-1881 note	***Method*** Seer stone in a hat. Characters appeared with the interpretation.
28. David Whitmer (*Reported 2nd hand in the St. Louis Republican*) **1884**. The understanding we have about it was that when the book was discovered an angel was present and pointed the place out. In translating from the plates, **Joseph Smith looked through the Urim and**	***Method*** Looked through the Urim and Thummim.

Thummim, consisting of two transparent pebbles set in the rim of a bow, fastened to a breastplate. He dictated by looking through them to his scribes. (*St. Louis Republican*, July 16, 1884; cited in Cook, *David Whitmer Interviews*, 143)	
29. David Whitmer (*interviewed by James H. Hart*) **1884**. "In regard to the translation," said Mr. Whitmer, "it was a laborious work for the weather was very warm, and the days were long and they worked from morning till night. But they were both young and strong and were soon able to complete the work. "The way it was done was thus: Joseph would place the seer-stone in a deep hat, and placing his face close to it, would see, not the stone, but what appeared like an oblong piece of parchment, on which the hieroglyphics would appear, and also the translation in the English language, all appearing in bright luminous letters. Joseph would then read it to Oliver, who would write it down as spoken. Sometimes Joseph could not pronounce the words correctly, having had but little education; and if by any means a mistake was made in the copy, the luminous writing would remain until it was corrected. It sometimes took Oliver several trials to get the right letters to spell correctly some of the more difficult words, but when he had written them correctly, the characters and the interpretation would disappear, and be replaced by other characters and their interpretation. "When the seer-stone was not placed in the hat, no characters or writing could be seen therein, but when so placed then the hieroglyphics would appear as before described. Some represented but one word, or name, some represented several, and some from one to two lines. "Emma, Joseph's wife, came to my father's house a short time after Joseph and Oliver came, and she wrote a little of the translation, my brother Christian wrote some, but Oliver wrote the greater portion of it." James H. Hart, "About the Book of Mormon," *Deseret Evening News*, March 25, 1884.	***Method*** Seer stone in a deep hat, saw a piece of parchment with English translation in bright luminous letters, corrected spelling.
30. David Whitmer (*Reported 2nd hand in the Chicago*	***Method***

Tribune) **1885**. Each time before resuming the work all present would kneel in prayer and invoke the Divine blessing on the proceeding. After prayer Smith would sit on one side of a table and the amanuenses, in turn as they became tired, on the other. Those present and not actively engaged in the work seated themselves around the room and then the work began. After **affixing the magical spectacles to his eyes, Smith would take the plates and translate the characters one at a time**. The graven characters would appear in succession to the seer, and directly under the character, when **viewed through the glasses**, would be the translation in English. ("The Book of Mormon;" *Chicago Tribune*, December 17, 1885, 3. The Tribune correspondent visited and interviewed Whitmer on December 15, 1885, at Whitmer's home in Richmond, Missouri) https://en.wikisource.org/wiki/Chicago_Daily_Tribune,_December_17,_1885	Affixed the spectacles to his eyes. Looked "through the glasses" at the plates and translated one character at a time.
31. David Whitmer *(Reported 2nd hand in the Chicago Tribune)* **1885**. In order to give privacy to the proceeding a blanket, which served as a portiere, was stretched across the family living room **to shelter the translators and the plates from the eyes of any who might call at the house while the work was in progress**. This, Mr. Whitmer says, was the only use made of the blanket, and it was not for the purpose of concealing the plates or the translator from the eyes of the amanuensis. In fact, Smith was at no time hidden from his collaborators, and the translation was performed in the presence of not only the persons mentioned, but of the entire Whitmer household and several of Smith's relatives besides. ("The Book of Mormon;" *Chicago Tribune*, December 17, 1885, 3. The Tribune correspondent visited and interviewed Whitmer on December 15, 1885, at Whitmer's home in Richmond, Missouri) https://en.wikisource.org/wiki/Chicago_Daily_Tribune,_December_17,_1885	***Method*** A privacy blanket was used only to shield the translator and scribes from those who might "call at the house."

32. David Whitmer [interviewed by Zenas H. Gurley]	***Method***
1885. Questions asked of David Whitmer at his home in Richmond Ray County Mo – January 14 – 1885 by Elder Z H Gurley [selected questions] 1 – Q Do you know that the plates seen with the Angel (on the table) were real metal, did you touch them? Ans – We did not touch nor handle the plates. 2 – Q Was the table literal wood; or was the whole a vision such as often occurs in dreams? Ans – The table had the appearance of literal wood as shown in the vision, in the glory of God. 3 – Q Did you see the Urim and Thummim, what was it? Ans – I saw the "Interpreters" in the holy vision, They looked like whitish stones put in the rim of a bow, looked like spectacles only much larger. 9 Q. Who was the Angel that showed the plates to you and Cowdery and have these plates been seen since? Ans – I do not know as no name was given. I have never seen the plates since. 20 Q. Did Joseph use his "peep stone" to finish up the translation? If so why? Ans – He used a stone called a "Seer stone," the "Interpreters" having been taken away from him because of transgression. 21 Q. Had you seen the plates at anytime before the Angel showed them to you? Ans – No. 25 Q. Were you present during any of the time of translation, if so, state how it was done. Ans – The "Interpreters" were taken away from Joseph after he allowed Martin Harris to carry away the 116 pages of Mx—of the Book of Mormon as a punishment, but he was allowed to go on and translate by the use of a "Seer stone" which he had, and which he placed in a hat into which he buried his face, stating to me and others that the original character appeared upon parchment and under it the translation in English, which enabled him to read it	Seer stone in a hat. Parchment appeared with ancient writing and under it, the interpretation in English

readily.

While Brother Whitmer was too feeble to write much, being unable to write the answers to the foregoing 25 questions in person—Yet it was with his consent and in his presence that I wrote and corrected them, as they appear here.

Jan. 21—1885. Z.H.Gurley

Gurley Collection, LDS Church Archives

Included in Cook, *David Whitmer Interviews*, 152-158.

1887. [The Eight Witnesses] are known to be reliable, and though after publishing this testimony they were widely separated in the earth, and in after years somewhat divided in spiritual faith, in their convictions of the gospel, yet they never denied this testimony; nor did they ever contradict it, but iterated and reiterated the same till death; than which no better proof could be offered of their competency according to the rules of evidence…

It would be very proper here to inquire after the Urim and Thummim; for of all instruments used in times past in the service of God, perhaps none are clothed with greater mystery and obscurity, and none endowed (if the term be permitted) with greater power. The Hebrew word Thummim--Tummim--means perfection, "symbolic figures in the high priest's breastplate." And the Hebrew word Urim means lights, "mentioned along with Thummim, as something in the high priest's breastplate that gave an oracular response."--Young's Analytical Concordance. See also Exodus 28:30; Leviticus 8:8; Numbers 27:21; Deuteronomy [Deuteronomy] 33:8; 1 Samuel 28:6; Ezra 2:63; Nehemiah 7:65.

Dr. Robinson in his Bible Encyclopedia says:--

"URIM AND THUMMIM, light and perfection, or doctrine and judgment, is supposed to have been an ornament in the high priest's habit, which was consulted as an oracle upon particular and difficult public questions. Some think it was the precious stones in his breastplate which made known the divine will, by casting an extraordinary lustre. Others assert that they were the words of manifestation and truth, written upon two precious stones, or upon a plate of gold. Various, in fact, are the conjectures upon this subject; and Moses has nowhere spoken of the Urim and Thummim in such terms as to remove the difficulty. When the Urim and Thummim was to be consulted, the high priest put on his robes; and, going into the holy place, stood before the curtain that separated the holy place from the most holy place; and then, turning his face directly toward the ark and the mercy-seat, upon which the divine presence rested, he proposed what he wanted to be resolved upon; and directly behind him, at some distance without the holy place, stood the person at whose command or entreaty God was consulted; and there, with all humility and devotion, expected the answer. According to Josephus, this oracle ceased about one hundred and twelve years before Christ."

Had the Book of Mormon been translated from "behind a blanket," **as its opponents assert**, it would even then be in harmony with that kind of practice among the high priests, as seen from the above quotation….

Joseph Smith declares that he soon found out why he had received such strict charges from the angel, as "every stratagem that could be invented was resorted to," to get the plates and Urim and Thummim away from him, even endangering his life, **for that reason on the one hand, and still greater on the other--that no person except permitted by command of God should view them. That Joseph had another stone called seers' stone, and "peep stone," is quite certain. This stone was frequently exhibited to different ones and helped to assuage their awful curiosity; but the Urim and Thummim never, unless possibly to Oliver Cowdery who, as early as September 7, 1834, in writing upon this subject testified:--**

"Day after day I continued, uninterruptedly, to write

from his mouth, as he translated, with the Urim and Thummim, or as the Nephites would have said, `Interpreters,' the history, or record, called `The Book of Mormon.'"--See Letter 1.

This agrees with Joseph Smith's account of the translation; and though Joseph lost the Urim and Thummim through transgression, the latter part of June (probably) 1828, yet they were returned to him in July of the same year; by which, according to his statement above, he accomplished by them what was required at his hand, when the heavenly messenger called for them, whereupon he delivered them all up.

Elder David Whitmer's idea was that the translation was made by the seers' stone, as he calls it, not the Interpreters, and Emma Smith's (Bidamon) statement accords with Whitmer as published in *Herald* some years since. The only discrepancy between the statements of the witnesses is that relating to the detail of the translation; and, as shown above, **David and Emma, in the nature of things, did not know just how the Urim and Thummim were used, as they had never seen them.** The reader will please bear in mind that no one was allowed to see either the plates or the Urim and Thummim, except as God commanded. The Eight Witnesses were allowed to see the plates and handle them as shown above; none else.

In January 1885, the writer visited Elder David Whitmer at Richmond, Missouri, and among other questions asked: "Were the plates from which the Book of Mormon was translated in Joseph Smith's possession while translating, and seen and handled by several different persons? If not, where were they? Answer: "I do not know." Question: Did you see the Urim and Thummim? Answer: **"I saw the Interpreters in the holy vision; they looked like whitish stones put in the rim of a bow; looked like spectacles only much larger."** Question: Had you seen the plates at any time before the angel

showed them to you? Answer: "No." Except in the holy vision referred to by Brother Whitmer, the reader may be sure that the Urim and Thummim was never shown to any person, **except possibly to Oliver Cowdery**, as he had desired to translate, and received permission to do so; but he lost the gift, evidently from a lack of faith. (See Supplement, page 14.) Also, Brother Whitmer stated to the writer in 1885, that "Joseph told him" that in the translation "the original characters appeared upon parchment, and under them the translation in English, which enabled him to read it readily." While this is probably correct, or approximately so, it should be taken for just what it purports to be, and goes to show that the theory advanced above is correct, that David, and all others, must depend on Joseph's statements as to how the translation was made. ZENAS H. GURLEY'S ACCOUNT OF THE TESTIMONIES OF WITNESSES OF THE BOOK OF MORMON Source: Zenas H. Gurley, "The Book of Mormon," *Autumn Leaves* 5 (1892):451-54. http://www.boap.org/LDS/Early-Saints/BOM-Witn.html Partially cited in Cook, *David Whitmer Interviews*, 152–58.	
33. David Whitmer (*an observer of the process (?) in his home in Fayette, New York; 1st hand account*) **1887**. I will now give you a description of the manner in which the Book of Mormon was translated. Joseph Smith would **put the seer stone into a hat, and put his face in the hat, drawing it closely around his face to exclude the light; and in the darkness the spiritual light would shine. A piece of something resembling parchment would appear, and on that appeared the writing. One character at a time would appear, and under it was the interpretation in English**. Brother	***Method*** Seer stone in a hat. Parchment appeared with ancient writing and under it, the interpretation in English.

Joseph would read off the English to Oliver Cowdery, who was his principal scribe, and when it was written down and repeated to Brother Joseph to see if it was correct, then it would disappear, and another character with the interpretation would appear. Thus the Book of Mormon was translated by the gift and power of God, and not by any power of man. (p. 12) After the translation of the Book of Mormon was finished, early in the spring of 1830, before April 6th, **Joseph gave the stone to Oliver Cowdery and told me as well as the rest that he was through with it, and he did not use the stone any more.** He said he was through with the work that God had given him the gift to perform, except to preach the gospel. (p. 32) (*An Address to All Believers in Christ*, (1887)) https://archive.org/details/addresstoallbeli00whit/page/12	
2nd Hand Accounts	
34. Jonathan A. Hadley (Printer of a Palmyra newspaper who had spoken to Joseph personally about the coming forth of the plates and the translation process) **1829**. Joseph Smith found the plates "together with a huge pair of Spectacles… By **placing the Spectacles in a hat, and looking into it, Smith could (he said so, at least,) interpret these characters**." ("Golden Bible," *Palmyra (NY) Freeman*, 11 Aug. 1829, [2]; quoted in *The Joseph Smith Papers: Documents, Volume 1*, xxxi). Online version here: http://www.sidneyrigdon.com/dbroadhu/NY/miscNYS1.htm Commentary here: https://www.josephsmithpapers.org/intro/introduction-to-documents-volume-1-july-1828-june-1831?p=1&highlight=golden%20bible#9174354092974015918	***Method*** Spectacles in a hat.
35. Shaker Richard McNemar (a Shaker from Union Village)	***Method*** Looked at the plates through

1830. In late 1830 Oliver Cowdery traveled through the Shaker community of Union Village, Ohio. One Shaker recorded that, while there, Oliver Cowdery explained the translation process as follows: "The engraving being unintelligible to learned & unlearned. there is said to have been in the box with the plates two transparent **stones in the form of spectacles thro which the translator looked on the engraving & afterwards put his face into a hat & the interpretation then flowed into his mind**. which he uttered to the amanuensis who wrote it down." (Goodwillie, "Shaker Richard McNemar," 143; quoted in *The Joseph Smith Papers: Documents, Volume 1*, xxxi-xxxii). https://www.josephsmithpapers.org/intro/introduction-to-documents-volume-1-july-1828-june-1831?p=1&highlight=golden%20bible#9174354092974015918	the spectacles, then looked into his hat.
36. Peter Bauder (*hostile interviewer of Joseph Smith*) **1830**. [Joseph Smith] went, and after the third or fourth time, which was repeated once a year, he obtained a parcel of plate resembling gold, on which were engraved what he did not understand, **only by the aid of a glass which he also obtained with the plate, by which means he was enabled to translate the characters on the plate into English** ... and after he had a part translated, the angel conmanded him to carry the plate into a certain piece of woods, which he did:—the angel took them and carried them to parts unknown to him. https://en.wikisource.org/wiki/Peter_Bauder_interview_with_Joseph_Smith	***Method*** By the aid of a glass.
37. Evangelical Magazine (*hostile magazine report*) **1831**. Oliver Cowdery, one of the three witnesses to the book, testified under oath [during the June 1830 Colesville trials], that said Smith found with the plates, from which he translated his book, **two transparent stones**, resembling glass, set in silver bows. That **by looking through these, he was able to read in English, the reformed Egyptian characters, which were engraved on the plates**. (*Evangelical Magazine and*	***Method*** Looking through two transparent stones. (Suggests that Joseph is looking at the plates)

Gospel Advocate, 9 April 1831. Note: that this is quoted by an unbeliever, in an antagonistic magazine, in a spirit of incredulity adds to the force of Oliver's statement) http://www.olivercowdery.com/smithhome/1877Purp.htm	
38. Illinois Patriot *(Newspaper article)* **Sept 1831.** A Preacher of this sect visited us last Saturday. We heard a part of his lecture, which occupied more than two hours. From account, this sect came into existence a little more than a year since in the following manner, -- A young man about 23 years of age, somewhere in Ontario county, N. Y., was visited by an angel! (here the preacher looked around him apparently to see if the credulity of the people in this enlightened age could be thus imposed on,) who informed him three times in one night that by visiting a certain place in that town he would have revealed to him something of importance. The young man was disturbed, but did not obey the summons until the following day, when the angel again visited him. At the place appointed he found in the earth a box which contained a set of thin plates resembling gold, with Arabic characters inscribed on them. The plates were minutely described as being connected with rings in the shape of the letter D, which facilitated the opening and shutting of the book. The preacher said **he found in the same place two stones, with which he was enabled, by placing them over his eyes and putting his head in a dark corner, to decypher the hieroglyphics on the plates!** -- This we were told was performed to admiration, and now, as the result, we have a book which the speaker informed us was the Mormon Bible -- a book second to no other -- without which the holy bible, he seemed to think, would be of little use. **"The Mormonites," Illinois Patriot, Sept. 16, 1831.** http://www.sidneyrigdon.com/dbroadhu/IL/miscill1.htm#091631	***Method*** Looking through two transparent stones, putting his head in a dark corner.
39. D. Marks *(traveler through Palmyra)* **Circa 1833.** During the time the book of Mormon was in press at Palmyra, I made particular inquiry, and was	***Method*** Spectacles in a hat

assured from respectable authority of the following particulars. That none were allowed to see the plates with Smith pretended to have dug up, except twelve chosen witnesses, and eight of these were connexions of two families: that the golden plates were said to be **engraved in a language that none but Smith could read -- and that an angel gave him a pair of spectacles which he put in a hat and thus read and translated**, while one of the witnesses wrote it down from his mouth. *Morning Star* VII/45, March 7, 1833. http://www.sidneyrigdon.com/dbroadhu/NE/miscMe01.htm#030733.	
40. Joseph Knight (*faithful friend to Joseph Smith*) **Circa 1835-1847**. Now the way he [Joseph Smith] translated was **he put the Urim and Thummim into his hat and darkened his eyes.** Then he would take a sentence and it would appear in bright Roman letters. Then he would tell the writer and he would write it. Then that would go away [and] the next sentence would come, and so on. But if it was not spelled right it would not go away till it was right. So we see, it was marvelous. Thus was the whole translated. ("Joseph Knight's Recollection of Early Mormon History," *BYU Studies*, Vol. 17, No. 1; spelling and grammar modernized) http://boap.org/LDS/Early-Saints/joseph-knigh-rec.html	***Method*** Urim and Thummim in his hat; word-by-word dictation.
41. W.W. Phelps (newspaper article) **1833.** "The Book of Mormon… was translated by the gift and Power of God, by an unlearned man, **through the aid of a pair of Interpreters, or spectacles**—(known, perhaps, in ancient days as Teraphim, or **Urim and Thummim**) and while it unfolds the history of the first inhabitants that settled this continent, it, at the same time, brings a oneness to scripture." ("Book of Mormon," *The Evening and the Morning Star*, Jan. 1833, 58.) https://archive.org/details/EveningAndMorningStar18321834/page/n57	***Method*** Gift and power of God; aid of pair of Interpreters, spectacles, or the Urim and Thummim
42. Lucy Mack Smith, interviewed by Henry Caswall	***Method***

1842 The angel of the Lord appeared to him fifteen years since, and shewed him the cave where the original golden plates of the book of Mormon were deposited. He shewed him also **the Urim and Thummim, by which he might understand the meaning of the inscriptions on the plates**, and he shewed him the golden breastplate of the high priesthood. My son received these precious gifts, he interpreted the holy record, and now the believers in that revelation are more than a hundred thousand in number. I have myself seen and handled the golden plates; they are about eight inches long, and six wide; some of them are sealed together and are not to be opened, and some of them are loose. They are all connected by a ring which passes through a hole at the end of each plate, and are covered with letters beautifully engraved. I have seen and felt also the Urim and Thummim. They resemble two large bright diamonds set in a bow like a pair of spectacles. **My son puts these over his eyes when he reads unknown languages, and they enable him to interpret them in English.** I have likewise carried in my hands the sacred breastplate. It is composed of pure gold, and is made to fit the breast very exactly. Henry Caswall, *The City of the Mormons; or, Three Days at Nauvoo*, in 1842 (London: J. G. F. and J. Rivington, 1842), 26–27, online at: https://archive.org/details/cityofmormonsort00casw/page/26	The Urim and Thummim
43. Lucy Mack Smith **1845. [Sept-Nov 1828]** For nearly two months after Joseph returned to his family in Pennsylvania we heard nothing from him; and becoming anxious about him, Mr. Smith [Joseph Smith Sr.] and myself set off to make him a visit. When we came withing [sic] three quarters of a mile of his house, Joseph started to meet us; telling his wife as he left, that "Father and mother were coming." When he met us his countenance wore so pleasant an aspect, that I was convinced he had something agreeable to communicate, in relation to the work in which he was engaged. And when I entered his house the first thing that	***Method*** Translated with the Urim and Thummim

attracted my attention was a red morocco trunk, that set on Emma's bureau; which trunk Joseph shortly informed me, **contained the Urim and Thummim and the plates**. In the evening he gave us the following relation of what had transpired since our separation: "After leaving you' said Joseph, "I returned immediately home; and soon after my travel which, I commenced humbling myself in mighty prayer before the Lord; and, as I was pouring out my soul to God, that, if possible I might obtain mercy at his hands, and be forgiven of all that I had done contrary to his will, an angel stood before me and answered me, saying, that I had sinned in delivering the manuscript into the hands of a wicked man; and, and as I had ventured to become responsible for his faithfulness, I would of necessity have to suffer the consequences of his indiscretion; and **must now give up the Urim and Thummim into his (the angels) hands. This I did as I was directed**. As I handed them to him, he said, 'If you are very jumble and penitent, it may be you will receive them again; if so, it will be on the 22d. of next September.'"... "After the angel left me', said he, "I continued my supplications to God without cessation; and, **on the 22d of September, I had the joy and satisfaction of again receiving the Urim and Thummim; and have commenced translating again**, and Emma writes for me; but the angel said that the Lord would send me a scribe, and <I> trust his promise will be verified. The angel He also seemed pleased with me, **when he gave me back the Urim and Thummim**; and he told me that the Lord loved me, for my faithfulness and humility... https://www.josephsmithpapers.org/paper-summary/lucy-mack-smith-history-1845/142	
44. Lucy Mack Smith **1844-5. [May 1829]** In the mean time Joseph was 150 miles distant and knew naught of the matter except an intimation that was given **through the urim and thumim for as he one morning applied them to his eyes to look upon the record instead of the words of the book**	***Method*** Urim and Thummim applied to his eyes

being given him he was commanded to write a letter to one David Whitmer this man Joseph had never seen but he was instructed to say him that he must come with his team immediately in order to convey Joseph and his family Oliver [Cowdery] back to his house which was 135 miles that they might remain with him there untill the translation should be completed for that an evil designing people were seeking to take away Joseph's life in order to prevent the work of God from going forth among the world. https://www.josephsmithpapers.org/paper-summary/lucy-mack-smith-history-1844-1845/100	
45. Lucy Mack Smith **1845. [May 1829]** Not far from this time, **as Joseph was translating by means of the Urim and Thummim, he received instead of the words of the Book**, a commandment to write a letter to a man by the name of David Whitmer, who lived in Waterloo; requesting him to come immediately with his team, and convey them [3 words illegible] (Joseph & Oliver) to Waterloo; as an evil designing people were seeking to take away his (Joseph's life), in order to prevent the work of God from going forth to the world. https://www.josephsmithpapers.org/paper-summary/lucy-mack-smith-history-1845/156	***Method*** By means of the Urim and Thummim
46. Oliver Cowdery *(Reported by Reuben Miller)* **1848**. [Oliver said:] Friends and brethren my name is Cowdrey, Oliver Cowdrey, In the early history of this church I stood Identified with her. And [was] one in her councils.... I wrote with my own pen the intire book of mormon (Save a few pages) as it fell from the Lips of the prophet [Joseph Smith]. **As he translated <it> by the gift and power of god, By [the] means of the urum and thummim, or as it is called by that book holy Interperters**. I beheld with my eyes. And handled with my hands the gold plates from which it was translated. I also beheld the Interperters. That book is true. Sidney Rigdon did not write it. Mr [Solomon] Spaulding did not write it. I wrote it myself as it fell from the Lips of the prophet.	***Method*** Gift and power of God; by means of the Urim and Thummim, or Interpreters

Richard Lloyd Anderson, "By the Gift and Power of God," *Ensign*, September 1977, online at https://www.churchofjesuschrist.org/study/ensign/1977/09/by-the-gift-and-power-of-god?lang=eng and https://catalog.churchofjesuschrist.org/assets/22222322-f4fe-41e3-aa86-bfc54b94df92/0/16	
47. Oliver Cowdery (Reported by Samuel W. Richards) **1848**. (Reported in 1907) "[Oliver] represented Joseph as sitting at a table with the plates before him, translating them by means of the Urim and Thummim, while he (Oliver) sat beside him writing every word as Joseph spoke them to him. This was done by holding the 'translators' over the hieroglyphics, the translation appearing distinctly on the instrument, which had been touched by the finger of God and dedicated and consecrated for the express purpose of translating languages. Every word was distinctly visible even to every letter; and if Oliver omitted a word or failed to spell a word correctly, the translation remained on the 'interpreter' until it was copied correctly." https://www.lds.org/study/ensign/1977/09/by-the-gift-and-power-of-god?lang=eng **Note:** the differences between this typewritten account and the original handwritten account are discussed in chapter 3.	***Method*** by means of the Urim and Thummim
48. Emma Smith (*Interviewed by Edmund C. Briggs*) **1856**. [Emma Smith said:] When my husband was translating the Book of Mormon, I wrote a part of it, **as he dictated each sentence, word for word**, and when he came to proper names he could not pronounce, or long words, he spelled them out, and while I was writing them, if I made any mistake in spelling, he would stop me and correct my spelling, although it was impossible for him to see how I was writing them down at the time. Even the word *Sarah* he could not pronounce at first, but had to spell it, and I would pronounce it for him. When he stopped for any purpose at any time he would, when he commenced again, begin where he left off	***Method*** Word-by-word dictation; spelling difficult words

without any hesitation, and one time while he was translating he stopped suddenly, pale as a sheet, and said, "Emma, did Jerusalem have walls around it?" When I answered "Yes," he replied "Oh! I was afraid I had been deceived." He had such a limited knowledge of history at that time that he did not even know that Jerusalem was surrounded by walls. (Edmund C. Briggs, "A Visit to Nauvoo in 1856," Journal of History 9 (October 1916): 454. Edmund C. Briggs and Samuel H. Gurley traveled to Nauvoo to visit Joseph Smith III and testify to him of the reorganization of the Church, which had recently occurred in Wisconsin. Briggs and Gurley arrived at the Mansion House in Nauvoo on December 5, 1856, and interviewed Emma Smith Bidamon three days later) http://www.mormonthink.com/files/a-visit-to-nauvoo-in-1856-elder-edmund-c-briggs-Journal-of-History-vol-9-no-2.pdf For a short bio of Joseph Smith III, see https://www.josephsmithjr.org/joseph-smith-jrs-family/joseph-smith-iii-biography/	

49. Martin Harris *(interview with John A. Clark)*	***Method***
[1840] [Martin remarked] that there had been a revelation made to [Joseph Smith] by which he had discovered this sacred deposit, **and two transparent stones, through which, as a sort of spectacles**, he could read the Bible, although the box or ark that contained it, had not yet been opened; and that **by looking through those mysterious stones**, he had transcribed from one of the leaves of this book, the characters which Harris had so carefully wrapped in the package which he was drawing from his pocket. . . . . . . [Joseph] was already in possession of the two transparent stones laid up with the GOLDEN BIBLE, by looking through which he was enabled to read the golden letters on the plates in the box. How he obtained these spectacles without opening the chest, Harris could not tell. But still he had them; and by means of them he could read all the book contained.... The way that Smith made his transcripts and transcriptions for Harris was the following. Although in the same room, a thick curtain or blanket was suspended between them, and Smith concealed behind the blanket, pretended to **look through his spectacles, or transparent stones**, and would then write down or repeat what he saw, which, when repeated aloud, was written down by Harris, who sat on the other side of the suspended blanket. Harris was told that it would arouse the most terrible divine displeasure, if he should attempt to draw near the sacred chest, or look at Smith while engaged in the work of decyphering the mysterious characters. This was Harris's own account of the matter to me. What other measures they afterwards took to transcribe or translate from these metallic plates, I cannot say, as I very soon after this removed to another field of labor where I heard no more of this matter till I learned the Book of Mormon was about being published. John A. Clark, *Gleanings By the Way* (Philadelphia: W. J. and J. K. Simon, 1842), 224, 228, 230-31. https://archive.org/details/gleaningsbyway00clarrich/page/224	plates translated "by looking through" two transparent stones "as a sort of spectacles"

50. Martin Harris *(interview with David B. Dille in 1853)* **[1859]** I know that the plates have been **translated by the gift and power of God**, for his voice declared it unto us; therefore I know of a surety that the work is true. For," continued Mr. Harris, "did I not at one time hold the plates on my knee an hour-and-a-half, whilst in conversation with Joseph, when we went to bury them in the woods, that the enemy might not obtain them? Yes, I did. And as many of the plates as Joseph Smith translated I handled with my hands, plate after plate.["] David B. Dille, "Additional Testimony of Martin Harris (One of the Three Witnesses) to the Coming Forth of the Book of Mormon," *Millennial Star* 21 (August 20, 1859): 545. Dille recorded the undated interview on Sept. 15, 1853, while in England. He said Martin was "about 58 years old" which indicates the interview took place around 1841, since Martin was born in 1783. https://archive.org/details/MStarVol21/page/n559	***Method*** plates translated "by the gift and power of God"
51. Martin Harris *(interview with Tiffany's Monthly)* **[1859]** Joseph did not dig for these plates. They were placed in this way: four stones were set up and covered with a flat stone, oval on the upper side and flat on the bottom. Beneath this was a little platform upon which the plates were laid; and **the two stones set in a bow of silver by means of which the plates were translated**, were found underneath the plates. These plates were seven inches wide by eight inches in length, and were of the thickness of plates of tin; and when piled one above the other, they were altogether about four inches thick; and they were put together on the back by three silver rings, so that they would open like a book. **The two stones set in a bow of silver were about two inches in diameter, perfectly round, and about five-eighths of an inch thick at the centre; but not so thick at the edges where they came into the bow. They were joined by a round bar of silver, about three-eighths of an inch in diameter, and about four inches long, which, with the two stones, would make eight inches. The stones were white, like polished marble, with a**	***Method*** plates translated "by means of" "two stones set in a bow of silver"

few gray streaks. I never dared to look into them by placing them in the hat, because Moses said that "no man could see God and live," and we could see anything we wished by looking into them; and I could not keep the desire to see God out of my mind. And beside, we had a command to let no man look into them, except by the command of God, lest he should "look aught and perish." These plates were usually kept in a cherry box made for that purpose, in the possession of Joseph and myself. **The plates were kept from the sight of the world, and no one, save Oliver Cowdrey, myself, Joseph Smith, jr., and David Whitmer, ever saw them.** Before the Lord showed the plates to me, Joseph wished me to see them. But I refused, unless the Lord should do it. At one time, before the Lord showed them to me, Joseph said I should see them. I asked him, why he would break the commands of the Lord? He said, you have done so much I am afraid you will not believe unless you see them. I replied, "Joseph, I know all about it. The Lord has showed to me ten times more about it than you know."-- Here we inquired of Mr. Harris--How did the Lord show you these things? He replied, "I am forbidden to say anything how the Lord showed them to me, except that by the power of God I have seen them." Mr. Harris continues: I hefted the plates many times, and should think they weighed forty or fifty pounds. "Mormonism—No. II," *Tiffany's Monthly* 5 (May 1859): 163, 165–66. http://boap.org/LDS/Early-Saints/MHarris-2.html https://archive.org/details/threewitnesses/page/n43	
52. Martin Harris (*Interview published in Iowa State Register*) **1870**. Mr. Harris describes the plates as being of thin leaves of gold, measuring seven by eight inches, and weighing altogether, from forty to sixty lbs. **There was also found in the chest, the Urim and Thummim, by means of which the writing upon the plates was translated... By means of the urim and thummim "a pair of large spectacles," as Mr. Harris termed them, the translation was made,** and Mr. Harris claims to	***Method*** By means of the Urim and Thummim – a pair of large spectacles

have written, of the translations as they were given by Smith, "116 solid pages of cap [foolscap]." The remainder was written by others. ("A Witness to the Book of Mormon," *Des Moines Iowa State Register*, August 28, 1870; cited in Vogel, *Early Mormon Documents*, 2:330. http://www.sidneyrigdon.com/dbroadhu/IA/misciow2.htm	
53. Martin Harris (*Reported by Edward Stevenson*) **1881**. Martin Harris related an instance that occurred during the time that he wrote that portion of the translation of the Book of Mormon, which he was favored to write direct from the mouth of the Prophet Joseph Smith. He said that the Prophet possessed a seer stone, by which he was enabled to translate as well as from the Urim and Thummim, and for convenience he then used the seer stone. Martin explained the translating as follows: By aid of the seer stone, sentences would appear and were read by the Prophet and written by Martin, and when finished he would say, "Written," and if correctly written, that sentence would disappear and another appear in its place, but if not written correctly it remained until corrected, so that the translation was just as it was engraven on the plates, precisely in the language then used. . . . Martin said further that the seer stone differed in appearance entirely from the Urim and Thummim that was obtained with the plates, which were two clear stones set in two rims, very much resembled spectacles, only they were larger. Martin said there were not many pages translated while he wrote; after which Oliver Cowdery and others did the writing. Edward Stevenson to the editor, November 30, 1881, *Deseret Evening News*, December 13, 1881, p.4, reporting Harris' Sept. 5, 1870, sermon, also reported by Jenson, below (#56). https://newspapers.lib.utah.edu/details?id=23174102	***Method*** Translated "by aid of the seer stone" as well as "from the Urim and Thummim" [Note: same account as #56 below]
54. Martin Harris (*Interviewed by Simon Smith*) **1884**. He [Martin Harris] also said, "I was Joseph Smith's scribe, and wrote for him a great deal; for he was such a poor writer, and could not even draw up a note of hand as	***Method*** Interpreted them by the Urim and Thummim

his education was so limited. I also wrote for him about one third of the first part of the translation of the plates as **he interpreted them by the Urim and Thummim.** Simon Smith to the editor, April 30, 1884, *Saints' Herald* 31 (May 24, 1884): 324, based on a July 1875 visit.	
55. Martin Harris *(Interviewed by Edward Stevenson)* **1886**. [Martin Harris] also stated that the Prophet translated a portion of the Book of Mormon, with the seer stone in his possession. The stone was placed in a hat that was used for that purpose, and with the aid of this seer stone the Prophet would read sentence by sentence as Martin wrote, and if he made any mistake the sentence would remain before the Prophet until corrected, when another sentence would appear. When they became weary, as it was confining work to translate from the plates of gold, they would go down to the river and throw stones into the water for exercise. Martin on one occasion picked up a stone resembling the one with which they were translating, and on resuming their work Martin placed the false stone in the hat. He said that the Prophet looked quietly for a long time, when he raised his head and said: "Martin, what on earth is the matter, all is dark as Egypt." Martin smiled and the seer discovered that the wrong stone was placed in the hat. When he asked Martin why he had done so he replied, to stop the mouths of fools who had declared that the Prophet knew by heart all that he told him to write, and did not see by the seer stone; when the true stone was placed in the hat, the translation was resumed, as usual. Edward Stevenson, relating what Martin Harris told him during the 1870 journey from Ohio to Utah, in "The Three Witnesses to the Book of Mormon, No. III," *Millennial Star* Vol. 48, No. 25 (June 21, 1886): 389–90. https://contentdm.lib.byu.edu/digital/collection/MStar/id/28210	***Method*** Translated "a portion of the Book of Mormon, with the seer stone in his possession"
56. Martin Harris *(Reported by Andrew Jenson)* **1887**. On Sunday, Sept. 4, 1870, Martin Harris addressed a congregation of Saints in Salt Lake City. He related an	***Method*** Translated "by aid of the seer

incident which occurred during the time that he wrote that portion of the translation of the Book of Mormon which he was favored to write direct from the mouth of the Prophet Joseph Smith, and said that **the Prophet possessed a seer stone, by which he was enabled to translate as well as from the Urim and Thummim, and for convenience he then used the seer stone.** Martin explained the translation as follows: **By aid of the seer stone**, sentences would appear and were read by the Prophet and written by Martin, and when finished he would say, "Written," and if correctly written, that sentence would disappear and another appear in its place; but if not written correctly it remained until corrected, so that the translation was just as it was engraven on the plates, precisely in the language then used. Martin said that after continued translation they would become weary, and would go down to the river and exercise by throwing stones out on the river, etc. While so doing, on one occasion, Martin Harris found a stone very much resembling the one used for translating, and on resuming their labor of translation, he put in place the stone that he had found. He said that the Prophet remained silent, unusually and intently gazing in darkness, no traces of the usual sentences appearing. Much surprised, Joseph excla[i]med, "Martin! What is the matter! All is as dark as Egypt!" Martin's countenance betrayed him, and the Prophet asked Martin why he had done so. Martin said, to stop the mouths of fools, who had told him that the Prophet had learned those sentences and was merely repeating them, etc. Martin said further that **the seer stones differed in appearance entirely from the Urim and Thummim obtained with the plates, which were two clear stones set in two rims, very much resembling spectacles,** only they were larger. Martin said, there were not many pages translated while he wrote, after which Oliver Cowdery and others did the writing. **Andrew Jenson, ed., "The Three Witnesses," *Historical Record* 6 (May 1887): 216–17.**	stone" as well as "from the Urim and Thummim"

57. Martin Harris *(Interviewed by R. W. Alderman)* **1888**. In February, 1852, I was snowbound in a hotel in Mentor, Ohio, all day. Martin Harris was there, and in conversation told me he saw Jo Smith translate the "Book of Mormon," with his peep-stone in his hat. Oliver Cowdery, who had been a school-teacher, wrote it down. Sidney Rigdon, a renegade preacher, was let in during the translation. Rigdon had stolen a manuscript from a printing office in Pittsburgh, Pa., which [Solomon] Spaulding, who had written it in the early part of the century, had left there to be printed, but the printers refused to publish it, but Jo and Rigdon did, as the "Book of Mormon." R.W.Alderman, statement made Dec. 25, 1884, in *Naked Truths about Mormonism* 1 (January 1888), p. 3.	***Method*** Translated "with his peep-stone in his hat"
58. Martin Harris *(as told to Gilbert in 1828)* **1892**. In the fall of 1827. he told us what wonderful discoveries Jo Smith had made, and of his finding plates in a hill in the town of Manchester, (three miles south of Palmyra,)-also found with the plates a large pair of " spectacles," by putting which on his nose and looking at the plates, the spectacles turned the hyroglyphics into good English. The question might be asked here whether Jo or the spectacles was the translator? https://scholarsarchive.byu.edu/cgi/viewcontent.cgi?article=1506&context=jbms	***Method*** Spectacles turned the hieroglyphics on the plates into English
59. Martin Harris *(Interviewed by William Pilkington)* **1934**. I offered my services as a scribe for the Prophet in the work of Translating. Joseph gladly accepted my Offer, it was the 12th day of April 1828, when I commenced to write for the Prophet from this time on until the 14th day of June 1828 Joseph dictated to me from the Plates of Gold as the characters thereon assumed through the Urim and Thummim the forms of Equivelent modern words, which were familiar to the understanding of the Prophet and Seer, from the 12th day of April until the 14th day of June he said he had written One Hundred and Sixteen pages Foolscap of the translation he said at this period of the Translation a	***Method*** Characters assumed through the Urim and Thummim the forms of modern words

circumstance happened that he was the cause of the One Hundred and Sixteen pages that he had written being lost, and never was found. . . . . . . Joseph was told in a Revelation to retranslate from the Small Plates of Nephi, and thereby thawart [thwart] the plans of wicked men, but I was never permitted to write for the Prophet anymore. Oliver Cowdery did all the rest of the writing. . . . William Pilkington, Affidavit, April 3, 1934, Church Archives; cited in Vogel, *Early Mormon Documents*, 2:353–56.	
60. Martin Harris (*Interviewed by Simon Smith*) **1875**. He [Martin Harris] also said, "I was Joseph Smith's scribe, and wrote for him a great deal; for he was such a poor writer, and could not even draw up a note of hand as his education was so limited. I also wrote for him about one third of the first part of the translation of the plates as **he interpreted them by the Urim and Thummim**. And I paid the printer about three thousand dollars for the first edition of the Book of Mormon." (Simon Smith to the editor, April 30, 1884, *Saints' Herald* 31 (May 24, 1884): 324. Smith visited Martin Harris in Clarkston, Utah, in July 1875)	***Method*** By the Urim and Thummim
61. Edward Stevenson (*interviewer*) **1881**. Martin Harris related an incident that occurred during the time that he wrote that portion of the translation of the Book of Mormon which he was favored to write direct from the mouth of the Prophet Joseph Smith. He said that the Prophet possessed a seer stone, by which he was enabled to translate as well as from the Urim and Thummim, and for convenience he then used the seer stone. Martin explained the translating as follows: By aid of the seer stone, sentences would appear and were read by the Prophet and written by Martin, and when finished he would say, "Written," and if correctly written, that sentence would disappear and another appear in its place, but if not written correctly it remained until corrected, so that the translation was just as it was engraven on the plates, precisely in the language then used.	***Method*** Joseph used the seer stone as well as the Urim and Thummim.

Martin said that after continued translation they would become weary and would go down to the river and exercise in throwing stones out on the river, etc. While so doing on one occasion, Martin found a stone very much resembling the one used for translating, and on resuming their labors of translation Martin put in place the stone that he had found. He said that the Prophet remained silent unusually and intently gazing in darkness, no trace of the usual sentences appearing. Much surprised Joseph exclaimed: "Martin! what is the matter? all is as dark as Egypt." Martin's countenance betrayed him, and the Prophet asked Martin why he had done so. Martin said, to stop the mouths of fools, who had told him that the Prophet had learned those sentences and was merely repeating them, etc. Martin said further that the seer stone differed in appearance entirely from the Urim and Thummim that was obtained with the plates, which were two clear stones set in two rims, very much resembled spectacles, only they were larger. Martin said there were not many pages translated while he wrote; after which Oliver Cowdery and others did the writing. (*Deseret Evening News*, December 13, 1881)	
62. William E. McLellin (*report of Elizabeth Whitmer Cowdery's words*) **1870**. On 15 February 1870, Elizabeth Ann (Whitmer) Cowdery (1815-1892), younger sister of David Whitmer and Oliver Cowdery's widow, prepared for an affidavit regarding the translation of the book of Mormon. That same month, William E. McLellin quoted the affidavit in a letter to friends. Unfortunately, the affidavit is lost, and McLellin's is the only known copy. In addition, the bottom half of the letter is missing beginning at the fold. Two years later, McLellin mentioned Elizabeth's affidavit again. (VI.F.10, WILLIAM E. MCLELLIN TO JOSEPH SMITH, III, JUL & SEP 1872).	***Method*** Placed the director in his hat. Words appeared.

In the first letter, McLellin introduced the affidavit with the following: I staid in Richmond two days and nights. I had a great deal of talk with widow Cowdry [Elizabeth Ann Whitmer Cowdery], and her amiable daughter. She is married to a Dr Johnson, but has no children. She gave me a certificate, And this is the copy. "Richmond, Ray Co., Mo. Feb 15, 1870———I cheerfully certify that I was familiar with the manner of Joseph Smith's translating the book of Mormon. He translated the most of it at my Father's house. And I often sat by and saw and heard them translate and write for hours together. Joseph never had a curtain drawn between him and his scribe while he was translating. **He would place the director in his hat, and then place his face in his hat, so as to exclude the light, and then [read?] to his scribe the words (he said) as they appeared before him.**" (William E. McLellin to "My Dear Friends," February 1870, Community of Christ Library-Archives; cited in Cook, *David Whitmer Interviews*, 233–34. Elizabeth Whitmer was the sister of David Whitmer. She was fourteen years old when the translation was completed at her parents' home in Fayette, New York. She married Oliver Cowdery in 1832. McLellin quoted the affidavit to support his claim that Joseph never had the Urim and Thummim. In his letter, he wrote "I am now looking for some man to rise with the Interpreters or Directors—those ancient eyes by which hidden treasures can and will come to light. (Joseph in his history and all L.D.S.ism call those interpreters the Urim and Thummim), but I prefer calling it by its proper name—it neer was Urim nor Thummim but LDSism nicknamed almost every holy thing which it touched.") http://theearlyanthology.tripod.com/18211827/id6.html	
63. Joseph Smith III (*interviewer of his mother, Emma Smith*) **1879**. [Emma Smith said:] In writing for your father I frequently wrote day after day, often sitting at the table close by him, he sitting with his face buried in his hat, with the stone in it, and dictating hour after hour with	***Method*** Dictated hour after hour with his head in his hat, looking at his stone. He did not

nothing between us.... The plates often lay on the table without any attempt at concealment, wrapped in a small linen table cloth, which I had given him to fold them in. I once felt of the plates, as they thus lay on the table, tracing their outline and shape. They seemed to be pliable like thick paper, and would rustle with a metalic sound when the edges were moved by the thumb, as one does sometimes thumb the edges of a book.... My belief is that the Book of Mormon is of divine authenticity—I have not the slightest doubt of it. I am satisfied that no man could have dictated the writing of the manuscripts unless he was inspired; for, when acting as his scribe, your father would dictate to me hour after hour; and when returning after meals, or after interruptions, he would at once begin where he had left off, without either seeing the manuscript or having any portion of it read to him. This was a usual thing for him to do. It would have been improbable that a learned man could do this; and, for one so ignorant and unlearned as he was, it was simply impossible. (Joseph Smith III, "Last Testimony of Sister Emma," *Saints' Herald* 26 (October 1, 1879): 289–90; and Joseph Smith III, "Last Testimony of Sister Emma," *Saints' Advocate* 2 (October 1879): 50–52. Joseph Smith III wrote that Emma reviewed the answers he had recorded for her. The answers "were affirmed by her" on the day before he left Nauvoo. Emma's husband Lewis C. Bidamon asserted that Emma's answers were "substantially what she had always stated" at times when they discussed the translation of the Book of Mormon) https://archive.org/stream/TheSaintsHerald_Volume_26_1879/the%20saints%20herald%20volume%2026%201879#page/n287/mode/2up	look directly at the plates, but they were nearby on the table.
64. ***Latter Day Saints Herald*** **1879** The proofs are clear and positive that the story of the Urim and Thummim Translation does not date back, for its origin further than 1833, or between that date and 1835; for it is not found in any printed document of the Church	***Method*** No Urim and Thummim.

of Christ up to the latter part of the year 1833, or the year 1834. The "Book of Commandments" to the Church of Christ, published in Independence, Mo., in 1833, does not contain any allusion to Urim and Thummim; though the term was inserted in some of the revelations in their reprint in the "Book of Doctrine and Covenants" in 1835. ***The True Latter Day Saints' Herald*, 26/22 (15 November 1879).**	
65. William Smith **1883.** In consequence of his vision, and his having the golden plates and refusing to show them, a great persecution arose against the whole family, and he was compelled to remove into Pennsylvania with the plates, where **he translated them by means of the Urim and Thummim, (which he obtained with the plates), and the power of God. The manner in which this was done was by looking into the Urim and Thummim, which was placed in a hat to exclude the light, (the plates lying near by covered up), and reading off the translation, which appeared in the stone by the power of God.** He was engaged in this business as he had opportunity for about two years and a half. In the winter of 1829 and thirty, the Book of Mormon, which is the translation of part of the plates he obtained, was published. He then showed the plates to my father and my brothers Hyrum and Samuel, who were witnesses to the truth of the book which was translated from them. I was permitted to lift them as they laid in a pillow-case; but not to see them, as it was contrary to the commands he had received. They weighed about sixty pounds according to the best of my judgment. https://archive.org/details/williamsmithonmo00smit/page/10	***Method*** By means of the Urim and Thummim, looking into them when placed in a hat and reading off the translation which appeared in the stone by the power of God.
66. David Whitmer, interviewed by Joseph Smith III **1884.** [David Whitmer] is a devout Christian, and speaks of Bro. Joseph, and the rise of the latter day work with endearing words of love. As he said: "The boys, Joseph and Oliver, worked hard, early and late, while translating the plates. It was slow work, and they could write only a	***Method*** Joseph put the Urim and Thummim

few pages a day." Of Joseph he continued; "He could not do a thing except he was humble, and just right before the Lord." I said, "Why not?" He replied: **"The Urim and Thummim would look dark**; he could not see a thing in them." "How did it appear in them?" we asked. His answer was: **"The letters appeared on them in light**, and would not go off until they were written correctly by Oliver. When Joseph could not pronounce the words he spelled them out letter by letter." E.C. Briggs, "Correspondence" *The Saints' Herald*, June 21, 1844. http://www.sidneyrigdon.com/dbroadhu/IA/sain1882.htm	
67. William Smith **1884.** When Joseph received the plates he also received the Urim and Thummim, which he would place in a hat to exclude all light, and with the plates by his side he translated the characters, which were cut into the plates with some sharp instrument, into English. And thus, letter by letter, word by word, sentence by sentence, the whole book was translated. "The Old Soldier's Testimony," Sermon preached by Bro. William Smith, Deloit, Iowa, June 8, 1844. *The Saints' Herald*, Oct. 4, 1884. http://www.sidneyrigdon.com/dbroadhu/IA/sain1882.htm	***Method*** Joseph put the Urim and Thummim in a hat
68. Edward Stevenson (*interviewer*) **1886**. Brother Harris ... stated that the Prophet translated a portion of the Book of Mormon, with the seer stone in his possession. The stone was placed in a hat that was used for that purpose, and with the aid of this seer stone the Prophet would read sentence by sentence as Martin wrote, and if he made any mistake the sentence would remain before the Prophet until corrected, when another sentence would appear. When they became weary, as it was confining work to translate from the plates of gold, they would go down to the river and throw stones into the water for exercise.	***Method*** Part of the Book of Mormon was translated with the seer stone by placing it in his hat. Words appeared.

<table>
<tr><td>Martin on one occasion picked up a stone resembling the one with which they were translating, and on resuming their work Martin placed the false stone in the hat. He said that the Prophet looked quietly for a long time, when he raised his head and said: "Martin, what on earth is the matter, all is dark as Egypt." Martin smiled and the seer discovered that the wrong stone was placed in the hat. When he asked Martin why he had done so he replied, to stop the mouths of fools who had declared that the Prophet knew by heart all that he told him to write, and did not see by the seer stone; when the true stone was placed in the hat, the translation was resumed, as usual. ("The Three Witnesses to the Book of Mormon," Millennial Star 48 (June 21, 1886): 389–90)</td><td></td></tr>
<tr><td>69. William Smith
1890. In an 1890 interview, William Smith, brother of Joseph Smith, reportedly described the Urim and Thummin.
"Explaining the expression as to the stones in the Urim and thummim being set in two rims of a bow he said: A silver bow ran over one stone, under the other, around over that one and under the first in the shape of a horizontal figure 8 much like a pair of spectacles. That they were much too large for Joseph and he could only see through one at a time using sometimes one and sometimes the other. By putting his head in a hat or some dark object it was not necessary to close one eye while looking through the stone with the other. In that way sometimes when his eyes grew tires [tired] he releaved them of the strain. He also said the Urim and Thummim was attached to the breastplate by a rod which was fastened at the outer shoulde[r] edge of the breastplate and to the end of the silver bow. This rod was just the right length so that when the Urim and thummim was removed from before the eyes it woul<d> reac<h> to a pocked [pocket] on the left side of the [p.509] breastplate where the instrument was kept when not in use by the Seer. I was not informed whether it was detacha<bl>e from the breastplate or not. From the fact that Joseph often had it</td><td>Method
Putting his head in a hat, looking through the stone</td></tr>
</table>

with him and sometimes when at work am of the opinion that it could be detached. He also informed us that the rod served to hold it before the eyes of the Seer." (William Smith interview with J.W. Peterson and W.S. Pender, 1890, from "Statement of J. W. Peterson Concerning William Smith," 1 May1921, Miscellaneous Letters and Papers, RLDS Church Library-Archives, Independence, Missouri. Available in "Early Mormon Documents, Vol 1, Vogel) No known online reference to the original.	
Other 2nd + Hand Accounts (Source Uncertain)	
70. Nancy Towle (*visiting critic*) **1832**. [*2nd-hand account. Reported by Nancy Towle*]. He accordingly went; and was directed by the angel to a certain spot of ground, where was deposited a "Box"—and in that box contained "Plates," which resembled gold; also, a pair of "interpreters," (as he called them,) that resembled spectacles; by looking into which, he could read a writing engraven upon the plates, though to himself, in a tongue unknown. (Nancy Towle, Vicissitudes Illustrated in the Experience of Nancy Towle, in Europe and America (Charleston: James L. Burges, 1832), 138–39. In October 1831, Towle visited Kirtland, where she attended Sabbath meetings, witnessed a baptism, and engaged in a contentious dialogue with W. W. Phelps, Martin Harris, and Sidney Rigdon. She also met Joseph Smith and watched him give the gift of the Holy Ghost to several women and children) https://archive.org/stream/vicissitudesill01towlgoog/vicissitudesill01towlgoog_djvu.txt	***Method*** Looks through the spectacles and reads the engraving on the plates.
71. Truman Coe (*unfriendly editorial*) **1836**. An angel descended and warned him that God was about to make an astonishing revelation to the world, and then directed him to go to such a place, and after prying up a stone he should find a number of plates of the color of gold inscribed with hieroglyphics, and under them a breastplate, and under that a transparent stone or stones	***Method*** Puts his finger on a character on the plates; looks into the Urim and Thummim; sees the word written

which was the Urim and Thummim mentioned by Moses.... The manner of translation was as wonderful as the discovery. **By putting his finger on one of the characters and imploring divine aid, then looking through the Urim and Thummin, he would see the import written in plain English on a screen placed before him**. After delivering this to his emanuensi, he would again proceed in the same manner and obtain the meaning of the next character, and so on till he came to a part of the plates which were sealed up, and there was commanded to desist: and he says he has a promise from God that in due time he will enable him to translate the remainder. (*Cincinnati Journal and Western Luminary* (25 August 1836). Reprinted from *Ohio Observer*, circa August 1836; see online version) https://contentdm.lib.byu.edu/digital/collection/BOMP/id/1323	in English on a "screen."
72. Orson Pratt **1859** If this book be of God, it must have sufficient evidence accompanying it to convince the minds of all reasonable persons that it is a Divine revelation. If it has been translated by the gift and power of God, **through the means of the Urim and Thummim**, and angels have been sent from heaven to bear testimony of its truth, then all the inhabitants of the world are concerned and have an interest in it. *Journal of Discourses*, Vol. 7, p. 22. http://jod.mrm.org/7/22	
73. Orson Pratt **1875** I will give you a very brief statement concerning the manner in which the Book of Mormon was found. In the year 1827, a young man, a farmer's boy, by the name of Joseph Smith, was visited by an holy angel, as he had been for several years prior to this time. But on this occasion, in the fall of 1827, he was permitted to take into his possession the plates from which the Book of Mormon was translated—the angel gave them into his	***Method*** Translate the record by the aid of the Urim and Thummim.

hands, permitted him to take them from the place of their deposit, which was discovered to Mr. Smith by the angel of God. With this book, called the Book of Mormon, was a very curious instrument, such a one, probably, as no person had seen for many generations; **it was called by the angel of God, the Urim and Thummim…. the Lord gave a special command to Joseph, unlearned as he was, that he should translate the record by the aid of the Urim and Thummim.** Mr. Smith commenced the work of translation. Mr. Harris, acting as his scribe, wrote from his mouth one hundred and sixteen pages of the first translation, given by the Prophet. *Journal of Discourses*, Vol. 18, p. 144. http://jod.mrm.org/18/155	
74. Orson Pratt **1875** When [the sealed portion of the record] is brought forth, I expect that the same Urim and Thummim which the Lord gave to Joseph Smith will come forth with these plates, and they will be translated, but by whom I know not. Who will be the favored Seer and Revelator that will be raised up among this people to bring this revelation to light, is not revealed to me." "King Limhi's Enquiry, Etc," *Journal of Discourses*, 19:217b https://jod.mrm.org/19/204	***Method*** Translate sealed portion in the future by the Urim and Thummim.
75. John Whitmer *(interviewed by Zenas H. Gurley)* **1879** He had seen the plates; and it was his especial pride and joy that he had written sixty pages of the Book of Mormon. . . . When the work of translation was going on he sat at one table with his writing material and Joseph at another with the breast-plate and Urim and Thummim. The latter were attached to the breast-plate and were two crystals or glasses, into which he looked and saw the words of the book. The words remained in sight till correctly written, and mistakes of the scribe in spelling the names were corrected by the seer without diverting his gaze from the Urim and Thummim.	***Method*** Translated with the breast-plate and the Urim and Thummim.

S.F. Walker, Synopsis of a Discourse Delivered at Lamoni, Iowa," *Saints' Herald* 26 (December 15, 1879) p. 370.	
76. Erastus Snow **1882** At first Joseph Smith received the gift of seeing visions and **the gift of translating dead languages by the Urim and Thummim**, and when he had exercised himself in these gifts for a season, he received the keys of the Aaronic Priesthood, together with his Brother Oliver, under the hands of John the Baptist, who was a resurrected being, and who was the last of the Jewish High Priests under the dispensation of the law, the only son of Zacharias the High Priest, and a child of promise, who was beheaded by order of Herod. *Journal of Discourses*, Vol. 23, p. 183. http://jod.mrm.org/23/181	***Method*** Translate dead languages by the Urim and Thummim.
77. Brigham Young **1841** I met with the Twelve at brother Joseph's. He conversed with us in a familiar manner on a variety of subjects, and explained to us the Urim and Thummim which he found with the plates, called in the Book of Mormon the Interpreters. He said that every man who lived on the earth was entitled to a seer stone, and should have one, but they are kept from them in consequence of their wickedness, and most of those who do find one make an evil use of it; he showed us his seer stone. Elden J. Watson, ed., *Manuscript History of Brigham Young 1801–1844* (Salt Lake City: Smith Secretarial Service, 1968), 112a.	***Method*** The Urim and Thummim Joseph found with the plates, called in the Book of Mormon the Interpreters.
78. Sarah (Sally) Conrad **1829, recorded in 1897 by Oliver B. Huntington** I conversed with one old lady 88 years old who lived with David Whitmer when Joseph Smith and Oliver Cowdery were translating the Book of Mormon in the upper room of the house, and she, only a girl, saw them come down from the translating room several times when they looked	***Method*** Joseph and Oliver translating upstairs in the Whitmer home

so exceedingly white and strange that she inquired of Mrs. Whitmer the cause of their unusual appearance, but Mr. Whitmer was unwilling to tell the hired girl, the true cause as it was a sacred holy event connected with a holy sacred work which was opposed and persecuted by nearly every one who heard of it. The girl felt so strangely at seeing so strange and unusual appearance, she finally told Mrs. Whitmer that she would not stay with her until she knew the cause of the strange looks of these men. Sister Whitmer then told her what the men were doing in the room above and that the power of God was so great in the room that they could hardly endure it; at times angels were in the room in their glory which nearly consumed them. Oliver B. Huntington, "History of the Life of Oliver B. Huntington," typescript, 49–50, Perry Special Collections, quoted in the *Era*, April 1970, p. 21, online at https://ia801606.us.archive.org/21/items/improvementera7304unse/improvementera7304unse.pdf	
79. Sarah (Sally) Conrad **1829, recorded in 1970 by Pearl Bunnell Newell** And she said they would go up into the attic, and they would stay all day. When they came down, they looked more like heavenly beings than they did just ordinary men. Interview by Carma Rose Anderson of Pearl Bunnell Newell (Sarah's granddaughter), Feb. 10, 1970, quoted in the *Era*, April 1970, p. 21, online at https://ia801606.us.archive.org/21/items/improvementera7304unse/improvementera7304unse.pdf	

Orson Pratt observed: "You will perceive, Latter-day Saints, how this Urim and Thummim was formed in the first place. It was not something that existed on the earth in a natural state, it was something made by the Lord.... those twenty-four plates of gold which contain the doings of the old Jaredite nation that inhabited this North American continent; at present we have only an abridgment, not a hundredth part of their history. These plates of gold will come forth, as well as many other records kept by the first nation—the Jaredites, that came here; and I have no doubt that the Lord will give the Urim and Thummim to translate them." Journal of Discourses, 19:217b. https://jod.mrm.org/19/204

Appendix 2: New Translation Timeline Supplement

Isaiah in 2 Nephi.

This section highlights the differences between 2 Nephi 19-20 and Isaiah 9-10. Omitted verses and parts of verses have no changes.

2 Nephi	Isaiah
2 Nephi 19:1 afterward did more **grieviously** afflict her by the way of the **Red Sea** beyond Jordan in Galilee of the nations.	Isaiah 9:1 afterward did more **grievously** afflict her by the way of the **sea** beyond Jordan in Galilee of the nations.
2 Nephi 19:3 Thou hast multiplied the nation and increased the joy	Isaiah 9:3 Thou hast multiplied the nation and **not** increased the joy
2 Nephi 19:4 For thou hast broken the yoke of his burden and the staff of his shoulder the rod of his oppressor	Isaiah 9:4 For thou hast broken the yoke of his burden and the staff of his shoulder the rod of his oppressor **as in the day of Midian**
2 Nephi 19:7 Of the increase of government and peace there **is** no end upon the throne of David	Isaiah 9:7 Of the increase of ***his*** government and peace there ***shall be*** no end upon the throne of David
2 Nephi 19:8 The Lord sent **his** word **unto** Jacob, and it hath lighted upon Israel.	Isaiah 9:8 The Lord sent **a** word **into** Jacob, and it hath lighted upon Israel.
2 Nephi 19:9 the **inhabitants** of Samaria that say in the pride and **the** stoutness of heart	Isaiah 9:9 the **inhabitant** of Samaria that say in the pride and stoutness of heart
2 Nephi 19:14 Therefore **will the Lord** cut off from Israel head and tail branch and rush in one day.	Isaiah 9:14 Therefore **the Lord will** cut off from Israel head and tail branch and rush in one day.

2 Nephi 19:15 The ancient he is the head and the prophet that teacheth lies he is the tail.	Isaiah 9:15 The ancient **and honourable** he is the head and the prophet that teacheth lies he is the tail.
2 Nephi 19:17 neither shall have mercy on their fatherless and widows for every one **of them** is **a** hypocrite and an evildoer	Isaiah 9:17 neither shall have mercy on their fatherless and widows for every one is **an** hypocrite and an evildoer
2 Nephi 19:18 it shall devour the briers and thorns and shall kindle in the thickets of the **forests** and they shall mount up like the lifting up of smoke	Isaiah 9:18 it shall devour the briers and thorns and shall kindle in the thickets of the **forest** and they shall mount up like the lifting up of smoke
2 Nephi 19:21 Manasseh Ephraim and Ephraim Manasseh they together *shall be* against Judah	Isaiah 9:21 Manasseh Ephraim and Ephraim Manasseh **and** they together *shall be* against Judah
2 Nephi 20:1 Woe unto them that decree unrighteous decrees and that write **grieviousness** which they have prescribed	Isaiah 10:1 Woe unto them that decree unrighteous decrees and that write **grievousness** which they have prescribed
2 Nephi 20:5 O Assyrian, the rod of mine anger, and the staff in their hand is **their** indignation.	Isaiah 10:5 O Assyrian, the rod of mine anger, and the staff in their hand is **mine** indignation.
2 Nephi 20:6 I will send him against **a** hypocritical nation, and against the people of my wrath will I give him a charge…	Isaiah 10:6 I will send him against **an** hypocritical nation, and against the people of my wrath will I give him a charge…
2 Nephi 20:7 Howbeit he meaneth not so neither doth his heart think so	Isaiah 10:7 Howbeit he meaneth not so neither doth his heart think so

but **in his heart it is** to destroy and cut off nations not a few.	but ***it is*** **in his heart** to destroy and cut off nations not a few.
2 Nephi 20:12 His whole work upon mount Zion And **upon** Jerusalem	Isaiah 10:12 His whole work upon mount Zion And **on** Jerusalem
2 Nephi 20:13 For he saith By the strength of my hand **And by my wisdom** I have done **these things** For I am prudent And I have removed The **borders** of the people And have robbed their treasures And I have put down the inhabitants Like a valiant man	Isaiah 10:13 For he saith By the strength of my hand I have done ***it*** **And by my wisdom** For I am prudent And I have removed The **bounds** of the people And have robbed their treasures And I have put down the inhabitants Like a valiant *man*
2 Ne. 20:17 And the light of Israel shall be for a fire and his Holy One for a flame and shall burn and **shall** devour his thorns and his briers in one day	Isaiah 10:17 And the light of Israel shall be for a fire and his Holy One for a flame and **it** shall burn and devour his thorns and his briers in one day
2 Ne. 20:30 Lift up **the** voice O daughter of Gallim cause it to be heard unto Laish O poor Anathoth.	Isaiah 10:30 Lift up **thy** voice O daughter of Gallim cause it to be heard unto Laish O poor Anathoth.
2 Ne. 20:34 And he shall cut down the thickets of the **forests** with iron and Lebanon shall fall by a mighty one	Isaiah 10:34 And he shall cut down the thickets of the **forest** with iron and Lebanon shall fall by a mighty one.

What Emma translated.

With Mosiah 1 as a starting point, there are four possible ending points for Emma's work as scribe. You might think of others.

Mosiah 18:19. This possibility is suggested from the PM itself.

As we saw in chapter 1, John Gilbert told James Cobb, "The most part of it was in Oliver Cowdery's handwriting. Some in Joseph's wife's; a small part, though."

Two years earlier, Gilbert had written three letters to Cobb in answer to Cobb's inquiries about the printing of the Book of Mormon. In a letter dated 10 February 1879, Cobb wrote

> I received your letter… and now answer your interrogations to the best of my recollection. But one copy of the manuscript was furnished the printer. I never heard of but one. As quick as Mr. Grandin got his type and got things all ready to commence the work, Hyrum Smith brought to the office 24 pages of manuscript on foolscap paper, closely written and legible, but not a punctuation mark from beginning to end….
>
> Oliver Cowdery was not engaged as compositor on the work or was not a printer. He was a frequent visitor to the office, and did several times take up a "stick" and set a part of a page—he may have set 10 or 12 pages, all told—he also a few times looked over the manuscript when proof was being read. In one instance he was looking over the manuscript, when the word "travail" occurred twice in the form, but spelling in the manuscript, travel. Mr. Grandin when reading the proof pronounced the word correctly, but Cowdery did not seem to know the difference.[286]

Some have interpreted Gilbert's letter to mean he was unaware that there were two manuscripts, but that doesn't make sense because he did use both the PM and the OM, as we'll discuss below. His wording is consistent with only one copy being given to the printer at a time.

Gilbert set the type mostly from the PM. We have the entire PM and

---

[286] John H. Gilbert to James T. Cobb, 10 February 1879, in Dan Vogel, *Early Mormon Documents*, (Signature Books, Salt Lake City, UT 1998), 2:522, underlining in the original.

we know that Emma's writing is not on it. Yet Gilbert said the manuscript he used included Emma's writing. That means Gilbert must have used some of the OM that had Emma's handwriting on it.

If we can determine what part of the OM Gilbert used, we might be able to tell what part Emma wrote. To do that, we need to understand how the typesetting worked.

Hyrum Smith brought in 24 pages at a time because Oliver Cowdery copied the OM onto sheets of paper that were sewn together as "gatherings" of 24 pages. Mosiah 1, which we assume is where Emma began writing, is on page 117, which is part of gathering #5. The following table shows the gatherings of the PM that include Mosiah.

Table 7 - Gatherings in the PM

Pages in PM	Chapter (1830)	Gathering
97-120	Jacob 2-Mosiah 1	5
121-144	Mosiah 1-Mosiah 9	6
145-168	Mosiah 9-Mosiah 13	7
169-188	Alma 1-Alma 6	8

From the corresponding portions of the OM, only a few partial pages and fragments from Jacob-Enos still exist. After Enos 1:14, none of the OM exists before Alma 10:31. All the fragments on the following list are in the handwriting of Oliver Cowdery.

Jacob 1:3-7 (lines 31-39)
Jacob 1:18-2:2 (lines 29-39)
Jacob 2:11-15 (lines 28-39)
Jacob 2:25-27 (lines 27-29)
Jacob 3:5
Jacob 4:3-5
Jacob 4:13-14

Jacob 5:46-48
Jacob 5:57-61
Jacob 5:69-70
Jacob 5:77
Jacob 6:11-7:6
Jacob 7:11-18
Jacob 7:24-Enos 1:1
Enos 1:9-14
Alma 10:31-11:4

Oliver was not copying the OM sheet by sheet but wrote the PM in a continuous flow.[287] As shown in the list above, Royal Skousen has determined from the fragments which lines of each sheet of the OM the text was written on. This allows us to see that text on the sheets in the PM do not correspond with the OM.

For example, Jacob 2:11-15 are on lines 28-30 in the OM, but they are on lines 14-23 on page 97 in the PM. The lack of page-by-page correlation between the OM and the PM makes it more challenging to determine when Gilbert set the type from each manuscript.

———

Skousen has explained that Gilbert used the OM for Helaman 13:17 through the end of Mormon. Skousen's methodology for discovering this detail offers clues for identifying another part of the OM that Gilbert used, the part containing Emma's handwriting.

Skousen discovered that a fragment of the OM (3 Nephi 26-27) "was full of the penciled-in punctuation marks that John Gilbert, the 1830 compositor, frequently added to his copytext before setting the type for the 1830 edition."[288] These marks include "pilcrows," which designate

[287] Compare this page from the OM https://www.josephsmithpapers.org/paper-summary/book-of-mormon-manuscript-excerpt-circa-june-1829-1-nephi-22b-318a/2 with the corresponding page from the PM https://www.josephsmithpapers.org/paper-summary/printers-manuscript-of-the-book-of-mormon-circa-august-1829-circa-january-1830/8

[288] See Royal Skousen's article here: https://journal.interpreterfoundation.org/why-

paragraph breaks.

Skousen also noticed that the 72 pages from Helaman 13:18 through Mormon in the PM *lacked* such markings. That was strong evidence that Gilbert used the OM instead of the PM. Other details corroborate Skousen's conclusion. For example, the 1830 edition misspelled *Cumorah* as *Camorah*, an error present in the OM but not in the PM.

Skousen concluded that in January 1830, Oliver took the entire PM to Canada to apply for a copyright. He left the OM with Gilbert to continue setting type while he was gone.

You can see Gilbert's pencil marks throughout the online version of the PM, but they are difficult to decipher. The Joseph Smith Papers has published an annotated facsimile of the PM.[289] The annotated facsimile provides a typewritten version of the handwritten text, along with every detectable mark on the PM, including corrections made by Oliver Cowdery as scribe and revisions made by Joseph Smith for newer editions of the Book of Mormon (including the 1837 edition).

There's another clue that curiously is not mentioned in the annotations.

As we saw above, the pages of the PM do not correspond exactly to the pages from the OM. If Gilbert marked and used the PM up to Helaman 13:18, and then used the OM after that through Mormon, there had to be a transition because the pages wouldn't line up.

If you can, go to page 356 of the PM online and look at the markings.[290] (This is page 191 in the printed book with the annotations.)

Figure 7 - PM page 356

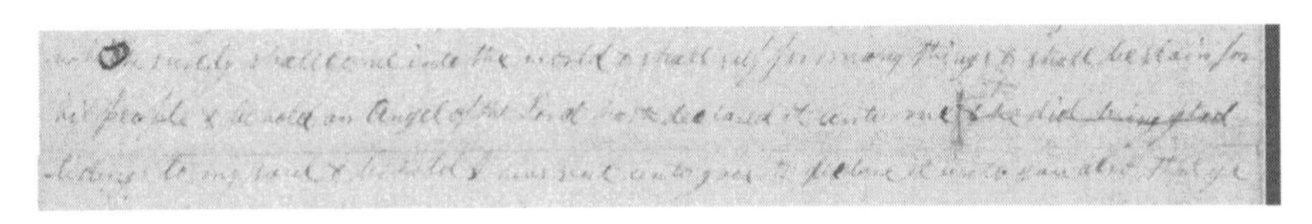

was-one-sixth-of-the-1830-book-of-mormon-set-from-the-original-manuscript/.

289 JSP, *Revelations and Translations*, Volume 3, Parts 1 and 2.

290 The page is here: https://www.josephsmithpapers.org/paper-summary/printers-manuscript-of-the-book-of-mormon-circa-august-1829-circa-january-1830/360.

The text above the line (the 11th row) reads like this:

*

his people & behold an Angel of the Lord hath declared it unto me || ~~& he did bring glad~~

Notice that the last five words of the 11th row ("& he did bring glad") are lined through and an asterisk occurs above "he." There is a double vertical line in front of these last five words There is a line below the 11th row of text with a large X over the lower portion.

The annotations point out that a mark on the top section "corresponds to the end of a paragraph on page 441 of the 1830 edition," but the double vertical lines "do not correspond to the end of a line in the 1830 edition."[291]

The annotation says "The page is cut horizontally below this line, likely for the convenience of the compositor as he set type from this page. Pinholes indicate that pins were used to hold the two pieces of the page together." Regarding the X, the annotation says "Compositor's large "X" may indicate the completion of typesetting for this portion of the page."

That explanation doesn't make sense to me. Why cut the page here, and why put an X through the text that was cut off from the upper part of the page?

The previous page (355) is the front side of p. 356, so it is also cut in the same place, but without the lined out words or asterisk. The top part of that page is marked with a large X.

I think someone—maybe Oliver or Hyrum—cut this page to merge it with the OM. I assume the page of the OM corresponding to page 356 ended with the words "declared it unto me" and the next page started with "& he did bring glad tidings," so they cut this page of the PM, crossed out "& he did bring glad tidings," and put an X through the bottom to avoid repeating the same text. This is part of Helaman 13:7 in the current edition. (I can't tell why Skousen says they used OM starting with verse 17 instead.)

In other words, the typesetter used the top part of page 356 of the

[291] You can see this on page 442 if you have a copy of the 1830 edition.

PM, cut off and crossed out the lower part of the page, and used the OM to continue. Later, they reassembled the page to have a complete copy.

The transition back from the PM to the OM at the end of Mormon is much easier because the copyist (not Oliver, but scribe 2, identified as Martin Harris) filled only the top one-third of the page. Oliver, copying separately, started Ether 1 on a new page. You can see that on page 428 of the PM.[292] All of this shows how Gilbert used the OM for a substantial part of the typesetting.

Now let's see if he did so for the part that Emma wrote.

As I examined the PM, I noted a separate unusual feature. There are no pilcrows on the PM after p. 99 (Jacob 4:1-12) through p. 129 (Mosiah 7:12-22). We don't have the OM for those pages so we cannot check if they have pilcrows on them, but this is possibly an indication that the OM was also used for some or all of these pages.

The lack of pilcrows may not be significant, though, because other parts of the PM also lack pilcrows.

Another unusual feature does look significant. In the entire PM, I noted 21 pilcrows that do not correspond to a new paragraph in the 1830 edition. All but three of these are found in the 15 pages between page 131 and 145, representing Mosiah 8:6-18:19.

Table 8 - Unused pilcrows in the PM

PM pages (modern versification)	# of pages	# pilcrows that do not correspond to a new paragraph - 1830 edition
1-130 (1 Ne. 1:1-Mosiah 8:5)	131	0
131-145 (Mosiah 8:6-18:19)	15	18
146-260 (Mosiah 18:19-Alma 35:16)	115	1
261-463 (Alma 35:17-Moro. 10:34)	203	2

292 https://www.josephsmithpapers.org/paper-summary/printers-manuscript-of-the-book-of-mormon-circa-august-1829-circa-january-1830/432

The large number of unused pilcrows from pages 131-145 stands out. To be sure, there are also many used pilcrows in this section. However, all these pilcrows, used and unused, were made by Oliver Cowdery (in ink). Before and after this section, the pilcrows are mostly attributed to the Compositor (presumably Gilbert, who used a pencil).

Remarkably, despite all the used and unused pilcrows in this section of Mosiah, there are paragraph breaks in the 1830 edition that are *not* marked on the PM.

Table 9 - Unmarked paragraph breaks

Paragraph breaks in the 1830 edition not indicated by pilcrows in the PM		text
PM page	1830 page	
137, line 13	180, line 41	And it shall come to pass that the life of king Noah
138, line 28	182, line 42	And it shall come to pass that ye shall be smitten
140, line 31	185, line 38	Surely he hath born
141, line 4	186, line 10	Yet it pleased the Lord
144, line 8	190, line 18	Now Abinadi saith unto
145, line 34	192, line 42	And it came to pass that whosoever was baptized

The combination of (i) unused pilcrows and (ii) paragraph breaks in the 1830 text that are not indicated by pilcrows in the PM, is strong evidence that at least these pages were not set with the PM.

True, many of the pilcrows in the PM do correspond with a new paragraph in the text, but that is not surprising when we realize that most new paragraphs in the text begin with a variation of "And it came to pass" or "And now...." Anyone who had read the text leading up to this section would recognize the pattern.

Notice that the unmarked paragraph breaks on pages 140 and 144 correspond to the paragraph breaks in the KJV of Isaiah 53:4 and 53:10, respectively. This is consistent with the Isaiah chapters in 1 and 2 Nephi, which are also divided into paragraphs that align with the paragraphs in the KJV Isaiah chapters.

In 1 Nephi 20 and 21, as well as in 2 Nephi 12-15, there are no pilcrows in the PM at all. From 2 Nephi 16 through 2 Nephi 23, the compositor placed pilcrows that correspond to a new paragraph of the 1830 edition and to a new paragraph in the KJV.

What is unique about Mosiah is the combination of used and unused pilcrows, plus unmarked paragraph breaks in the text.

Royal Skousen suggested that "Oliver Cowdery added paragraph marks as he prepared this manuscript, but by page 145 he stopped this practice, probably because he had realized that the compositor was ignoring his suggested paragraph breaks."[293]

That's a possible explanation, but John Gilbert never said the text was punctuated or marked. Instead, he said, "Every chapter, if I remember correctly, was one solid paragraph, without a punctuation mark, from beginning to end." Gilbert also said that marking the text was time consuming.

> After working a few days, I said to [Hyrum] Smith on his handing me the manuscript in the morning: "Mr. Smith, if you would leave this manuscript with me, I would take it home with me at night and read and punctuate it, and I could get along faster in the day time, for now I have frequently to stop and read half a page to find how to punctuate it." His reply was, "We are commanded not to leave it." A few mornings after this, when Smith handed me the manuscript, he said to me: "If you will give your word that this manuscript shall be returned to us when you get through with it, I will leave it with you." I assured Smith that it should be returned all right when I got through with it. For two or three nights I took it home with me and read it, and punctuated it with a lead pencil. This will account for the punctuation marks in pencil.[294]

---

[293] Royal Skousen, "Worthy of Another Look: John Gilbert's 1892 Account of the 1830 Printing of the Book of Mormon," *Journal of Book of Mormon Studies* 21:2 (2012):66 https://scholarsarchive.byu.edu/cgi/viewcontent.cgi?article=1506&context=jbms
[294] Ibid, 65.

It is difficult to believe that Gilbert would have forgotten Oliver's punctuation marks, let alone rejected them. It seems more plausible that Gilbert never saw them because he was using the OM for these pages instead of the PM Oliver marked.

———

Unlike with Helaman 13, there are no cut pages here. I infer that Oliver (or Hyrum) marked the OM instead of the PM to show where to merge the two. For example, instead of giving Gilbert gathering #6 of the PM, maybe they gave him the corresponding pages of the OM, marked with the beginning and end points.

The last unused pilcrow marked by Oliver is on page 145, corresponding to page 191 in the 1830 edition (Mosiah 18:6). This is the first page of Gathering #7. Starting on page 146, the pilcrows are marked by the Compositor and correspond to new paragraphs in the text (although there continue to be unmarked new paragraphs in the text).

Apart from the lack of Compositor markings in Gatherings 5 and 6, the unused pilcrows and the unmarked paragraph breaks in the text, I cannot find a way to tell where the transitions from the PM to the OM and back took place.

There may be clues in the text itself, such as where the text varies from the PM.

As we noted above, Gilbert said Oliver set "10 or 12 pages" of type. Maybe Oliver set these 15 pages that had the high number of unused pilcrows, but it is difficult to explain why he would not use the paragraph breaks he marked.

I could find no Compositor marks from page 106 through 134, a single bracket on p. 135, and no more until page 140, which was a correction to the chapter number (8) that Oliver had numbered as chapter IX. The next correction was on page 143, correcting Oliver's chapter X to IX. Starting on page 146, the Compositor began writing the pilcrows again.

The lack of compositor marks in most of Gatherings 5 and 6, combined with the unused pilcrows inserted by Oliver Cowdery and the paragraph breaks in the text not indicated on the PM, leads me to suggest that Gilbert probably set these pages from a manuscript he marked—the OM written by Emma. He would have inserted his own paragraph breaks, which differed from those Oliver marked.

I propose that Oliver may have added pilcrows when he copied these pages to help him make sense of the text because he was unfamiliar with the content on the OM. Why would he be unfamiliar with these passages?

Because Emma wrote the OM for this section.

Gilbert also mentioned that when proofreading, Oliver didn't notice the difference between *travail* and *travel. Travail* appears in the text in four places: Mosiah 14:11, Mosiah 27:33, Alma 18:37, and 3 Nephi 22:1. Presumably Oliver was in Canada when they set 3 Nephi, so it had to be one of the earlier passages. Oliver would have written Alma 18:37 in the OM. Therefore, the passages in Mosiah are the only plausible ones that could have confused Oliver.

If you go through the annotated facsimile of the PM, you will notice another possible clue.

Mosiah 25:14. When Oliver copied the OM to create the PM, he copied all of the Fayette translation (which had been originally written by Oliver and the other scribes). Oliver continued copying Mosiah up to Mosiah 25:14 (page 208 in the 1830 edition). Martin took over at that point and, alternating with Hyrum Smith, copied until Alma 13:20, when Oliver resumed copying.

One possible explanation for the hand-off at Mosiah 25:14 is that Oliver copied parts of the OM he did not write. This meant there was at least one complete copy in his handwriting, which presumably would make it easier for the typesetter, John Gilbert.[295]

[295] Gilbert typeset from the part of the PM that included the handwriting of Hyrum and Martin, but Oliver's OM for that section was available if needed.

Table 10 - Scribes of the Printer's Manuscript

Scribes of the Printer's Manuscript[296]		
Oliver	**Martin**	**Hyrum**
Title Page; 1Ne. 1:0 - Mosiah 25:14	Mosiah 25:14 - 28:0	Mosiah 28:1
	Mosiah 28:1-19	Mosiah 18:20 – 29:19
	Mosiah 29:19-28	Mosiah 29:29-35
	Mosiah 29:35-Alma 2:38	Alma 2:38-3:1
	Alma 3:1-5:0	Alma 5:1
	Alma 5:1-13:20	
Alma 13:20-3 Ne. 19:20	3 Ne. 19:21-Morm. 9:37	
Ether – Moroni Witness Statements		

In that scenario, it made sense for him to copy the Fayette translation because the writing of the other scribes was interspersed with his. It could also mean that Emma (and the other pre-Oliver scribes) had written the OM through Mosiah 25:14. If so, then Hyrum and Martin took over where Oliver had begun the OM (because Oliver had previously written that part).

Oliver resumed copying the OM at Alma 13:20, not because he had not written the OM at that point (he had started at least at Alma 10:31), but presumably because he was the better scribe.

Note that Martin copied 3 Ne. 19:21-Morm. 9:37. He apparently did this at the same time as Oliver copied Ether and Moroni. They doubled up on the copying so Oliver could take the entire Printer's Manuscript to Canada to pursue a copyright there, as we discussed earlier in this chapter. When Oliver was gone, Grandin used the Original Manuscript for typesetting.

All of Mosiah. Elden Watson proposes[297] that Emma wrote all of Mosiah (62 pages, through the top of p. 221 in the 1830 edition), based on that being a natural stopping place. The last few pages of Mosiah

---

[296] Skousen, *Part 6*, pages 32-33.

[297] Search for "D&C 5" at https://www.eldenwatson.net/BoM.htm.

would be the "few more pages" the Lord mentioned in D&C 5:30. Because the revelation was received sometime in March, the "season" in D&C 5:30 could be only the following few weeks before Oliver arrived in Harmony on April 5.

In this scenario, Oliver would have begun scribing at Alma 1.

Alma 10:31. Because Alma 10:31 is the first part of the OM that we know Oliver wrote, it is theoretically possible Emma wrote everything up to that point. However, it seems unlikely that a mere coincidence would have led to the destruction of all of Emma's work, right up to the time Oliver took over.

These scenarios are speculation based on limited evidence. We have no record that Emma or anyone else ever said what, exactly, she wrote while Joseph dictated. So far as I know, there are no other clues about what pages Emma would have written in the OM.

All we know is that she (and the other pre-Oliver scribes) wrote something before Oliver arrived in Harmony.

Conclusion. I think the physical evidence supports Elden Watson's proposal, but anywhere within the ranges discussed above is feasible.

Appendix 3: Gospel Topics Essay Comments

This Appendix consists of my annotations, from a faithful perspective, to the Gospel Topics Essay on Book of Mormon Translation found at this web page:

https://www.churchofjesuschrist.org/manual/gospel-topics-essays/book-of-mormon-translation?lang=eng

The essay thoughtfully tackles an issue that has no readily apparent resolution. As you read the essay, however, you will notice that although it quotes many observers and commentators, it never quotes what Joseph Smith and Oliver Cowdery taught about the Urim and Thummim.

Not even once.

The essay edits the few quotations from Joseph and Oliver it does provide to *omit* their references to the term *Urim and Thummim.*

This is a strange editorial decision for an essay that is intended to educate people about this important topic.

Although the essay has undergone undocumented changes over time, the online version as of December 2019 makes speculative assumptions that lead to speculative conclusions. The essay omits important facts. It does not acknowledge, let alone discuss, alternative interpretations of the known facts.

Except as indicated, all footnotes to the essay are original. My annotations are in brackets and **bold** typeface.

Book of Mormon Translation

Joseph Smith said that the Book of Mormon was "the most correct of any Book on earth & the keystone of our religion & a man would get nearer to God by abiding by its precepts than by any other Book."[298]

[It is good to see the original source cited here. As indicated in the footnote, this is a quotation from Wilford Woodruff's summary of a day's teaching, not a direct quotation of something Joseph said. Woodruff did not put the sentence in quotation marks, as he usually did when recording a direct quotation. Nevertheless, Church historians converted it into a first-person quotation in History of the Church and other publications. I hope this is a first step toward correcting the misquotation that appears still today in the Introduction to the Book of Mormon[299] in every copy.]

The Book of Mormon came into the world through a series of miraculous events. Much can be known about the coming forth of the English text of the Book of Mormon through a careful study of statements made by Joseph Smith, his scribes, and others closely associated with the translation of the Book of Mormon.

[Although this paragraph encourages a careful study of Joseph Smith's statements, the essay actually omits every one of Joseph's statements in which he used the term *Urim and Thummim*.]

"By the Gift and Power of God"

Joseph Smith reported that on the evening of September 21, 1823, while he prayed in the upper room of his parents' small log home in

---

[298] Wilford Woodruff journal, Nov. 28, 1841, Church History Library, Salt Lake City., https://www.josephsmithpapers.org/paper-summary/remarks-28-november-1841/1.

[299] https://www.churchofjesuschrist.org/study/scriptures/bofm/introduction?lang=eng

Palmyra, New York, an angel who called himself Moroni appeared and told Joseph that "God had a work for [you] to do."[300]

[The quotation is from what is now Joseph Smith—History 1:33. That verse identifies the angel as Moroni.

The original version was published in the *Times and Seasons* on 15 April 1842.[301] There, the angel who visited was identified as Nephi. Lucy Mack Smith's history quoted the *Times and Seasons*, also identifying the angel as Nephi.[302]

Some have wondered why the compilers of this history would have identified the angel as "Nephi" and why Joseph, supposedly the active editor of the *Times and Seasons* when this account was published, would not have "corrected" the identification. One reason could be that Joseph was merely the nominal editor; i.e., someone else was the actual editor. (That's what I think the evidence shows.[303]) Another could be that the compilers knew Joseph interacted with both Moroni and Nephi and weren't sure which one appeared in 1823.

Brigham Young taught that Joseph had interactions with Nephi (one of the unnamed three Nephites from 3 Nephi 28) as well as with Moroni.

One such incident can be pieced together from the historical record. Before leaving Harmony in May/June 1829, Joseph gave the plates to a divine messenger he later identified as "one of the Nephites." The same messenger later showed the Fayette plates to Mary Whitmer. She said he identified himself as Brother Nephi.

---

300 On the identity of the angel, see Karen Lynn Davidson, David J. Whittaker, Mark Ashurst-McGee, and Richard L. Jenson, eds., *Histories, Volume 1: Joseph Smith Histories, 1832–1844*, vol. 1 of the Histories series of The Joseph Smith Papers, edited by Dean C. Jessee, Ronald K. Esplin, and Richard Lyman Bushman (Salt Lake City: Church Historian's Press, 2012), 223 n 56.

301 Online at https://www.josephsmithpapers.org/paper-summary/times-and-seasons-15-april-1842/3

302 Online at https://www.josephsmithpapers.org/paper-summary/lucy-mack-smith-history-1845/86

303 See my books *The Lost City of Zarahemla, Brought to Light,* and *The Editors: Joseph, William, and Don Carlos Smith.*

The essay's footnote discusses the identity of the angel, citing a note in the Joseph Smith Papers that in turn quotes President Oliver Cowdery's 1835 Letter IV as authority for the identity of the angel as Moroni.]

He informed Joseph that "there was a book deposited, written upon gold plates, giving an account of the former inhabitants of this continent, and the source from whence they sprang."

[The quotation is from Joseph Smith—History 1:33.]

The book could be found in a hill not far from the Smith family farm.

[This is an uncredited paraphrase of President Cowdery's 1835 Letter IV, in which Moroni tells Joseph "this history was written and deposited not far from that place [the Smith family farm near Palmyra]." Letter IV gives additional details from this visit that relate to the translation, but these details are omitted in this essay. The angel "proceeded and gave a general account of the promises made to the fathers, and also gave a history of the aborigenes of this country, and said they were literal descendants of Abraham.... He said this history was written and deposited not far from that place, and that it was our brother's privilege, if obedient to the commandments of the Lord, to obtain and translate the same by the means of the Urim and Thummim, which were deposited for that purpose with the record.[304]]

This was no ordinary history, for it contained "the fullness of the everlasting Gospel as delivered by the Savior."[305]

[This is another quotation from Joseph Smith—History 1:34.

---

[304] Letter IV, online at https://www.josephsmithpapers.org/paper-summary/history-1834-1836/68

[305] Davidson et al., *Joseph Smith Histories,* 223; punctuation regularized; Joseph Smith, "Church History," *Times and Seasons* 3 (March 1, 1842): 706-7. See also Joseph Smith—History 1:33–34.

Oddly, the next verse, 35, is never quoted or cited in the essay. That verse explains what accompanied the plates: "Also, that there were two stones in silver bows—and these stones, fastened to a breastplate, constituted what is called the Urim and Thummim—deposited with the plates; and the possession and use of these stones were what constituted "seers" in ancient or former times; and that God had prepared them for the purpose of translating the book."]

The angel charged Joseph Smith to translate the book from the ancient language in which it was written.

[While true, this sentence omits Moroni's explanation that Joseph would translate the plates by means of the Urim and Thummim that came with the plates. The Urim and Thummim was specifically prepared for a seer to translate the unknown language.]

The young man, however, had very little formal education and was incapable of writing a book on his own, let alone translating an ancient book written from an unknown language, known in the Book of Mormon as "reformed Egyptian."[306]

[Joseph's formal education was limited to three years, but he knew the many Biblical passages Moroni quoted well enough to discern that Moroni had quoted some exactly and changed the wording in other passages. Joseph was also "intimately familiar" with Christian doctrines and writings.]

Joseph's wife Emma insisted that, at the time of translation, Joseph "could neither write nor dictate a coherent and well-worded letter, let alone dictat[e] a book like the Book of Mormon."[307]

[Emma purportedly related this statement to her son, Joseph

---

306 Mormon 9:32. See also 1 Nephi 1:2.
307 "Last Testimony of Sister Emma," *Saints' Herald* 26 (Oct. 1, 1879), 290.

Smith III, in 1879. The account was published after her death. Emma never publicly acknowledged the statement. We discussed it in Chapter 9. The full statement is in Appendix 6.]

Joseph received the plates in September 1827 and the following spring, in Harmony, Pennsylvania, began translating them in earnest, with Emma and his friend Martin Harris serving as his main scribes.

[Emma apparently served as a scribe for the 116 pages, the first part of Mosiah, and some of the translation in Fayette, probably in 2 Nephi. Her "Last Testimony" claims she wrote while Joseph stared at a stone in a hat, but Joseph said she wrote for him after the messenger returned the Urim and Thummim and the plates in 1828 *after* the 116 pages were lost. See quotations below.]

The resulting English transcription, known as the Book of Lehi and referred to by Joseph Smith as written on 116 pages, was subsequently lost or stolen. As a result, Joseph Smith was rebuked by the Lord and lost the ability to translate for a short time.[308]

[The essay doesn't explain what "lost the ability to translate" means, but Lucy Mack Smith explained that Joseph had to give up the Urim and Thummim after losing the 116 pages.

Later, Joseph told her that "on the 22d of September [1828], I had the joy and satisfaction of again receiving the Urim and Thummim; and have commenced translating again, and Emma writes for me; but the angel said that the Lord would send me a scribe, and I trust his promise will be verified. He also seemed pleased with me, when he gave me back the Urim and Thummim; and he told me that the Lord loved me, for my faithfulness and humility.

---

[308] Joseph Smith History, 1838–ca. 1841, 8–11 (draft 2), in Karen Lynn Davidson, David J. Whittaker, Mark Ashurst-McGee, and Richard L. Jenson, eds., *Histories, Volume 1: Joseph Smith Histories, 1832–1844*, vol. 1 of the Histories series of *The Joseph Smith Papers*, edited by Dean C. Jessee, Ronald K. Esplin, and Richard Lyman Bushman (Salt Lake City: Church Historian's Press, 2012), 252–3; available at josephsmithpapers.org; Doctrine and Covenants 3:5–15.

"Soon after I received them I inquired of the Lord, and obtained the following revelation": "Now, behold I say unto you, that, because <you> delivered up those writings, which you had power given you to translate, by the means of the Urim and Thummim into the hands of a wicked man, you have lost them; and you also lost your gift at the same time, and your mind became darkened;"[309]

Notice how the Urim and Thummim was directly linked to Joseph's ability to translate throughout this incident. The essay explains none of this; it merely says Joseph "lost the ability to translate for a short time."]

Joseph began translating again in 1829, and almost all of the present Book of Mormon text was translated during a three-month period between April and June of that year.

[Some portion or all of the Book of Mosiah was translated before Oliver Cowdery arrived in Harmony in April.]

His chief 'scribe during these months was Oliver Cowdery, a schoolteacher from Vermont who learned about the Book of Mormon while boarding with Joseph's parents in Palmyra. Called by God in a vision, Cowdery traveled to Harmony to meet Joseph Smith and investigate further. Of his experience as scribe, Cowdery wrote, "These were days never to be forgotten—to sit under the sound of a voice dictated by the *inspiration* of heaven."[310]

[This quotation is from President Cowdery's Letter I, now canonized as a footnote to Joseph Smith – History 1:71.[311] The

---

[309] D&C 10:1-2; Lucy Mack Smith, *History, 1845*, online at https://www.josephsmithpapers.org/paper-summary/lucy-mack-smith-history-1845/143

[310] Joseph Smith History, ca. summer 1832, in *Joseph Smith Histories,* 16; Oliver Cowdery to William W. Phelps, Sept. 7, 1834, in *Messenger and Advocate* 1 (Oct. 1834): 14; italics in original.

[311] The essay's footnote refers to the obscure *Messenger and Advocate*, but Joseph had his scribes copy Oliver's letters into his personal history, which is available online

essay terminates the quotation just before the following sentence that directly pertains to the translation:

"Day after day I continued, uninterrupted, to write from his mouth, as he translated with the Urim and Thummim, or, as the Nephites would have said, 'Interpreters,' the history or record called 'The Book of Mormon.'"

Oliver said the entire text was translated with the Urim and Thummim. This is consistent with Letter IV, quoted above, in which Moroni told Joseph he would "translate the same by the means of the Urim and Thummim, which were deposited for that purpose with the record." Oliver does not mention any seer stone or hat.

The essay omits other relevant passages from Joseph Smith—History. Besides JS-H 1:35 (quoted above), the essay omits these verses:

JS-H 1:42 Again, he told me, that when I got those plates of which he had spoken—for the time that they should be obtained was not yet fulfilled—I should not show them to any person; neither the breastplate with the Urim and Thummim; only to those to whom I should be commanded to show them; if I did I should be destroyed.

JS-H 1:62 By this timely aid was I enabled to reach the place of my destination in Pennsylvania; and immediately after my arrival there I commenced copying the characters off the plates. I copied a considerable number of them, and by means of the Urim and Thummim I translated some of them, which I did between the time I arrived at the house of my wife's father, in the month of December, and the February following.]

The manuscript that Joseph Smith dictated to Oliver Cowdery and others is known today as the original manuscript, about 28 percent of which still survives.[312] This manuscript corroborates Joseph Smith's

---

here: https://www.josephsmithpapers.org/paper-summary/history-1834-1836/49

[312] Most of the manuscript disintegrated or became otherwise unreadable due to water damage between 1841 and 1882, as a result of being placed in the cornerstone of the Nauvoo House in Nauvoo, Illinois. Most of the surviving pages were later archived in the historian's office of The Church of Jesus Christ of Latter-day Saints in Salt Lake

statements that the manuscript was written within a short time frame and that it was dictated from another language. For example, it includes errors that suggest the scribe heard words incorrectly rather than misread words copied from another manuscript.[313]

In addition, some grammatical constructions that are more characteristic of Near Eastern languages than English appear in the original manuscript, suggesting that the base language of the translation was not English.[314]

City. The extant original manuscript has been published in *The Original Manuscript of the Book of Mormon: Typographical Facsimile of the Extant Text*, ed. Royal Skousen (Provo, UT: Foundation for Ancient Research and Mormon Studies, 2001). A complete copy of this original, known as the printer's manuscript, was made by Oliver Cowdery and two other scribes between August 1829 and early 1830. It was used to set the type for most of the printing in Palmyra. The printer's manuscript is published in *The Printer's Manuscript of the Book of Mormon: Typological Facsimile of the Entire Text in Two Parts*, ed. Royal Skousen (Provo, UT: Foundation for Ancient Research and Mormon Studies, 2001). Both the printer's manuscript and the original manuscript will be published in future volumes of *The Joseph Smith Papers*. (Dean C. Jessee, "The Original Book of Mormon Manuscript," *BYU Studies* 10, no. 3 [Spring 1970]: 261–72; Royal Skousen, "Piecing Together the Original Manuscript," *BYU Today* 46, no. 3 [May 1992]: 18–24.)

313 For example, when Joseph translated the text that is now in 1 Nephi 13:29, the scribe wrote "&" in one place where he should have written "an." At 1 Nephi 17:48, the scribe wrote "weed" where he should have written "reed." (See Royal Skousen, "Translating the Book of Mormon: Evidence from the Original Manuscript," in Noel B. Reynolds, ed., *Book of Mormon Authorship Revisited: The Evidence for Ancient Origins* [Provo, UT: Foundation for Ancient Research and Mormon Studies, 1997], 67; see also Grant Hardy, "Introduction," in *The Book of Mormon: The Earliest Text*, ed. Royal Skousen [New Haven: Yale University Press, 2009], xv–xix.)

314 John A. Tvedtnes, "Hebraisms in the Book of Mormon" and "Names of People: Book of Mormon," in Geoffrey Kahn, ed., *Encyclopedia of Hebrew Language and Linguistics* (Brill Online, 2013); M. Deloy Pack, "Hebraisms," in *Book of Mormon Reference Companion*, ed. Dennis L. Largey (Salt Lake City: Deseret Book, 2003), 321–25; John A. Tvedtnes, "The Hebrew Background of the Book of Mormon," in John L. Sorenson and Melvin J. Thorne, eds., *Rediscovering the Book of Mormon* (Salt Lake City and Provo, UT: Deseret Book and Foundation for Ancient Research and Mormon Studies, 1991), 77–91; Donald W. Parry, "Hebraisms and Other Ancient Peculiarities in the Book of Mormon," in Donald W. Parry and others, eds., *Echoes and Evidences of the Book of Mormon* (Provo, UT: Foundation for Ancient Research and Mormon Studies, 2002), 155–89.

Unlike most dictated drafts, the original manuscript was considered by Joseph Smith to be, in substance, a final product. To assist in the publication of the book, Oliver Cowdery made a handwritten copy of the original manuscript. This copy is known today as the printer's manuscript. Because Joseph Smith did not call for punctuation, such as periods, commas, or question marks as he dictated, such marks are not in the original manuscript. The typesetter later inserted punctuation marks when he prepared the text for the printer.[315] With the exceptions of punctuation, formatting, other elements of typesetting, and minor adjustments required to correct copying and scribal errors, the dictation copy became the text of the first printed edition of the book.[316]

Translation Instruments

Many accounts in the Bible show that God transmitted revelations to His prophets in a variety of ways. Elijah learned that God spoke not to him through the wind or fire or earthquake but through a "still small voice."[317] Paul and other early apostles sometimes communicated with angels and, on occasion, with the Lord Jesus Christ.[318] At other times, revelation came in the form of dreams or visions, such as the revelation to Peter to preach the gospel to the Gentiles, or through sacred objects

---

[315] On the role of the typesetter John Gilbert, see Royal Skousen, "John Gilbert's 1892 Account of the 1830 Printing of the Book of Mormon," in Stephen D. Ricks and others, eds., *The Disciple as Witness: Essays on Latter-day Saint History and Doctrine in Honor of Richard Lloyd Anderson* (Provo, UT: Foundation for Ancient Research and Mormon Studies, 2000), 383–405.

[316] Some grammatical constructions that sound odd to English speakers were edited out of later editions of the Book of Mormon by Joseph Smith or others in order to render the translation into more standard current English. See Richard E. Turley Jr. and William W. Slaughter, *How We Got the Book of Mormon* (Salt Lake City: Deseret Book, 2011), 44–45. Approximately five-sixths of the 1830 first edition of the Book of Mormon was typeset from the printer's manuscript. The other one-sixth was typeset from the original manuscript. (Royal Skousen, "Editor's Preface," in *The Book of Mormon: The Earliest Text,* xxx.)

[317] 1 Kings 19:11–12.

[318] Acts 9:1–8; 12:7–9.

like the Urim and Thummim.[319]

Joseph Smith stands out among God's prophets, because he was called to render into his own language an entire volume of scripture amounting to more than 500 printed pages, containing doctrine that would deepen and expand the theological understanding of millions of people. For this monumental task, God prepared additional, practical help in the form of physical instruments.

Joseph Smith and his scribes wrote of two instruments used in translating the Book of Mormon.

[This is a misleading sentence. Joseph never wrote of any instrument other than the Urim and Thummim. Second, Oliver Cowdery, his main scribe for all but a few pages of the Book of Mormon we have today, never wrote of any instrument other than the Urim and Thummim. Another scribe, John Whitmer, also spoke only of the Urim and Thummim. That leaves only Martin Harris and Emma Smith as scribes, but Martin never wrote about the translation, and Emma wrote only a brief letter in which she mentioned two instruments. Additional statements of varying reliability have been attributed to Martin and Emma.]

According to witnesses of the translation, when Joseph looked into the instruments, the words of scripture appeared in English.

[The only person who looked into the instruments was Joseph Smith. We have no record of a direct statement by Joseph about what he saw or how he used the instruments, except that he used them to translate. The witness statements reflect inference, assumption, and conjecture.

Furthermore, these witnesses could not have seen the actual translation because Joseph was forbidden to show them either the plates or the Urim and Thummim. Instead, the evidence suggests they merely observed a demonstration. All of their statements are

319 Acts 11:4–17; 16:9–10; Exodus 28:30; Leviticus 8:8; Numbers 21:9.

consistent with having observed a demonstration, not the actual translation of the plates.]

One instrument, called in the Book of Mormon the "interpreters," is better known to Latter-day Saints today as the "Urim and Thummim." Joseph found the interpreters buried in the hill with the plates.[320]

[If the "interpreters" are "better known today as the "Urim and Thummim" it is because Joseph himself referred to the Nephite interpreters as the "Urim and Thummim," as is plain throughout Joseph Smith—History and his other accounts of Moroni's visit. The essay consistently evades that important point. Furthermore, they were not "buried." They were "deposited" in a stone box. "Buried" implies a false connection with "buried treasure."]

Those who saw the interpreters described them as a clear pair of stones bound together with a metal rim. The Book of Mormon referred to this instrument, together with its breastplate, as a device "kept and preserved by the hand of the Lord" and "handed down from generation to generation, for the purpose of interpreting languages."[321]

---

[320] Michael Hubbard MacKay, Gerrit J. Dirkmaat, Grand Underwood, Robert J. Woodford, and William G. Hartley, eds., *Documents, Volume 1: July 1828–June 1831,* vol. 1 of the Documents series of *The Joseph Smith Papers,* edited by Dean C. Jessee, Ronald K. Esplin, Richard Lyman Bushman, and Matthew J. Grow (Salt Lake City: Church Historian's Press, 2013), xxix.

[321] Mosiah 28:14–15, 20; see also Mosiah 8:13, 19; and Ether 4:5. Joseph Smith seems to have used the terms "interpreters" and "spectacles" interchangeably during the early years of the Church. Nancy Towle, an itinerant Methodist preacher, recounted Joseph Smith telling her about "a pair of 'interpreters,' (as he called them,) that resembled spectacles, by looking into which, he could *read* a writing engraven upon the plates, though to himself, in a tongue unknown." (Nancy Towle, *Vicissitudes Illustrated in the Experience of Nancy Towle, in Europe and America* [Charleston: James L. Burges, 1832], 138-39.) Joseph's 1832 history referred to "spectacles." (Joseph Smith History, ca. summer 1832, in *Joseph Smith Histories,* 16.) In January 1833, the Latter-day Saint newspaper *The Evening and the Morning Star,* edited by William W. Phelps, equated "spectacles" and "interpreters" with the term "Urim and Thummim": the Book of Mormon "was translated by the gift and power of God, by an unlearned man, through the aid of a pair of Interpreters, or spectacles— (known, perhaps, in ancient days as

[Important: this is the only instrument that Oliver and Joseph ever said that Joseph used during the translation.

As indicated in the footnote, some scholars assume it was W.W. Phelps who coined the term "Urim and Thummim" for the interpreters because Phelps' article in the 1833 *Evening and Morning Star* is the earliest extant published account that uses that term. However, Phelps' article is also consistent with prior use of the term, whether verbal or printed; i.e., Phelps was providing an explanation of the term for readers who were familiar with the Bible. Besides, the first known use of the term *Urim and Thummim* to refer to the Nephite interpreters was reported on August 5, 1832, when Orson Hyde and Samuel Smith told an audience in Boston that the translation "was made known by the spirit of the Lord through the medium of the Urim and Thummim."[322] Of course, Orson and Samuel undoubtedly heard that from someone else—presumably Joseph or Oliver.

Letter IV portrays Moroni telling Joseph that it was his privilege "to obtain and translate the same by the means of the Urim and Thummim, which were deposited for that purpose with the record." When Oliver wrote these letters, he explained he was using original documents then in their possession. He could have referred to the notebook he kept during the translation process, in which he recorded the things Joseph told him. In other words, it could have been Moroni, not W.W. Phelps, who first identified

---

Teraphim, or Urim and Thummim)." ("The Book of Mormon," *The Evening and the Morning Star,* January 1833, [2].) By 1835 Joseph Smith most often used the term "Urim and Thummim" when speaking of translation and rarely, if ever, used the terms "interpreters" or "spectacles." (Joseph Smith, Journal, Nov. 9-11, 1835, in *Journals: Volume 1: 1832-1839,* 89; Joseph Smith, History, 1834-1836, in Davidson et al., *Histories, Volume 1,* 116; John W. Welch, "The Miraculous Translation of the Book of Mormon," in John W. Welch, ed., with Erick B. Carlson, *Opening the Heavens: Accounts of Divine Manifestations, 1820–1844* [Provo, UT, and Salt Lake City: Brigham Young University Press and Deseret Book, 2005], 123-28.)

322 "Questions Proposed to the Mormonite Preachers and Their Answers Obtained Before the Whole Assembly at Julian Hall, Sunday Evening, August 5, 1832," ***Boston Investigator*** Vol. II, No. 20 (August 10, 1832). Online at http://www.sidneyrigdon.com/dbroadhu/NE/miscne01.htm

the interpreters as the Urim and Thummim.

The footnote observes that Joseph "*most often* used the term "Urim and Thummim," but does not explain that we have no record of Joseph ever using the term "seer stone" to explain his translation of the Book of Mormon.]

The other instrument, which Joseph Smith discovered in the ground years before he retrieved the gold plates, was a small oval stone, or "seer stone."[323] As a young man during the 1820s, Joseph Smith, like others in his day, used a seer stone to look for lost objects and buried treasure.[324] As Joseph grew to understand his prophetic calling, he learned that he could use this stone for the higher purpose of translating scripture.[325]

[The last sentence is pure speculation, portrayed here as fact. There are no historical records in which Joseph says or implies anything like this.]

Apparently for convenience, Joseph often translated with the single seer stone rather than the two stones bound together to form the interpreters.

---

323 Joseph Smith probably possessed more than one seer stone; he appears to have found one of the stones while digging for a well around 1822. (Richard L. Bushman, *Joseph Smith and the Beginnings of Mormonism* [Urbana: University of Illinois Press, 1984], 69–70.)

324 According to Martin Harris, an angel commanded Joseph Smith to stop these activities, which he did by 1826. (See Bushman, *Joseph Smith and the Beginnings of Mormonism,* 64–76; and Richard Lloyd Anderson, "The Mature Joseph Smith and Treasure Searching," *BYU Studies* 24, no. 4 [Fall 1984]: 489–560.) Joseph did not hide his well-known early involvement in treasure seeking. In 1838, he published responses to questions frequently asked of him. "Was not Jo Smith a money digger," one question read. "Yes," Joseph answered, "but it was never a very profitable job to him, as he only got fourteen dollars a month for it." (Selections from *Elders' Journal,* July 1838, 43, available at josephsmithpapers.org.) For the broader cultural context, see Alan Taylor, "The Early Republic's Supernatural Economy: Treasure Seeking in the American Northeast, 1780–1830," *American Quarterly* 38, no. 1 (Spring 1986): 6–33.

325 Mark Ashurst-McGee, "A Pathway to Prophethood: Joseph Smith Junior as Rodsman, Village Seer, and Judeo-Christian Prophet," (Master's Thesis, Utah State University, 2000).

[This is also pure speculation, portrayed as fact. Neither Joseph nor Oliver ever said he used one seer stone to translate the text. As we discussed in Chapter 6, others observed Joseph dictating words, but none of them reported what the words were. No one quoted Joseph saying he was translating the plates during these occasions. These accounts are consistent with people who observed a demonstration and inferred it was the actual translation. But they also said Joseph did not use the Urim and Thummim or the plates, so by their own admission, they did not observe what Joseph and Oliver claimed about the actual translation.]

These two instruments—the interpreters and the seer stone—were apparently interchangeable and worked in much the same way such that, in the course of time, Joseph Smith and his associates often used the term "Urim and Thummim" to refer to the single stone as well as the interpreters.[326]

[Although the essay claims Joseph and his associates "often" used the term to refer to a seer stone, the footnote gives only one example, and that example doesn't support the claim.

Over a decade after the translation, on December 27, 1841, Wilford Woodruff recorded in his journal "The Twelve or a part of them spent the day with Joseph the seer + he unfolded unto them many glorious things of the kingdom of God the privileges + blessings of the priesthood + I had the privilege of seeing for the first time in my day the URIM & THUMMIM."[327]

Woodruff does not describe the object, leaving historians to *surmise* he was referring to the seer stone so many people

---

326 For example, when Joseph Smith showed a seer stone to Wilford Woodruff in late 1841, Woodruff recorded in his journal: "I had the privilege of seeing for the first time in my day the URIM & THUMMIM." (Wilford Woodruff journal, Dec. 27, 1841, Church History Library, Salt Lake City.) See also Doctrine and Covenants 130:10.

327 The journal is online at https://catalog.lds.org/assets/28b53d73-2ba2-418b-8ef7-dafcc935bee3/0/125

reported seeing Joseph use years previously. But if Woodruff was referring to the seer stone that many people had already seen, he doesn't explain why it was such a privilege. Brigham Young recorded the same occasion differently.

> I met with the Twelve at brother Joseph's. He conversed with us in a familiar manner on a variety of subjects, and explained to us the Urim and Thummim which he found with the plates, called in the Book of Mormon the Interpreters. He said that every man who lived on the earth was entitled to a seer stone, and should have one, but they are kept from them in consequence of their wickedness, and most of those who do find one make an evil use of it; he showed us his seer stone.[328]

This quotation contradicts the main thesis of SITH. Brigham Young made an explicit distinction between "the Urim and Thummim which he [Joseph] found with the plates," and the "seer stone" Joseph had, which Joseph displayed to explain that "every man who lived on earth was entitled to" such a seer stone. Every man on earth was not entitled to the Urim and Thummim that Joseph found with the plates.

Woodruff didn't mention two separate objects. His statement can be interpreted several ways, including the possibility that he didn't care much about the seer stone but was impressed because Joseph still had the actual Urim and Thummim.

On February 19, 1842, Woodruff recorded in his journal that "the Lord is Blessing Joseph with Power to reveal the mysteries of the kingdom of God; to translate through the Urim and Thummim Ancient records."

Lucy Mack Smith wrote that "Joseph kept the Urim and Thummim constantly about his person." She was writing about an event that occurred in 1827, but Joseph Smith—History 1:60, he says nothing about him delivering the Urim and Thummim to the messenger.

Years later, Heber C. Kimball declared in General Conference that Brigham Young had the Urim and Thummim. Some say this referred to a seer stone, which is possible. But it is also congruent

---

[328] "History of Brigham Young," *Millennial Star* 26 (20 February 1864): 118–119.

with Woodruff's journal entry to infer that what Woodruff saw and what Brigham Young possessed was the Urim and Thummim that Joseph obtained with the plates.

All of Joseph's contemporaries and successors in Church leadership, including Brigham and Wilford, taught that Joseph translated the plates with the Urim and Thummim. None said or implied that he used a seer stone instead.]

In ancient times, Israelite priests used the Urim and Thummim to assist in receiving divine communications. Although commentators differ on the nature of the instrument, several ancient sources state that the instrument involved stones that lit up or were divinely illumined.[329] Latter-day Saints later understood the term "Urim and Thummim" to refer exclusively to the interpreters.

[Joseph's contemporaries and successors all understood the term this way, but Joseph's history shows it was Moroni who identified the interpreters as Urim and Thummim. JS-H 1:52.]

Joseph Smith and others, however, seem to have understood the term more as a descriptive category of instruments for obtaining divine revelations and less as the name of a specific instrument.

["Seem to have understood" is mindreading—and unsupportable historical revisionism. By 1843, usage had developed this way (D&C 130:8-10), but not before Nauvoo.

In 1834, there was no confusion about the two terms. The 1834 book *Mormonism Unvailed* spelled out the two distinct and alternative explanations for the translation: SITH and U&T.

In response to *Mormonism Unvailed*, Oliver Cowdery and Joseph Smith declared unequivocally that Joseph used the Urim and Thummim. They published Letter I (now the footnote to Joseph Smith—History 1:71 that we discussed above). Thereafter, Joseph and Oliver consistently taught that Joseph used the Urim

---

329 Cornelius Van Dam, *The Urim and Thummim: A Means of Revelation in Ancient Israel* (Winona Lake, IN: Eisenbrauns, 1997), 9–26.

and Thummim. All of Joseph's contemporaries and successors did likewise. There are no known instances in which Joseph or Oliver used the term Urim and Thummim to refer to anything Joseph used for the translation of the Book of Mormon except the instrument Moroni put in the stone box.]

Some people have balked at this claim of physical instruments used in the divine translation process, but such aids to facilitate the communication of God's power and inspiration are consistent with accounts in scripture. In addition to the Urim and Thummim, the Bible mentions other physical instruments used to access God's power: the rod of Aaron, a brass serpent, holy anointing oils, the Ark of the Covenant, and even dirt from the ground mixed with saliva to heal the eyes of a blind man.[330]

The Mechanics of Translation

In the preface to the 1830 edition of the Book of Mormon, Joseph Smith wrote: "I would inform you that I translated [the book], by the gift and power of God." When pressed for specifics about the process of translation, Joseph repeated on several occasions that it had been done "by the gift and power of God"[331] and once added, "It was not intended to tell the world all the particulars of the coming forth of the book of Mormon."[332]

[The first statement quoted here establishes Joseph's claim that he <u>actually translated</u> ancient records. The full statement is more explicit: "the which I took from the Book of Lehi," referring to the plates. He did *not* say "the which I read on a stone."

The last statement quoted here does not explicitly refer to the translation. While "the coming forth of the book of Mormon"

---

[330] Exodus 7:9-12; 30:25; 40:9; Leviticus 8:10-12; Numbers 21:9; Joshua 3:6-8; John 9:6.

[331] Preface to the Book of Mormon, 1830 edition.

[332] Minutes, Church conference, Orange, OH, Oct. 25–26, 1831, in Minute Book 2, Church History Library, Salt Lake City, available at josephsmithpapers.org; Welch, "Miraculous Translation," 121–9.

could include the manner of translation, those present at the meeting did not apparently understand it that way. David Whitmer and Martin Harris were both present, and both later discussed details about the translation. If Joseph meant "it is not intended to tell the world all the particulars _of the translation_ of the Book of Mormon," then these two men violated Joseph's instructions. There is no record of anyone stating that Joseph told them not to talk about the mechanics of the translation.

The "coming forth of the Book of Mormon" involved more than the translation. People never told "the particulars" of Joseph being tutored by divine messengers, including Moroni and Nephi. They didn't give "the particulars" about the plates, the breastplate, and the interpreters, or such things as where the Title Page was published.]

Nevertheless, the scribes and others who observed the translation left numerous accounts that give insight into the process.

[This statement assumes these witnesses saw the actual translation instead of merely a demonstration of the concept. Oliver Cowdery was the principal scribe for the current text, and he always said Joseph used the Urim and Thummim to translate. John Whitmer concurred. Only Emma claimed otherwise, for reasons we discussed in Chapter 9.]

Some accounts indicate that Joseph studied the characters on the plates. Most of the accounts speak of Joseph's use of the Urim and Thummim (either the interpreters or the seer stone), and many accounts refer to his use of a single stone.

[This analysis conflates the accounts. Joseph said he studied the characters. Joseph and Oliver consistently said that Joseph translated the plates with the U&T that Moroni put in the stone box. Neither of them ever said or implied that Joseph used a seer stone. Other observers who described SITH may or may not have observed the translation. They did not record what words they heard Joseph dictate, so we can't tell what parts, if any, of the text

they witnessed being translated, although evidence I've presented in this book suggests Joseph dictated some of the Isaiah chapters in 2 Nephi during this demonstration.

Dan Vogel, a critic of Joseph Smith, agrees with the anonymous authors of this essay.

Eyewitness testimony confirms that Joseph Smith translated the Book of Mormon in the same manner that he once hunted for buried treasure: that is, with his brown-colored seer stone placed in the crown of his white top hat and his face snug to its brim. Rather than seeing treasures in the bowels of the earth, Smith claimed he saw luminous words on the stone, which he read to a scribe. In this manner the entire Book of Mormon as we have it came into existence. This fact conflicts with Joseph Smith's official history, which claims that he used magic spectacles—which he euphemistically called Urim and Thummim—attached to a breastplate.[333]

I agree with Vogel that SITH conflicts with the official history, as well as every other statement Joseph and Oliver made.

But I disagree with Vogel—and this Gospel Topics Essay—when they claim the other witnesses observed Joseph translating the Book of Mormon.]

According to these accounts, Joseph placed either the interpreters or the seer stone in a hat, pressed his face into the hat to block out extraneous light, and read aloud the English words that appeared on the instrument.[334]

[Here again, the essay simply assumes the witnesses were

---

[333] http://www.mormonthink.com/essays-bom-translation.htm

[334] Virtually all of the accounts of the translation process are reproduced in Welch, "Miraculous Translation." Two accounts of the translation process, including the use of a seer stone, have been written by members of the Quorum of the Twelve Apostles and published in Church magazines. Historians have also written about the seer stone in Church publications, both in the *Ensign* and in *The Joseph Smith Papers*. (See Neal A. Maxwell, "'By the Gift and Power of God,'" *Ensign*, Jan. 1997, 36–41; Russell M. Nelson, "A Treasured Testament," *Ensign*, July 1993, 61–63; Richard Lloyd Anderson, "'By the Gift and Power of God,'" *Ensign*, Sept. 1977, 78–85; and *Documents, Volume 1: July 1828–June 1831*, xxix–xxxii.)

describing the actual translation of the Book of Mormon instead of a demonstration.

The essay's footnote claims two Apostles have written accounts of the translation process, but each involve isolated quotations from the historical record, not rejections of what Joseph and Oliver taught about the Urim and Thummim.

Elder Maxwell wrote, "The Prophet Joseph alone knew the full process, and he was deliberately reluctant to describe details. We take passing notice of the words of David Whitmer, Joseph Knight, and Martin Harris, who were observers, not translators…. Oliver Cowdery is reported to have testified in court that the Urim and Thummim enabled Joseph 'to read in English, the reformed Egyptian characters, which were engraved on the plates.'"[335]

This statement by Oliver is consistent with everything else he taught; i.e., that Joseph translated the characters with the Urim and Thummim.

Many years before becoming President of the Church, Elder Russell M. Nelson wrote, "The details of this miraculous method of translation are still not fully known. Yet we do have a few precious insights." He then quoted David Whitmer and Emma Smith without further comment.

These statements are "precious insights," but insights into what? David and Emma apparently coordinated their statements more than 40 years after the events. Both focused on SITH to refute the Spalding theory.]

The process as described brings to mind a passage from the Book of Mormon that speaks of God preparing "a stone, which shall shine forth in darkness unto light."[336]

[The passage in Alma (37:21-25) refers twice to "interpreters," but that was a change made in the 1920 edition. Earlier editions, including the original 1830 edition, used the term "directors"

---

335 https://www.churchofjesuschrist.org/study/ensign/1997/01/by-the-gift-and-power-of-god?lang=eng

336 Alma 37:23-24.

instead. That suggests a meaning different from the "interpreters" mentioned in Ether 4:5 and Mosiah 8 and 28, to which Oliver Cowdery referred in Letter 1 ("the Urim and Thummim, or, as the Nephites would have said, 'Interpreters'").

The scriptural phrase doesn't necessarily refer to shining words appearing on a stone.

Consider the other instances of the phrase "shine forth" in the scriptures. "Thou shalt shine forth" (Job 11:17). "Thou that dwellest between the cherubims, shine forth" (Psalms 80:1). "Then shall the righteous shine forth as the sun" (Matthew 13:43). "The King of heaven shall very soon shine forth among all the children of men" (Alma 5:50). "Then shall the righteous shine forth in the kingdom of God" (Alma 40:25). "It shall be brought out of the earth, and it shall shine forth out of darkness" (Mormon 8:16). "Prepare them [stones] that they may shine forth in darkness" (Ether 3:4). "Thy church may... shine forth" (D&C 109:73. "Arise and shine forth..." (D&C 115:5).

The teachings of the Book of Mormon "shine forth" regardless of the method of translation.]

The scribes who assisted with the translation unquestionably believed that Joseph translated by divine power. Joseph's wife Emma explained that she "frequently wrote day after day" at a small table in their house in Harmony, Pennsylvania. She described Joseph "sitting with his face buried in his hat, with the stone in it, and dictating hour after hour with nothing between us."[337]

---

[337] "Last Testimony of Sister Emma," *Saints' Herald* 26 (Oct. 1, 1879), 289–90. Some outside reports describe the spectacles being placed in the hat during the translation process. A Palmyra newspaper published the earliest known account of the translation in August 1829: Jonathan Hadley, a Palmyra printer who may have spoken with Joseph Smith about translation, claimed that the plates were found with a "huge pair of Spectacles," and that "by placing the Spectacles in a hat, and looking into it, Smith could (he said so, at least,) interpret these characters." ("Golden Bible," *Palmyra Freeman*, Aug. 11, 1829, [2].) In the winter of 1831, a Shaker in Union Village, Ohio, spoke of "two transparent stones in the form of spectacles" through which the translator "looked on the engraving & afterwards put his face into a hat & the interpretation then flowed into his mind." (Christian Goodwillie, "Shaker Richard McNemar: The Earliest Book of Mormon Reviewer," *Journal of Mormon History* 37, no.

[Other than claiming to write "day after day," Emma never specified when she wrote or what portion of the text she recorded. She may have written during Joseph's early attempts to translate before Martin Harris arrived, but that would mean she wrote while Joseph translated with the Urim and Thummim because in her 1870 letter, she wrote, "Now the first that my husband translated was translated by the use of the Urim and Thummim, and that was the part that Martin Harris lost, after that he used a small stone, not exactly, black, but was rather a dark color."

Joseph said Emma wrote for him after he recovered the Urim and Thummim in 1828 (they had been taken because of the lost 116 pages). Presumably Emma wrote part or all of the Book of Mosiah, but again, Emma would have written while Joseph translated with the Urim and Thummim. Lucy Mack Smith wrote in her history that while Joseph and Oliver were working in Harmony, Joseph applied the Urim and Thummim to his eyes and looked on the plates. This was before they left for Fayette.

Emma may also have written part of 2 Nephi in Fayette when Joseph demonstrated the process with a stone in a hat. That could have provided the basis for her statements 40+ years later, especially if she sought to counter the Spalding theory.]

According to Emma, the plates "often lay on the table without any attempt at concealment, wrapped in a small linen table cloth."

[This statement has been taken to mean Joseph never used the plates *during the translation*, but that is not what it says. Joseph could leave the plates on the table and also use them when he translated. This is not complicated.]

When asked if Joseph had dictated from the Bible or from a manuscript he had prepared earlier, Emma flatly denied those possibilities: "He had neither manuscript nor book to read from."

---

2 [Spring 2011]: 143.)

[This is part of the refutation of the Spalding theory, which was the original purpose for the interview. Emma volunteered her comments about the manner of translation; they were not in response to specific questions.]

Emma told her son Joseph Smith III, "The Book of Mormon is of divine authenticity—I have not the slightest doubt of it. I am satisfied that no man could have dictated the writing of the manuscripts unless he was inspired; for, when acting as his scribe, your father would dictate to me for hour after hour; and when returning after meals, or after interruptions, he would at once begin where he had left off, without either seeing the manuscript or having any portion of it read to him."[338]

Another scribe, Martin Harris sat across the table from Joseph Smith and wrote down the words Joseph dictated. Harris later related that as Joseph used the seer stone to translate, sentences appeared. Joseph read those sentences aloud, and after penning the words, Harris would say, "Written."

[After he would say "Written," Martin claimed that "if correctly written that sentence would disappear and another appear in its place, but if not written correctly it remained until corrected, so that the translation was just as it was engraven on the plates, precisely in the language then used."

The reference to the engravings on the plates is consistent with the language of D&C 10.

Martin's statement seems to imply a literal translation, but Joseph said only that the Title Page was a literal translation.

Martin never claimed to have seen what Joseph saw when he translated. He also didn't claim that Joseph told him what he saw. Instead, Martin apparently made this claim based on his own inference of what occurred. This statement has led some to conclude that the translation was "tightly controlled," but we do not have the 116 pages to see if there were misspellings and other errors of the type present in the OM.

Martin wrote the 116 pages, so the process may have been

---

[338] "Last Testimony of Sister Emma," 289–90.

different for the translation we have today.]

An associate who interviewed Harris recorded him saying that Joseph "possessed a seer stone, by which he was enabled to translate as well as from the Urim and Thummim, and for convenience he then used the seer stone."[339]

[The essay's footnote here points out that Martin Harris recognized the distinction between the Urim and Thummim (the Nephite interpreters) and the seer stone. Like his contemporaries, Martin didn't use the term to apply to both. Of course, Martin's statement here contradicts Emma's statement that Joseph used the stone after the 116 pages were lost. Martin first spoke about the seer stone in 1881 after David and Emma had used the seer stone scenario to refute the Spalding theory.]

The principal scribe, Oliver Cowdery, testified under oath in 1831 that Joseph Smith "found with the plates, from which he translated his book, two transparent stones, resembling glass, set in silver bows. That by looking through these, he was able to read in English, the reformed Egyptian characters, which were engraved on the plates."[340]

[This is consistent with every statement by Joseph and Oliver about the translation, although it contradicts the SITH narrative.]

In the fall of 1830, Cowdery visited Union Village, Ohio, and spoke about the translation of the Book of Mormon. Soon thereafter, a village resident reported that the translation was accomplished by means of "two transparent stones in the form of spectacles thro which the translator looked on the engraving."[341]

---

339 "One of the Three Witnesses," *Deseret Evening News,* Dec. 13, 1881, 4. Here Martin Harris uses the term "Urim and Thummim" to refer to the interpreters found with the plates.

340 A. W. B., "Mormonites," *Evangelical Magazine and Gospel Advocate* 2 (Apr. 19, 1831): 120.

341 Goodwillie, "Shaker Richard McNemar," 143. For additional accounts of translation by one of the Three Witnesses, see *David Whitmer Interviews: A Restoration*

[This report has Joseph looking on the engraving instead of having the plates resting nearby under a cloth. This is consistent with what Lucy Mack Smith wrote about how Joseph translated the plates. The phrase "two transparent stones" is the description always given of the Nephite interpreters.]

Conclusion

Joseph Smith consistently testified that he translated the Book of Mormon by the "gift and power of God." His scribes shared that testimony. The angel who brought news of an ancient record on metal plates buried in a hillside and the divine instruments prepared especially for Joseph Smith to translate were all part of what Joseph and his scribes viewed as the miracle of translation.

[The term "buried" is ahistorical and implies a false connection to "buried treasure." Moroni explained that the plates were "deposited."]

When he sat down in 1832 to write his own history for the first time, he began by promising to include "an account of his marvelous experience."[342] The translation of the Book of Mormon was truly marvelous.

The truth of the Book of Mormon and its divine source can be known today. God invites each of us to read the book, remember the mercies of the Lord and ponder them in our hearts, "and ask God, the Eternal Father, in the name of Christ, if these things are not true." God promises that "if ye shall ask with a sincere heart, with real intent, having faith in Christ, he will manifest the truth of it unto you, by the power of the Holy Ghost."[343]

Witness, ed. Lyndon W. Cook (Orem, UT: Grandin Book, 1991).

342 Joseph Smith History, ca. Summer 1832, 1, in *Histories, Volume 1, 1832–1844,* 10; available at josephsmithpapers.org. Spelling modernized.

343 Moroni 10:3–5

Appendix 4: Gospel Topics Essay – Proposed Revision

This Appendix consists of my proposed revision to the Gospel Topics Essay on Book of Mormon Translation found at this web page:

https://www.churchofjesuschrist.org/manual/gospel-topics-essays/book-of-mormon-translation?lang=eng

Except as indicated, all footnotes to the essay are original. My proposed revisions are in **bold** typeface.

Book of Mormon Translation

Wilford Woodruff reported that Joseph Smith **taught** that the Book of Mormon was "the most correct of any Book on earth & the keystone of our religion & a man would get nearer to God by abiding by its precepts than by any other Book."[344]

The Book of Mormon came into the world through a series of miraculous events. Much can be known about the coming forth of the English text of the Book of Mormon through a careful study of statements made by Joseph Smith, his scribes, and others closely associated with the translation of the Book of Mormon.

"By the Gift and Power of God"

Joseph Smith reported that on the evening of September 21, 1823, while he prayed in the upper room of his parents' small log home in Palmyra, New York, an angel who called himself Moroni appeared and

[344] Wilford Woodruff journal, Nov. 28, 1841, Church History Library, Salt Lake City.

told Joseph that "God had a work for [you] to do."[345]

He informed Joseph that "there was a book deposited, written upon gold plates, giving an account of the former inhabitants of this continent, and the source from whence they sprang." The book contained the fullness of the everlasting Gospel as delivered by the Savior to the ancient inhabitants.[346]

The messenger **"said this history was written and deposited not far from that place [the Smith farm near Palmyra], and that it was [Joseph's] privilege, if obedient to the commandments of the Lord, to obtain and translate the same by the means of the Urim and Thummim, which were deposited for that purpose with the record.**[347]

The young man had little formal education, **but between the ages of 12 and 15, he had been "searching the scriptures believeing as I was taught, that they contained the word of God thus applying myself to them and my intimate acquaintance with those of differant denominations,"[348] so he was conversant with Christian teachings.** He knew no languages other than English. He was incapable of translating an ancient book written in an unknown language (known in the Book of Mormon as "reformed Egyptian"[349]) into English. Joseph's wife Emma later explained that, at the time of translation, Joseph "could neither write nor dictate a

---

[345] On the identity of the angel, see Karen Lynn Davidson, David J. Whittaker, Mark Ashurst-McGee, and Richard L. Jenson, eds., *Histories, Volume 1: Joseph Smith Histories, 1832–1844*, vol. 1 of the Histories series of The Joseph Smith Papers, edited by Dean C. Jessee, Ronald K. Esplin, and Richard Lyman Bushman (Salt Lake City: Church Historian's Press, 2012), 223 n 56.

[346] Davidson et al., *Joseph Smith Histories,* 223; punctuation regularized; Joseph Smith, "Church History," *Times and Seasons* 3 (March 1, 1842): 706-7. See also Joseph Smith—History 1:33–34.

[347] Letter IV, online at https://www.josephsmithpapers.org/paper-summary/history-1834-1836/68

[348] Smith, *History*, circa Summer 1832, https://www.josephsmithpapers.org/paper-summary/history-circa-summer-1832/2.

[349] Mormon 9:32. See also 1 Nephi 1:2.

coherent and well-worded letter, let alone dictat[e] a book like the Book of Mormon."[350]

How was he to translate the record?

The angel explained "that there were two stones in silver bows—and these stones, fastened to a breastplate, constituted what is called the Urim and Thummim—deposited with the plates; and the possession and use of these stones were what constituted "seers" in ancient or former times; and that God had prepared them for the purpose of translating the book."[351]

Joseph received the plates in September 1827 and the following spring, in Harmony, Pennsylvania, began translating them in earnest, with Emma and his friend Martin Harris serving as his main scribes. The resulting English transcription, known as the Book of Lehi and referred to by Joseph Smith as written on 116 pages, was subsequently lost or stolen. As a result, Joseph Smith was rebuked by the Lord and lost the ability to translate for a short time.[352]

Joseph reported that "on the 22d of September [1828], I had the joy and satisfaction of again receiving the Urim and Thummim; and have commenced translating again." [353] Joseph began translating in earnest in 1829. Most of the present Book of Mormon text was translated during a three-month period between April and June of that year. His chief scribe during these months was Oliver Cowdery,

---

350 "Last Testimony of Sister Emma," *Saints' Herald* 26 (Oct. 1, 1879), 290.

351 Joseph Smith—History 1:35.

352 Joseph Smith History, 1838–ca. 1841, 8–11 (draft 2), in Karen Lynn Davidson, David J. Whittaker, Mark Ashurst-McGee, and Richard L. Jenson, eds., *Histories, Volume 1: Joseph Smith Histories, 1832–1844,* vol. 1 of the Histories series of *The Joseph Smith Papers,* edited by Dean C. Jessee, Ronald K. Esplin, and Richard Lyman Bushman (Salt Lake City: Church Historian's Press, 2012), 252–3; available at josephsmithpapers.org; Doctrine and Covenants 3:5–15.

353 D&C 10:1-2; Lucy Mack Smith, *History,* 1845, available online at https://www.josephsmithpapers.org/paper-summary/lucy-mack-smith-history-1845/143

a schoolteacher from Vermont who learned about the Book of Mormon while boarding with Joseph's parents in Palmyra. Called by God in a vision, Cowdery traveled to Harmony to meet Joseph Smith and investigate further. Of his experience as scribe, Cowdery wrote, "These were days never to be forgotten—to sit under the sound of a voice dictated by the *inspiration* of heaven....Day after day I continued, uninterrupted, to write from his mouth, as he translated with the Urim and Thummim, or, as the Nephites would have said, 'Interpreters,' the history or record called 'The Book of Mormon.'"[354]

The manuscript that Joseph Smith dictated to Oliver Cowdery and others is known today as the original manuscript, about 28 percent of which still survives.[355] This manuscript corroborates Joseph Smith's statements that the manuscript was written within a short time frame and that it was dictated from another language. For example, it includes errors that suggest the scribe heard words incorrectly rather than misread words copied from another manuscript.[356]

---

[354] Joseph Smith History, ca. summer 1832, in *Joseph Smith Histories,* 16; Oliver Cowdery to William W. Phelps, Sept. 7, 1834, in *Messenger and Advocate* 1 (Oct. 1834): 14; italics in original.

[355] Most of the manuscript disintegrated or became otherwise unreadable due to water damage between 1841 and 1882, as a result of being placed in the cornerstone of the Nauvoo House in Nauvoo, Illinois. Most of the surviving pages were later archived in the historian's office of The Church of Jesus Christ of Latter-day Saints in Salt Lake City. The extant original manuscript has been published in *The Original Manuscript of the Book of Mormon: Typographical Facsimile of the Extant Text,* ed. Royal Skousen (Provo, UT: Foundation for Ancient Research and Mormon Studies, 2001). A complete copy of this original, known as the printer's manuscript, was made by Oliver Cowdery and two other scribes between August 1829 and early 1830. It was used to set the type for most of the printing in Palmyra. The printer's manuscript is published in *The Printer's Manuscript of the Book of Mormon: Typological Facsimile of the Entire Text in Two Parts,* ed. Royal Skousen (Provo, UT: Foundation for Ancient Research and Mormon Studies, 2001). Both the printer's manuscript and the original manuscript will be published in future volumes of *The Joseph Smith Papers.* (Dean C. Jessee, "The Original Book of Mormon Manuscript," *BYU Studies* 10, no. 3 [Spring 1970]: 261–72; Royal Skousen, "Piecing Together the Original Manuscript," *BYU Today* 46, no. 3 [May 1992]: 18–24.)

[356] For example, when Joseph translated the text that is now in 1 Nephi 13:29, the scribe wrote "&" in one place where he should have written "an." At 1 Nephi 17:48, the scribe wrote "weed" where he should have written "reed." (See Royal Skousen,

In addition, some grammatical constructions that are more characteristic of Near Eastern languages than English appear in the original manuscript, suggesting that the base language of the translation was not English.[357]

Unlike most dictated drafts, the original manuscript was considered by Joseph Smith to be, in substance, a final product. To assist in the publication of the book, Oliver Cowdery made a handwritten copy of the original manuscript. This copy is known today as the printer's manuscript. Because Joseph Smith did not call for punctuation, such as periods, commas, or question marks as he dictated, such marks are not in the original manuscript. The typesetter later inserted punctuation marks when he prepared the text for the printer.[358] With the exceptions of punctuation, formatting, other elements of typesetting, and minor adjustments required to correct copying and scribal errors, the dictation copy became the text of the first printed edition of the book.[359]

"Translating the Book of Mormon: Evidence from the Original Manuscript," in Noel B. Reynolds, ed., *Book of Mormon Authorship Revisited: The Evidence for Ancient Origins* [Provo, UT: Foundation for Ancient Research and Mormon Studies, 1997], 67; see also Grant Hardy, "Introduction," in *The Book of Mormon: The Earliest Text,* ed. Royal Skousen [New Haven: Yale University Press, 2009], xv–xix.)

[357] John A. Tvedtnes, "Hebraisms in the Book of Mormon" and "Names of People: Book of Mormon," in Geoffrey Kahn, ed., *Encyclopedia of Hebrew Language and Linguistics* (Brill Online, 2013); M. Deloy Pack, "Hebraisms," in *Book of Mormon Reference Companion,* ed. Dennis L. Largey (Salt Lake City: Deseret Book, 2003), 321–25; John A. Tvedtnes, "The Hebrew Background of the Book of Mormon," in John L. Sorenson and Melvin J. Thorne, eds., *Rediscovering the Book of Mormon* (Salt Lake City and Provo, UT: Deseret Book and Foundation for Ancient Research and Mormon Studies, 1991), 77–91; Donald W. Parry, "Hebraisms and Other Ancient Peculiarities in the Book of Mormon," in Donald W. Parry and others, eds., *Echoes and Evidences of the Book of Mormon* (Provo, UT: Foundation for Ancient Research and Mormon Studies, 2002), 155–89.

[358] On the role of the typesetter John Gilbert, see Royal Skousen, "John Gilbert's 1892 Account of the 1830 Printing of the Book of Mormon," in Stephen D. Ricks and others, eds., *The Disciple as Witness: Essays on Latter-day Saint History and Doctrine in Honor of Richard Lloyd Anderson* (Provo, UT: Foundation for Ancient Research and Mormon Studies, 2000), 383–405.

[359] Some grammatical constructions that sound odd to English speakers were edited out of later editions of the Book of Mormon by Joseph Smith or others in order to

Translation Instruments

Many accounts in the Bible show that God transmitted revelations to His prophets in a variety of ways. Elijah learned that God spoke not to him through the wind or fire or earthquake but through a "still small voice."[360] Paul and other early apostles sometimes communicated with angels and, on occasion, with the Lord Jesus Christ.[361] At other times, revelation came in the form of dreams or visions, such as the revelation to Peter to preach the gospel to the Gentiles, or through sacred objects like the Urim and Thummim.[362]

Joseph Smith stands out among God's prophets, because he was called to render into his own language (English) an entire volume of scripture amounting to more than 500 printed pages, containing doctrine that would deepen and expand the theological understanding of millions of people. For this monumental task, God prepared additional, practical help in the form of physical instruments.

Joseph Smith and Oliver Cowdery provided several accounts of the translation during their lifetimes.[363] They always explained that Joseph Smith translated the plates with the Urim and Thummim. Neither of them described the process in detail, but

---

render the translation into more standard current English. See Richard E. Turley Jr. and William W. Slaughter, *How We Got the Book of Mormon* (Salt Lake City: Deseret Book, 2011), 44–45. Approximately five-sixth of the 1830 first edition of the Book of Mormon was typeset from the printer's manuscript. The other one-sixth was typeset from the original manuscript. (Royal Skousen, "Editor's Preface," in *The Book of Mormon: The Earliest Text,* xxx.)

360 1 Kings 19:11–12.

361 Acts 9:3-8; 12:7–9.

362 Acts 10:9–17; 16:9–10; Exodus 28:30; Leviticus 8:8; Numbers 21:9.

363 For example, in his 1842 article "Church History," commonly known as the Wentworth letter, Joseph wrote "With the records was found a curious instrument, which the ancients called "Urim and Thummim," which consisted of **two transparent stones** set in the rim of a **bow** fastened to a breastplate. Through the medium of the Urim and Thummim I translated the record by the gift and power of God." ("Church History," *Times and Seasons,* March 1, 1842.)

two accounts reported that Oliver explained Joseph looked through the Urim and Thummim to read the characters on the plates. (These accounts are discussed below.)

Joseph recalled that when the angel first visited him, "he told me, that when I got those plates of which he had spoken—for the time that they should be obtained was not yet fulfilled—I should not show them to any person; neither the breastplate with the Urim and Thummim; only to those to whom I should be commanded to show them; if I did I should be destroyed."[364]

Pursuant to this command, only three witnesses besides Joseph Smith were permitted to see the Urim and Thummim: Oliver Cowdery, David Whitmer, and Martin Harris. Joseph's mother felt it through a cloth and described it. Those who saw the interpreters described them as a clear pair of stones bound together with a metal rim. The Book of Mormon referred to this instrument, together with its breastplate, as a device "kept and preserved by the hand of the Lord" and "handed down from generation to generation, for the purpose of interpreting languages."[365]

---

364 JS-H 1:42.

365 Mosiah 28:14–15, 20; see also Mosiah 8:13, 19; and Ether 4:5. Joseph Smith seems to have used the terms "interpreters" and "spectacles" interchangeably during the early years of the Church. Nancy Towle, an itinerant Methodist preacher, recounted Joseph Smith telling her about "a pair of 'interpreters,' (as he called them,) that resembled spectacles, by looking into which, he could *read* a writing engraven upon the plates, though to himself, in a tongue unknown." (Nancy Towle, *Vicissitudes Illustrated in the Experience of Nancy Towle, in Europe and America* [Charleston: James L. Burges, 1832], 138-39.) Joseph's 1832 history referred to "spectacles." (Joseph Smith History, ca. summer 1832, in *Joseph Smith Histories,* 16.) A Boston newspaper reported on August 5, 1832, that Orson Hyde and Samuel Smith told an audience that the translation "was made known by the spirit of the Lord through the medium of the Urim and Thummim." ("Questions Proposed to the Mormonite Preachers and Their Answers Obtained Before the Whole Assembly at Julian Hall, Sunday Evening, August 5, 1832," *Boston Investigator*, Vol. II, No. 20 (August 10, 1832).) In January 1833, the Latter-day Saint newspaper *The Evening and the Morning Star,* edited by William W. Phelps, equated "spectacles" and "interpreters" with the term "Urim and Thummim": the Book of Mormon "was translated by the gift and power of God, by an unlearned man, through the aid of a pair of Interpreters, or spectacles— (known, perhaps, in

Although Joseph and Oliver always taught that Joseph translated with the Urim and Thummim that came with the plates, others claimed that Joseph used another instrument to produce the Book of Mormon. This other instrument, which Joseph Smith discovered in the ground years before he retrieved the gold plates, was a small oval stone, or "seer stone,"[366] also referred to as a "peep stone."[367] As a young man during the 1820s, Joseph Smith, like others in his day, allegedly used a seer stone to look for lost objects and buried treasure.[368]

The existence of two alternative explanations for the translation was apparent by 1834. The book *Mormonism Unvailed* described the alternatives as "the old 'peep stone'" and

---

ancient days as Teraphim, or Urim and Thummim)." ("The Book of Mormon," *The Evening and the Morning Star*, January 1833, [2].) By 1835 Joseph Smith most often used the term "Urim and Thummim" when speaking of translation and rarely, if ever, used the terms "interpreters" or "spectacles." (Joseph Smith, Journal, Nov. 9-11, 1835, in *Journals: Volume 1: 1832-1839*, 89; Joseph Smith, History, 1834-1836, in Davidson et al., *Histories, Volume 1*, 116; John W. Welch, "The Miraculous Translation of the Book of Mormon," in John W. Welch, ed., with Erick B. Carlson, *Opening the Heavens: Accounts of Divine Manifestations, 1820–1844* [Provo, UT, and Salt Lake City: Brigham Young University Press and Deseret Book, 2005], 123-28.)

366 Joseph Smith may have possessed more than one seer stone; he appears to have found one of the stones while digging for a well around 1822. (Richard L. Bushman, *Joseph Smith and the Beginnings of Mormonism* [Urbana: University of Illinois Press, 1984], 69–70.)

367 "Peep stone" is a pejorative term used by critics such as the 1834 book *Mormonism Unvailed.*

368 According to Martin Harris, an angel commanded Joseph Smith to stop these activities, which he did by 1826. (See Bushman, *Joseph Smith and the Beginnings of Mormonism*, 64–76; and Richard Lloyd Anderson, "The Mature Joseph Smith and Treasure Searching," *BYU Studies* 24, no. 4 [Fall 1984]: 489–560.) Joseph did not hide his well-known early involvement in treasure seeking. In 1838, he published responses to questions frequently asked of him. "Was not Jo Smith a money digger," one question read. "Yes," Joseph answered, "but it was never a very profitable job to him, as he only got fourteen dollars a month for it." (Selections from *Elders' Journal*, July 1838, 43, available at josephsmithpapers.org.) For the broader cultural context, see Alan Taylor, "The Early Republic's Supernatural Economy: Treasure Seeking in the American Northeast, 1780–1830," *American Quarterly* 38, no. 1 (Spring 1986): 6–33.

the "big spectacles… Urim and Thummim."[369]

When they responded to *Mormonism Unvailed* in the series of eight essays or letters published in the *Messenger and Advocate*,[370] Joseph and Oliver claimed Joseph used the Urim and Thummim to translate the plates. They reaffirmed that teaching throughout the rest of their lives. Neither of them claimed that Joseph merely read words that appeared on a seer/peep stone, that he didn't actually translate the plates, or that he had power to translate the plates with anything other than the Urim and Thummim.

Church leaders, including both Joseph's contemporaries and his successors, have consistently reaffirmed that Joseph translated the plates with the Urim and Thummim.

However, the existence of alternative accounts in the historical record has led scholars to seek a reconciliation between the two narratives. The analysis involves a comparison of the relative credibility, reliability and consistency of the various witnesses, as well as any motives for their statements.

One author proposed that as Joseph grew to understand his prophetic calling, he learned that he could use this seer stone for the higher purpose of translating scripture.[371] Some authors propose that, for convenience, Joseph translated with the single

---

369 "Instead of looking at the characters inscribed upon the plates, the prophet was obliged to resort to the old "peep stone," which he formerly used in money-digging. This he placed in a hat, or box, into which he also thrust his face…. Another account they give of the transaction, is, that it was performed with the big spectacles before mentioned, and which were in fact, the identical Urim and Thumim." E.D. Howe, *Mormonism Unvailed*, p. 18.

370 Oliver Cowdery's Letter I, now a note at the end of Joseph Smith—History in the Pearl of Great Price, was first published in October 1834, the same month that *Mormonism Unvailed* was released.

371 Mark Ashurst-McGee, "A Pathway to Prophethood: Joseph Smith Junior as Rodsman, Village Seer, and Judeo-Christian Prophet," (Master's Thesis, Utah State University, 2000).

seer stone rather than the two stones bound together to form the interpreters. Others propose that, assuming these two instruments—the interpreters and the seer stone—were interchangeable and worked in much the same was, in the course of time, Joseph Smith and his associates often used the term "Urim and Thummim" to refer to the single stone as well as the interpreters.[372]

Still others propose that Joseph conducted a demonstration of the process by using the well-known stone-in-the-hat technique, which witnesses inferred was the actual translation, although none of them quoted Joseph saying as much or recorded what he dictated on those occasions.[373] Witness statements based on such a "seer stone" demonstration may have been used to refute the once-popular theory that Joseph produced the Book of Mormon by reading, from behind a curtain, a manuscript originating with Solomon Spalding.

It is unlikely that the existing historical sources can be reconciled to everyone's satisfaction. Each individual may choose what to believe. The larger point is that Joseph could translate the ancient record only by the gift and power of God.

The use of divine instruments has historical precedent. In ancient times, Israelite priests used the Urim and Thummim to assist in receiving divine communications. Although commentators differ on the nature of the instrument, several ancient sources state that the

---

[372] For example, in late 1841, Wilford Woodruff recorded in his journal: "I had the privilege of seeing for the first time in my day the URIM & THUMMIM." (Wilford Woodruff journal, Dec. 27, 1841, Church History Library, Salt Lake City.) https://catalog.churchofjesuschrist.org/assets?id=28b53d73-2ba2-418b-8ef7-dafcc935bee3&crate=0&index=125. See also Doctrine and Covenants 130:10. Some assume Woodruff saw a seer stone, while others assume Joseph had retained the Urim and Thummim that he found with the plates.

[373] If, as he and Oliver always claimed, Joseph translated the plates with the Urim and Thummim, he could not display these interpreters to anyone. By definition, therefore, none of the seer stone witnesses could have observed the actual translation. See Jonathan Neville, *A Man that Can Translate* (Legends Library 2020).

instrument involved stones that lit up or were divinely illumined.[374]

Some people have balked at this claim of physical instruments used in the divine translation process, but such aids to facilitate the communication of God's power and inspiration are consistent with accounts in scripture. In addition to the Urim and Thummim, the Bible mentions other physical instruments used to access God's power: the rod of Aaron, a brass serpent, holy anointing oils, the Ark of the Covenant, and even dirt from the ground mixed with saliva to heal the eyes of a blind man.[375]

The Mechanics of Translation

In the preface to the 1830 edition of the Book of Mormon, Joseph Smith wrote: "I would inform you that I translated [the book], by the gift and power of God." When pressed for specifics about the process of translation, Joseph repeated on several occasions that it had been done "by the gift and power of God"[376] **and that he translated "through the medium of the Urim and Thummim" that came with the plates.**[377]

Joseph once stated that "It was not intended to tell the world all the particulars of the coming forth of the book of Mormon."[378] That statement does not appear to have been understood to apply to the translation, however; Oliver Cowdery, David Whitmer and Martin Harris were all present in that meeting and went on to discuss "particulars" about the translation itself.

---

374 Cornelius Van Dam, *The Urim and Thummim: A Means of Revelation in Ancient Israel* (Winona Lake, IN: Eisenbrauns, 1997), 9–26.
375 Exodus 7:9-12; 30:25; 40:9; Leviticus 8:10-12; Numbers 21:9; Joshua 3:6-8; John 9:6.
376 Preface to the Book of Mormon, 1830 edition.
377 Wentworth letter.
378 Minutes, Church conference, Orange, OH, Oct. 25–26, 1831, in Minute Book 2, Church History Library, Salt Lake City, available at josephsmithpapers.org; Welch, "Miraculous Translation,",121–9.

The most authoritative explanation of the process appears in the Doctrine and Covenants. The Lord granted Oliver Cowdery the privilege of translating, but Oliver was unable to accomplish the task. The Lord explained the cause of that failure this way:

> **7 Behold, you have not understood; you have supposed that I would give it unto you, when you took no thought save it was to ask me.**
> **8 But, behold, I say unto you, that you must study it out in your mind; then you must ask me if it be right, and if it is right I will cause that your bosom shall burn within you; therefore, you shall feel that it is right.**
> **9 But if it be not right you shall have no such feelings, but you shall have a stupor of thought that shall cause you to forget the thing which is wrong; therefore, you cannot write that which is sacred save it be given you from me.**
> **10 Now, if you had known this you could have translated; nevertheless, it is not expedient that you should translate now.**
> **(Doctrine and Covenants 9:7–10)**

Joseph explained that he prepared for the translation by studying the characters on the plates. He explained that in Harmony, Pennsylvania, in December 1827, "I commenced copying the characters off the plates. I copied a considerable number of them, and by means of the Urim and Thummim I translated some of them, which I did between the time I arrived at the house of my wife's father, in the month of December, and the February following." (Joseph Smith—History 1:62)

The historical record contains numerous accounts from Joseph contemporaries spanning over 50 years. Witnesses claimed Joseph placed either the Urim and Thummim or the seer stone in a hat, pressed his face into the hat to block out extraneous light, and read aloud the English words that appeared on the instrument.[379] **It is difficult to tell**

379 Virtually all of the accounts of the translation process are reproduced in Welch, "Miraculous Translation." Two accounts of the translation process, including the use of a seer stone, have been written by members of the Quorum of the Twelve Apostles and published in Church magazines. Historians have also written about the seer stone in Church publications, both in the *Ensign* and in *The Joseph Smith Papers*. (See Neal A.

whether these witnesses reported their own first-hand observations of the translation or a demonstration, or whether they stated as fact things they heard from others.

For these reasons, Church members generally accept what Joseph and Oliver taught; i.e., that Joseph Smith translated the plates by the gift and power of God, using the Urim and Thummim that came with the plates. This teaching has been reaffirmed by Church leaders for over 150 years.

In the fall of 1830, the principal scribe, Oliver Cowdery visited Union Village, Ohio, and spoke about the translation of the Book of Mormon. Soon thereafter, a village resident reported that the translation was accomplished by means of "two transparent stones in the form of spectacles thro which the translator looked on the engraving."[380]

Oliver reportedly testified under oath in 1831 that Joseph Smith "found with the plates, from which he translated his book, two transparent stones, resembling glass, set in silver bows. That by looking through these, he was able to read in English, the reformed Egyptian characters, which were engraved on the plates."[381]

Other scribes who assisted with the translation unquestionably believed that Joseph translated by divine power. Joseph Smith's son, Joseph Smith III, interviewed his mother Emma 50 years

---

Maxwell, "'By the Gift and Power of God,'" *Ensign,* Jan. 1997, 36–41; Russell M. Nelson, "A Treasured Testament," *Ensign,* July 1993, 61–63; Richard Lloyd Anderson, "'By the Gift and Power of God,'" *Ensign,* Sept. 1977, 78–85; and *Documents, Volume 1: July 1828–June 1831,* xxix–xxxii.)

380 Goodwillie, "Shaker Richard McNemar," 143. For additional accounts of translation by one of the Three Witnesses, see *David Whitmer Interviews: A Restoration Witness,* ed. Lyndon W. Cook (Orem, UT: Grandin Book, 1991).

381 A. W. B., "Mormonites," *Evangelical Magazine and Gospel Advocate* 2 (Apr. 19, 1831): 120. This is not a direct quotation but merely a summary of Oliver's testimony as understood by the newspaper reporter.

after the events. He published the interview six months after her death as "The Last Testimony of Sister Emma." The interview began by focusing on the Spalding theory and progressed to a discussion of the translation. The "Last Testimony" claimed that Emma "frequently wrote day after day" at a small table in their house in Harmony, Pennsylvania, with Joseph "sitting with his face buried in his hat, with the stone in it, and dictating hour after hour with nothing between us."[382]

According to this statement, the plates "often lay on the table without any attempt at concealment, wrapped in a small linen table cloth."

When asked if Joseph had dictated from the Bible or from a manuscript he had prepared earlier, Emma flatly denied those possibilities: "He had neither manuscript nor book to read from… The Book of Mormon is of divine authenticity—I have not the slightest doubt of it. I am satisfied that no man could have dictated the writing of the manuscripts unless he was inspired; for, when acting as his scribe, your father would dictate to me for hour after hour; and when returning after meals, or after interruptions, he would at once begin where he had left off, without either seeing the manuscript or having any portion of

382 "Last Testimony of Sister Emma," *Saints' Herald* 26 (Oct. 1, 1879), 289–90. This statement was recorded shortly before Emma died in April 1879 but not published until six months later. She never signed or publicly acknowledged it. Some outside reports describe the spectacles being placed in the hat during the translation process. A Palmyra newspaper published the earliest known account of the translation in August 1829: Jonathan Hadley, a Palmyra printer who may have spoken with Joseph Smith about translation, claimed that the plates were found with a "huge pair of Spectacles," and that "by placing the Spectacles in a hat, and looking into it, Smith could (he said so, at least,) interpret these characters." ("Golden Bible," *Palmyra Freeman,* Aug. 11, 1829, [2].) In the winter of 1831, a Shaker in Union Village, Ohio, spoke of "two transparent stones in the form of spectacles" through which the translator "looked on the engraving & afterwards put his face into a hat & the interpretation then flowed into his mind." (Christian Goodwillie, "Shaker Richard McNemar: The Earliest Book of Mormon Reviewer," *Journal of Mormon History* 37, no. 2 [Spring 2011]: 143.)

it read to him."[383]

Another scribe, Martin Harris sat across the table from Joseph Smith and wrote down the words Joseph dictated. Although he spoke only of the Urim and Thummim for decades, late in life Harris related that Joseph used a seer stone to translate. Joseph read sentences aloud, and after penning the words, Harris would say, "Written."

An associate who interviewed Harris recorded him saying that Joseph "possessed a seer stone, by which he was enabled to translate as well as from the Urim and Thummim, and for convenience he then used the seer stone."[384]

Conclusion

Joseph Smith consistently testified that he translated the Book of Mormon by the "gift and power of God" through the medium of the Urim and Thummim. His scribes shared that testimony. The angel who brought news of an ancient record on metal plates deposited in a hillside and the Urim and Thummim prepared especially for Joseph Smith to translate were all part of what Joseph and his scribes viewed as the miracle of translation. When he sat down in 1832 to write his own history for the first time, he began by promising to include "an account of his marvelous experience."[385] The translation of the Book of Mormon was truly marvelous.

The truth of the Book of Mormon and its divine source can be known today. God invites each of us to read the book, remember the mercies of the Lord and ponder them in our hearts, "and ask God, the Eternal Father, in the name of Christ, if these things are not true." God promises that "if ye shall ask with a sincere heart, with real intent,

---

383 "Last Testimony of Sister Emma," 289–90.

384 "One of the Three Witnesses," *Deseret Evening News,* Dec. 13, 1881, 4. Here Martin Harris distinguishes between the seer stone and the "Urim and Thummim" as *Mormonism Unvailed* did.

385 Joseph Smith History, ca. Summer 1832, 1, in *Histories, Volume 1, 1832–1844,* 10; available at josephsmithpapers.org. Spelling modernized.

having faith in Christ, he will manifest the truth of it unto you, by the power of the Holy Ghost."[386]

386 Moroni 10:3–5.

Appendix 5: Interpreters vs. Directors

When Oliver Cowdery rejoined the Church in 1848, he reiterated the testimony he had given on previous occasions, adding an important detail. When you read this, keep in mind that Oliver possessed Joseph's brown seer stone, the one people claimed Joseph used to produce the Book of Mormon. After Oliver died in 1850, his wife gave the stone to Phineas Young. This is the one displayed by the Church in recent years.[387] It was in his pocket or on his person as he stood and spoke.

Did he hold it up and display it? No.

Did he refer to it as the instrument Joseph used to translate the plates? No.

Did he even mention it? No.

Instead, he reaffirmed his testimony that Joseph used the U&T.

> I wrote with my own pen the entire Book of Mormon (save a few pages) as it fell from the lips of the Prophet as he translated it by the gift and power of God by means of the Urim and Thummim, or as it is called by that book, holy interpreters. I beheld with my eyes and handled with my hands the gold plates from which it was translated. I also beheld the Interpreters.[388]

Whether Oliver handled the plates and beheld the interpreters during the translation process or later as one of the Three Witnesses, or both, he spoke with the authority that comes from personal experience.

Consider how closely this final testimony tracks with what he wrote in 1834:

> These were days never to be forgotten—to sit under the sound of a voice dictated by the inspiration of heaven, awakened the utmost gratitude of this bosom! Day after day I continued, uninterrupted, to write from his mouth, as **he translated with the Urim and**

---

[387] See https://www.josephsmithpapers.org/topic/seer-stone.

[388] Reuben Miller's account of Oliver's speech. See Item #46 in Appendix 1.

> **Thummim**, or, as the Nephites would have said, '**Interpreters**,' the history or record called 'The Book of Mormon.'
>
> (Joseph Smith—History, Note, 1)

Only four verses in the 1830 edition of the Book of Mormon refer to "interpreters."

> Now Ammon said unto him: I can assuredly tell thee, O king, of a man that can translate the records; for he has wherewith that he can look, and translate all records that are of ancient date; and it is a gift from God. And the things are called **interpreters**, and no man can look in them except he be commanded, lest he should look for that he ought not and he should perish. And whosoever is commanded to look in them, the same is called seer. (Mosiah 8:13)

> And now, when Ammon had made an end of speaking these words the king rejoiced exceedingly, and gave thanks to God, saying: Doubtless a great mystery is contained within these plates, and these **interpreters** were doubtless prepared for the purpose of unfolding all such mysteries to the children of men. (Mosiah 8:19)

> And now, as I said unto you, that after king Mosiah had done these things, he took the plates of brass, and all the things which he had kept, and conferred them upon Alma, who was the son of Alma; yea, all the records, and also the **interpreters**, and conferred them upon him, and commanded him that he should keep and preserve them, and also keep a record of the people, handing them down from one generation to another, even as they had been handed down from the time that Lehi left Jerusalem. (Mosiah 28:20)

> Wherefore the Lord hath commanded me to write them; and I have written them. And he commanded me that I should seal them up; and he also hath commanded that I should seal up the interpretation thereof; wherefore I have sealed up the **interpreters**, according to the commandment of the Lord. (Ether 4:5)

The current edition of the Book of Mormon contains two additional references to the "interpreters" in Alma 37.

> 21 And now, I will speak unto you concerning those twenty-four plates, that ye keep them, that the mysteries and the works of darkness, and their secret works, or the secret works of those people who have been destroyed, may be made manifest unto this people; yea, all their murders, and robbings, and their plunderings, and all their wickedness and abominations, may be made manifest unto this people; yea, and that ye preserve these **interpreters**.
>
> 24 And now, my son, these **interpreters** were prepared that the word of God might be fulfilled, which he spake, saying:

In the 1830 edition, these verses read "yea, and that ye preserve these **directors**… And now my son, these **directors** were prepared…" It wasn't until the 1920 edition that the term *directors* was changed to *interpreters.*

This means that **Oliver Cowdery was not referring to the directors in Alma 37**.

This is important because some historians cite Alma 37 to support the stone-in-a-hat theory.

Why was the term changed in the 1920 edition?

One reasonable interpretation of Alma 37 is that when Alma referred to the *directors*, he was referring to the same objects called *interpreters* in Mosiah and Ether. That's the gist of an article in the *Interpreter*, which you can read here:

https://www.mormoninterpreter.com/reflections-of-urim-hebrew-poetry-sheds-light-on-the-directors-interpreters-mystery/

The comments below the article raise several interesting points and provide additional references for those who want to know more about all of this.

The article in the *Interpreter* magazine makes a point that in Chapter 37, Alma refers to the *directors*, plural, but Alma also discusses the liahona, a compass, a ball, or *director* (singular).

The article doesn't mention that, in today's editions of the scriptures, the only reference to *directors* is in D&C 17:1. That verse makes a clear distinction between the Urim and Thummim and the directors (plural).

> Behold, I say unto you, that you must rely upon my word, which if you do with full purpose of heart, you shall have a view of the plates, and also of the breastplate, the sword of Laban, the **Urim and Thummim**, which were given to the brother of Jared upon the mount, when he talked with the Lord face to face, and the miraculous **directors** which were given to Lehi while in the wilderness, on the borders of the Red Sea. (D&C 17:1)

Of course, it's possible that D&C 17:1 is simply an error; i.e., that it should have read "the miraculous director" (singular). On the other hand, it's possible that Lehi was given both a ball or compass, *and* an interpretive seer stone. In that case, Alma could be referring to both when he used the plural, and then later focused only on the liahona. I won't get into the details of that here, but you can get some background on this in the comments to the article in the *Interpreter* magazine.

For purposes of this appendix, though, it seems obvious that Oliver Cowdery understood and made it clear that the *interpreters* referred to in the Book of Mormon, which he equated to the Urim and Thummim, had nothing to do with a seer stone Joseph found in a well.

Appendix 6: Emma's Last Testimony

This Appendix includes the complete "Last Testimony of Sister Emma," as published in the *Saints' Herald.*

Emma's "Last Testimony" was controversial when first published and remains so today. LDS leaders and members in Utah responded promptly, publishing rebuttals in the Deseret News in October 1879 just a few weeks after the "Last Testimony" was published. They questioned the legitimacy of the documents.

As published in *The Saints' Herald*, the "Last Testimony" takes the form of a question-and-answer session. The contemporaneous notes differ by listing eight questions at the outset, followed by several pages of answers. With respect to the topics of polygamy and Book of Mormon translation, the published version accurately reflects what is written in the notes, except for the change to the Q&A format.

Saints' Herald, Vol. 26, No 19 p. 289 (1 October 1879).[389]

LAST TESTIMONY OF SISTER EMMA.

In a conversation held in the Herald office during the early days of the present year, between Bishop Rogers, Elders W. W. Blair, H. A. Stebbins and a few others, leading minds in the Church, it was thought advisable to secure from Mother Bidamon, (Sister Emma Smith), her testimony upon certain points upon which various opinions existed; and to do this, it was decided to present to her a few prominent questions, which were penned and agreed upon, the answers to which might, so far as she was concerned, **settle these differences of opinion**. In accordance with this understanding the senior editor of the HERALD visited Nauvoo, in February last, arriving on the 4th and remaining until the 10th. Sister Emma answered the questions freely and

[389] https://archive.org/stream/TheSaintsHerald_Volume_26_1879/the%20saints%20herald%20volume%2026%201879#page/n287/mode/2up

in the presence of her husband, Major Lewis C. Bidamon, who was generally present in their sitting- room where the conversation took place. We were more particular in this because it had been frequently stated to us: "Ask your mother, she knows." "Why don't you ask your mother; she dare not deny these things." "You do not dare to ask your mother!"

Our thought was, that if we had lacked courage to ask her, because we feared the answers she might give, we would put aside that fear; and, whatever the worst might be, we would hear it. The result is given below; it having been decided to give the statements to the readers of the HERALD, in view of the death of Sister Emma having occurred so soon after she made them, thus giving them the character of a last testimony.

It is intended to incorporate these questions and answers in the forthcoming history of the reorganization.

We apologized to our mother for putting the questions respecting polygamy and plural wives, as we felt we ought to do.

Question. Who performed the marriage ceremony for Joseph Smith and Emma Hale? When? Where?

Answer. I was married at South Bainbridge, New York; at the house of Squire Tarbell, by him, when I was in my 22d or 23d year.

We here suggested that Mother Smith's history gave the date of the marriage as January 18, 1827. To this she replied:

I think the date correct. My certificate of marriage was lost many years ago, in some of the marches we were forced to make.

In answer to a suggestion by us that she might mistake about who married father and herself; and that it was rumored that it was Sidney Rigdon, or a Presbyterian clergyman, she stated:

It was not Sidney Rigdon, for I did not see him for years after that. It was not a Presbyterian clergyman. I was visiting at Mr. Stowell's who lived in Bainbridge, and saw your father there. I had no intention of marrying when I left home; but, during my visit at Mr. Stowell's, your father visited me there. My folks were bitterly opposed to him; and, being importuned by your father, sided by Mr. Stowell, who urged me to marry him, and preferring to marry him (than) to any other man I knew, I consented. We went to Squire Tarbell's and were married. Afterward, when father found that I was married, he sent for us. The account in Mother Smith's history is substantially correct as to date and place. Your father bought your Uncle Jesse's (Hale) place, off father's farm, and we lived there until the Book of Mormon was translated; and I think published. I was not in Palmyra long.

Q. How many children did you lose, mother, before I was born?

A. There were three. I buried one in Pennsylvania, and a pair of twins in

Ohio.

Q. Who were the twins that died?

A. They were not named.

Q. Who were the twins whom you took to raise?

A. I lost twins. Mrs. Murdock had twins and died. Brother Murdock came to me and asked me to take them, and I took the babes. Joseph died at 11 months. They were both sick when your father was mobbed. The mob who tarred and feathered him, left the door open when they went out with him, the child relapsed and died. Julia lived, though weaker than the boy.

Q. When did you first know Sidney Rigdon? Where?

A. I was residing at father Whitmer's when I first saw Sidney Rigdon. I think he came there.

Q. Was this before or after the publication of the Book of Mormon?

A. The Book of Mormon had been translated and published some time before. Parley P. Pratt had united with the Church before I knew Sidney Rigdon, or heard of him. At the time of Book of Mormon was translated there was no church organized, and Rigdon did not become acquainted with Joseph and me till after the Church was established in 1830. How long after that I do not know, but it was some time.

Q. Who were scribes for father when translating the Book of Mormon?

A. Myself, Oliver Cowdery, Martin Harris, and my brother Reuben Hale.

Q. Was Alva Hale one?

A. I think not. He may have written some; but if he did, I do not remember it.

Q. What about the revelation on polygamy? Did Joseph Smith have anything like it? What of spiritual wifery?

A. There was no revelation on either polygamy or spiritual wives. There were some rumors of something of the sort, of which I asked my husband. He assured me that all there was of it was, that, in a chat about plural wives, he had said, "Well, such a system might possibly be, if everybody was agreed to it, and would behave as they should; but they would not; and besides, it was contrary to the will of heaven." No such thing as polygamy or spiritual wifery was taught, publicly or privately, before my husband's death, that I have now, or ever had any knowledge of.

Q. Did he not have other wives than yourself?

A. He had no other wife but me; nor did he to my knowledge ever have.

Q. Did he not hold marital relations with women other than yourself?

A. He did not have improper relations with any woman that ever came to my knowledge.

Q. Was there nothing about spiritual wives that you recollect?

A. At one time my husband came to me and asked me if I had heard certain rumors about spiritual marriages, or anything of the kind; and assured me that if I had, that they were without foundation; that there was no such doctrine, and never should be with his knowledge or consent. I know that he had no other wife or wives than myself, in any sense, either spiritual or otherwise.

Q. What of the truth of Mormonism?

A. I know Mormonism to be the truth; and believe the Church to have been established by divine direction. I have complete faith in it. In writing for your father I frequently wrote day after day, often sitting at the table close by him, he sitting with his face buried in his hat, with the stone in it, and dictating hour after hour with nothing between us.

Q. Had he not a book or manuscript from which he read, or dictated to you?

A. He had neither manuscript nor book to read from.

Q. Could he not have had, and you not know it?

A. If he had had anything of the kind he could not have concealed it from me.

Q. Are you sure that he had the plates at the time you were writing for him?

A. The plates often lay on the table without any attempt at concealment, wrapped in a small linen tablecloth, which I had given him to fold them in. I once felt of the plates, as they thus lay on the table, tracing their outline and shape. They seemed to be pliable like thick paper, and would rustle with a metallic sound when the edges were moved by the thumb, as one does sometimes thumb the edges of a book.

Q. Where did father and Oliver Cowdery write?

A. Oliver Cowdery and your father wrote in the room where I was at work.

Q. Could not father have dictated the Book of Mormon to you, Oliver Cowdery and the others who wrote for him, after having first written it, or having first read it out of some book?

A. Joseph Smith (and for the first time she used his name direct, having usually used the words, "your father" or "my husband") could neither write nor dictate a coherent and well-worded letter, let alone dictate a book like the Book of Mormon. And, though I was an active participant in the scenes that transpired, and was present during the translation of the plates, and had cognizance of things as they transpired, it is marvelous to me, "a marvel and a wonder," as much so as to anyone else.

Q. I should suppose that you would have uncovered the plates and examined them?

A. I did not attempt to handle the plates, other than I have told you, nor uncover them to look at them. I was satisfied that it was the work of God, and therefore did not feel it to be necessary to do so;

Major Bidamon here suggested: Did Mr. Smith forbid your examining the plates?

A. I do not think he did. I knew that he had them, and was not specially curious about them. I moved them from place to place on the table, as it was necessary in doing my work.

Q. Mother, what is your belief about the authenticity, or origin, of the Book of Mormon?

A. My belief is that the Book of Mormon is of divine authenticity - I have not the slightest doubt of it. I am satisfied that no man could have dictated the writing of the manuscripts unless he was inspired; for, when acting as his scribe, your father would dictate to me hour after hour; and when returning after meals, or after interruptions, he could at once begin where he had left off, without either seeing the manuscript or having any portion of it read to him. This was a usual thing for him to do. It would have been improbable that a learned man could do this; and, for one so ignorant and unlearned as he was, it was simply impossible.

Q. What was the condition of feeling between you and father?

A. It was good.

Q. Were you in the habit of quarreling?

A. No. There was no necessity for any quarreling. He knew that I wished for nothing but what was right; and, as he wished for nothing else, we did not disagree. He usually gave some heed to what I had to say. It was quite a grievous thing to many that I had any influence with him.

Q. What do you think of David Whitmer?

A. David Whitmer I believe to be an honest and truthful man. I think what he states may be relied on.

Q. It has been stated sometimes that you apostatized at father's death, and joined the Methodist Church. What do you say to this?

A. I have been called apostate; but I have never apostatized nor forsaken the faith I at first accepted; but was called so because I would not accept their new-fangled notion.

Q. By whom were you baptized? Do you remember?

A. I think by Oliver Cowdery, at Bainbridge.

Q. You say that you were married at South Bainbridge, and have used the word Bainbridge. Were they one and the same town?

A. No. There was Bainbridge and South Bainbridge; some distance apart, how far I don't know. I was in South Bainbridge.

These questions and the answers she had given to them were read to my mother by me, the day before my leaving Nauvoo for home, and were

affirmed by her. Major Bidamon stated that he had frequently conversed with her on the subject of the translation of the Book of Mormon, and her present answers were substantially what she had always stated in regard to it.
JOSEPH SMITH.

Critiques of the "Last Testimony" compiled in *The Historical Record*, Andrew Jenson, Ed., Church Encyclopaedia, Book 1 (Salt Lake City, Utah) 1889, p. 220 f.[390]

A section of the Historical Record titled "Plural marriage" addressed the claims of Emma Smith's "Last Testimony" regarding polygamy. Although the question of the translation of the Book of Mormon was not addressed, the treatment of the polygamy claims in the "Last Testimony" suggest that Emma's testimony may not have been her own.

---

[390] Available on google books. A less readable version is available at https://mormonpolygamydocuments.org/wp-ontent/uploads/2015/01/JS1000.pdf

Appendix 7: Affirmations of the Urim and Thummim

For many years, LDS Church leaders have reiterated the teachings of Joseph and Oliver that Joseph translated the engravings on the plates with the Urim and Thummim, or Interpreters, that he obtained from Moroni's stone box along with the plates. Here are some examples from contemporaries of Joseph Smith, taken from the Journal of Discourses and Conference Reports.[391]

1859, Aug. 14. Elder Orson Pratt. "In the year 1827 he was permitted to take those plates from their long deposit, and **with them the Urim and Thummim**—a sacred instrument such as was used by ancient Prophets among Israel to inquire of the Lord. He was commanded of the Lord, notwithstanding his youth and inexperience, **to translate the engravings upon those plates into the English language.** He did so, and others wrote from his mouth."
https://jod.mrm.org/7/210

1864, June 4. President Brigham Young. "The Lord had not spoken to the inhabitants of this earth for a long time, until He spoke to Joseph Smith, committed to him the plates on which the Book of Mormon was engraved, and **gave him a Urim and Thummim to translate a portion of them**, and told him to print the Book of Mormon, which he did, and sent it to the world, according to the word of the Lord."
https://jod.mrm.org/10/299

1864, Nov. 6. President Brigham Young. "The first act that Joseph Smith was called to do by the angel of God, was, to get the plates from the hill Cumorah, and then translate them, and he got Martin Harris and Oliver Cowdery to write for him. **He would read the plates, by the aid of the Urim and Thummim, and they would write.** They had to either raise their bread from the ground, or buy it, and they had to eat and drink, and sleep, and toil, and rest, while they were engaged in bringing forth the great Work

[391] The best resource for the *Journal of Discourses* is WordCruncher, but that software has to be downloaded. Here I cite jod.mrm.org an easy-to-use website that some perceive as "anti-Mormon" but is merely offering a resource.

of the last days. All these were temporal acts, directed by the spirit of revelation."
https://jod.mrm.org/10/358

1869, Feb 24. Elder Orson Pratt said, "He uncovered the spot of ground, took off the crowning stone on the stone box, and there beheld the sacred record of the ancient inhabitants of this continent; **by its side lay the Urim and Thummim, an instrument for its translation**.... **The work of translation was done with the Urim and Thummim**, for Mr. Smith was not a learned man, and in fact was scarcely in possession of an ordinary common school education. He could write a little, but was by no means an expert penman, and, in the work of translation, he had to employ first one and then another to write the words of the records **as he translated them with the Urim and Thummim**, consequently the manuscripts of the Book of Mormon were written by different scribes. Not long before the time he obtained the plates, Mr. Smith got married, and he employed his wife to write some of it. Martin Harris also wrote some portion of it; but the greater part was written by Oliver Cowdery—a still younger man than Joseph—and that the manuscript is in his handwriting, anyone can satisfy himself by appealing to the original."
https://jod.mrm.org/12/352

1870, Nov. 27. Elder Orson Pratt. "And having revealed this book, and it having been translated by the gift and power of the Holy Ghost—the same gift and spirit which **enabled Joseph Smith to interpret the language of this record by the use of the Urim and Thummim**."
http://jod.mrm.org/14/289

1872, Sept. 22. Elder Orson Pratt. "**The Prophets who deposited those plates in the hill Cumorah were commanded of the Lord to deposit the Urim and Thummim with them**, so that when the time came for them to be brought forth, the individual who was entrusted with them might be able to translate them by the gift and power of God."
https://jod.mrm.org/15/178

1874, June 21. President Brigham Young. "We have passed from one thing to another, and I may say from one degree of knowledge to another. When Joseph first received the knowledge of the plates that were in the hill Cumorah, he did not then receive the keys of the Aaronic Priesthood, he merely received the knowledge that the plates were there, and that the Lord would bring them forth, and that they contained the history of the aborigines of this country. He received the knowledge that they were once in possession of the Gospel, and from that time he went on, step by step, until he obtained the plates, **and the Urim and Thummim, and had power to translate them.**

This did not make him an Apostle, it did not give to him the keys of the kingdom, nor make him an Elder in Israel. He was a Prophet, and had the spirit of prophecy, and had received all this before the Lord ordained him. And when the Lord, by revelation, told him to go to Pennsylvania, he did so, and finished the translation of the Book of Mormon; and **when the Lord, in another revelation**, told him to come back, into New York State, and to go to old Father Whitmer's, who lived in a place opposite Waterloo, and there stop, he did so, and had meetings, and gathered up the few who believed in his testimony."

http://jod.mrm.org/18/235

[Note: Lucy Mack Smith explained that Joseph received this revelation through the U&T, after he applied it to his eyes and looked on the plates. This occurred in May 1829 while Joseph and Oliver were translating in Harmony.]

1875, Sept. 12. Elder Wilford Woodruff. "And what I wish to say to the Elders and to the Latter-day Saints is—Have we faith in God and in his revelations? Have we faith in our own religion? Have we faith in Jesus Christ? Have we faith in the words of the Prophets? **Have we faith in Joseph Smith, who, by the aid of the Urim and Thummim, translated the Book of Mormon**, giving a record of the ancient inhabitants of this country, and through whom the Lord gave the revelations contained in the Book of Doctrine and Covenants? If we have faith in these things, then we certainly should prepare ourselves for the fulfillment of them."

https://jod.mrm.org/18/109

1877, Dec. 2. Elder Orson Pratt. "The time having fully arrived, in this the 19th century, for the prophecies to be fulfilled, in regard to the setting up of the latter-day kingdom, the Lord and his angel, as predicted in the 14th chapter of John's Revelation, revealed the original plates from which **the Book of Mormon was translated by inspiration and the aid of the Urim and Thummim**, is found to contain the fullness of the Gospel of the Son of God, as revealed in ancient times to the Israelites of this western hemisphere, the forefathers of our Indian race."

https://jod.mrm.org/19/168

1878, June 30. Elder Wilford Woodruff. "For by faith Joseph Smith received the ministration of God out of heaven. By faith he received the records of Nephi, and **translated them through the Urim and Thummim into our own language**, and which have since been translated into many different languages."
https://jod.mrm.org/19/357

1879, Sept 7, Elder Orson Pratt. "The record was translated, as the Latter-day Saints understand, and as the world generally have been informed, by revelation, by the inspiration of the Holy Ghost, **through the aid of an instrument that was used anciently and called the Urim and Thummim.** The Lord did not, in revealing this work to us, require us to receive it blindly and enthusiastically, but to receive it on good, substantial, sound evidence, such as we cannot controvert, such as we cannot contradict—evidence that no reasonable person, having the common reasoning faculties of man, can consistently reject. JD 21:129. https://jod.mrm.org/21/128

1879, Sept 21, Elder Orson Pratt. This angel committed, as I have always said, the plates of the Book of Mormon, **together with the Urim and Thummim,** into the hands of this youth, and also gave him many instructions informing him that he must be very strict in keeping the commandments of God, and that he must do with these plates as he was counseled from time to time, not to shew them to everybody that might wish to see them, but **was strictly forbidden, by the angel, to shew them unto any person until the Lord should give him commandment so to do.** JD 21:169.
https://jod.mrm.org/21/168

1880, Oct 10, Elder Orson Pratt. Authority was bestowed before there was any Church. First (not the authority of the Priesthood) but **the authority to bring forth the plates of the Book of Mormon, and to translate them by the Urim and Thummim, by the inspiration of the Holy Ghost.** This was the first authority conferred upon the one whom the Lord chose to commence this great work. The authority of the Priesthood was not conferred upon him at that time, but He revealed unto him concerning the everlasting Gospel contained in the ancient records kept by the Nephites, or Israelites, upon this great Western Continent.

Joseph Smith, **when he translated these records by the aid of the Urim and Thummim,** had not yet received any Priesthood, so far as his temporal existence was concerned. JD 22:28. https://jod.mrm.org/22/27

1882, March 5, President John Taylor. "We have here on the ceiling of this building pictured to us, Moroni making known to Joseph Smith **the plates, from which the Book of Mormon was translated**, which plates had been hidden up in the earth; and **in connection with them was the Urim and Thummim, by which sacred instrument Joseph was enabled to translate the ancient characters,** now given unto us in the form of the Book of Mormon; in which is set forth the theories, doctrines, principles, organizations, etc., of these peoples who lived upon this continent. People talk about their disbelief regarding these things. That is a matter of no moment to us. I do not intend to bring any argument upon this question, caring nothing about what people believe. **We know certain things, and knowing them we regard them as matters of fact."**
https://jod.mrm.org/23/28

1882, May, Elder Erastus Snow. "At first Joseph Smith received the gift of seeing visions and the **gift of translating dead languages by the Urim and Thummim**, and when he had exercised himself in these gifts for a season, he received the keys of the Aaronic Priesthood, together with his Brother Oliver, under the hands of John the Baptist, who was a resurrected being…"
https://jod.mrm.org/23/181

1895, October, Elder Franklin D. Richards. "The stick of Joseph, in the hands of Ephraim—which is the Book of Mormon—was translated into English from the Reformed Egyptian, **by means of the Urim and Thummim**, in the hands of Joseph Smith … its existence is already widely known in Christendom.

The Book of Mormon has special and peculiar claim upon the faith of all true Christian people, because **it was translated by the power of God through the Urim and Thummim, word by word and sentence by sentence**.

1909, April, Elder Anthony W. Ivins. "The Prophet Joseph Smith did not undertake to establish the divine authenticity of this book by reference to the evidences which exist in this continent, by which it may be corroborated—not at all. He gave us the book as a truth; it was a truth that God revealed these things to him; it was a truth that Moroni delivered the plates into his hands**; it was a truth that this book was translated by the gift and power of God, through the medium of the Urim and Thummim**. Now, we spend a good deal of time trying to determine how that was brought about. What does it matter how it was brought about? It was done by the gift and power of God, that is sufficient for me. **It was done by means of the Urim and Thummim**—not a new method either of learning the will of the Lord, for the ancients had it."

1962, April, Elder Spencer W. Kimball, "Is it difficult to believe that the Urim and Thummim carried down through the ages by the prophets, even in the hands of our own modern-day prophet, could be that precision instrument which would transmit messages from God himself to his supreme creation—man?

1974, April, Elder Boyd K. Packer, "When we announce that we have scripture other than the Bible, we are asked of course, "Well, where did you get these revelations? Where did these books come from?"

In response to these questions, we immediately speak of **translation through the use of the urim and thummim** of records prepared by ancient prophets; we speak of visions; we speak of visitations of angelic messengers from the presence of God; and we speak without hesitation of interviews with the Lord himself.

1989, April, President Gordon B. Hinckley, "My name is Cowdery—Oliver Cowdery. In the history of the Church I stood ... in her councils. Not because I was better than other men was I called ... He called me to a high and holy calling. I wrote with my own pen the entire Book of Mormon (save a few pages) as it fell from the lips of the Prophet Joseph Smith, and he translated it by the power and gift of God, **by means of the Urim and Thummim**, or as it is called by that book, 'Holy Interpreter.'

2003, October, Elder Robert D. Hales, "After four years of continued obedience, Joseph received the plates on September 22, 1827, at the age of 21. He also received **an ancient instrument for translating them, called the Urim and Thummim. Using this sacred interpreter,** along with the Holy Ghost, Joseph began the work of translation in December of that year."

2007, April, Elder L. Tom Perry, "Oliver wrote of this remarkable experience: "These were days never to be forgotten—to sit under the sound of a voice dictated by the inspiration of heaven, awakened the utmost gratitude of this bosom! Day after day I continued, uninterrupted, to write from his mouth, as he translated, **with the Urim and Thummim** ... the history, or record, called 'The book of Mormon.'"

Appendix 8: Expanding the text

As I noted in Chapter 11, once we recognize the influence of Jonathan Edwards and the other sources Joseph drew upon to translate the plates, we see additional meaning for several passages in the Book of Mormon, the Doctrine and Covenants, and the Pearl of Great Price.

The Book of Mormon assumes readers are already familiar with the Bible. It cites biblical passages, refers to biblical events, and mentions biblical names and places, all without explanation.

For example, a reader unfamiliar with the Bible would not understand Book of Mormon references to the Law of Moses, because the Book of Mormon never defines or explains the Law of Moses in any detail. To understand the Book of Mormon references to the Law of Moses, a reader must consult the Bible. The better a reader knows the Bible, the more he/she will appreciate and understand the Book of Mormon.

What about *non-biblical* passages in the Book of Mormon (and Doctrine and Covenants and Pearl of Great Price)?

Our understanding of these passages will be enhanced once we know the sources to which they refer. Here we consider two examples.

The Natural Man.

The term "natural man" appears once in the Bible.

> But the **natural man** receiveth not the things of the Spirit of God: for they are foolishness unto him: neither can he know them, because they are spiritually discerned. (1 Corinthians 2:14).

The term appears three times in the Book of Mormon and once in the Doctrine and Covenants.

> For the **natural man** is an enemy to God, and has been from the fall of Adam, and will be, forever and ever, unless he yields to the enticings of the

> Holy Spirit, and putteth off the **natural man** and becometh a saint through the atonement of Christ the Lord, and becometh as a child, submissive, meek, humble, patient, full of love, willing to submit to all things which the Lord seeth fit to inflict upon him, even as a child doth submit to his father. (Mosiah 3:19)

> And now behold, my brethren, what **natural man** is there that knoweth these things? I say unto you, there is none that knoweth these things, save it be the penitent. (Alma 26:21)

> For no man has seen God at any time in the flesh, except quickened by the Spirit of God. Neither can any **natural man** abide the presence of God, neither after the carnal mind. (Doctrine and Covenants 67:11–12)

At first glance, we might infer that when Joseph was translating the plates (and receiving the D&C 67), he alluded to 1 Corinthians 2:14. Many LDS writers and speakers have made that assumption. Alma 26:21 seems to paraphrase Paul's language about knowing spiritual things.

But King Benjamin declared that the natural man is an "enemy to God." This non-biblical phrase[392] appears four times in the Book of Mormon. Many have expressed their opinions about exactly how and in what ways "the natural man is an enemy to God," but the Book of Mormon doesn't spell it out. *It makes the statement as though readers already are familiar with the idea.*

Instead of explaining what he means by the statement, King Benjamin focuses on how to solve the problem; i.e., how to no longer be an enemy to God.

To better understand the concept, we look to an earlier source, just like we look to the Bible to understand what the Law of Moses is.

In this case, we can look to Jonathan Edwards' sermon titled "Men Naturally God's Enemies." Over several pages of text, Edwards explains in detail how the natural man is an enemy to God. Here are a

---

[392] The closest verse is "enemy of God" in James 4:4. "Ye adulterers and adulteresses, know ye not that the friendship of the world is enmity with God? whosoever therefore will be a friend of the world is the enemy of God."

few excerpts:

> Hence, natural men are enemies to God's government. They are not loyal subjects, but enemies to God, considered as Lord of the world. They are entire enemies to God's authority. They are enemies to God in their affections. **There is in every natural man a seed of malice against God**.... Natural men are enemies to the dominion of God... Yea, they are enemies to the being of God.... **Natural men do not generally conceive themselves to be so bad:** They have not this notion of themselves, that they are enemies to God. And therefore when they hear such doctrine as this taught them, they stand ready to make objections.[393]

This sermon does not appear to be included in the database of the Jonathan Edwards Center at Yale University, but it was included in the 8-volume set of Edwards' works that was advertised for sale in the *Palmyra Register* newspaper in Palmyra, NY, from 1818-1821. Joseph visited the printing shop weekly to purchase the newspaper for his father; these books were readily available to him. He said that, between the ages of 12-15, he applied himself to searching the scriptures and had an intimate acquaintance with those of different denominations.

In addition to the specific sermon, Edwards' 8-volume set contains dozens of references to the "natural man" that explain various applications of the term, including the roles of mercy and justice.

Armed with that enhanced understanding, King Benjamin's discourse on how to "put off" the natural man has deeper meaning.

The worth of souls.

While Joseph and Oliver were translating the plates of Nephi in Fayette in June 1829, Joseph received a revelation now known as D&C 18. Verse 10 contains an important phrase not found in the Bible or the Book of Mormon.

> Remember the worth of souls is great in the sight of God;

393 Jonathan Edwards, "Natural Men are God's Enemies," in *Works of President Jonathan Edwards*, Worcester, MA, 1808.

The term "remember" appears 357 times in the scriptures, always in reference to a specific precedent. E.g., "O remember, remember, my sons, the words which king Benjamin spake unto his people" (Helaman 5:9) and "remember ye the words which were spoken before of the apostles of our Lord Jesus Christ (Jude 1:17).

However, "worth of souls" is not found in the Bible or Book of Mormon (neither the words nor the concept). To what source was the Lord referring?

I propose that the Lord was reminding Joseph of something he had read earlier in his life. Obvious examples are teachings of Jonathan Edwards from the Palmyra bookstore such as these.

> The man Christ Jesus when he was upon earth, had doubtless as great a sense of the **infinite greatness** and importance of eternal things, and **the worth of souls**, as any have nowadays…

> They [the devils] have a great sense of the worth of salvation, and **the worth of immortal souls**, and the vast importance of those things that concern men's eternal welfare… Unregenerate men may have a sense of the importance of the **things of eternity**, and the vanity of the things of time; **the worth of immortal souls**; the preciousness of time and means of grace, and the follow the way of allowed sin…

With this background, we can understand D&C 18 as a more intimate interaction between the Lord and Joseph Smith. It is a complement to what the Lord told Oliver Cowdery in D&C 6:22-3.

> Verily, verily, I say unto you, if you desire a further witness, cast your mind upon the night that you cried unto me in your heart, that you might know concerning the truth of these things. Did I not speak peace to your mind concerning the matter? What greater witness can you have than from God?

Many other passages in the Book of Mormon, Doctrine and Covenants, and Pearl of Great Price, as well as other writings and sermons of Joseph Smith, are enhanced once we recognize the way the Lord prepared Joseph Smith by having him acquire a mental language bank upon which they—the Lord and Joseph Smith—could draw to translate the Nephite records and express these revelations.

Appendix 9: Annotation of 1 Nephi 1:1-3

While preparing my book on Jonathan Edwards, I've annotated several chapters from the Book of Mormon, as well as Joseph's 1832 history and some passages from the Doctrine and Covenants and Pearl of Great Price, with references to the five categories of sources mentioned in Chapter 11.

Many passages blend biblical sources, and I've annotated those, but I'm more interested in non-biblical language. Non-biblical phrases are more useful than words because they are more complex and therefore less likely to be random.

Relative frequency is also of interest; low-frequency biblical terms and phrases that appear in the Book of Mormon in high frequencies often appear in the works of Jonathan Edwards in high frequencies.

The following example from 1 Nephi 1:1-3, the first two sentences in the 1830 Book of Mormon (presumably the first words Joseph translated in Fayette from the plates of Nephi), has several nonbliblical terms and phrases that are found in the work of Jonathan Edwards. I have also searched other books on sale in Palmyra, such as Wesley's Sermons, with few matches.

Non-biblical terms are shown as 0 OT, 0 NT, and bolded. Because some of these terms may appear in DC or PGP, terms unique to BM are so indicated in the notes. I put the verses in a form of poetic parallelism characteristic of Hebrew writing, with parallel terms and concepts underlined. Edwards focused on Hebrew parallel structures.

Besides the normal abbreviations for scriptures, I use the following:

JE = Jonathan Edwards

AmRev = The American Revolution

Nap = First Book of Napoleon

LW = The Late War

Shakes = Shakespeare

Herv = James Hervey

I, Nephi, **having been born**[394] of goodly parents,[395] therefore I was[396] **taught somewhat**[397] in all the learning[398] of my father;[399] and having seen[400] **many afflictions**[401] **in the course**[402] of my days,[403] nevertheless, having been[404] highly favored[405] of the Lord in **all my days;**[406]

yea, having had[407] a **great knowledge**[408] of the goodness[409] and the mysteries of God,[410]

---

394 "having been born" **unique to BM**, but it appears 5 times in Edwards (shown as 5 JE)

395 "goodly parents" **unique to BM**. "goodly" 31 OT, 4 NT, 2 BM, 4 DC, 0 PGP, 52 JE, 3 AmRev, 3 Nap, 87 Shakes.

396 "therefore I was" 1 OT, 0 NT, 4 BM, 0 DC, 0 PGP, 3 JE.

397 "taught somewhat" **unique to BM**. "somewhat" 14 OT, 10 NT, 44 BM, 0 DC, 1 PGP-JS-H, 260 JE. High prevalence in LDS = JE. Edwards: "It appears to me obvious, also, that, in connection with all this, they should be **taught somewhat** relating to the chronology of events, which would make the story so much the more distinct…"

398 "the learning" 1 OT, 0 NT, 4 BM, 0 DC, 0 PGP, 27 JE.

399 "of my father" 13 OT, 15 NT, 41 BM, 22 DC, 0 PGP, 103 JE. High prevalence in LDS = JE.

400 "having seen" 0 OT, 2 NT, 5 BM, 0 DC, 0 PGP, 19 JE.

401 "many afflictions" **0 OT, 0 NT**, 8 BM, 1 DC, 0 PGP, 1 JST, 7 JE. Edwards: "it may be God's hand is upon them in **many afflictions**."

402 "in the course" **0 OT, 0 NT**, 3 BM, 0 DC, 0 PGP, 231 JE. Edwards: "the same is now proposed **in the course** of a sinner's convictions in these days…"

403 "my days" 18 OT, 0 NT, 14 BM, 0 DC, 0 PGP, 34 JE. "of my days" 3 OT, 0 NT, 3 BM, 0 DC, 0 PGP, 8 JE.

404 "having been" 0 OT, 1 NT, 53 BM, 1 DC, 6 PGP (1 AB, 5 JS-H), 286 JE. High prevalence in LDS = JE.

405 "highly favored" 0 OT, 1 NT, 7 BM, 0 DC, 0 PGP, 19 JE; "highly favored of" **0 OT, 0 NT**, 3 BM, 0 DC, 0 PGP, 2 JE. Edwards: "highly favored by the Lord."

406 "all my days" **0 OT, 0 NT**, 3 BM, 0 DC, 0 PGP, 2 JE. Edwards: "resolving to live devoted to God all my days."

407 "having had" 0 OT, 1 NT, 7 BM, 0 DC, 0 PGP, 56 JE.

408 "great knowledge" **0 OT, 0 NT**, 6 BM, 0 DC, 1 PGP, 27 JE. Edwards: "they have a very great knowledge of the natural glory of God."

409 "goodness" 41 OT, 9 NT, 31 BM, 2 DC, 1 PGP, 2897 JE.

410 "mysteries of God" 0 OT, 1 NT, 8 BM, 3 DC, 0 PGP, 0 JE (mysteries of God's providence, mysteries of God's universe, mysteries of God's eternal duration)

therefore I make a record[411] of my **proceedings**[412] in my days;

Yea, I make a record[413] in the language of[414] my father,

which consists[415] of **the learning of the Jews**[416]

and the **language of** the[417] Egyptians.

And I know that the record which I make, **to be true;**[418] and **I make it**[419] according to my own hand; and **I make it** according to

my knowledge.

---

411 "a record" 1 OT, 1 NT, 19 BM, 4 DC, 0 PGP, 42 JE. Edwards: "how much more may we expect that God gives the world a record of the dispensations of his divine government that doubtless is infinitely more worthy of an history..."

412 "proceedings" **0 OT, 0 NT**, 10 BM, 2 DC, 1 PGP (JS-H), 207 JE. "my proceedings" **unique to BM** (3x). Edwards: "A Just & faithful account of my Proceedings & Conduct…"

413 "make a record" 0 OT, 0 NT, 7 BM, 1 DC, 0 PGP, 0 JE.

414 "language of" 4 OT, 0 NT, 17 BM, 0 DC, 2 PGP, 402 JE.

415 "which consists" **unique to BM**; 146 JE. "which consists of" 12 JE.

416 "the learning of the Jews" **unique to BM**; Edwards: "the apostle Paul, who was famed for his much learning, as you may see, Acts 26:24; and was not only skilled in the learning of the Jews"

417 "language of the" **unique to BM** (8x); 110 JE. Edwards "the language of the people," "the language of the Indians."

418 "to be true" 0 OT, 0 NT, 3 BM, 2 DC, 1 PGP, 203 JE

419 "I make it" **unique to BM** (3x); 3 JE. Edwards "I make it my rule"

INDEX